PRESENTED TO

_____

FROM

_____

DATE

THE ACTION
BIBLE

THE ACTION BIBLE

GOD'S REDEMPTIVE STORY

ILLUSTRATIONS BY **SERGIO CARIELLO**

GENERAL EDITOR **DOUG MAUSS**

David C Cook®

transforming lives together

THE ACTION BIBLE
Published by David C. Cook
4050 Lee Vance View
Colorado Springs, CO 80918 U.S.A.

David C. Cook Distribution Canada
55 Woodslee Avenue, Paris, Ontario, Canada N3L 3E5

David C. Cook U.K., Kingsway Communications
Eastbourne, East Sussex BN23 6NT, England

LCCN 2010923224
ISBN 978-0-7814-4499-6
eISBN 978-1-4347-0239-5

General Editor: Doug Mauss
Art Director: Kevin Mullins
Bible Editor: Shawn Yost, M. Div.
Cover Design: Rule29 Creative, Inc.
Letterers: Dave Lanphear, Dave Rothe
Colorists: Patrick Gama, and
Wellington Marçal, Priscila Ribeiro, Fabrício Sampaio Guerra,
MaxFlan Araujo, Alex Guim of Impacto Studio

Printed in the United States of America
First Edition 2010

2 3 4 5 6 7 8 9 10

092910

STEEL YOURSELF FOR ACTION...

People don't usually think of God like this, but God is the original action hero. Everyone is so impressed when Superman blows a car over with his breath, yet God created the whole universe with His breath. Superman may save the day with his strength, but Jesus saved the whole world with His death.

And then there are the humans God chose to fulfill His divine plan—they were pretty awesome (though imperfect) action heroes themselves. Read about Samson wading into an army of Philistines, killing them all with nothing more than a donkey's jawbone. Discover how Esther risked the wrath of a temperamental king to save God's people. Every few years there's another action movie about Robin Hood or King Arthur—but Hollywood always forgets about King David, a shepherd boy who lived as an outlaw before he became king. He was a part of history long before both of those legends.

But here's the thing: *The Action Bible* is more than just the exciting stories of the past. Here and now, today, it inspires us to be God's next generation of difference-makers. The heroes in the Bible were flawed and chosen; you and I are flawed and chosen. The action you read about in these 750 pages is nothing compared to the action that will occur once you put this book down.

How will you answer God's call to action?

Doug Mauss
General Editor

I tell you the truth, anyone who has faith in me will do what I have been doing.
He will do even greater things than these ...
—Jesus Christ (John 14:12)

TABLE of CONTENTS

JOSHUA

GOD'S JUDGES

THE KINGS

THE PROPHETS

THE EXILES

NEW TESTAMENT

JESUS' BIRTH AND MINISTRY

JESUS' FINAL DAYS

THE CHURCH IS BORN

PAUL

In the Beginning ...

... THERE WAS NOTHING.

EXCEPT GOD.

Day 1

GOD'S SPIRIT MOVED THROUGH
THE VOID. THEN GOD SPOKE:

LET THERE
BE LIGHT!

Day 2

THEN GOD SEPARATED THE WATERS OF THE NOTHINGNESS INTO THE MOISTURE AND CLOUDS OF THE SKY ABOVE, AND THE DROPS AND WAVES OF THE OCEAN BELOW. GOD NAMED THE SKY "HEAVENS."

Day 3

GOD NAMED THE LOWER WATERS THE "SEA." HE GATHERED TOGETHER THE WATERS OF THE SEA, EXPOSING DRY GROUND. HE NAMED THE DRY LAND "EARTH." ON THIS LAND, HE MADE GRASS AND FLOWERS AND TREES. HE MADE THEM WITH SEEDS SO THEY COULD GROW MORE GRASS AND FLOWERS AND TREES. THE FRUITFUL EARTH WAS A PLACE OF BEAUTY.

AND GOD KNEW THAT IT WAS GOOD.

Day 4

THEN GOD FASHIONED THE SUN,
THE MOON, AND THE STARS TO
LIGHT THE EARTH. AND HE SET
THEM IN THE HEAVENS TO MARK
THE DAYS, SEASONS, AND YEARS.

Day 5

GOD SAID, "LET THE WATER BE
FILLED WITH LIVING CREATURES!"
AND THE SEAS AND RIVERS
SWARMED WITH WHALES AND FISH.

GOD SAID, "LET BIRDS FLY THROUGH
THE SKY." AND THE OPEN SKY ABOVE THE
EARTH WAS FILLED WITH EVERY KIND
OF FLYING BIRD.

"BE FRUITFUL AND FILL THE EARTH,"
GOD SAID AS HE BLESSED THE LIVING
CREATURES OF THE SEA AND SKY.

AND GOD KNEW THAT IT WAS GOOD.

Day 6

THEN GOD SAID, "LET THE EARTH BRING FORTH LIVING CREATURES." AND GOD MADE ALL KINDS OF ANIMALS: WILD ONES, TAME ONES—EVEN THOSE THAT CRAWL ON THE GROUND.

THEN GOD CREATED THE FIRST MAN, ADAM, AND THE FIRST WOMAN, EVE. THEY WERE THE GREATEST OF ALL GOD'S CREATIONS BECAUSE HE MADE THEM IN HIS OWN IMAGE, TO BE A REFLECTION OF WHAT HE IS LIKE. GOD MADE ADAM AND EVE WITH SOULS THAT WOULD LIVE FOREVER. AND HE PLANNED FOR PEOPLE TO RULE AND LIVE IN HARMONY WITH EVERY LIVING THING ON EARTH.

GOD LOOKED AT EVERYTHING THAT HE HAD MADE, AND HE KNEW IT WAS ALL VERY, VERY GOOD.

Day 7

AND ON THE SEVENTH DAY, GOD RESTED.

GOD SHOWED ADAM AND EVE THE BEAUTY AND FRUITFULNESS OF THE GARDEN THEY LIVED IN. HE TOLD THEM, "YOU MAY EAT FROM EVERY TREE EXCEPT ONE, THE TREE OF KNOWLEDGE OF GOOD AND EVIL. IF YOU EAT FROM THAT TREE, YOU WILL DIE."

Tempted in the Garden
BASED ON GENESIS 3

LOOK, ADAM! THE LITTLE BIRD COMES WHEN I CALL!

GOD IS GOOD TO US. HE HAS GIVEN US EVERYTHING.

EVERYTHING EXCEPT FRUIT FROM THE TREE OF KNOWLEDGE OF GOOD AND EVIL.

YES, THAT IS FORBIDDEN!

BUT EVE WONDERS. AND ONE DAY SHE GOES TO THE TREE AND GAZES AT THE FORBIDDEN FRUIT.

BUT THE FORBIDDEN FRUIT HAS FAR DIFFERENT EFFECTS THAN THE SERPENT PROMISED. SUDDENLY ADAM AND EVE REALIZE THEY HAVE DISOBEYED GOD. THEIR INNOCENCE IS TAKEN AWAY AS WELL.

WE'RE NOT WISE—WE'RE JUST NAKED!

COVER YOURSELF WITH THESE LEAVES! WE MUST HIDE.

IN THE STILLNESS OF THE GARDEN, GOD COMES TO ADAM AND EVE.

HOW DID YOU KNOW YOU WERE NAKED? HAVE YOU EATEN THE FRUIT I TOLD YOU NOT TO EAT?

I ONLY ATE IT BECAUSE THE WOMAN *YOU* GAVE ME HANDED IT TO ME.

THE SERPENT *YOU* CREATED TRICKED ME!

BECAUSE YOU DISOBEYED ME, YOU MUST LEAVE THIS BEAUTIFUL GARDEN. FROM NOW ON, YOU'LL HAVE TO WORK HARD TO SURVIVE.

GOD MAKES CLOTHES FOR ADAM AND EVE OUT OF ANIMAL SKINS AND SENDS THEM AWAY.

LOOK! A FLAMING SWORD BLOCKS THE ENTRANCE TO THE GARDEN. WE CAN NEVER GO BACK NOW!

WHERE CAN WE GO? WHAT CAN WE DO?

GOD'S PROMISE OF SALVATION

THE PERFECT UNITY BETWEEN GOD AND HIS BELOVED CREATION IS NOW BROKEN FOR ALL TIME. ADAM AND EVE ARE FORCED TO CREATE A NEW LIFE OUT OF THEIR KNOWLEDGE AND SHAME.

BUT ALREADY, GOD HAS A PLAN TO REDEEM HIS CREATION. GOD PROMISES THAT ONE DAY HE WILL SEND A SAVIOR FOR HIS PEOPLE.

Brother's Blood Cry

BASED ON GENESIS 4—5

OUTSIDE THE GARDEN OF EDEN, THE LAND IS BARREN, HOT, AND DRY. WEARY, ALONE, AND FRIGHTENED, ADAM AND EVE SEARCH UNTIL THEY FIND A PLACE TO MAKE A HOME.

REMEMBER HOW BEAUTIFUL EDEN WAS? IF ONLY ...

IT IS OUR OWN FAULT FOR DISOBEYING GOD. BUT I WILL TEACH OUR CHILDREN TO OBEY AND LOVE GOD. IF I CAN HELP IT, THEY WON'T REPEAT OUR MISTAKE.

SO ADAM TEACHES THEIR SONS, CAIN AND ABEL, ABOUT GOD.

GOD MADE THE EARTH AND EVERYTHING WE HAVE.

GOD EVEN GAVE ME MY LITTLE LAMB!

SHEEP ARE DUMB.

BUT GOD CALLS OUT TO CAIN.

CAIN! WHERE IS YOUR BROTHER?

I ... I DON'T KNOW. AM I SUPPOSED TO KEEP TRACK OF MY BROTHER?

HE KNOWS!

YOUR BROTHER'S BLOOD CRIES OUT TO ME FROM THE GROUND. FROM NOW ON, THE GROUND WILL YIELD NO FRUIT FOR YOU, AND YOU WILL WANDER THE EARTH UNTIL YOUR DEATH.

PLEASE, GOD, THIS PUNISHMENT IS MORE THAN I CAN TAKE!

YOUR WICKEDNESS CANNOT CONTINUE! TURN AWAY FROM YOUR IDOL WORSHIP.

RETURN TO GOD, WHO CREATED YOU AND GAVE US EVERYTHING WE HAVE.

GOD DIDN'T GIVE ME EVERYTHING I HAVE. I STOLE IT! HA!

NOAH THINKS HE'S BETTER THAN EVERYONE ELSE.

BUT NOAH REMAINS TRUE TO GOD. ONE DAY GOD SPEAKS TO HIM.

I'M SORRY THAT I EVER MADE HUMANS. THEY ARE CORRUPT AND VIOLENT. SO I'M GOING TO DESTROY THEM. NOAH, YOU HAVE BEEN FAITHFUL; BUILD YOURSELF A SHIP, BECAUSE I'M GOING TO FLOOD THE WHOLE EARTH.

NOAH OBEYS AND BEGINS BUILDING AN ARK. HE FOLLOWS THE INSTRUCTIONS THAT GOD GIVES HIM.

THAT CRAZY NOAH THINKS HE CAN FLOAT A BOAT ON DRY LAND.

WHAT WILL HE THINK OF NEXT?

WHEN THE ARK IS FINISHED, GOD TELLS NOAH TO TAKE SEVEN PAIRS OF EACH KIND OF ANIMAL AND BIRD THAT IS USED FOR FOOD, AND ONE PAIR OF EACH KIND THAT IS NOT USED FOR FOOD. NOAH AND HIS FAMILY ENTER THE ARK.

WATER FLOWS OVER THE LAND AND RISES ABOVE THE MOUNTAINTOPS. ALL THE EARTH IS COVERED. ONLY NOAH'S GREAT ARK SURVIVES. THE FLOOD DESTROYS EVERYTHING EVIL.

AS THE RAIN POURS WITHOUT STOPPING, NOAH AND HIS FAMILY WORK HARD TO CARE FOR THE ANIMALS IN THE ARK.

HAVE YOU FED THE COWS AND SHEEP YET, SHEM?

YES, I JUST FINISHED. NOW I'M GOING TO FEED THE REPTILES.

AND NOW I HAVE TO CLEAN UP AFTER THE COWS AND SHEEP ...

... AND THEN THE REPTILES.

ONE DAY THE RAIN STOPS! BUT THE ARK STILL FLOATS ABOVE THE FLOODED EARTH. LAND IS NOWHERE IN SIGHT.

LOOK! THE DOOR OF NOAH'S ARK IS CLOSING.

BUT WHO IS SHUTTING IT? COULD IT BE NOAH'S GOD?

BUT IT IS TOO LATE. THE PEOPLE WHO HAVE SPENT THEIR LIVES REJECTING GOD NOW SEE THAT GOD HAS FINALLY REJECTED THEM. AND THE RAINS POUR STEADILY FOR 40 DAYS AND 40 NIGHTS.

A Rainbow Promise

BASED ON GENESIS 8—10

MONTH AFTER MONTH, NOAH'S FAMILY WAITS ...

WE'VE BEEN IN THIS ARK FOR SIX MONTHS NOW. WHEN WILL WE EVER SEE LAND AGAIN?

IT COULD BE ANOTHER SIX MONTHS. AND WHAT WILL WE FIND WHEN WE FINALLY GET OUT?

FINALLY THE WATER LEVEL BEGINS TO DROP. THE ARK COMES TO REST ON TOP OF THE MOUNTAINS OF ARARAT.

I'LL SEND OUT A DOVE. IF IT DOESN'T COME BACK, WE'LL KNOW IT HAS FOUND LAND.

THE DOVE DISAPPEARS FROM SIGHT. NOAH WATCHES THE SKIES ...

AFTER LONG HOURS SWIRLING THROUGH THE SKY, THE DOVE RETURNS. A FEW DAYS LATER, NOAH AGAIN SENDS OUT A DOVE, AND AGAIN IT RETURNS.

AN OLIVE BRANCH! THAT MEANS SOME LAND MUST BE DRY AGAIN.

SEVEN DAYS LATER, NOAH SENDS OUT A DOVE FOR THE THIRD TIME. THIS TIME, THE BIRD DOES NOT RETURN. IT HAS FOUND A PLACE TO NEST.

NOAH AND HIS FAMILY ARE ANXIOUS TO LEAVE THE ARK. THEY LOOK EVERY DAY FOR SIGNS OF DRY LAND.

LOOK!

A LITTLE OVER A YEAR AFTER THE FLOOD STARTED, NOAH STEPS OUT ONTO DRY LAND ONCE MORE. ONLY EIGHT PEOPLE HAVE SURVIVED THE FLOOD: NOAH, HIS WIFE, THEIR THREE SONS, AND THEIR SONS' WIVES.

THE WARM SUN ON MY FACE, THE GRASS UNDER MY FEET—IT FEELS WONDERFUL!

EVERYTHING EVIL IS GONE. THROUGH US, GOD IS GIVING HUMAN BEINGS A NEW START. WE MUST OBEY GOD AND TEACH EVERYONE WHO FOLLOWS US TO OBEY.

OH, GROUND! HOW I'VE MISSED YOU!!

A Babbling Tower

BASED ON GENESIS 11:1-9

A TOWER THAT WILL REACH TO HEAVEN—WE RULE!!

PEOPLE CAN SEE IT FOR MILES. IN TIMES OF DANGER, WE'LL RALLY OUR FORCES AROUND IT. NO ONE IS GOING TO CONQUER AND SCATTER US. WITH THIS TOWER, WE'LL BE INVINCIBLE!

BUT GOD IS DISPLEASED WITH THE PEOPLE'S QUEST FOR FAME AND POWER. TO STOP THEIR WORK ON THE TOWER, HE CAUSES THE PEOPLE TO SPEAK IN DIFFERENT LANGUAGES.

BECAUSE THEY CANNOT UNDERSTAND EACH OTHER, THE BUILDERS ARE CONFUSED. THEY STOP WORKING ON THE TOWER. ONE BY ONE, FAMILIES WHO SPEAK THE SAME LANGUAGE MOVE AWAY. THE GIANT TOWER, CALLED BABEL, BEGINS TO CRUMBLE ...

YOU'RE TALKING GIBBERISH!! HOW CAN I WORK WITH A MAN I CAN'T UNDERSTAND?

DIFFERENT CIVILIZATIONS SPRING UP, SPEAKING DIFFERENT LANGUAGES, AND SOON THE TOWER IS COMPLETELY FORGOTTEN.

God's Wager

BASED ON JOB

IN A DISTANT LAND, JOB, A MAN WHO LOVES GOD, HAS EVERYTHING HE NEEDS. HE HAS 7,000 SHEEP, 3,000 CAMELS, 1,000 OXEN, 500 DONKEYS AND SERVANTS TO TAKE CARE OF ALL HIS NEEDS. HE ALSO HAS A WONDERFUL FAMILY—A WIFE, SEVEN SONS, AND THREE DAUGHTERS ...

THE LORD HAS BLESSED ME TO OVERFLOWING!

UP IN HEAVEN, GOD IS PROUD OF HIS RIGHTEOUS SERVANT. BUT SATAN HATES TO SEE A HAPPY ENDING.

JOB ONLY WORSHIPS YOU BECAUSE YOU MAKE SURE NOTHING BAD EVER HAPPENS TO HIM. IF YOU DIDN'T GIVE HIM SUCH RICHES AND BLESSINGS—

—HE WOULD TURN FROM YOU IN AN INSTANT AND CURSE YOUR NAME.

YOU THINK SO? VERY WELL. YOU MAY TEST HIM. TAKE AWAY HIS BLESSINGS, BUT DO NOT HURT HIM.

SATAN WASTES NO TIME IN STRIKING JOB WITH CATASTROPHE. ONE DAY A MESSENGER COMES TO JOB ...

THE SABEANS ATTACKED! THEY STOLE THE OXEN AND DONKEYS AND KILLED THE PEOPLE WORKING IN YOUR FIELDS. I'M THE ONLY ONE WHO ESCAPED.

THAT SAME MOMENT, ANOTHER MESSENGER ARRIVES ...

LIGHTNING STRUCK THE SHEEP AND SHEPHERDS. THEY'RE ALL DEAD. I'M THE ONLY ONE WHO ESCAPED.

THEN A THIRD MESSENGER COMES ...

CHALDEANS RAIDED THE CAMELS AND KILLED THE CAMEL DRIVERS. I'M THE ONLY ONE WHO ESCAPED.

YET ANOTHER MESSENGER ARRIVES WITH BAD NEWS ...

YOUR OLDEST SON'S HOUSE COLLAPSED, KILLING ALL OF YOUR CHILDREN. I'M THE ONLY ONE WHO ESCAPED.

JOB IS SADDENED BY THE LOSS OF HIS PROPERTY AND LIVESTOCK. BUT HE IS DEVASTATED AT THE DEATH OF HIS CHILDREN!

HE SHAVES OFF ALL HIS HAIR IN GRIEF, AND RIPS HIS CLOTHES TO TATTERS. BUT HE DOES NOT BLAME GOD FOR THIS MISFORTUNE.

I CAME INTO THIS WORLD WITH NOTHING, AND I WILL LEAVE IT WITH NOTHING. GOD GAVE, AND GOD TOOK AWAY. PRAISE BE TO GOD!

SEE, SATAN? HE IS A BETTER MAN THAN YOU THOUGHT.

WELL, SURE. SINCE I DIDN'T DO ANYTHING TO HIM OR HIS HEALTH. BUT NO ONE PRAISES GOD WHEN THEY'RE SICK.

SO YOU THINK. RUIN HIS HEALTH, IF YOU THINK THAT WILL HAVE ANY EFFECT ON THIS RIGHTEOUS MAN. BUT DO NOT KILL HIM.

SATAN IMMEDIATELY RETURNS TO EARTH AND STRIKES JOB WITH TERRIBLE OPEN SORES FROM HEAD TO FOOT. HE CURSES JOB WITH INSOMNIA AND—WHEN JOB DOES SLEEP—SATAN TERRIFIES HIM WITH NIGHTMARES. JOB CAN'T KEEP HIS FOOD DOWN AND LOSES SO MUCH WEIGHT, HE CAN HARDLY MOVE.

STILL, JOB DOES NOT COMPLAIN. BUT HIS WIFE ...

EVERYTHING WE OWNED AND EVERYONE WE LOVED IS GONE. SURELY THIS DISEASE WILL KILL YOU. YOU SHOULD JUST CURSE GOD AND DIE!

JOB LOOKS AT HIS WIFE OUT OF PAINFUL, BLEARED EYELIDS.

DON'T BE A FOOL. WE CANNOT ACCEPT THE GOOD THINGS FROM GOD WITHOUT ALSO ACCEPTING THE BAD.

WHEN JOB'S FRIENDS HEAR ABOUT HIS TROUBLES, THEY COME TO SIT WITH HIM IN THE GARBAGE DUMP AT THE EDGE OF TOWN. THE DISEASE HAS AFFECTED JOB SO STRONGLY, HIS FRIENDS ALMOST DON'T EVEN RECOGNIZE HIM. FOR SEVEN DAYS, NO ONE SPEAKS. THEY JUST SIT TOGETHER WITH THEIR FRIEND. FINALLY, AFTER A WEEK, JOB BREAKS OUT WITH A CRY OF GRIEF.

I HAVE DONE NOTHING WRONG! WHY IS GOD LETTING ALL THESE TERRIBLE THINGS HAPPEN TO ME?

ELIPHAZ IS SHOCKED AT JOB'S HARSH QUESTION.

NOW, DON'T GET UPSET, JOB, BUT FROM EVERYTHING I'VE SEEN, GOD DOESN'T PUNISH INNOCENT PEOPLE. YOU MUST HAVE DONE SOMETHING WRONG.

BUT I HAVEN'T SINNED! AND EVEN IF I HAVE, GOD KNOWS MY HEART AND WOULD FORGIVE ME.

BUT BILDAD IS NOT CONVINCED.

IT SOUNDS LIKE YOU'RE BLAMING GOD FOR BEING UNFAIR, JOB! I'M SORRY, BUT IF YOUR KIDS WERE KILLED, IT'S BECAUSE THEY MUST HAVE DESERVED IT. YOU HAVE A CHANCE TO CONFESS YOUR SINS—YOU SHOULD TAKE IT.

I WOULD CONFESS MY SINS, IF GOD WOULD COME AND TELL ME WHAT I HAD DONE WRONG.

JOB'S INSISTENCE THAT HE IS INNOCENT OFFENDS HIS THIRD FRIEND, ZOPHAR.

YOU WINDBAG! YOU DON'T KNOW ANYTHING ABOUT GOD! YOU STUBBORNLY INSIST THAT YOU HAVE DONE NO WRONG, WHEN THE ONLY THING THAT CAN SAVE YOU IS TO APOLOGIZE TO GOD FOR YOUR SINS.

SOME FRIENDS YOU ARE! YOU DO NOT COMFORT ME AT THE WORST TIME OF MY LIFE. YOU THINK YOU SPEAK FOR GOD? I ONLY WISH HE WOULD COME SPEAK FOR HIMSELF. EVEN IF HE KILLED ME, I WOULD TRUST IN HIM.

God Calls Abram
BASED ON GENESIS 11–12

MANY YEARS PASS. PEOPLE FORGET ABOUT THE GOD WHO CREATED THEM. THEY MOVE DOWN THE EUPHRATES RIVER AND BUILD THE GREAT TRADING CITY OF UR. UR IS A LAND OF PLENTY— WITH PLENTY OF DIFFERENT GODS. BUT THE ONE TRUE GOD SPEAKS TO A YOUNG MAN NAMED ABRAM.

SARAI, GOD HAS SPOKEN TO ME. HE SAID TO LEAVE MY FATHER'S FAMILY, MY COUNTRY, AND THE FALSE GODS OF UR BEHIND ME. HE SAID TO TRAVEL TO A LAND THAT HE WILL SHOW ME. THERE HE WILL MAKE OUR FAMILY A GREAT NATION, AND ALL THE PEOPLE ON THE EARTH WILL BE BLESSED THROUGH ME.

ABRAM! WHY ARE YOU OUT HERE IN THE MIDDLE OF THE NIGHT?

IT WILL BE SCARY TO LEAVE EVERYTHING WE KNOW—AND OUR FAMILY! BUT WE WILL TRUST THE LORD TO KEEP HIS PROMISES.

HOW DO YOU THINK YOUR FATHER WILL TAKE THE NEWS?

NOT WELL ...

ABRAM CAN'T LEAVE ME BEHIND IN MY OLD AGE! AND, LOT—YOU'RE HIS NEPHEW. SINCE YOUR FATHER IS DEAD, IT'S ABRAM'S RESPONSIBILITY TO TAKE CARE OF YOU TOO! WE'RE GOING WITH HIM.

ABRAM LEADS HIS TRIBE THROUGH THE SURROUNDING LANDS. FOR SEVERAL YEARS, HE AND HIS EXTENDED FAMILY LIVE THE LIFE OF WANDERING NOMADS.

BUT THEN A FAMINE SWEEPS THROUGH THE LAND. ABRAM DOESN'T HAVE ENOUGH FOOD TO SUPPORT HIS TRIBE. HE DECIDES HIS ONLY CHOICE IS TO LEAD HIS PEOPLE TO EGYPT, A POWERFUL NATION WITH PLENTY OF FOOD.

BUT HE HAS SOME FEARS ABOUT HIS PLAN ...

SARAI, YOU ARE THE MOST BEAUTIFUL WOMAN I'VE EVER SEEN. I'M AFRAID THAT WHEN PHARAOH SEES YOU, HE WILL FALL IN LOVE WITH YOU. SINCE I'M YOUR HUSBAND, HE'LL KILL ME SO THAT HE CAN MARRY YOU. WE MUST PRETEND TO BE BROTHER AND SISTER.

THAT SOUNDS VERY UNLIKELY ... BUT I'LL DO WHAT YOU ASK.

BUT ABRAM'S PREDICTION COMES TRUE. PHARAOH FALLS FOR SARAI'S LOVELINESS. THINKING ABRAM IS HER BROTHER, PHARAOH GIVES HIM LOTS OF MONEY AND GIFTS AND ASKS SARAI TO BE HIS WIFE.

BUT BEFORE PHARAOH CAN MARRY HER, GOD INTERVENES TO SAVE HIS CHOSEN FAMILY.

PLAGUES!

A Lot Is Too Much

BASED ON GENESIS 13

ABRAM HAS LEFT EGYPT WITH GREAT WEALTH. BUT THIS BLESSING FROM EGYPT TURNS OUT TO BE A CURSE IN DISGUISE.

IS THERE A PROBLEM?

NOW THAT THE TRIBE HAS TASTED WEALTH, THEIR OLD NOMAD WAYS DON'T SEEM SO GREAT.

YOUR NEPHEW LOT IS CLAIMING THAT HIS FAMILY SHOULD GET FIRST CHOICE OF THE RICHES FROM EGYPT.

IN SPITE OF THIS, ABRAM AND LOT BOTH PROSPER, AND THEIR FLOCKS INCREASE. BUT SOON THE QUARRELING SPREADS TO THEIR WORKERS.

MAKE ROOM FOR LOT'S SHEEP.

NO! ABRAM IS THE CHIEF. HIS FLOCKS COME FIRST.

Insufficient Sons

BASED ON GENESIS 15—18

MANY YEARS PASS. ABRAM AND SARAI ARE NOW OLD, AND THEY HAVE NO CHILDREN. BUT GOD REPEATS HIS PROMISE.

YOU WILL HAVE MORE DESCENDANTS THAN THERE ARE STARS IN THE HEAVENS!

AS A SIGN OF HIS PROMISE, GOD CHANGES ABRAM'S NAME TO ABRAHAM, WHICH MEANS "FATHER OF MANY."

GOD ALSO CHANGES SARAI'S NAME TO SARAH—WHICH MEANS "PRINCESS"—BECAUSE SHE WOULD BE THE MOTHER OF NATIONS. BUT SARAH IS TOO OLD TO HAVE CHILDREN. WITHOUT ANY SONS, HOW COULD ABRAHAM'S DESCENDANTS BE AS NUMBERLESS AS THE STARS?

GOD HAS PROMISED ME AN HEIR. PERHAPS THIS IS THE WAY.

MAYBE GOD JUST MEANS *YOU* WILL HAVE CHILDREN, AND NOT ME. YOU SHOULD TAKE MY SERVANT, HAGAR, AS A WIFE. SHE MIGHT HAVE A SON FOR ME.

HAGAR HAS A SON, AND HE IS THE PRIDE OF ABRAHAM'S HEART.

MY ISHMAEL IS A TALENTED BOY.

REMEMBER, HAGAR, YOU HAD A SON FOR ME. I ADOPTED HIM.

BUT IN HER HEART, SARAH KNOWS THAT ISHMAEL ISN'T REALLY HERS. AS ISHMAEL GROWS TO BOYHOOD, HE IS THE CENTER OF ATTENTION THROUGHOUT THE CAMP ...

... AND THE SOURCE OF TROUBLE BETWEEN HAGAR AND SARAH.

SOMEDAY MY SON WILL RULE THIS WHOLE TRIBE.

HAGAR GETS MORE SURE OF HERSELF EVERY DAY.

ABRAHAM WORRIES ABOUT THE TROUBLE IN HIS CAMP. ONE DAY WHILE HE IS RESTING AND THINKING ABOUT ISHMAEL, HAGAR, AND SARAH, HE LOOKS UP ...

THREE STRANGERS APPROACH ABRAHAM'S CAMP. HE GREETS THEM AND INVITES THEM TO REST AND EAT WITH HIM.

YOUR WIFE, SARAH, WILL HAVE A SON.

HA HA! I AM TOO OLD TO HAVE CHILDREN NOW.

WHEN THE STRANGERS LEAVE, ABRAHAM WALKS WITH THEM FOR A WHILE.

THAT CITY OF SODOM IS SO WICKED THAT GOD WILL HAVE TO DESTROY IT.

THESE MUST BE MESSENGERS FROM GOD! THEY ARE TALKING ABOUT THE PLACE WHERE LOT LIVES!

ABRAHAM PLEADS TO GOD TO SAVE SODOM.

WOULD YOU REALLY DESTROY THE RIGHTEOUS ALONG WITH THE WICKED? WHAT IF THERE ARE EVEN 50 GOOD PEOPLE IN THAT CITY? DO THEY DESERVE TO BE DESTROYED?

GOD AGREES TO SAVE SODOM FOR THE SAKE OF 50 GOOD MEN. BUT ABRAHAM CONTINUES TO BARGAIN WITH GOD. WHAT IF THERE ARE 30 GOOD MEN? FINALLY HE GETS GOD TO PROMISE THAT THE CITY WILL BE SAVED EVEN IF THERE ARE ONLY TEN GOOD MEN IN IT.

A Lot Is Not Enough *BASED ON GENESIS 19*

OUTSIDE LOT'S HOUSE IN SODOM, THE MOB GOES WILD.

AS THE MEN PUSH AGAINST LOT'S DOOR, THE ANGELS—SHOWING THEIR POWER—STRIKE THE RIOTERS BLIND.

HELP! I CAN'T SEE!

MY EYES! WHO HIT ME?

INSIDE LOT'S HOUSE ...

THERE ARE NO RIGHTEOUS PEOPLE LEFT IN THIS TOWN. RUN FOR YOUR LIVES! THE LORD SENT US TO DESTROY THIS WICKED CITY.

MY FAMILY! I MUST SAVE THEM.

Too Many Sons
BASED ON GENESIS 21:1-21

AFTER THE DESTRUCTION OF SODOM, ABRAHAM DECIDES TO MOVE TO A NEW PLACE. HE LEADS HIS GROWING CLAN TO THE NEGEV REGION, NEAR THE DESERT.

THE ANGELS WHO VISITED ABRAHAM HAD TOLD HIM SARAH WOULD HAVE A SON. ONE YEAR LATER, THEIR PREDICTION COMES TRUE.

WHO WOULD HAVE THOUGHT THAT I WOULD EVER HAVE A SON? I'M TOO OLD, BUT I'M HOLDING MY BABY IN MY ARMS.

I'LL NEVER DOUBT GOD'S PROMISES AGAIN.

ABRAHAM HAS NAMED HIS SECOND SON ISAAC.

WHAT WILL BECOME OF ISHMAEL, HIS FIRST SON? HE MIGHT HAVE BECOME OUR RULER. BUT NOW THE BABY, ISAAC, WILL BE NEXT IN LINE AFTER ABRAHAM.

I'M SURE IT WON'T BE A PROBLEM.

TENSION GROWS BETWEEN SARAH AND HAGAR OVER THEIR SONS. AT BABY ISAAC'S FIRST FEAST ...

HA HA! LOOK HOW CLUMSY LITTLE ISAAC IS!

ISHMAEL! BE QUIET!

SARAH IS ANGRY. WHAT WILL SHE DO ABOUT ISHMAEL?

HAGAR'S SON CAN'T MAKE FUN OF MINE! ABRAHAM, YOU MUST SEND ISHMAEL AND HAGAR AWAY BEFORE THEY CAUSE REAL TROUBLE IN THE TRIBE.

NIGHT AFTER NIGHT, ABRAHAM ASKS GOD HOW TO SOLVE THIS FAMILY PROBLEM. FINALLY, GOD ANSWERS HIM:

DO WHAT SARAH SAYS, BECAUSE I WILL FULFILL MY PROMISE THROUGH ISAAC. BUT DON'T WORRY ABOUT YOUR FIRST SON, ISHMAEL. I WILL TAKE CARE OF HIM AND HIS MOTHER.

DAY AFTER DAY, HAGAR AND ISHMAEL WANDER THROUGH THE BURNING SAND. ONE FEAR POUNDS IN HAGAR'S MIND.

EARLY ONE MORNING ...

BECAUSE OF SARAH'S JEALOUSY, IT IS BETTER THAT YOU AND ISHMAEL LEAVE. DON'T BE AFRAID. GOD WILL WATCH OVER YOU.

WILL WE HAVE ENOUGH WATER UNTIL WE FIND AN OASIS?

AT LAST THE DREADED MOMENT COMES ...

THERE'S NO MORE WATER, MOTHER! I'M DYING OF THIRST!

I KNOW, SON. SO AM I. LIE DOWN IN THE SHADE OF THE BUSH.

O GOD, DON'T MAKE ME WATCH MY CHILD DIE!

DEAD TIRED AND CHOKING WITH THIRST, HAGAR TURNS HER BACK ON HER SON, ISHMAEL. SHE CANNOT STAND TO WATCH HIM DIE. SUDDENLY SHE HEARS A VOICE. THE ANGEL OF GOD SAYS, "LIFT THE BOY UP. I WILL MAKE HIM A GREAT NATION."

HAGAR STARTS TOWARD HER SON ...

... AND SEES A SPRING OF WATER!

WATER! WE WILL NOT DIE! ISHMAEL, GOD HAS SAVED US!

KNOWING GOD IS WITH THEM, HAGAR AND ISHMAEL CONTINUE THEIR JOURNEY. THEY BUILD A HOME IN THE WILDERNESS. YEARS PASS. EVENTUALLY ISHMAEL MARRIES AN EGYPTIAN GIRL AND BECOMES THE HEAD OF A GREAT DESERT TRIBE.

A Father's Sacrifice

BASED ON GENESIS 22–23

SADDLE THE HORSES!

ISAAC AND I MUST GO ON A JOURNEY.

BUT THIS IS A JOURNEY LIKE NO OTHER. NO ONE KNOWS THAT—AS A TEST OF FAITH—GOD HAS TOLD ABRAHAM TO SACRIFICE HIS SON. OVER A LIFETIME OF FAITHFULNESS, ABRAHAM HAS LEARNED TO OBEY GOD, BUT HE DOES NOT UNDERSTAND THIS PERPLEXING COMMAND.

HOW COULD GOD ASK SUCH A THING? I KNOW IT'S ABSURD, BUT I MUST BELIEVE THAT EVEN IF I SACRIFICE ISAAC, GOD WILL GIVE HIM BACK TO ME SOMEHOW—EVEN IF IT MEANS RAISING HIM FROM THE DEAD.

LEAVING THE SERVANTS BEHIND, THEY TREK UP TO THE MOUNTAINTOP, BUT ISAAC'S CURIOSITY GROWS ...

SOMETHING IS WRONG. THIS ISN'T HOW WE USUALLY DO IT.

SUDDENLY, ABRAHAM HEARS THE VOICE OF GOD.

DON'T LAY A HAND ON YOUR SON! I WOULD NEVER TRULY LET YOU DO SUCH A THING. BUT YOU HAVE PROVEN THAT YOU ARE FULLY DEVOTED TO ME. YOU DIDN'T HOLD BACK EVEN YOUR SON.

AS ABRAHAM BREATHES A HUGE SIGH OF RELIEF, HE SPOTS A RAM CAUGHT IN A NEARBY BUSH.

A RAM FOR THE SACRIFICE! THANK YOU, GOD!

QUICKLY ABRAHAM RELEASES ISAAC AND PUTS THE RAM IN HIS PLACE ON THE ALTAR.

FATHER, YOU GAVE ME TO GOD—AND HE GAVE ME BACK TO YOU.

YES, MY SON. IT WAS A TEST OF FAITH.

ISAAC, NEVER DOUBT THE WISDOM AND LOVE OF GOD.

WITH JOYOUS HEARTS, ABRAHAM AND ISAAC GIVE THANKS TO GOD.

I SWEAR— IN THE NAME OF MYSELF— THAT BECAUSE YOU OBEYED ME I WILL BLESS THE WHOLE WORLD THROUGH YOUR CHILDREN.

ON THE WAY HOME, ISAAC WALKS AHEAD—AND ALONE. THROUGH HIS MIND FLASH SCENES OF THE DAY. HE CAN STILL FEEL THE ROPES THAT TIED HIM ON THE ALTAR ... SEE HIS FATHER'S KNIFE ... FEEL THE JOY OF KNOWING HE WOULD NOT BE KILLED.

SARAH RUSHES OUT OF THE CAMP TO GREET THEM.

ISAAC, WHAT HAPPENED? YOU LEFT HERE A BOY, BUT YOU HAVE RETURNED A MAN—LIKE YOUR FATHER, STRONG AND WISE.

FROM MY FATHER I LEARNED THE COST OF FAITH— AND FROM GOD I LEARNED THE REWARD OF FAITH.

IN THE YEARS THAT FOLLOW, THE TRIBE OF ABRAHAM PROSPERS. THEN ONE DAY, SAD NEWS SPREADS QUICKLY THROUGH THE CAMP. SARAH HAS DIED.

ABRAHAM'S SERVANT REACHES HARAN IN THE EVENING. HE RESTS BY THE WELL JUST OUTSIDE TOWN AND SEES YOUNG WOMEN OF THE CITY COMING TO GET WATER.

GOD, LET THIS BE THE TEST: WHOEVER GIVES WATER TO ME *AND* MY CAMELS WILL BE ISAAC'S BRIDE.

SHE'S BEAUTIFUL! IS SHE THE ONE?

MISS? COULD I PLEASE HAVE A DRINK?

I'LL BE GLAD TO GET YOU A DRINK.

... AND I'LL DRAW WATER FOR YOUR CAMELS, TOO.

SHE IS THE ONE!

WHEN THE GIRL FINISHES WATERING THE CAMELS, ELIEZAR GIVES HER A NOSE RING AND GOLD BRACELETS.

WHAT IS YOUR NAME?

DO YOU THINK THERE IS ROOM FOR ME TO STAY IN YOUR FATHER'S HOUSE?

THESE ARE BEAUTIFUL! MY NAME IS REBEKAH. WE HAVE PLENTY OF ROOM FOR YOU AT OUR HOUSE. JUST A MINUTE ...

REBEKAH RUNS TO TELL HER FAMILY. WHEN SHE SHOWS THEM THE PRESENTS, HER BROTHER, LABAN, GOES OUT TO MEET ABRAHAM'S SERVANT.

COME WITH ME! MY FATHER HAS ROOM FOR YOU AND YOUR CARAVAN.

ABRAHAM'S SERVANT TELLS EVERYONE WHO HE IS AND EXPLAINS THAT GOD HAS CHOSEN REBEKAH TO BE THE BRIDE OF ISAAC, SON AND HEIR OF ABRAHAM, HER GREAT-UNCLE.

TAKE REBEKAH TO BE THE WIFE OF MY UNCLE'S SON. DO IT JUST THE WAY THE LORD HAS SAID.

EARLY THE NEXT MORNING, THE CARAVAN GETS READY TO RETURN TO ABRAHAM'S CAMP. REBEKAH SAYS GOOD-BYE TO HER FAMILY, AND THE CARAVAN BEGINS ITS LONG JOURNEY.

DAYS LATER, THE CARAVAN NEARS ABRAHAM'S CAMP. REBEKAH WONDERS ...

WHAT WILL ISAAC BE LIKE?

TALL AND STRONG LIKE A CHIEF'S SON? I WONDER IF HE WILL LOVE ME ...

WHO IS THE MAN COMING TO MEET US?

THAT'S ISAAC!

HE IS HANDSOME!

IS THIS THE WOMAN I'M GOING TO MARRY?

WHEN ISAAC SEES REBEKAH, HE FALLS IN LOVE WITH HER AT ONCE AND TAKES HER TO HIS FATHER FOR HIS BLESSING. THEY GET MARRIED IMMEDIATELY, AND THE WHOLE CAMP REJOICES THAT GOD CONTINUES TO WATCH OVER ABRAHAM'S FAMILY.

Birthright Stew

BASED ON GENESIS 25–26

AFTER A LONG AND HAPPY LIFE, ABRAHAM FINALLY JOINS HIS WIFE IN DEATH. ISAAC LEADS ABRAHAM'S TRIBE TO THE BURIAL CAVE OF MACHPELAH TO PLACE THE BODY OF ITS GREAT CHIEFTAIN BESIDE HIS WIFE, SARAH.

BUT ISAAC, LIKE HIS FATHER, HAS GONE A LONG TIME WITHOUT HAVING ANY CHILDREN.

REBEKAH IS BARREN. WE'VE TRIED EVERY REMEDY KNOWN TO MAN. NOTHING HAS WORKED. NOW I MUST PRAY TO GOD AND TRUST HIS PROMISE.

THE LORD ANSWERS ISAAC'S PRAYERS, AND REBEKAH BECOMES PREGNANT. BUT HER PREGNANCY SEEMS UNUSUAL. WHEN THEY INQUIRE OF THE LORD, HE TELLS REBEKAH THAT SHE IS PREGNANT WITH TWINS! "YOU WILL GIVE BIRTH TO TWO NATIONS. ONE WILL BE STRONGER THAN THE OTHER, AND THE YOUNGER WILL RULE THE OLDER."

WHEN REBEKAH GIVES BIRTH, HER FIRST SON IS REDDISH AND HAIRY. THEY NAME HIM ESAU. BUT CLUTCHING ESAU'S HEEL IS JACOB, WHO DOES NOT WANT TO BE LEFT BEHIND. AS THE BOYS GROW UP, ISAAC EARNS A REPUTATION AS A MAN WHO AVOIDS CONFLICT. BUT ISAAC FAILS TO SEE THE CONFLICT GROWING BETWEEN HIS OWN TWIN SONS.

WHICH ONE WILL BE OUR RULER AFTER ISAAC?

ESAU IS STRONGER— BUT JACOB IS MORE CLEVER. ESAU HAS THE BIRTHRIGHT BECAUSE HE IS THE OLDEST. BUT I'D BE SURPRISED IF JACOB DOESN'T DO SOMETHING TRICKY.

IF I WERE ISAAC, I'D PAY MORE ATTENTION TO THE COMPETITION BETWEEN THOSE TWO BOYS.

ONE DAY, WHEN ESAU RETURNS WITH FRESH FOOD FROM HUNTING, ISAAC PRAISES HIM.

ESAU IS A MIGHTY HUNTER!

YES, HE'S STRONG AS AN OX—AND DUMB AS ONE TOO.

JACOB BIDES HIS TIME. ONE MORNING, DURING A HOT SPELL, ESAU SETS OUT FOR A HUNTING TRIP. THIS IS THE CHANCE JACOB HAS BEEN WAITING FOR.

ESAU WILL FIND GAME AT THE WATER HOLE, MILES AWAY FROM HERE. WHEN HE GETS BACK FROM THE LONG DAY'S HUNT, HE'LL BE TIRED AND HUNGRY. I'LL BE READY FOR HIM.

TOWARD SUNDOWN, JACOB WAITS FOR HIS BROTHER OUTSIDE CAMP.

HERE HE COMES—AND WITHOUT ANY GAME. DIDN'T HE CATCH ANYTHING?

CAMP WITH ITS FOOD IS ONLY A SHORT DISTANCE AWAY, BUT ESAU IS SO HUNGRY, HE CAN'T WAIT ...

I'M STARVING. GIVE ME SOME OF THE STEW YOU'RE MAKING.

WILL YOU TRADE YOUR BIRTHRIGHT FOR IT?

WELL, THAT'S A DUMB QUESTION.

IS A BIRTHRIGHT TASTY AND FILLED WITH SAVORY MEAT? I'LL TAKE THE STEW.

HERE IS THE STEW. SWEAR THAT YOUR BIRTHRIGHT IS MINE!

I PROMISE—THE BIRTHRIGHT IS YOURS. I'M DYING OF HUNGER. LET ME EAT!

HERE, EAT ALL YOU WANT.

ESAU'S BIRTHRIGHT IS MINE! SOMEDAY I WILL INHERIT A DOUBLE SHARE OF MY FATHER'S WEALTH. I WILL RULE THE TRIBE, NOT ESAU.

BUT JACOB HAS A LONG TIME TO WAIT. HIS FATHER IS STILL STRONG AND POWERFUL. AND AS ISAAC GROWS OLDER, IT BECOMES CLEAR THAT ESAU IS HIS FAVORITE SON. JACOB REALIZES THAT TRICKING ESAU INTO GIVING HIM THE BIRTHRIGHT IS NOT ENOUGH. SOMEHOW HE MUST CONVINCE HIS FATHER TO GIVE HIM THE FAMILY BLESSING AS WELL. FOR ALL HIS TRICKY PLOTS, JACOB CAN'T DISOBEY HIS FATHER. HIS FATHER, ISAAC, IS THE HEAD OF THE FAMILY; HIS MOTHER, REBEKAH, HOWEVER, IS THE BRAINS ...

ISAAC DOESN'T KNOW THAT JACOB HAS ALREADY CLAIMED THE BIRTHRIGHT THAT BELONGS TO ESAU.

FIND MY SON ESAU. TELL HIM THAT I MUST SEE HIM RIGHT AWAY.

ISAAC'S THOUGHTS GO BACK OVER THE YEARS TO THE DAY HE FIRST SAW REBEKAH. HE ALSO KNOWS THERE WILL BE TROUBLE BETWEEN THE SONS. HE SENDS FOR JACOB.

ASHAMED BUT FRIGHTENED BY ESAU'S ANGER, JACOB COMES TO HIS FATHER.

GO TO YOUR UNCLE LABAN. FIND A WIFE FROM AMONG HIS FAMILY. GOD BLESS YOU, MY SON.

A FEW HOURS LATER, AT THE EDGE OF THE CAMP ...

GOOD-BYE, JACOB. I'LL SEND WORD WHEN IT'S SAFE FOR YOU TO COME BACK.

MY FATHER IS OLD—I MAY NEVER SEE HIM AGAIN! ESAU WANTS TO KILL ME. YOU ARE THE ONLY ONE I WILL BE ABLE TO COME BACK TO.

ONE PUNISHMENT FOR THEIR DECEIT IS THAT JACOB AND REBEKAH NEVER SEE EACH OTHER AGAIN.

TRAVELING FARTHER AND FARTHER FROM HIS FAMILY, JACOB IS TORTURED BY LONELINESS. HE ESPECIALLY MISSES HIS MOTHER, WHO HAS ALWAYS PROTECTED AND ADVISED HIM. AS NIGHT APPROACHES, JACOB COLLAPSES IN WEARINESS.

THAT NIGHT, HE DREAMS OF A SHINING STAIRWAY REACHING UP TO HEAVEN. ON THE STAIRWAY, ANGELS GO UP AND DOWN AS IF BRINGING HELP FROM GOD. AND JACOB HEARS GOD SPEAK TO HIM, PROMISING TO TAKE CARE OF HIM AND BRING HIM SAFELY HOME AGAIN.

THE NEXT MORNING, JACOB WAKES UP, STILL AWED BY HIS DREAM.

SURELY GOD IS IN THIS PLACE. AND THIS IS THE GATE OF HEAVEN.

JACOB REALIZES THE WRONG HE HAS DONE. BUT HE KNOWS THAT GOD WILL HELP HIM IF HE OBEYS HIM. QUICKLY, HE TURNS A STONE ON END FOR AN ALTAR AND WORSHIPS GOD. HE CALLS THE PLACE BETHEL, WHICH MEANS "THE HOUSE OF GOD."

IF GOD WILL GO WITH ME, I'LL BE GOD'S MAN.

JACOB GOES ON HIS WAY A STRONGER, NOBLER YOUNG MAN. HE IS EAGER TO PUT BEHIND HIM THE DISHONESTY OF HIS PAST AND TO SHARE GOD'S LOVE AND CARE.

Wife Swap BASED ON GENESIS 29

JACOB CONTINUES HIS JOURNEY. AT LAST HE GETS CLOSE TO HARAN.

MAYBE THOSE SHEPHERDS AT THE WELL CAN HELP ME FIND MY UNCLE LABAN.

CAN YOU TELL ME HOW TO FIND THE CHIEFTAIN, LABAN?

LABAN? SURE! THAT FLOCK OF SHEEP IS HIS. THAT'S HIS DAUGHTER RACHEL WITH THEM.

SHE'S GORGEOUS!

QUICKLY JACOB ROLLS THE STONE FROM THE WELL AND HELPS RACHEL WATER THE SHEEP. WHEN HE TELLS HER WHO HE IS, SHE RUNS TO FIND HER FATHER.

THAT NIGHT, LABAN HOLDS A FEAST FOR HIS NEPHEW JACOB. LEAH, THE OLDER DAUGHTER, SERVES THE FOOD, WHILE RACHEL, THE YOUNGER DAUGHTER, LISTENS TO JACOB TELL ABOUT HIS HOME AND THE LONG JOURNEY TO HARAN.

Leavin' Laban
BASED ON GENESIS 31

SO JACOB MARRIES RACHEL AND BEGINS ANOTHER SEVEN YEARS OF WORK FOR LABAN. BUT GOD BLESSES JACOB AND MAKES HIM RICH WITH HIS OWN FLOCKS. ONE DAY JACOB CALLS HIS WIVES TOGETHER.

HAVE YOU NOTICED THAT YOUR FATHER KEEPS SCOWLING AT ME—EVEN WHILE HE'S CHEATING ME? I THINK IT'S TIME TO GO. GOD IS TELLING ME TO RETURN HOME.

JACOB LOADS EVERYTHING ON CAMELS AND HERDS HIS FLOCKS TOGETHER. SOON THE CARAVAN IS ON ITS WAY.

LABAN MAY FOLLOW, SO KEEP WATCH AND TELL ME IF YOU SEE HIM COMING.

AS THEY TRAVEL, JACOB GUARDS THE CAMEL CARRYING RACHEL AND HER ONLY SON, JOSEPH. JACOB'S OTHER TEN SONS WATCH WITH JEALOUS EYES. WITHOUT REALIZING IT, JACOB SOWS SEEDS OF TROUBLE FOR THE SON HE LOVES BEST.

SEVERAL DAYS AFTER LEAVING LABAN ...

LOOK— RIDERS! LABAN AND HIS MEN! QUICK—TELL JACOB!

JACOB IS READY WHEN HIS FATHER-IN-LAW ARRIVES.

JACOB, WHY DID YOU LEAVE WITHOUT GIVING ME A CHANCE TO SAY GOOD-BYE?

I WAS AFRAID YOU MIGHT HAVE KEPT YOUR DAUGHTERS FROM GOING.

WELL, YOU'RE PROBABLY RIGHT.

BUT THE GOD OF YOUR FATHERS HAS TOLD ME NOT TO HURT YOU.

LABAN IS FURIOUS, BUT HE DOESN'T DARE GO AGAINST JACOB'S GOD. SO LABAN AND JACOB SET UP A PILE OF STONES TO MARK A BORDER AND MAKE AN AGREEMENT TO GO THEIR SEPARATE WAYS.

YOU STAY ON YOUR SIDE, AND I'LL STAY ON MINE.

Touched by an Angel

BASED ON GENESIS 32–33

EAGERLY, JACOB CONTINUES HIS JOURNEY HOME. ON THE WAY, HE HAS A WONDERFUL VISION ...

AN ARMY OF ANGELS! THE ARMY OF GOD IS CAMPED BESIDE ME!

THE ANGELS COMFORT JACOB. BUT AS HE GETS CLOSER TO HOME, HE BEGINS TO WORRY ABOUT HIS BROTHER, ESAU, WHO ONCE PLANNED TO MURDER HIM.

RIDE AHEAD OF ME AND LOOK FOR ESAU. TELL HIM I'M COMING HOME WITH MY FAMILY AND FLOCKS. TELL HIM I HOPE HE WILL FORGIVE ME.

JACOB WAITS ANXIOUSLY FOR THE RIDERS TO COME BACK. HE REMEMBERS THE TIME HE LIED TO HIS FATHER AND STOLE HIS BROTHER'S BLESSING—AND WHEN ESAU THREATENED TO KILL HIM.

FINALLY, THE SCOUTS RETURN ...

WE SAW ESAU! HE'S COMING TO MEET YOU—WITH 400 MEN!

JACOB IS FRIGHTENED, BUT HE IS ALSO SHREWD. HE DIVIDES HIS CARAVAN INTO TWO PARTS. THEN HE SENDS SERVANTS AHEAD WITH PRESENTS FOR ESAU.

IF ESAU ATTACKS ONE GROUP, THE OTHER CAN GET AWAY.

AND WHEN WE MEET ESAU, WE WILL GIVE HIM YOUR GENEROUS GIFTS OF GOATS, CAMELS, COWS, AND DONKEYS. HE WILL BE VERY IMPRESSED!

THAT NIGHT JACOB PRAYS, CONFESSING HIS SINS, ADMITTING HIS FEAR, AND ASKING FOR GOD'S HELP. BUT STILL HE CANNOT SLEEP.

SO IN THE MIDDLE OF THE NIGHT, JACOB MOVES HIS FAMILY ...

MY FAMILY WOULD BE SAFER ON THE OTHER SIDE OF THE RIVER.

YOU WILL BE SAFER ON THE OTHER SIDE, RACHEL.

I WISH YOU WOULD STAY WITH US.

BUT JACOB NEEDS TO BE ALONE. LATER THAT NIGHT, AS HE PRAYS, HE FEELS HIMSELF WRESTLING WITH A MYSTERIOUS STRANGER. THE STRUGGLE IS FIERCE, BUT JACOB DOES NOT GIVE UP UNTIL THE STRANGER BLESSES HIM: "YOUR NAME WILL NOT BE JACOB ANY LONGER. INSTEAD, YOU WILL BE ISRAEL, WHICH MEANS "GOD-WRESTLER."

THE NEXT MORNING, JACOB IS LIMPING BECAUSE HE HURT HIS HIP WRESTLING WITH THE ANGEL. BUT JACOB IS HAPPY BECAUSE HE KNOWS GOD HAS BLESSED HIM. JACOB GOES CONFIDENTLY TO MEET HIS BROTHER, ESAU.

JACOB, MY BROTHER! I'M HAPPY TO SEE YOU AGAIN!

ESAU! I'M SO GLAD YOU DON'T HATE ME ANYMORE.

PROUDLY JACOB PRESENTS HIS FAMILY— WELL, THE ONES HE LOVES MOST, ANYWAY ...

THIS IS MY WIFE RACHEL AND MY SON JOSEPH.

IT'S GOOD TO SEE MY BROTHER'S FAMILY. GOD HAS REALLY BLESSED YOU.

JACOB'S HAND TREMBLES AS HE SHADES HIS EYES AND LOOKS TOWARD THE DISTANT CITY OF HEBRON.

IS THAT WHERE GRANDFATHER ISAAC LIVES?

YES, JOSEPH. I PRAY WE ARE NOT TOO LATE. HE IS VERY OLD ...

GOD ANSWERS JACOB'S PRAYERS. AT THE SIGHT OF HIS OLD AND BLIND FATHER, JACOB FALLS TO HIS KNEES.

FATHER! I AM JACOB, YOUR SON! THANK GOD I AM WITH YOU AGAIN.

JACOB! I HAVE PRAYED FOR YOUR RETURN. DO YOU HAVE CHILDREN NOW?

PROUDLY JACOB PRESENTS HIS 12 SONS TO THEIR GRANDFATHER ISAAC.

FATHER, THIS IS JOSEPH AND THIS IS BENJAMIN, THE SONS OF MY BELOVED RACHEL.

BE STRONG, MY CHILDREN, AND ALWAYS OBEY GOD.

WITH THESE FINAL WORDS, ISAAC GOES TO BE WITH HIS GOD, THE GOD OF HIS FATHERS.

BUT JOSEPH DOESN'T GET THE HINT.

JACOB SOON FORGETS HIS OWN ANGER TOWARD JOSEPH, BUT THE SECOND DREAM WHIPS THE OLDER BROTHERS' HATRED INTO A BURNING RAGE.

Dreamer for Sale BASED ON GENESIS 37:12-36

JOSEPH'S DREAMS HAVE MADE HIS BROTHERS HATE HIM, BUT HIS FATHER IS BLIND TO THE DANGER. WHILE THE OLDER BROTHERS ARE TENDING SHEEP FAR AWAY IN THE LAND OF SHECHEM, JACOB SENDS JOSEPH TO FIND THEM.

GO CHECK ON THE FLOCKS—AND YOUR BROTHERS—AND LET ME KNOW HOW THINGS ARE GOING.

BUT WHEN THE BROTHERS SEE JOSEPH APPROACHING ...

HERE COMES THAT ARROGANT DREAMER.

I'VE HAD ENOUGH OF HIS TALK. LET'S GET RID OF HIM.

JOSEPH'S BROTHERS POUNCE ON HIM, STRIP HIM OF HIS FINE COAT, AND THROW HIM DOWN AN EMPTY WELL. THEN THEY TALK ABOUT HOW TO GET RID OF HIM FOR GOOD ...

Management Crisis

BASED ON GENESIS 39:1-20

O GOD, PLEASE HELP ME! HOW IS THIS IN YOUR PLAN?

AND SO JACOB'S FAVORITE SON BECOMES THE SLAVE OF POTIPHAR, CAPTAIN OF THE KING'S GUARD. BUT JOSEPH DOES NOT BEG FOR PITY. HE PUTS HIS TRUST IN GOD AND HOLDS UP HIS HEAD PROUDLY.

SOON THE SPOILED YOUNG BOY BECOMES A HARDWORKING YOUNG MAN.

JOSEPH HAS BECOME MY BEST SLAVE.

HE DOESN'T ACT LIKE A SLAVE. TELL ME MORE ABOUT HIM.

SOME TRADERS BROUGHT HIM FROM CANAAN. HE'S STRONG— INTELLIGENT, TOO.

AND HANDSOME! IN THE RIGHT CLOTHES, HE WOULD PASS FOR A PRINCE.

YEARS PASS, AND POTIPHAR EVENTUALLY MAKES JOSEPH MANAGER OF ALL HIS PROPERTY.

THINGS ARE BETTER WITH JOSEPH IN CHARGE.

HE PRAYS EVERY DAY, ASKING HIS GOD TO HELP HIM.

BUT JOSEPH'S SUCCESS ALSO LEADS TO TROUBLE. POTIPHAR'S WIFE FALLS IN LOVE WITH THE HANDSOME YOUNG SLAVE. ONE DAY WHILE POTIPHAR IS AWAY...

JOSEPH, COME SIT BESIDE ME AND TELL ME WHERE YOU CAME FROM. WHY ARE YOU HERE IN EGYPT?

THANK YOU, BUT I HAVE WORK TO FINISH BEFORE POTIPHAR RETURNS.

DO YOU ALWAYS HAVE TO THINK OF POTIPHAR?

HE'S MY MASTER! I WON'T BE DISLOYAL TO HIM OR DISOBEY MY GOD!

NO MAN CAN TREAT ME LIKE THAT—AND LIVE!

SHE WAITS WITH JOSEPH'S ROBE IN HER HANDS. WHEN POTIPHAR RETURNS, SHE GREETS HIM WITH TEARS IN HER EYES AND A LIE ON HER LIPS.

YOUR HEBREW SLAVE TRIED TO KISS ME! I SCREAMED AND HE LEFT—BUT HE DROPPED HIS ROBE. HERE, SEE IT?

I'LL THROW HIM INTO PRISON FOR THIS!

LOOK WHO WE HAVE COMING TO JOIN US IN SUCH FANCY CLOTHES.

WHEN HE'S BEEN HERE AS LONG AS I HAVE, HE'LL FORGET WHAT IT'S LIKE TO WEAR SUCH NICE CLEAN CLOTHES.

Jailhouse Shock

BASED ON GENESIS 39:20—41:43

FALSELY ACCUSED, JOSEPH FACES HIS FIRST NIGHT IN PRISON. BUT HE IS NOT AFRAID, AND HE IS NOT ALONE, BECAUSE GOD IS WITH HIM. JOSEPH PRAYS JUST AS HE HAS DONE EVERY OTHER NIGHT OF HIS LIFE.

WHAT GOD CAN SAVE HIM?

LEAVE HIM ALONE! HE'S BRAVER THAN THE REST OF US.

ONE LONG, HOT DAY FOLLOWS ANOTHER. THE PRISONERS QUARREL OVER FOOD, WATER, AND THE BEST PLACE TO SLEEP. ONE DAY A FIGHT BREAKS OUT ...

STOP IT! FIGHTING WON'T MAKE LIFE ANY BETTER.

EVEN IN PRISON, GOD IS WITH JOSEPH. THROUGH THESE TRIALS, GOD IS FORCING JOSEPH TO LEARN PATIENCE AND LEADERSHIP. WHEN THE KEEPER OF THE JAIL DISCOVERS THAT JOSEPH MAINTAINS PEACE IN THE PRISON, HE PUTS JOSEPH IN CHARGE OF THE OTHER PRISONERS.

ONE DAY, THE KING'S BAKER AND BUTLER ARE THROWN INTO PRISON FOR OFFENDING THE KING. BOTH MEN HAVE DREAMS THAT DISTURB THEM AND COME TO JOSEPH FOR HELP.

WHAT DO YOU THINK MY DREAM MEANS?

NOW TELL ME WHAT MY DREAM MEANS. LIKE HIS WOULD BE NICE!

I'M VERY SORRY. YOUR DREAM SHOWS THAT IN THREE DAYS YOUR HEAD WILL BE LIFTED OFF—YOU WILL BE HANGED UP HIGH BY PHARAOH.

IN THREE DAYS, YOUR HEAD WILL BE LIFTED UP, AND PHARAOH WILL GIVE YOU BACK YOUR HIGH POSITION. YOU WILL BE THE KING'S BUTLER AGAIN. AND PLEASE, WHEN MY WORDS COME TRUE, ASK PHARAOH TO RELEASE ME FROM PRISON. I AM AN INNOCENT CAPTIVE.

JOSEPH'S WORDS COME TRUE. THREE DAYS LATER, ONE MAN IS EXECUTED AND THE OTHER RETURNS TO SERVE THE KING. BUT THE BUTLER FORGETS HIS PROMISE TO PUT IN A GOOD WORD FOR JOSEPH. TWO YEARS GO BY. ONE DAY PHARAOH SUMMONS HIS BUTLER.

NO WINE FOR ME TODAY. I HAVE HAD A DISTURBING DREAM, AND NO ONE IN MY WHOLE KINGDOM CAN TELL ME WHAT IT MEANS.

PHARAOH, I KNOW OF A HEBREW PRISONER WHO CAN TELL THE MEANING OF DREAMS. HE EXPLAINED MINE!

WELL, WHAT ARE YOU WAITING FOR?!

Pharaoh's Man
BASED ON GENESIS 41:44–42:38

IN A SINGLE MOMENT, PHARAOH ELEVATES JOSEPH FROM PRISONER TO PRIME MINISTER. FROM THE THRONE ROOM, JOSEPH GOES OUTSIDE AND KNEELS IN PRAYER, THANKING GOD FOR HIS PROTECTION AND GUIDANCE.

JOSEPH ORDERS THE PEOPLE TO START PREPARING FOR THE FAMINE. HE BECOMES FAMOUS, AND EVERYONE REJOICES WHEN HE MARRIES THE BEAUTIFUL DAUGHTER OF THE PRIEST OF ON.

I AM PROUD TO BE YOUR WIFE, JOSEPH. YOU HAVE DONE SO MUCH FOR OUR PEOPLE.

THERE IS STILL A LOT TO DO. THE GOOD YEARS WILL PASS QUICKLY.

ALL TOO SOON, THE BAD YEARS BEGIN. AS THE FAMINE CONTINUES, PEOPLE COME FROM OTHER COUNTRIES THAT HAVE RUN OUT OF FOOD. ONLY EGYPT, WARNED BY GOD, HAS STORES OF GRAIN. PEOPLE FROM EVERY COUNTRY COME TO EGYPT, HOPING TO BUY SOME OF THE EXTRA FOOD. ONE DAY, TRIBESMEN FROM CANAAN ENTER JOSEPH'S CITY.

IN ORDER TO BUY GRAIN, THEY APPEAR BEFORE THE GOVERNOR OF EGYPT. THEN, JUST AS JOSEPH DREAMED MANY YEARS BEFORE, THEY BOW BEFORE HIM.

MY BROTHERS! THEY DO NOT RECOGNIZE ME AFTER ALL THESE YEARS.

WHY SHOULD HE THINK WE ARE SPIES?

I DON'T KNOW—BUT IT WAS STRANGE THAT THE GOVERNOR WANTED TO KNOW HOW MANY SONS OUR FATHER HAD.

HOURS PASS ... THEN DAYS. THE BROTHERS TRY TO UNDERSTAND WHAT HAS HAPPENED. NEVER ONCE DO THEY SUSPECT THAT THEIR BROTHER JOSEPH IS THE GOVERNOR OF EGYPT.

ON THE THIRD DAY, JOSEPH CALLS FOR THE BROTHERS TO BE BROUGHT TO HIM.

YOU MAY BUY GRAIN. BUT TO MAKE SURE YOU ARE NOT SPIES, I WILL HOLD ONE OF YOU IN PRISON UNTIL YOU BRING YOUR YOUNGEST BROTHER TO ME.

ME—IN PRISON?

THIS MUST BE PUNISHMENT FOR WHAT WE DID TO JOSEPH LONG AGO.

I TOLD YOU NOT TO HURT HIM!

HAS IT TAKEN YOU ALL THESE YEARS TO REGRET THE EVIL YOU DID THAT DAY?

SIMEON IS QUICKLY BOUND AND TAKEN BACK TO PRISON AS A HOSTAGE. FRIGHTENED AND EAGER TO LEAVE EGYPT, THE OTHER BROTHERS HURRY TO THE STOREHOUSE TO BUY GRAIN.

PAY ME FIRST. THEN I'LL FILL YOUR SACKS.

THEIR GRAIN SACKS FILLED, THE BROTHERS LEAVE EGYPT AT ONCE. BUT WHEN THEY GET HOME, THEY DISCOVER THAT THEIR SACKS ARE FILLED NOT ONLY WITH GRAIN BUT ALSO WITH ALL OF THEIR MONEY!

WHY DO YOU HAVE MONEY IN YOUR GRAIN SACKS? AND WHERE IS SIMEON?

THE WHOLE TRIP WAS VERY STRANGE. THE GOVERNOR SAID WE WERE SPIES. HE PUT US ALL IN PRISON. THEN HE RELEASED EVERYONE EXCEPT SIMEON. SIMEON HAS TO STAY THERE ... UNTIL ... WE TAKE BENJAMIN TO EGYPT.

TAKE BENJAMIN TO EGYPT? NEVER! I LOST JOSEPH LONG AGO. I'M NOT ABOUT TO LOSE ANOTHER SON. I WILL NOT LET YOU TAKE BENJAMIN.

BUT FATHER, WHAT ABOUT SIMEON?

YES, WHAT ABOUT SIMEON? AND WHAT ABOUT US IF THE GRAIN RUNS OUT AND WE HAVE TO GO BACK FOR MORE? WE CAN'T GO WITHOUT BENJAMIN.

THE FAMILY USES THE GRAIN SPARINGLY. BUT ONE DAY, JACOB'S HUNGRY TRIBE HAS TO FACE THE TRUTH ...

THE GRAIN IS ALMOST GONE. WHAT ARE WE GOING TO DO?

Bringing Benjamin

BASED ON GENESIS 43—44

JACOB, THE OLD CHIEFTAIN, FACES A HARD DECISION ...

BUT WHY SHOULD THE GOVERNOR OF EGYPT HOLD SIMEON IN PRISON UNTIL HE SEES BENJAMIN? WHAT DOES HE WANT WITH MY YOUNGEST SON?

NOBODY KNOWS, FATHER. BUT IF I DON'T GO, SIMEON WILL DIE IN PRISON—AND WE WILL STARVE. I HAVE TO GO!

BENJAMIN IS RIGHT.

THEN GO. BUT THIS TIME, TAKE DOUBLE THE AMOUNT OF MONEY FOR GRAIN. TAKE GIFTS FOR THE GOVERNOR. AND MAY GOD BE MERCIFUL TO US!

DAYS LATER, JACOB'S SONS LEAD THEIR PACK ANIMALS THROUGH THE GATES OF THE EGYPTIAN CITY.

DON'T WORRY, BENJAMIN. WE'LL DO EVERYTHING WE CAN TO PROTECT YOU.

I'M NOT AFRAID. GOD WILL TAKE CARE OF US HERE JUST LIKE HE DOES IN OUR OLD FIELDS AT HOME.

BUT EVEN AS THEY WONDER, THE GOVERNOR HAS THE BROTHERS SERVED. HE GIVES THE LARGEST PORTION TO BENJAMIN. THIS IS A SIGN OF GREAT HONOR.

DO YOU SEE THAT?

I HOPE THAT MEANS BENJAMIN IS SAFE!

THE BANQUET ENDS. THE NEXT MORNING, THE BROTHERS BUY THEIR GRAIN AND LEAVE. BUT THEY ARE HARDLY OUT OF THE CITY BEFORE A CHARIOT OVERTAKES THEM.

STOP! ONE OF YOU HAS STOLEN MY MASTER'S SILVER CUP.

YOUR MASTER'S CUP? WE ARE INNOCENT! SEARCH US IF YOU WANT TO.

IF I FIND THE CUP, THE MAN WHOSE SACK IT IS HIDDEN IN WILL BE PUNISHED SEVERELY.

ONE BY ONE THE SACKS ARE SEARCHED. AT LAST THE OFFICER OPENS BENJAMIN'S ...

THE CUP!

BUT I WILL BE MERCIFUL. THE ONE WHO HAD THE CUP WILL BE MY SLAVE. THE REST OF YOU CAN RETURN TO YOUR FATHER.

IF BENJAMIN DOESN'T COME HOME, OUR FATHER WILL DIE OF GRIEF. LET ME BE YOUR SLAVE INSTEAD OF BENJAMIN.

FOR A MOMENT, THERE IS SILENCE. THEN THE GOVERNOR TURNS TO HIS GUARDS.

GO!

LEAVE ME ALONE WITH THESE MEN.

THE TERRIFIED BROTHERS WAIT. FINALLY JOSEPH SPEAKS ...

I CAN'T KEEP THE SECRET ANY LONGER— I AM JOSEPH, YOUR BROTHER. YOU SOLD ME AS A SLAVE MANY YEARS AGO. GOD HAS BLESSED ME, AND NOW WE ARE TOGETHER AGAIN.

Family Reunion

BASED ON GENESIS 45—47

JACOB'S SONS ARE SHOCKED TO REALIZE THAT THE GOVERNOR OF ALL EGYPT IS ACTUALLY THEIR LONG-LOST BROTHER. THEN THEY REMEMBER HOW THEY LAST TREATED HIM ...

JOSEPH!

HE MUST HATE US. WHAT WILL HE DO NOW?

I BELIEVE IT WAS GOD'S WILL FOR ME TO COME TO EGYPT SO I COULD SAVE YOUR LIVES—AND THE LIVES OF EVERYONE SUFFERING FROM THE FAMINE.

WE DON'T DESERVE GOD'S MERCY. JOSEPH, CAN YOU FORGIVE US?

I FORGAVE YOU ALL YEARS AGO. BUT I HAD TO BE SURE YOU HAD CHANGED. WHEN YOU SHOWED YOUR LOYALTY AND LOVE FOR BENJAMIN, I KNEW YOU HAD.

LOOK, THIS FAMINE WILL LAST FIVE MORE YEARS. GO HOME AND BRING OUR FATHER TO BE NEAR ME. I WILL PROVIDE FOR ALL OF YOU.

THANK GOD FOR A BROTHER LIKE YOU.

The End of an Era

FOR 17 YEARS, JACOB AND HIS SONS LIVE HAPPILY IN EGYPT. THEN ONE DAY A MESSENGER BRINGS SAD NEWS TO JOSEPH ...

SIR, YOUR FATHER IS VERY ILL. HE WANTS YOU AND YOUR SONS TO COME RIGHT AWAY!

THEY HURRY TO JACOB'S BEDSIDE.

BRING YOUR SONS TO ME SO I CAN BLESS THEM BEFORE I DIE.

MAY GOD, WHO HAS GUIDED ME ALL OF MY LIFE, BLESS MY GRANDSONS.

THEN JACOB CALLS ALL OF HIS SONS TO HIM AND BLESSES THEM. JACOB DIES AND HIS SONS CARRY THE OLD CHIEFTAIN'S BODY BACK TO HIS HOMELAND OF CANAAN.

AFTER JACOB'S FUNERAL, JOSEPH WALKS AWAY FROM THE CAMP ALONE. HIS BROTHERS WATCH HIM IN HIS GRIEF.

EVEN AFTER ALL THESE YEARS, JOSEPH WAS CLOSEST WITH OUR FATHER.

AND WE HAVE NO WAY TO COMFORT HIM.

BECAUSE OF THE WICKEDNESS OF HIS OLDER SONS, JACOB GIVES THE FAMILY BIRTHRIGHT TO JOSEPH AND HIS SONS. REMEMBERING HOW HE WAS THE YOUNGEST, JACOB CROSSES HIS ARMS WHEN HE BLESSES MANASSEH AND EPHRAIM. THIS GIVES THE LARGER SHARE OF THE BIRTHRIGHT TO THE YOUNGER EPHRAIM.

JOSEPH, YOU ARE THE HEAD OF OUR TRIBE NOW. WE WILL BE YOUR SLAVES IF YOU WISH IT.

NO, NO. YOU DID EVIL, BUT GOD USED IT FOR GOOD.

FOR YEARS, THE SONS OF JACOB LIVE HAPPILY IN EGYPT.

GOD HAS BEEN GOOD TO US—MORE THAN WE DESERVE.

AS LONG AS I LIVE, I'LL THANK GOD AND SEEK HIS FORGIVENESS.

WHEN JOSEPH IS VERY OLD, HE CALLS HIS RELATIVES TO SEE HIM.

GOD WILL BRING YOU OUT OF THIS LAND TO THE LAND HE GAVE TO ABRAHAM, TO ISAAC, AND TO JACOB. WHEN YOU RETURN, TAKE MY BODY WITH YOU. I WANT TO BE BURIED IN THE LAND OF MY FATHERS.

SOON AFTER THIS, JOSEPH DIES.

ALL OF EGYPT MOURNS JOSEPH'S DEATH. BUT AS NEW RULERS COME TO THE THRONE, THEY FORGET HOW JOSEPH AND HIS GOD SAVED EGYPT. THEY ONLY NOTICE HOW LARGE THE TRIBE OF HEBREWS HAS BECOME ...

Baby in a Basket

BASED ON EXODUS 1:1–2:10

THERE ARE TOO MANY HEBREWS IN EGYPT! IF WE HAD A WAR, THEY MIGHT TURN AGAINST US. I MUST FIND A WAY TO KEEP THEM FROM CAUSING TROUBLE.

THE NEW PHARAOH IN EGYPT HAS FORGOTTEN THAT THE HEBREWS' ANCESTOR JOSEPH SAVED EGYPT FROM THE FAMINE. FROM HIS ROYAL YACHT ON THE NILE, THE KING FROWNS AS HE WATCHES THE HEBREW SHEPHERDS WITH THEIR RICH FLOCKS.

THE NEXT DAY, THE KING INSPECTS A NEW BUILDING PROJECT.

WE NEED THOUSANDS MORE WORKERS TO GET THIS JOB DONE.

THIS SOUNDS LIKE A PERFECT JOB FOR THE HEBREWS. THEY WILL WORK AS SLAVES. IT WILL SAVE US MONEY, AND THEN THOSE FOREIGNERS WON'T BE ABLE TO CAUSE TROUBLE.

SO FROM DAYLIGHT TO DARK, HEBREW MEN AND BOYS ARE DRIVEN FROM THEIR HOMES AND FORCED TO WORK UNDER WHIP-CRACKING SLAVE DRIVERS.

BUT WITH GOD'S BLESSING, THE HEBREWS FLOURISH AND GROW STRONGER—EVEN UNDER THE HARSH CONDITIONS!

WE WORK THEM HARDER EVERY DAY, BUT THERE ARE MORE HEBREWS THAN BEFORE. THE KING WILL NOT BE HAPPY ABOUT THIS ...

WHEN PHARAOH HEARS THE REPORT ...

I'LL TAKE CARE OF THE SLAVES! THROW EVERY HEBREW BOY BABY INTO THE NILE RIVER!

THE CRUEL ORDER IS CARRIED OUT. HEBREW MOTHERS AND FATHERS RISK THEIR LIVES TO PROTECT THEIR SONS, BUT THE KING'S MEN NEVER GIVE UP ON THEIR SEARCH.

NIGHT AFTER NIGHT, AMRAM, A HEBREW FROM THE TRIBE OF LEVI, HURRIES HOME FROM WORK—AFRAID THAT THE SOLDIERS HAVE VISITED HIS HOME.

O GOD, HELP US KEEP OUR NEW BABY BOY SAFE FROM THE EGYPTIANS.

THERE'S MIRIAM! THE SOLDIERS MUST NOT HAVE COME.

QUICKLY AMRAM ENTERS THE HOUSE—AND BOLTS THE DOOR.

SURELY GOD IS WITH US. OUR BABY IS THREE MONTHS OLD AND STILL PHARAOH'S SOLDIERS HAVE NOT FOUND HIM.

GOD WILL HELP ME FIND A WAY TO SAVE OUR SON!

THE NEXT DAY, JOCHEBED PREPARES A LITTLE BASKET.

KEEP WATCH, MIRIAM, I'M ALMOST FINISHED.

THEN, CAREFULLY AVOIDING THE EGYPTIAN SOLDIERS, SHE TAKES THE BASKET AND HER TINY SON TO THE RIVER.

HIS BASKET WILL FLOAT LIKE A LITTLE BOAT!

KEEP WATCH OVER HIM, MIRIAM. OH, MY SON, IT TEARS MY HEART TO SEND YOU AWAY. MAY GOD WATCH OVER YOU AND PROTECT YOU.

MIRIAM HIDES IN THE BULRUSHES AND WATCHES ...

THE PRINCESS! WILL SHE SEE THE BABY'S BASKET?

LOOK— WHAT A STRANGE LITTLE BASKET! I WONDER WHAT'S INSIDE IT.

Prince on the Run BASED ON EXODUS 2

SO THE HEBREW BABY IS RETURNED TO HIS OWN HOME—BUT NOW UNDER THE PROTECTION OF THE KING'S DAUGHTER. THAT NIGHT, AMRAM AND JOCHEBED GATHER MOSES WITH HIS SISTER, MIRIAM, AND BROTHER, AARON. THEY KNEEL AND PRAY.

O GOD, WE THANK YOU FOR SAVING OUR LITTLE SON. HELP US TO TRAIN HIM TO SERVE YOU.

YOUNG MOSES LIVES IN HIS HOME UNTIL HE IS ABOUT FOUR YEARS OLD. THEN HIS MOTHER TAKES HIM TO THE PALACE TO LIVE WITH THE PRINCESS, WHO ADOPTS HIM.

YEARS PASS, AND THE BOY MOSES LIVES THE LIFE OF A YOUNG PRINCE IN PHARAOH'S PALACE. ONE DAY HE DRIVES THROUGH THE CITY ...

... TO A PLACE WHERE HEBREW SLAVES ARE WORKING. AS HE WATCHES THE SLAVES TOIL, HE IS STARTLED BY A MAN'S SCREAM ...

TIRED AFTER HIS FLIGHT FROM PHARAOH, MOSES RESTS BY A WELL.

GET AWAY FROM HERE UNTIL WE WATER OUR SHEEP!

NO! WE WERE HERE FIRST. YOU LEAVE US ALONE!

I THINK YOU SHOULD LET THE WOMEN GO FIRST. AFTER ALL, THAT'S THE CIVILIZED THING TO DO.

THE COWARDLY SHEPHERDS RETREAT—AND MOSES HELPS THE WOMEN WATER THEIR FLOCKS.

WHEN THE WOMEN RETURN TO THEIR CAMP, ONE OF THEM TELLS HER FATHER WHAT HAPPENED AT THE WELL.

A MAN SAVED YOU AND YOU CAME STRAIGHT HOME? WHY DIDN'T ANY OF YOU ASK HIM TO DINNER?

I AM ZIPPORAH. MY FATHER, JETHRO, INVITES YOU TO EAT WITH US.

MOSES ACCEPTS THE INVITATION, AND THAT NIGHT AFTER SUPPER ...

I NEED A SHEPHERD—A GOOD MAN I CAN TRUST. WHY DON'T YOU STAY WITH US?

THANK YOU, I WILL.

THIS WILL BE A GOOD PLACE TO HIDE FROM PHARAOH.

A Burning Bush!

BASED ON EXODUS 2:21—4:17

MOSES STAYS WEEKS AND THEN MONTHS. HE MARRIES ZIPPORAH AND THEY HAVE TWO SONS.

GERSHOM HANDLES HIS SLING VERY WELL.

HE'LL MAKE A GOOD SHEPHERD—LIKE HIS FATHER.

MOSES WORKS AS A SHEPHERD FOR HIS FATHER-IN-LAW FOR 40 YEARS. YEAR AFTER YEAR, THE FLOCKS OF JETHRO INCREASE. BUT ONE YEAR, THE GRASSES DRY UP AND MOSES LEADS HIS SHEEP TO PASTURES NEAR THE MOUNTAIN OF SINAI.

BUT EVEN AFTER ALL THESE YEARS, MOSES CANNOT FORGET THE HEBREW PEOPLE IN EGYPT.

I WONDER IF PHARAOH IS STILL ALIVE. AND WHAT HAS BECOME OF MY SISTER, MIRIAM, AND MY BROTHER, AARON?

MOSES WONDERS TOO ABOUT THE HEBREW SLAVES STILL STRUGGLING UNDER THE WHIPS OF EGYPTIAN RULERS. ONE DAY, HE LOOKS UP TO SEE A STRANGE SIGHT ON MOUNT SINAI.

A BUSH ON FIRE— YET IT'S NOT BURNING UP!

HE STEPS CLOSER—AND THEN STOPS. A VOICE FROM THE FIERY BUSH CALLS OUT, "MOSES!"

121

I'M HERE!

ONCE AGAIN, MOSES STARTS TOWARD THE BUSH, BUT THE SAME VOICE WARNS HIM:

DON'T COME ANY NEARER. TAKE OFF YOUR SHOES BECAUSE YOU ARE STANDING ON HOLY GROUND.

I AM THE GOD OF YOUR FATHER AND THE GOD OF YOUR ANCESTORS ABRAHAM, ISAAC, AND JACOB.

MOSES HIDES HIS FACE IN FEAR AT BEING ADDRESSED BY THE ONE TRUE GOD.

I HAVE SEEN MY PEOPLE SUFFER IN EGYPT, AND I HAVE COME DOWN TO SAVE THEM. I WANT YOU TO BRING THEM OUT OF THAT LAND. THEN YOU WILL LEAD THEM TO A NEW HOME, A LAND FLOWING WITH MILK AND HONEY. NOW, GO! I AM SENDING YOU TO PHARAOH.

WHO AM I TO SPEAK TO PHARAOH OF EGYPT? WHO AM I TO LEAD THE HEBREWS? I AM NOT A LEADER.

I AM YOUR LEADER, AND I AM WITH YOU. BELIEVE ME THAT YOU AND THE ISRAELITES WILL COME TO WORSHIP ME ON THIS VERY MOUNTAIN.

I AM NOT A PROPHET OR A PRIEST. WHAT IF THEY ASK ME YOUR NAME?

I AM WHO I AM. AND I WILL PERFORM MY WONDERS AGAINST THE EGYPTIANS.

WHAT IF THEY DON'T BELIEVE ME?

THROW YOUR STAFF ON THE GROUND.

MOSES' STAFF IMMEDIATELY TURNS INTO A VENOMOUS SNAKE. HE RUNS IN TERROR.

Spokesmen for God
BASED ON EXODUS 4:27—7:11

MEANTIME, IN THE SLAVE HUTS OF EGYPT, THE HEBREWS ARE CRYING OUT TO GOD TO HELP THEM.

WHILE AARON, THE BROTHER OF MOSES, IS PRAYING, GOD SPEAKS TO HIM.

GO INTO THE WILDERNESS TO MEET MOSES.

AARON IS SURPRISED AT THE STRANGE COMMAND. BUT, UNLIKE MOSES, HE OBEYS WITHOUT COMPLAINT. HE HEADS OUT ALONE INTO THE WILDERNESS.

I DON'T EVEN KNOW WHERE IN THE WILDERNESS MOSES *IS*. I HOPE I'M GOING THE RIGHT WAY.

AARON EVENTUALLY WINDS UP AT MOUNT SINAI. MOSES IS WAITING FOR HIM.

BROTHER?

BROTHER! I'VE BEEN WATCHING FOR YOU. GOD TOLD ME YOU WOULD COME.

QUICKLY, MOSES EXPLAINS THAT GOD HAS CALLED THEM TO LEAD THE HEBREWS OUT OF SLAVERY IN EGYPT. THEY TRAVEL TOGETHER TO TALK TO THE ELDERS OF ISRAEL IN EGYPT. MOSES PERFORMS THE MIRACLES GOD GAVE HIM, AND THE ELDERS BELIEVE.

TOMORROW, WE'LL TAKE GOD'S MESSAGE TO PHARAOH.

THE NEXT DAY ...

YOU'LL DO ALL THE TALKING, RIGHT, AARON?

I'M JUST HERE FOR MORAL SUPPORT. YOU'RE THE ONE WHO KNOWS EGYPTIAN POLITICS.

THE ISRAELITES NO LONGER BELIEVE MOSES. AND WHEN HE COMPLAINS TO GOD, GOD ONLY TELLS HIM TO VISIT PHARAOH AGAIN. THOUGH MOSES IS SURE PHARAOH WILL NOT LISTEN TO HIM, HE OBEYS.

HAVE YOU COME BACK TO BEG FOR MERCY?

NO, BUT TO SHOW YOU THE POWER OF OUR GOD.

AARON THROWS HIS STAFF TO THE GROUND, WHERE IT IS TRANSFORMED INTO A SERPENT.

SEE?

VERY CLEVER, BUT MY MAGICIANS CAN DO THE SAME THING.

The Plagues
BASED ON EXODUS 7:12—10:20

BUT WHILE PHARAOH WATCHES, THE SERPENT OF AARON SWALLOWS THE SERPENTS OF THE EGYPTIAN MAGICIANS. THOUGH DISAPPOINTED, PHARAOH REFUSES TO ADMIT THAT MOSES' GOD IS MORE POWERFUL THAN THE GODS OF EGYPT.

AGAIN MOSES ASKS FOR GOD'S HELP. AND AGAIN GOD TELLS HIM WHAT TO DO. IN THE MORNING, MOSES AND AARON MEET PHARAOH ON THE BANK OF THE NILE RIVER.

DON'T YOU HAVE ANYTHING BETTER TO DO THAN BOTHER ME DURING MY MORNING BATH?

BECAUSE YOU WON'T LET THE HEBREWS GO, THE RIVER WILL BE TURNED TO BLOOD.

[MOSES' COMMAND, AARON [STR]IKES THE WATER WITH HIS ROD, [AND] THE WATER TURNS RED.

MY SORCERERS CAN DO THE SAME THING.

IF THEY'RE SUCH GREAT SORCERERS, WHY DON'T THEY TURN THE NILE BACK INTO WATER?

BUT THIS THEY CANNOT DO, AND THE NILE REMAINS BLOOD FOR SEVEN DAYS.

EVEN IN THE PALACE ...

I CAN'T STAND THESE FILTHY CREATURES! SEND FOR MOSES AND AARON!

ASK YOUR GOD TO TAKE AWAY THE FROGS, AND I WILL LET THE HEBREWS GO.

IT WILL BE AS YOU SAY.

BUT WHEN THE FROGS ARE GONE, PHARAOH BREAKS HIS PROMISE. SO GOD PROCEEDS WITH HIS NEXT "WONDER."

GOD TORMENTS THE EGYPTIANS WITH A PLAGUE OF GNATS. THEY INFEST EVERYTHING. THE EGYPTIANS CAN'T GET THEM OUT OF THEIR HOUSES, THEIR HAIR—EVEN THEIR BEDS!

PHARAOH TRIES TO BARGAIN WITH MOSES, BUT MOSES STANDS FIRM IN HIS REQUEST. ONCE AGAIN, PHARAOH PROMISES TO FREE THE HEBREWS. BUT WHEN THE GNATS ARE GONE, HE HARDENS HIS HEART AGAIN.

AS IF THE GNATS WEREN'T BAD ENOUGH, GOD FOLLOWS THEM WITH A PLAGUE OF FLIES. FLIES ARE IN EVERYTHING—THE EGYPTIANS CAN'T KEEP THEM OFF THEIR FOOD OR OFF THEIR FACES. BUT NO FLIES TROUBLE THE HEBREWS IN GOSHEN.

CAN'T YOU WORSHIP YOUR GOD HERE?

NO.

OKAY, OKAY. YOU CAN GO.

BUT, LIKE BEFORE, PHARAOH CHANGES HIS MIND. THEN GOD SENDS DISEASE UPON THE EGYPTIANS' ANIMALS AND LIVESTOCK.

MANY OF THEM DIE. BUT PHARAOH'S HEART IS UNYIELDING.

GOD GIVES MOSES HIS NEXT INSTRUCTIONS. HE AND AARON INTERRUPT PHARAOH'S COURT AND THROW SOOT IN THE AIR.

IMMEDIATELY PHARAOH AND HIS ADVISERS BREAK OUT IN PAINFUL SORES AND BOILS. THE REST OF EGYPT IS STRUCK WITH THE SAME DISEASE AS WELL. BUT PHARAOH STUBBORNLY REFUSES TO RECOGNIZE GOD'S POWER AND AUTHORITY.

HOW LONG WILL YOU REFUSE TO HUMBLE YOURSELF? LET MY PEOPLE GO, OR I WILL SEND LOCUSTS TO DESTROY ANYTHING THAT'S LEFT ALIVE IN THIS LAND.

PHARAOH'S ADVISERS AGREE WITH MOSES.

PLEASE, JUST LET THE HEBREWS GO ALREADY!

DON'T YOU REALIZE THAT THESE PLAGUES HAVE LEFT EGYPT IN RUINS?

ALREADY IT WILL TAKE US YEARS TO RECOVER FROM THEM.

BEGRUDGINGLY, PHARAOH CALLS MOSES BACK TO HIM.

FINE, GO WORSHIP YOUR LORD. WHO WERE YOU PLANNING ON TAKING?

WE WILL TAKE OUR YOUNG AND OLD, OUR SONS AND DAUGHTERS, OUR FLOCKS AND HERDS.

HA HA! NO. JUST THE MEN.

LOCUSTS, IT IS!

GOD SENDS LOCUSTS, WHICH DEVOUR ANYTHING THAT WASN'T DESTROYED BY THE HAILSTORM. THEN, WHEN PHARAOH'S HEART REMAINS HARDENED AGAINST THE ISRAELITES, GOD MAKES THE DAY AS DARK AS NIGHT.

The Final Plague

BASED ON EXODUS 10:21–12:51

AFTER THREE DAYS OF DARKNESS, PHARAOH CALLS FOR MOSES AND AARON AGAIN.

FINE. YOU MAY TAKE YOUR WOMEN AND CHILDREN—BUT YOUR SHEEP AND CATTLE MUST REMAIN IN EGYPT.

NO! WE WON'T LEAVE A SINGLE HOOF BEHIND WHEN WE GO.

THEN YOU'LL ALL STAY RIGHT WHERE YOU ARE. GET OUT OF MY SIGHT! IF I SEE YOUR FACE AGAIN, YOU WILL DIE!

BUT MOSES IS NO LONGER AFRAID OF PHARAOH.

THAT'S WHAT YOU SAY—HERE'S WHAT THE LORD SAYS:

"TONIGHT EVERY FIRSTBORN SON IN EGYPT WILL DIE—INCLUDING YOURS, O PHARAOH. YOU WILL KNOW GRIEF WORSE THAN ANY EGYPT HAS EVER EXPERIENCED. AND THEN YOU WILL COME TO ME ON YOUR HANDS AND KNEES, AND YOU WILL BEG FOR MY PEOPLE TO LEAVE."

QUICKLY, MOSES CALLS FOR A MEETING OF THE HEBREW LEADERS.

GOD TOLD ME THAT THE ANGEL OF DEATH WILL STRIKE EGYPT AND TAKE THE FIRSTBORN OF EVERY FAMILY.

FIRSTBORN OF EVERY FAMILY?

135

MOSES INSTRUCTS THE HEBREWS ON HOW TO PROTECT THEIR FAMILIES ...

SURELY THIS WILL BRING OUR RELEASE FROM SLAVERY.

NINE TIMES PHARAOH HAS BROKEN HIS PROMISE TO LET US GO—WHAT WILL HE DO THIS TIME?

WHY ARE YOU PUTTING LAMB'S BLOOD ON OUR DOORPOST?

GOD TOLD MOSES IT WOULD BE A SIGN TO LET THE ANGEL OF DEATH KNOW TO PASS OVER OUR HOUSE.

THAT EVENING, EVERY HEBREW FAMILY PACKS ALL OF THEIR POSSESSIONS, HOPING THAT THEY WILL FINALLY BE ABLE TO LEAVE EGYPT. THEY EAT A MEAL CALLED THE PASSOVER BECAUSE THE ANGEL OF DEATH WILL PASS OVER THEIR HOMES.

20,000 Egyptians Under the Sea

BASED ON EXODUS 13:17—15:21

THE NEXT DAY, THE GREAT EXODUS FROM EGYPT IS UNDERWAY. JOYFULLY THE HEBREWS MARCH TOWARD THE LAND GOD PROMISED WOULD BE THEIR HOME. DURING THE DAY, A BRIGHT CLOUD GUIDES THEM ...

... AND AT NIGHT A PILLAR OF FIRE LEADS THEM.

BUT IN THEIR RUSH FOR FREEDOM, THEY DO NOT FORGET TO TAKE WITH THEM THE BODY OF THEIR ANCESTOR JOSEPH.

HE WAS A GREAT MAN IN EGYPT, BUT HE WANTED TO BE BURIED IN HIS OWN LAND.

PHARAOH AND HIS ARMY LOOK AT THE HEBREWS CAMPED BESIDE THE RED SEA.

TRAPPED! JUST AS I SAID.

GOOD! THEY'LL SOON SEE WHO IS MIGHTIER— PHARAOH OR THE GOD THEY WORSHIP!

AT THE SAME TIME IN THE HEBREW CAMP ...

I'D RATHER BE AN EGYPTIAN SLAVE THAN DIE THIS WAY!

DON'T BE AFRAID! AFTER TODAY, YOU WILL NEVER SEE THESE EGYPTIANS AGAIN. THE LORD WILL FIGHT ON OUR BEHALF. JUST BE STILL, AND SEE WHAT GOD IS GOING TO DO.

AS MOSES SPEAKS, THE CLOUD THAT LEADS THEM MOVES TO THE BACK OF THE CAMP.

LOOK! THE CLOUD IS HIDING US FROM THE EGYPTIANS!

THEN MOSES HOLDS OUT HIS STAFF TOWARD THE RED SEA, AS GOD TOLD HIM TO DO. A STRONG EAST WIND BLOWS ALL NIGHT AND ROLLS BACK THE WATERS OF THE SEA ...

AWED BY THE SIGHT, THE HEBREWS RUSH JOYFULLY ACROSS THE PATH IN THE SEA.

The Complaining Begins

BASED ON EXODUS 15:22—17:7

FROM THE RED SEA, THE ISRAELITES MARCH ACROSS THE DESERT. BUT AFTER DAYS OF TRAVEL THEY FORGET WHAT GOD HAS DONE FOR THEM. AND THEY BEGIN TO COMPLAIN ...

I'M THIRSTY.

THREE DAYS AND NO WATER IN SIGHT!

AT LAST THEY FIND A SPRING, BUT ...

IT'S BITTER! WE CAN'T DRINK THIS!

WE'LL ALL DIE OF THIRST.

THE PEOPLE COMPLAIN TO MOSES WHILE HE IS SITTING AS A JUDGE. MOSES PRAYS TO GOD FOR HELP—AND GOD POINTS OUT A NEARBY BRANCH. MOSES THROWS IT INTO THE SPRING.

NOW TASTE THE WATER AND KNOW THE POWER OF GOD!

IT'S CLEAN NOW.

GOD HAS SAVED US AGAIN. NOW I *KNOW* GOD IS GUIDING MOSES.

145

EARLY THE NEXT MORNING, THE PEOPLE ARE SURPRISED TO FIND A STRANGE WHITISH COVERING ON THE GROUND.

WHAT IS IT? IT LOOKS LIKE FROST.

WHAT IS IT? IT'S FOOD THAT GOD HAS SENT YOU. CALL IT MANNA, WHATEVER IT IS.

GOD IS SO GOOD TO US.

GATHER WHAT YOU NEED JUST FOR TODAY.

HOW CAN I BE SURE THERE WILL BE MORE TOMORROW? I'M GOING TO COLLECT AS MUCH AS I CAN.

SEE! I'LL PUT THIS EXTRA ASIDE FOR TOMORROW. NO MATTER WHAT HAPPENS TO THE OTHERS, WE'LL HAVE SOMETHING TO EAT.

BUT THE NEXT MORNING ...

UGH! IT'S SPOILED!

MOSES WARNED US. WE HAVE TO HAVE FAITH THAT GOD WILL TAKE CARE OF US.

ON THE SIXTH DAY OF THE WEEK, THE PEOPLE GATHER FOOD FOR THAT DAY AND THE SABBATH. THE FOOD KEPT FOR THE SABBATH DOES NOT SPOIL, AND NO NEW MANNA APPEARS ON THE GROUND.

WITH RENEWED FAITH IN GOD, THE ISRAELITES CONTINUE THEIR JOURNEY. THEY TRAVEL TOWARD MOUNT SINAI, WHERE MOSES WAS CALLED BY GOD TO SET THEM FREE FROM SLAVERY. MOSES SENDS HIS WIFE AND TWO SONS ON AHEAD TO VISIT THEIR OLD HOME.

TELL YOUR FATHER, JETHRO, WHAT GOD HAS DONE FOR OUR PEOPLE.

FARTHER ON ... WHILE THE ISRAELITES CAMP IN A PEACEFUL VALLEY, FIERCE TRIBESMEN WATCH FROM THE HILLS ...

THIS WILL BE EASY— A SURPRISE ATTACK, AND THE CAMP IS OURS!

"Armed" Battle

BASED ON EXODUS 17:8-16

AMALEKITES HAVE ATTEMPTED TO AMBUSH THE ISRAELITES. BUT THE ISRAELITE SENTINELS SEE THE DANGER ...

RAIDERS! PREPARE FOR AN ATTACK!

MOSES CALLS TO JOSHUA, SON OF NUN, HIS FAITHFUL AIDE.

JOSHUA, CHOOSE OUR BEST SOLDIERS AND FIGHT OFF THOSE RAIDERS. I'LL STAND ON TOP OF THE HILL WITH THE STAFF OF GOD IN MY HAND.

THE BATTLE RAGES ALL DAY. AS LONG AS MOSES KEEPS HIS HANDS IN THE AIR, THE TIDE OF THE BATTLE GOES IN FAVOR OF THE ISRAELITES.

BUT WHEN MOSES' WEARY ARMS DROP ...

... THE ISRAELITE SOLDIERS FALL BACK IN FEAR AND RETREAT BEFORE THE SAVAGE ATTACK OF THE RAIDERS.

TO WIN THE FIGHT, MOSES MUST KEEP HIS ARMS RAISED. BUT MOSES CANNOT HOLD UP HIS ARMS ALL DAY. HIGH ON THE HILL, AARON AND HUR ARE FORCED TO HOLD UP MOSES' TIRED ARMS SO THAT THE ISRAELITES WILL WIN THE BATTLE.

LOOK! MOSES IS HOLDING THE STAFF OF GOD ABOVE US!

FIGHT, MEN! WE WON'T FAIL NOW.

AFTER A TIRING DAY, BOTH FOR THE SOLDIERS AND FOR MOSES' ARMS, GOD GIVES THEM THE VICTORY.

AT SUNSET, JOSHUA'S MEN RETURN VICTORIOUS ...

HERE COME THE VICTORS!

GIVE YOUR PRAISE TO GOD. WITHOUT HIS HELP, WE WOULD HAVE FAILED.

THEN MOSES BUILDS AN ALTAR AND LEADS THE PEOPLE IN A PRAYER OF THANKSGIVING TO GOD.

FRESH FROM THEIR FIRST MILITARY VICTORY, THE ISRAELITES EAGERLY PUSH ON.

ONLY A FEW WEEKS AGO, WE WERE SLAVES IN EGYPT. NOW WE ARE FREE—AND STRONG ENOUGH TO DEFEND OURSELVES!

WHEN WE GET TO THE PROMISED LAND, WE'LL BUILD A NATION MIGHTIER THAN ALL EGYPT.

Good Advice

BASED ON
EXODUS 18–19

WHEN THEY REACH
THE WILDERNESS AT
MOUNT SINAI, MOSES
SETS UP CAMP. ONE
DAY A MESSENGER
BRINGS HIM GOOD
NEWS ...

YOUR
FATHER-IN-LAW,
JETHRO, YOUR WIFE,
AND YOUR SONS
ARE ON THEIR WAY
TO SEE YOU.

MOSES GOES OUT
IMMEDIATELY TO
MEET THEM ...

I'M SO
GLAD TO SEE
YOU!

I'VE HEARD
THE WONDERFUL THINGS
GOD HAS DONE FOR YOU
AND YOUR PEOPLE.

PROUDLY, MOSES
SHOWS JETHRO
AROUND THE CAMP. AS
THE DAY GOES BY,
JETHRO NOTICES THAT
PEOPLE BRING THEIR
COMPLAINTS TO
MOSES ALL DAY LONG.

THIS IS
REMARKABLY
INEFFICIENT.

MOSES,
YOU CAN'T SERVE
AS JUDGE TO ALL
THESE PEOPLE BY
YOURSELF.

YOU NEED TO
LEARN A LITTLE THING
CALLED DELEGATING.
FIND OTHER WISE MEN,
TEACH THEM THE WAY OF
THE LORD, AND LET
THEM JUDGE FOR ALL
OF THESE PEOPLE IN
YOUR PLACE.

MOSES TAKES HIS FATHER-IN-LAW'S ADVICE.

YOU WERE RIGHT. THIS GIVES ME MORE TIME TO TEACH MY PEOPLE ABOUT GOD.

SOON AFTER THIS, MOSES GOES UP THE MOUNTAIN TO TALK WITH GOD.

WHEN HE RETURNS, HE HAS NEWS FOR HIS PEOPLE.

PREPARE YOURSELVES, FOR ON THE THIRD DAY, THE LORD WILL COME DOWN IN THE SIGHT OF ALL THE PEOPLE ON MOUNT SINAI.

ON THE MORNING OF THE THIRD DAY, THUNDER ROLLS ACROSS THE SKY. LIGHTNING FLASHES. THEN THE SOUND OF A TRUMPET FILLS THE AIR.

THIS IS THE SIGNAL TO LEAVE CAMP!

STAY RIGHT BESIDE ME. DON'T GO BEYOND THE BOUNDARIES MOSES SET FOR US.

MOSES SAYS IF WE EVEN TOUCH THE MOUNTAIN, WE WILL DIE!

God's Commandments

BASED ON EXODUS 20

WHILE THE PEOPLE OF ISRAEL STAND BEFORE
MOUNT SINAI, GOD SPEAKS FROM THE MOUNTAIN
AND GIVES THEM THE TEN COMMANDMENTS:

I am the Lord your God. You must not worship other gods.

You must not make any idols.

You must not use the name of the Lord your God wrongly.

Remember the Sabbath day and keep it holy.

Respect your father and your mother.

You must not murder.

You must not cheat on your husband or wife.

You must not steal.

You must not lie.

You must not be jealous of other people's possessions.

A Golden Calf BASED ON EXODUS 32

GOD GIVES MOSES MORE LAWS, AND WHEN THESE ARE WRITTEN DOWN, MOSES BUILDS AN ALTAR. HE AND HIS PEOPLE MAKE AN AGREEMENT, OR "COVENANT," WITH GOD. THE PEOPLE PROMISE TO FOLLOW ALL OF THE LORD'S COMMANDS.

LATER, GOD CALLS MOSES TO COME AGAIN TO MOUNT SINAI, WHERE HE WILL GIVE MOSES THE LAW WRITTEN ON STONE TABLETS. JOSHUA GOES PARTWAY WITH HIM. DAYS PASS, AND MOSES DOES NOT RETURN.

WHEN IS MOSES COMING BACK?

CAN WE GO LOOK FOR HIM?

WE DON'T KNOW WHEN MOSES WILL BE BACK. BUT YOU MUST NOT FOLLOW HIM UP THE MOUNTAIN. HE IS ALONE WITH GOD.

WHO KNOWS, MAYBE MOSES ISN'T COMING BACK ...

IF HE DOESN'T COME BACK, WHAT WILL WE DO?

LET'S ASK AARON TO LET US MAKE A STATUE TO WORSHIP.

YES! WE WANT A GOD WE CAN SEE.

FEELING LOST WITHOUT THEIR LEADER, THE PEOPLE FORGET GOD'S COMMANDMENTS AND THEIR PROMISE TO WORSHIP ONLY GOD. THEY BRING THEIR JEWELRY TO AARON, WHO MELTS IT AND MAKES A GOLDEN STATUE OF A CALF.

MOSES MELTS THE IDOL, GRINDS UP THE GOLD, AND DUMPS IT IN THE RIVER.

NOW, ALL OF YOU DRINK THIS WATER!

DRINK IT?

IT'S AWFUL!

UGH! THIS WILL MAKE US SICK.

JUST DRINK IT. LET THIS BE A LESSON TO YOU! PONDER YOUR FAITHLESSNESS WHILE I GO BACK UP THE MOUNTAIN AND ASK GOD TO FORGIVE YOU.

HIGH ON THE MOUNTAIN, WHERE HE RECEIVED GOD'S COMMANDMENTS, MOSES KNEELS TO PRAY.

THESE ARE A STUBBORN, REBELLIOUS PEOPLE. LEAVE ME, MOSES, SO I MAY DESTROY THEM.

LORD, PLEASE FORGIVE THEM. YOU PROMISED ABRAHAM, ISAAC, AND JACOB TO BLESS THEIR DESCENDANTS. I KNOW THEY DON'T DESERVE IT. BUT IF YOU DESTROY THEM, THE OTHER NATIONS WILL THINK THAT YOU CAN'T FULFILL YOUR PROMISES.

The Tent of Meeting
BASED ON EXODUS 34:29–40:38

GOD HAS FORGIVEN HIS PEOPLE FOR THEIR FAITHLESSNESS. HE GIVES MOSES MORE LAWS AND WRITES THE TEN COMMANDMENTS ON TWO NEW TABLETS OF STONE. BUT GOD HAS MORE IN STORE FOR THE ISRAELITES TO DO ...

GOD HAS GIVEN ME PLANS FOR A TENT-HOUSE OF WORSHIP. BRING YOUR OFFERINGS AND WE WILL ALL WORK TOGETHER TO MAKE IT.

THE PEOPLE GLADLY BRING JEWELRY, CLOTH, SKINS, RARE METALS, AND WOOD SO THAT GOD'S HOUSE WILL BE BEAUTIFUL.

AFTER MANY WEEKS OF CAREFUL, LOVING WORK, THE HOUSE OF GOD—THE TENT OF MEETING—IS READY. JOYOUSLY, THE PEOPLE WATCH AS MOSES CARRIES THE SACRED ARK—A BOX CONTAINING THE TEN COMMANDMENTS—INTO THE TENT OF MEETING, WHERE GOD MEETS HIS PEOPLE. MOSES PLACES THE ARK IN A SPECIAL ROOM CALLED THE HOLY OF HOLIES. THEN A CLOUD COVERS THE TENT OF MEETING AND THE GLORY OF THE LORD FILLS IT.

NOW THE ISRAELITES ARE NO LONGER A MOB OF FLEEING SLAVES. IN THE YEAR SINCE THEY LEFT EGYPT, THEY HAVE FINALLY BECOME A NATION OF THEIR OWN—WITH LAWS, JUDGES, AND A PLACE OF WORSHIP.

Sacrifice and Blessing

BASED ON LEVITICUS AND NUMBERS

GOD APPOINTS AARON AND THE REST OF THE TRIBE OF LEVI TO BE HIS PRIESTS. AND HE TEACHES AARON THE WORDS OF BLESSING TO SHARE WITH THE PEOPLE.

MAY THE LORD BLESS YOU AND KEEP YOU; MAY THE LORD MAKE HIS FACE SHINE ON YOU AND BE GRACIOUS TO YOU; MAY THE LORD TURN HIS FACE TOWARD YOU AND GIVE YOU PEACE.

GOD GIVES HIS PEOPLE RULES FOR LIVING SO THEY WILL FORGET THE EGYPTIAN WAYS OF LIVING AND THINK ABOUT GOD'S WAYS.

GOD WANTS HIS PEOPLE TO BE HOLY BECAUSE HE IS HOLY. HE TELLS THEM HOW TO MAKE SACRIFICES TO SHOW THAT THEY ARE SORRY FOR THEIR SINS.

I WANT TO SACRIFICE TO GOD, BUT ALL I CAN AFFORD IS THIS PIGEON.

DEAR WOMAN, GOD DOES NOT CARE ABOUT THE SIZE OF THE ANIMAL, ONLY THE SINCERITY OF YOUR HEART.

THERE ARE MANY DIFFERENT SACRIFICES GOD ASKS THE ISRAELITES TO PERFORM. ONE IS THE OFFERING OF THE SCAPEGOAT. AARON STANDS BEFORE THE CROWD AND CASTS LOTS BETWEEN THE GOATS.

MOMMY, WHY ARE THERE TWO GOATS UP THERE?

ONE GOAT WILL BE A SACRIFICE TO THE LORD.

BUT THE OTHER WILL TAKE ALL OF OUR SINS UPON IT.

I TAKE ALL THE WICKEDNESS AND SINS OF ISRAEL AND PUT THEM ON YOUR HEAD.

NOW GO, BE BANISHED INTO THE DESERT AND TAKE OUR SINS FAR AWAY FROM US.

THROUGH SACRIFICES AND SPECIAL FEAST DAYS, GOD REMINDS THE ISRAELITES OF WHAT HE HAS DONE FOR THEM AND TEACHES THEM HOW THEY SHOULD LIVE.

Counting the Numbers

EXCITEMENT SPREADS THROUGH THE CAMP AS THE PEOPLE TALK MORE AND MORE ABOUT THE PROMISED LAND GOD WILL LEAD THEM TO. ONE DAY, THE BLAST OF TWO GREAT SILVER TRUMPETS FILLS THE AIR ...

THIS IS THE SIGNAL FOR ALL THE PEOPLE TO COME TO THE TENT OF MEETING. SOMETHING IMPORTANT IS GOING TO HAPPEN.

THE PEOPLE DROP WHAT THEY ARE DOING AND HURRY TO THE TENT OF MEETING.

DOES THIS MEAN WE ARE GOING TO MOVE?

I DON'T KNOW. WE'LL HAVE TO WAIT AND SEE. OUR ORDERS COME FROM GOD.

RISE UP, O LORD! MAY YOUR ENEMIES FLEE BEFORE YOU!

LOOK! THE CLOUD IS LIFTING!

THIS IS THE SIGN! EAGERLY THE PEOPLE LINE UP TO MARCH TOWARD THE PROMISED LAND. THE PRIESTS LEAD THE FORMATION, CARRYING THE SACRED ARK OF THE COVENANT. AND MOSES COUNTS THE NUMBER OF ISRAELITES AS THEY PASS BY, FOLLOWING GOD'S INSTRUCTIONS.

GOD'S RAGE BURNS AT THE ISRAELITES' PETTY COMPLAINTS—AND THEN SO DO THEIR TENTS. FIRE BREAKS OUT IN THE ISRAELITE CAMP, AND THE PEOPLE ARE FORCED TO PAUSE THEIR COMPLAINING WHILE THEY TRY TO BEAT BACK THE FLAMES.

DID GOD SEND THE LIGHTNING TO BURN OUR TENTS?

MAYBE IT'S A WARNING FOR US TO STOP GRUMBLING ABOUT THE FOOD HE HAS GIVEN US.

HELP US, MOSES! WE'LL LOSE THE WHOLE CAMP!

ONLY GOD'S MERCY CAN HELP YOU NOW. I'LL PRAY FOR YOU.

AND AS MOSES PRAYS, THE FIRE GOES OUT ON ITS OWN.

AS THE QUAIL LAND ON THE DESERT, THE ISRAELITES PICK UP ALL THEY CAN CARRY.

MEAT! ALL WE CAN EAT!

LET'S SAVE ENOUGH TO EAT LATER ON.

HOW MANY MORE BASKETS DO I HAVE TO GATHER?

GET AS MANY AS YOU CAN. AT LEAST WE'LL HAVE ALL THE MEAT WE NEED.

THE PEOPLE STUFF THEMSELVES UNTIL MANY OF THEM ARE SICK.

IT SERVES ME RIGHT. I WAS TOO GREEDY.

SOON AFTER THIS, THE ORDER COMES TO CONTINUE THE JOURNEY. ONCE AGAIN A CLOUD LEADS THE PEOPLE BY DAY AND A PILLAR OF FIRE LEADS THEM AT NIGHT. THEY TRAVEL TO A CAMPSITE CLOSER TO THE HOMELAND GOD PROMISED THEM.

NO SOONER IS CAMP SET UP THAN MOSES' OWN BROTHER AND SISTER TURN AGAINST HIM.

MOSES ACTS AS IF HE IS THE ONLY SPOKESMAN FOR GOD.

HE SEEMS TO FORGET, AARON, THAT *YOU* ARE THE HIGH PRIEST.

Sibling Rivalry
BASED ON NUMBERS 12

AFTER ALL THESE YEARS, AARON AND MIRIAM ARE TIRED OF ALWAYS FOLLOWING THE COMMAND OF THEIR LITTLE BROTHER, MOSES. WHY DOES GOD FAVOR HIM?

YOU'RE RIGHT, MIRIAM. IT'S TIME WE HAVE A TALK WITH OUR LITTLE BROTHER.

IN ANGER, THEY GO TO MOSES ...

WE'RE TIRED OF HAVING YOU RUN EVERYTHING, MOSES.

DO YOU THINK YOU ARE THE ONLY ONE WHO CAN SPEAK FOR GOD? DIDN'T GOD CALL AARON TO BE THE HIGH PRIEST?

AND DON'T FORGET, I'M A PROPHETESS TOO!

BEFORE MOSES CAN ANSWER, GOD CALLS THE THREE OF THEM TO THE TENT OF MEETING.

I HAVE ALWAYS SPOKEN TO MY PEOPLE THROUGH DREAMS AND VISIONS.

MOSES IS THE FIRST PROPHET I HAVE EVER SPOKEN WITH FACE-TO-FACE.

DOESN'T THAT TELL YOU SOMETHING? DON'T YOU THINK YOU SHOULD BE AFRAID TO DISRESPECT MY CHOSEN DELIVERER?

THEN THE CLOUD DISAPPEARS. WHEN MIRIAM AND AARON LOOK AROUND, THEY GET THE SHOCK OF THEIR LIVES ...

MIRIAM DISCOVERS THAT SHE SUDDENLY HAS LEPROSY—THE DISEASE THE ISRAELITES DREAD MOST.

OH NO! WHY DID I SPEAK AGAINST MOSES? HELP ME! *HELP ME!*

WE WERE WRONG, MOSES. BUT DON'T HOLD IT AGAINST US. PLEASE! CAN'T YOU HELP MIRIAM?

ONLY GOD CAN HEAL HER, AARON. BUT I WILL PRAY FOR HER.

HEAL HER NOW, O GOD, I BEG YOU.

GOD AGREES TO HEAL MIRIAM, BUT FIRST SHE IS BANISHED FROM THE CAMP FOR SEVEN DAYS.

ON THE SEVENTH DAY, MIRIAM RETURNS. AS HIGH PRIEST, AARON ACCEPTS HER BACK INTO THE CAMP.

I HAVE LEARNED MY LESSON, AARON. MY SELFISH PRIDE WAS A SIN.

SO WAS MINE. WE SHOULD NEVER QUESTION GOD'S WISDOM AGAIN.

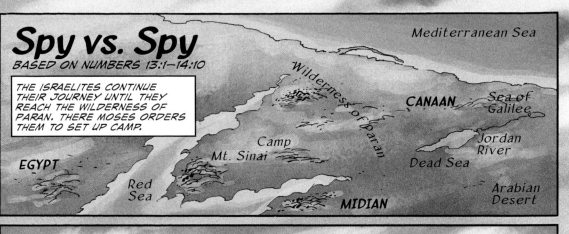

Spy vs. Spy
BASED ON NUMBERS 13:1–14:10

THE ISRAELITES CONTINUE THEIR JOURNEY UNTIL THEY REACH THE WILDERNESS OF PARAN. THERE MOSES ORDERS THEM TO SET UP CAMP.

Mediterranean Sea

Wilderness of Paran

CANAAN

Sea of Galilee

Camp

Jordan River

Mt. Sinai

EGYPT

Dead Sea

Red Sea

Arabian Desert

MIDIAN

MOSES CALLS ONE MAN FROM EACH TRIBE TO ATTEND AN IMPORTANT MEETING.

WE ARE ON THE BORDER OF CANAAN, THE LAND GOD HAS PROMISED TO US.

BUT BEFORE WE GO INTO IT, WE MUST KNOW WHAT LIES AHEAD.

WHAT ARE YOUR PLANS?

WE NEED TO EXPLORE THE LAND, JOSHUA.

WE MUST FIND OUT WHAT THE PEOPLE ARE LIKE, HOW MANY RIVERS WE WILL HAVE TO CROSS, HOW WELL THE CITIES ARE FORTIFIED.

IT'S A DANGEROUS JOB, BUT IT MUST BE DONE.

EACH MAN HERE CAN ACT AS A SCOUT, AND WE'LL GET STARTED RIGHT AWAY.

LOOK AT THAT CITY!

AND THE SIZE OF THOSE WALLS!

LET'S GO TAKE THE LAND!

YES! WITH GOD'S HELP, WE CAN DO IT.

BUT THE OTHER TEN SCOUTS DISAGREE WITH JOSHUA AND CALEB.

NO! WE'RE PUNY GRASSHOPPERS COMPARED TO THE SIZE OF THOSE GIANTS.

THEY'D WIPE OUT ALL THE MEN AND MAKE OUR CHILDREN BE SLAVES AGAIN.

WE CAN'T STAY HERE, BUT WE CAN'T GO INTO CANAAN.

I DON'T KNOW WHAT WE SHOULD DO.

I SAY WE GO BACK TO EGYPT!

GOD LED US HERE. TRUST HIM AND HE WILL HELP US CONQUER THE LAND HE PROMISED US.

BUT CAN WE BE SURE?

WHERE IS YOUR COURAGE? AND YOUR FAITH IN GOD?

THERE IS ONLY ONE WAY TO STOP JOSHUA'S WILD TALK!

175

PLANS ARE QUICKLY MADE, AND THE MEN GO TO TELL MOSES.

YOU CAN GO BACK TO THE WILDERNESS, BUT *WE'RE* GOING ON TO CANAAN.

YOU HAVE SWITCHED FROM COWARDS TO FOOLS. NO! DON'T TRY IT. IN FEAR, YOU REJECTED GOD'S PROMISES, AND NOW SUDDENLY YOU THINK YOU CAN WIN A BATTLE ON YOUR OWN AGAINST THE VERY GIANTS YOU FEARED?

YOU ALWAYS SAY THINGS IN THE WORST WAY, MOSES!

THE REBELLIOUS IDIOTS FORM AN ARMY AND SET OUT IMMEDIATELY TO CONQUER CANAAN.

WE FOUGHT OFF RAIDERS. WE CAN CONQUER THIS LAND, TOO.

AND WE CAN DO IT WITHOUT MOSES.

BUT AS THEY GO UP A HILL, THE DEFENDING ARMY ATTACKS!

IF WE GET BACK ALIVE, I'LL OBEY EVERY WORD MOSES SAYS.

THIS IS A MASSACRE! LET'S GET OUT OF HERE.

THE BATTLE IS SOON OVER. THE DEFEATED ISRAELITES LIMP BACK TO CAMP.

WHAT HAPPENED?

WE DIDN'T HAVE A CHANCE.

THE ENEMY CAME AT US FROM EVERY DIRECTION. OUR LEADERS WERE THE FIRST TO RUN.

THE PEOPLE SEE THE RESULTS OF DISOBEYING GOD—AND FOR A TIME THEY GLADLY FOLLOW MOSES.

BUT THEN A MAN NAMED KORAH AND OTHERS WHO HELP IN THE TENT OF MEETING GROW JEALOUS OF MOSES' LEADERSHIP.

WE ARE AS GOOD AS MOSES! WHY SHOULD HE TELL US WHAT TO DO?

LET'S TELL MOSES WE'LL TAKE CARE OF THINGS OURSELVES.

KORAH AND HIS FOLLOWERS GO TO MOSES, AND MOSES CALLS ALL THE PEOPLE TOGETHER.

TOMORROW THE LORD WILL SHOW US WHOM HE HAS CHOSEN TO LEAD OUR PEOPLE!

THE NEXT DAY MOSES STANDS BEFORE THE ISRAELITES.

GET AWAY FROM KORAH AND THESE MEN WHO WILL LEAD YOU TO EVIL. IF YOU DON'T, YOU'LL LOSE YOUR LIVES. HERE IS PROOF OF MY AUTHORITY: IF GOD HAS CHOSEN ME TO LEAD YOU, THE EARTH WILL OPEN AND SWALLOW THEM UP.

AS MOSES SPEAKS, A GREAT EARTHQUAKE SPLITS THE GROUND OPEN. THE TENTS OF KORAH AND HIS FOLLOWERS FALL INTO A DEEP CRACK IN THE EARTH.

THE FRIGHTENED PEOPLE TURN ONCE AGAIN TO MOSES. AS GOD COMMANDED, MOSES LEADS THEM AWAY FROM THE PROMISED LAND ... TO WANDER IN THE WILDERNESS FOR 40 YEARS.

Two Strikes— You're Out!

BASED ON NUMBERS 20:1-13

WHEN HARDSHIPS COME, THE PEOPLE FORGET THAT IT WAS THEIR FEAR THAT KEPT THEM FROM TAKING THE GOOD LAND GOD HAD PROMISED THEM. AGAIN AND AGAIN THEY COMPLAIN ...

NO WATER! NOW WHAT WILL I DO?

THE SPRING IS DRY! HOW CAN I COOK— OR WASH?

I'LL HAVE OUR TRIBAL LEADERS TAKE THIS UP WITH MOSES.

WELL, MOSES, WHERE ARE WE GOING TO GET WATER?

DID YOU LEAD US OUT HERE TO DIE OF THIRST?

WE'VE HAD ENOUGH. LET'S GO BACK TO EGYPT. AT LEAST THERE WE HAD FOOD AND WATER.

YOU WANT WATER? I'LL GIVE YOU WATER!!

IN A FIT OF ANGER, MOSES STRIKES A NEARBY ROCK WITH HIS STAFF—TWICE! WATER POURS OUT, BUT GOD IS NOT HAPPY. HOW CAN MOSES TEACH THE PEOPLE TO OBEY IF HE DOESN'T OBEY? BECAUSE OF HIS BAD EXAMPLE, GOD TELLS MOSES THAT HE WILL NOT ENTER THE PROMISED LAND.

The Bronze Snake

BASED ON NUMBERS 20:22–21:22

THE ISRAELITES TRAVEL ON. WHEN THEY COME TO MOUNT HOR, GOD TELLS MOSES THAT AARON WILL SOON DIE, AND HE SHOULD TAKE AARON AND HIS SON ELEAZAR TO THE MOUNTAINTOP.

ELEAZAR, TAKE YOUR FATHER'S ROBES. YOU WILL TAKE HIS PLACE AS HIGH PRIEST OF ALL ISRAEL.

AARON DIES ON MOUNT HOR, AND THE ISRAELITES MOURN FOR 30 DAYS. THEN THEY MOVE ON. A CLOUD LEADS THEM BY DAY, AND A PILLAR OF FIRE LEADS BY NIGHT.

BUT THE PEOPLE SOON FORGET GOD'S CARE ... AND AGAIN THEY COMPLAIN ...

THERE'S NOT ENOUGH WATER. I'M ALWAYS THIRSTY.

HASN'T GOD ALWAYS GIVEN US WATER WHEN WE NEEDED IT?

YES, BUT THE FOOD—I'M SICK OF THIS STUFF THAT WE HAVE TO GATHER EVERY DAY AND MAKE INTO BREAD. I WANT FOOD LIKE WE HAD IN EGYPT— MELONS, FRUIT ...

IN EGYPT YOU WERE BEATEN AND FORCED TO WORK AS SLAVES—AND YOU CRIED OUT FOR YOUR FREEDOM!

MOSES PRAYS AND GOD TELLS HIM TO MAKE A BRONZE SNAKE AND PUT IT ON A POLE.

LISTEN TO ME, EVERYONE WHO HAS BEEN BITTEN BY THE SNAKES. GOD SAID THAT IF YOU LOOK AT THIS BRONZE SNAKE, YOU WILL BE WELL AGAIN.

I'M WELL! GOD HAS HEALED ME.

EVERYONE WHO LOOKS UP AT THE SNAKE IS HEALED.

MOSES AND HIS PEOPLE CONTINUE THEIR JOURNEY. THIS TIME NO ONE COMPLAINS OR QUESTIONS MOSES' RIGHT TO LEAD. WHEN THEY REACH THE BORDER OF THE AMORITES, MOSES SUMMONS TWO MESSENGERS.

GO SPEAK TO KING SIHON. ASK HIM IF WE MAY PASS THROUGH HIS LAND IN PEACE.

The Wonderful Win Against Og

BASED ON NUMBERS 21:21-35

AT DAYBREAK, KING SIHON STRIKES. HE IS SURPRISED BY A STRONG COUNTERATTACK FROM THE ISRAELITES.

THE AMORITES ARE DEFEATED IN A SWIFT BATTLE. THEN JOSHUA GOES ON TO TAKE THE ENEMY'S CAPITAL CITY OF HESHBON.

THE ISRAELITE SOLDIERS ARE EAGER TO PUSH ON AFTER THIS VICTORY. BUT JOSHUA GOES TO MOSES FOR ADVICE.

SHALL WE MOVE NORTH INTO BASHAN? IT'S A POWERFUL COUNTRY AND THEIR KING OG IS A GIANT.

SEND OUT SOME SCOUTS TO EXPLORE THE LAND FIRST. THEN WE'LL DECIDE.

JOSHUA'S SCOUTS ARE DISCOVERED, AND A MESSENGER HURRIES TO TELL KING OG OF BASHAN.

O KING, I SAW SOME STRANGE MEN SPYING OUT OUR LAND.

THEY MUST BE THE ISRAELITES. THEY JUST CONQUERED THE AMORITES, BUT WE'LL TEACH THEM A LESSON ...

BOLDLY, THE GIANT KING OG OF BASHAN SETS OUT TO TEACH THE ISRAELITES A LESSON IN WARFARE. BUT INSTEAD, JOSHUA AND HIS MEN TEACH OG ABOUT DEFEAT. THE ISRAELITES ARE NOW CAMPED JUST ACROSS THE RIVER FROM THE LAND GOD HAS PROMISED THEM!

A Stubborn Mule— and His Donkey

BASED ON NUMBERS 22–24

KING BALAK SEES THE DEFEAT OF SIHON AND OG AND KNOWS HE IS NEXT. IN FEAR, HE SENDS FOR A POWERFUL SORCERER NAMED BALAAM.

BUT LITTLE DOES ISRAEL KNOW THAT OTHER COUNTRIES ARE WATCHING THEIR VICTORIES AND SCHEMING AGAINST THEM.

IF YOU CAN PUT A CURSE ON THE ISRAELITES, KING BALAK WILL GREATLY REWARD YOU.

BALAAM SETS OUT ON HIS FAITHFUL DONKEY TO MEET WITH KING BALAK. BUT GOD SENDS AN ANGEL TO STOP HIM.

BALAAM DOESN'T NOTICE ANYTHING, BUT WHEN BALAAM'S DONKEY SEES THE FEARSOME ANGEL, SHE SCAMPERS INTO THE FIELD TO AVOID ITS FIERY SWORD.

STUPID BEAST!

THEN THE ANGEL OF THE LORD MOVES AHEAD TO A NARROW PATH BETWEEN TWO STONE WALLS.

THE DONKEY PRESSES CLOSE AGAINST ONE OF THE WALLS TO DODGE THE ANGEL'S SWORD.

BUT BALAAM'S FOOT IS SMASHED AGAINST THE WALL, AND HE BEATS HER AGAIN.

OW!! CURSE YOU!

187

A New Leader

BASED ON NUMBERS 27:12-23;
DEUTERONOMY 31—34; JOSHUA 1

FOR THE SECOND TIME, THE ISRAELITES HAVE COME TO THE BORDER OF THE PROMISED LAND. THIS TIME, THEY ARE NOT AFRAID. MEN TALK OF THE FLOCKS AND HERDS THEY WILL HAVE, AND WOMEN DREAM OF PEACEFUL HOMES. BUT MOSES' FEELINGS ARE BITTERSWEET. HE CALLS THE PEOPLE TOGETHER.

I AM 120 YEARS OLD.

I CAN NO LONGER LEAD YOU.

AND GOD HAS ALREADY TOLD ME THAT I WILL NOT ENTER THE PROMISED LAND.

SO GOD HAS APPOINTED A NEW LEADER.

JOSHUA! COME AND STAND BEFORE THE ASSEMBLY.

THE PEOPLE CHEER MOSES' SUCCESSOR. JOSHUA HAS PROVEN HIMSELF FAITHFUL TO GOD AND A BRAVE LEADER. AT THAT MOMENT, THE LORD SPEAKS, CONFIRMING HIS CHOICE OF JOSHUA.

BE STRONG AND COURAGEOUS, JOSHUA.

FOR YOU WILL BRING THE ISRAELITES INTO THE LAND I PROMISED THEM, A LAND FLOWING WITH MILK AND HONEY. AND I MYSELF WILL BE WITH YOU!

THEN THE AGED LEADER CLIMBS MOUNT NEBO AND GAZES DOWN ON THE LAND GOD HAS PROMISED HIS PEOPLE. THERE—ALONE WITH GOD—HE DIES. THE LORD HIMSELF BURIES MOSES, AND TO THIS DAY, NO ONE KNOWS WHERE HIS GRAVE IS.

189

THE ISRAELITES MOURN THE DEATH OF MOSES FOR 30 DAYS. JOSHUA PRAYS TO GOD FOR HELP, AND THE LORD ANSWERS: "DON'T BE AFRAID, FOR THE LORD YOUR GOD IS WITH YOU."

GET THE PEOPLE READY TO GO ACROSS THE JORDAN RIVER. I WANT YOU TO GO INTO THE LAND I AM GOING TO GIVE YOU.

THEN JOSHUA, THE NEW LEADER, CALLS A MEETING.

THE CAMPAIGNS AHEAD WILL BE HARD AND DANGEROUS. BUT I'LL SEEK GOD'S GUIDANCE IN EVERYTHING WE DO.

AND WE WILL FOLLOW YOU AS WE DID MOSES!

I HOPE NOT! I'D PREFER LESS COMPLAINING.

JOSHUA SENDS WORD THROUGH THE CAMP ...

GET YOUR SUPPLIES READY.

WE'RE GOING IN TO TAKE THE LAND!

THREE DAYS FROM NOW WE'LL CROSS THE JORDAN RIVER. THEN WE MUST CAPTURE THE CITY OF JERICHO— BUT FIRST WE NEED TO LEARN EVERYTHING WE CAN ABOUT IT.

ARE WE SURE WE CAN TAKE JERICHO?

YES! FORTY YEARS AGO, OUR FATHERS TURNED BACK BECAUSE THEY WERE AFRAID. LET'S TRUST IN GOD—AND THE MAN HE HAS CHOSEN TO LEAD US!

The Roof of Rahab

BASED ON JOSHUA 2

THAT NIGHT AT THE RIVER'S EDGE ...

YOU SCOUTS WILL BE IN DANGER EVERY MINUTE. BE CAREFUL. LEARN ALL YOU CAN AND COME BACK SOON!

THE NEXT DAY, INSIDE THE CITY OF JERICHO ...

THESE WALLS ARE THICK AND HIGH— AND WELL FORTIFIED!

AND THE SOLDIERS ARE WELL ARMED.

LET'S SEE IF WE CAN FIND A ROOM TO STAY IN AT THIS HOUSE.

THOSE STRANGERS LOOK SUSPICIOUS. I'M GOING TO REPORT THEM TO THE CAPTAIN OF THE GUARD.

THE SCOUTS PROMISE SAFETY FOR RAHAB AND HER FAMILY.

HIDE OUT IN THE MOUNTAINS FOR THREE DAYS. AFTER THAT IT WILL BE SAFE FOR YOU TO CROSS THE RIVER TO YOUR OWN CAMP.

WHEN THE ATTACK COMES, KEEP YOUR FAMILY IN THE HOUSE. AND TIE THIS RED ROPE IN YOUR WINDOW SO OUR MEN WILL KNOW WHERE YOU LIVE.

THE SCOUTS OBEY RAHAB. AFTER THREE DAYS, THEY REPORT TO JOSHUA.

THE CITY IS WELL DEFENDED WITH TWO WALLS. EACH WALL IS THIRTY FEET HIGH. THE OUTER WALL IS SIX FEET THICK AND THE INNER WALL IS TWELVE FEET THICK.

BUT THE PEOPLE HAVE HEARD OF US, AND THEY ARE AFRAID.

GOOD WORK! WE'LL GO AHEAD WITH OUR PLANS TO CROSS THE JORDAN AND TAKE JERICHO.

THE RIVER IS WIDE AND HAS A SWIFT CURRENT. HOW CAN WE GET ALL THE PEOPLE ACROSS?

GOD HELPED OUR PEOPLE CROSS THE RED SEA. LET'S TRUST HIM TO HELP US NOW.

WHEN ALL HAVE CROSSED, JOSHUA ORDERS A MAN FROM EACH OF THE TRIBES TO BRING A LARGE STONE FROM THE RIVERBED.

CARRY THESE STONES TO CAMP. THEY WILL REMIND US OF HOW GOD STOPPED THE JORDAN SO THAT WE COULD CROSS OVER SAFELY.

JOSHUA SETS UP 12 MORE STONES IN THE MIDDLE OF THE JORDAN, AT THE PLACE WHERE THE PRIESTS HOLD THE ARK. THEN HE TELLS THE PRIESTS TO CARRY THE ARK ACROSS THE RIVER. WHEN THEY REACH THE BANK, THE FLOODWATERS OF THE JORDAN RUSH THROUGH THE RIVERBED ...

THE ISRAELITES SET UP THEIR FIRST CAMP AT GILGAL. HERE THEY CELEBRATE THEIR FIRST PASSOVER FEAST IN THE PROMISED LAND.

... AND THE WALLS OF THE MIGHTY CITY COLLAPSE TO THE GROUND.

IN ALL OF JERICHO, ONLY RAHAB, THE WOMAN WHO BELIEVED IN GOD AND HELPED THE SCOUTS, IS SAVED.

THE ISRAELITE SOLDIERS SEARCH THE CITY FOR IRON, BRASS, SILVER, AND GOLD FOR THE TENT OF MEETING TREASURY.

LOOK AT THIS BEAUTIFUL ROBE.

WHY SHOULD I FIGHT AND NOT TAKE SOMETHING? I'LL HIDE SOMETHING, AND NO ONE WILL KNOW ...

FORGET IT. JOSHUA SAID WE CAN'T KEEP ANYTHING FOR OURSELVES.

AFTER THE VICTORY OF JERICHO, JOSHUA CALLS SOME OF THE SCOUTS TO HIM.

HERE IS THE CITY OF AI. IT GUARDS THE APPROACH OF OUR FUTURE CAMPAIGNS.

WE MUST FIND OUT HOW STRONG THE CITY IS BEFORE WE ATTACK.

WE'LL SCOUT IT OUT THE WAY WE DID JERICHO.

EARLY THE NEXT MORNING, JOSHUA CALLS THE LEADERS OF THE TRIBES TO HIM.

SOMEONE DISOBEYED GOD'S ORDER AND KEPT PART OF THE SPOILS OF JERICHO. THIS MAN MUST BE PUNISHED OR WE WILL DIE AT THE HANDS OF THE ENEMY.

GOD POINTS OUT ACHAN AS THE GUILTY ONE.

IT'S TRUE. I SINNED AGAINST GOD AND MY PEOPLE.

NOW WE STAND RIGHT WITH GOD AGAIN.

NOW WITH GOD'S SUPPORT, JOSHUA LEADS SOLDIERS AGAINST AI. JOSHUA RAISES HIS SPEAR TO GIVE THE SIGNAL FOR THE ISRAELITES TO RUSH IN AND SET FIRE TO THE CITY. THE SOLDIERS OF AI ARE CAUGHT IN A TRAP AND QUICKLY DEFEATED.

Stop the Sun BASED ON JOSHUA 9—10

NEWS OF JOSHUA'S VICTORIES SPREADS. THE GIBEONITES KNOW THAT THEY ARE NEXT. SO THEY COME UP WITH A PLAN. THEY SEND A DELEGATION TO MEET WITH JOSHUA. THEY WEAR OLD AND DIRTY CLOTHING, AND PUT MOLDY BREAD IN THEIR SADDLEBAGS.

WE COME FROM A FARAWAY COUNTRY. VERY FAR. SO FAR THAT YOU WON'T HAVE HEARD OF IT.

WE CAME BECAUSE WE HAVE HEARD ABOUT THE GREATNESS OF YOUR GOD. WE WANT TO SIGN A PEACE TREATY WITH YOU.

SHOULD WE MAKE A TREATY WITH THEM? WHAT IF THEY REALLY LIVE IN THE PROMISED LAND, AND WE'RE SUPPOSED TO CONQUER THEM?

LOOK AT HOW WORN THEIR SANDALS AND CLOTHES ARE. AND THE BREAD IN THEIR SADDLEBAGS—IT'S GONE MOLDY.

IT'S DISGUSTING! THEY MUST HAVE TRAVELED FROM MANY MILES AWAY FOR THEIR POSSESSIONS TO GET THIS BEAT UP.

NEITHER JOSHUA NOR HIS MEN THINK TO PRAY AND ASK THE LORD ABOUT THESE TRAVELERS. SO JOSHUA PROMISES TO LIVE IN PEACE WITH THEIR PEOPLE.

A FEW DAYS LATER, THE ISRAELITES COME TO THE CITY OF GIBEON. THERE THEY SEE THE MEN THEY'D JUST SIGNED A TREATY WITH! THIS TIME, THE MEN ARE WEARING MUCH NICER CLOTHES.

YOU LIED TO US!

WE KNEW IF WE DIDN'T DO SOMETHING, YOU WOULD CONQUER US ALL.

THAT IS WHY WE TRICKED YOU. BUT NOW OUR LIVES ARE IN YOUR HANDS.

DO WHATEVER YOUR HONOR REQUIRES YOU TO DO.

WE CAN'T KILL THEM NOW; WE PROMISED.

BUT FROM NOW ON THEY WILL BE OUR SERVANTS.

THE ISRAELITES MOVE ON. BUT A FEW DAYS LATER, THEY RECEIVE A MESSAGE THAT THEIR NEW SERVANTS ARE BEING ATTACKED BY THE FIVE AMORITE KINGS!

A Division Problem

BASED ON JOSHUA 11:1—24:18

UNDER JOSHUA THE ISRAELITES CONQUER ALL THE CITIES OF SOUTHERN CANAAN. THEN THEY GO BACK TO THEIR CAMP AT GILGAL. WHEN JOSHUA LEARNS THAT THE NORTHERN KINGS ARE FORMING A GREAT ARMY, HE MAKES A QUICK MARCH NORTH AND CATCHES THEM OFF GUARD. HIS LIGHTNING ATTACK THROWS THE ENEMY INTO PANIC.

WHAT'S HAPPENING?

I THOUGHT WE WEREN'T FIGHTING UNTIL TOMORROW!

WITH QUICK, DECISIVE BLOWS, JOSHUA TAKES THE CAMP. SOME OF THE ENEMY TRY TO ESCAPE, BUT ISRAELITE SOLDIERS FOLLOW IN CLOSE PURSUIT. THE FIGHTING LASTS THROUGHOUT THE DAY, BUT BY NIGHTFALL THE ENEMY IS IN JOSHUA'S HANDS.

WHEN THE WAR IS OVER, THE ISRAELITES REJOICE AND GIVE THANKS TO GOD FOR THEIR VICTORIES. THEN JOSHUA CALLS THE LEADERS TO A SPECIAL MEETING.

WE HAVE WON MUCH OF THE LAND GOD PROMISED US. IT'S TIME FOR US TO DIVIDE IT AMONG THE TRIBES.

CALEB, JOSHUA'S FRIEND, SPEAKS FIRST.

BECAUSE I WAS ONE OF THE SCOUTS WHO WAS NOT AFRAID TO TAKE CANAAN 45 YEARS AGO, GOD PROMISED THAT SOMEDAY I COULD HAVE THE LAND I SAW.

GIVE ME THE LAND AROUND MOUNT HEBRON, AND I'LL DRIVE OFF THE GIANTS WHO LIVE THERE AND MAKE IT MY HOME.

YOUR WISH IS GRANTED, CALEB, AND MAY GOD BLESS YOU.

SOME YEARS AFTER THE PEOPLE ARE SETTLED IN THEIR NEW HOMELAND, JOSHUA AGAIN CALLS THE TRIBAL LEADERS TO HIM.

I AM OLD AND DON'T HAVE MUCH TIME LEFT. LET ME REMIND YOU OF ALL THAT GOD HAS DONE FOR YOU. CHOOSE THIS DAY WHO YOU WILL SERVE. WILL IT BE GOD OR FALSE IDOLS?

WE WILL SERVE THE LORD OUR GOD, AND WE WILL OBEY HIS VOICE.

"You know with all your heart and soul that not one of all the good promises the LORD your God gave you has failed. Every promise has been fulfilled; not one has failed."

Cities of Refuge

BASED ON NUMBERS 35;
DEUTERONOMY 19;
AND JOSHUA 20

ASHER

NAPHTALI

KEDESH

GOLAN

MANASSEH

Sea of
Galilee

Mediterranean Sea

ZEBULUN

ISSACHAR

RAMOTH

SHECHEM

Jordan River

EPHRAIM

GAD

BEZER

BENJAMIN

Dead Sea

REUBEN

DAN

HEBRON

JUDAH

SIMEON

JOSHUA DIVIDES THE LAND AMONG THE TRIBES
AND SETS UP SIX CITIES OF REFUGE WHERE
PEOPLE CAN GO TO RECEIVE MERCY—EVEN IF
THEY DO SOMETHING AS BAD AS KILLING A
PERSON.

Left-Handed Judge

BASED ON JUDGES 1–3

JOSHUA DIES, AND FOR A LONG TIME HIS LEADERS KEEP THEIR PROMISE TO GOD. THEY BUILD UP STRONG CITIES AND CHOOSE JUDGES TO RULE OVER THEM. BUT WHEN JOSHUA'S FRIENDS GROW OLD AND DIE, MANY OF THE ISRAELITES FORGET GOD ...

... AND BEGIN TO WORSHIP THE IDOLS OF THEIR NEIGHBORS. SO GOD ALLOWS THEM TO BE CONQUERED BY THE DOUBLY WICKED KING OF CUSH. BUT THE ISRAELITES ARE EVENTUALLY SAVED BY CALEB'S SON-IN-LAW OTHNIEL, THE FIRST OF THE HEROIC HEBREW JUDGES.

OTHNIEL RULES ISRAEL IN PEACE FOR 40 YEARS. BUT WHEN HE DIES, THE ISRAELITES TURN AGAIN TO WORSHIP HEATHEN IDOLS. SO GOD LETS THEM BE INVADED BY THE FAT KING EGLON OF MOAB. HE SETS UP HIS CAPITAL IN JERICHO, THE CITY GOD CURSED. FOR 18 YEARS, KING EGLON RULES OVER THE ISRAELITES FROM THE CITY OF PALMS. FINALLY THEY CRY OUT TO GOD FOR A DELIVERER.

GOD HEARS THE ISRAELITES' PRAYERS AND RAISES UP A DELIVERER FROM THE TRIBE OF BENJAMIN—A TRIBE KNOWN FOR BEING LEFT-HANDED. WHEN KING EGLON DEMANDS TRIBUTE FROM THE BENJAMITES, A MAN NAMED EHUD STEPS FORWARD.

LET ME DELIVER THE GOLD TO THIS TYRANT!

HOPEFULLY THEY WON'T SEARCH ME FOR A WEAPON.

IN EGLON'S THRONE ROOM, EHUD DELIVERS THE BENJAMITES' GOLD AND TURNS TO LEAVE.

OH, WAIT! I ALMOST FORGOT. GOD HAS A MESSAGE FOR YOU.

BUT IT'S A SECRET; I HAVE TO TELL YOU PRIVATELY.

EVERYBODY OUT! BUT FIRST, MAKE SURE HE DOESN'T HAVE A WEAPON.

SEARCH HIM!

THE GUARDS SEARCH THE LEFT SIDE OF HIS BODY FOR A WEAPON. BUT THEY DON'T SEARCH HIS OTHER SIDE, NEVER SUSPECTING HE MIGHT BE LEFT-HANDED.

AFTER THE GUARDS LEAVE, EHUD APPROACHES EGLON ON THE THRONE.

THIS IS GOD'S MESSAGE TO YOU!

EHUD STABS KING EGLON IN THE BELLY. BUT EGLON IS SO FAT THAT EHUD CAN'T PULL HIS SWORD BACK OUT. THE FAT OF EGLON'S STOMACH COVERS UP THE HANDLE COMPLETELY.

QUICKLY, EHUD LOCKS THE DOORS OF THE UPPER ROOM AND THEN SNEAKS OUT THROUGH THE SEWER SYSTEM. THE SMELL IN THE ROOM IS SO BAD THAT EGLON'S SERVANTS THINK HE IS GOING TO THE BATHROOM, SO NO ONE DISCOVERS THE ASSASSINATION FOR MANY HOURS.

IN THE MEANTIME, EHUD RALLIES THE ISRAELITES. THEY STAND AT THE FORDS OF THE JORDAN, THE SHALLOWEST PART OF THE RIVER. WITH THE WATER UP TO THEIR KNEES, THEY FIGHT OFF THE MOABITES, KILLING MANY OF THEM.

AFTER THIS VICTORY, THE LAND HAS PEACE FOR 80 YEARS.

The Song of Deborah

BASED ON JUDGES 4–5

THE ANGRY FARMERS TAKE THEIR STORY TO DEBORAH, WHO HOLDS COURT UNDER A PALM TREE IN EPHRAIM.

WHAT CAN WE DO? THE CANAANITES ARE STEALING OUR FOOD.

TAKE A MESSAGE TO CAPTAIN BARAK IN THE NORTH COUNTRY. TELL HIM TO COME AT ONCE.

DOES SHE MEAN WAR?

WE DON'T HAVE A CHANCE AGAINST THE CANAANITES. THEY HAVE 900 IRON CHARIOTS, AND WE HAVE ONLY A FEW CRUDE WEAPONS.

A FEW DAYS LATER ...

BARAK, THIS IS THE PLAN GOD GAVE ME. TAKE 10,000 MEN TO MOUNT TABOR. WHEN KING JABIN HEARS OF THIS, HE WILL ORDER HIS ARMY, UNDER SISERA, TO COME OUT AND DESTROY US. BUT WITH GOD'S HELP YOU WILL DEFEAT THEM.

I'LL LEAD THE ARMY, BUT ONLY IF YOU'LL GO WITH US. GOD SPEAKS THROUGH YOU. AND IF YOU ARE THERE, I KNOW GOD WILL HELP US.

I AM SORRY THAT YOU LACK THE FAITH TO LEAD BY YOURSELF. VERY WELL, I WILL GO WITH YOU. BUT SINCE YOU NEED A WOMAN TO HELP YOU FIGHT YOUR BATTLES, A WOMAN WILL WIN YOUR BATTLE FOR YOU AS WELL.

AFTER A QUICK MARCH, THE ISRAELITES REACH MOUNT TABOR. DEBORAH'S PROPHECY COMES TRUE—THE CANAANITE ARMY COMES TO MEET THEM.

HAVE FAITH! THIS IS THE DAY THE LORD WILL DELIVER US.

DEBORAH GIVES THE SIGNAL, AND BARAK CHARGES DOWN THE MOUNTAIN LEADING HIS TROOPS. ABOVE THEM LIGHTNING FLASHES ...

A CLOUDBURST TURNS THE PLAIN INTO A SEA OF MUD. THE IRON CHARIOTS OF THE CANAANITES SINK INTO THE MIRE. TRAPPED, THEY ARE AT THE MERCY OF THE ISRAELITES, WHO ATTACK WITH SPEED AND COURAGE.

TO THE RIVER!

THE CANAANITES TRY TO RETREAT. BUT THE KISHON RIVER IS ALREADY OVERFLOWING ITS BANKS. AND THE CANAANITES WHO TRY TO SWIM TO SAFETY SINK UNDER THE WEIGHT OF THEIR HEAVY ARMOR.

SISERA TRIES TO ESCAPE. ON THE WAY HE STOPS TO REST IN A TENT THAT HE THINKS IS FRIENDLY. BUT THE WOMAN WHO LIVES THERE, JAEL, IS LOYAL TO ISRAEL AND KILLS SISERA WHILE HE IS ASLEEP.

WHEN DEBORAH LEARNS THAT THE CANAANITES HAVE BEEN DEFEATED, SHE SINGS A SONG OF VICTORY ...

IN THE HEAVENS, EVEN THE STARS FIGHT FOR THE LORD. MAY ALL THE LORD'S ENEMIES PERISH. AND MAY THOSE WHO LOVE THE LORD BE LIKE THE SUN SHINING IN ALL ITS MIGHT.

THE PEOPLE REJOICE AND SING PRAISES TOO. AND FOR 40 YEARS THERE IS PEACE IN ISRAEL. FAMILIES WORK IN THEIR FIELDS AND HARVEST THEIR CROPS. BUT IN TIME THEY AGAIN FORGET GOD AND FIND THEMSELVES IN MORE TROUBLE THAN EVER BEFORE.

Cowardly Judge BASED ON JUDGES 6—7

IN THE YEARS OF PLENTY THAT FOLLOW DEBORAH'S VICTORY OVER THE CANAANITES, THE ISRAELITES AGAIN FORGET GOD. ONE BY ONE, THEY JOIN THEIR NEIGHBORS IN WORSHIPPING THE IDOL BAAL. AT LAST ONLY A FEW PEOPLE IN ALL OF ISRAEL REMEMBER THAT IT WAS GOD WHO HAD RESCUED THEM FROM THEIR ENEMIES.

EVERY HARVEST SEASON, JUST WHEN THE ISRAELITES ARE READY TO GATHER THEIR FOOD FOR THE YEAR, ROVING BANDS OF MIDIANITES STEAL THEIR HARVEST. FOR YEARS, THE DESERT TRIBESMEN TERRORIZE THE ISRAELITE VILLAGES AND RAID THEIR FIELDS.

RUN FOR YOUR LIVES!

IF THEY FIND WHERE I HID MY GRAIN, WE'LL STARVE.

BUT WHEN THE RAID IS OVER ...

IT'S GONE! OUR GRAIN IS GONE!

FOR SEVEN LONG YEARS THE ISRAELITES SUFFER AT THE HANDS OF THE DESERT TRIBESMEN. THEY HIDE OUT IN CAVES AND THRESH THEIR GRAIN IN SECRET PLACES ... BUT THE RAIDERS ALWAYS RETURN.

THEN EVEN MORE FRIGHTENING NEWS COMES ...

THE MIDIANITES ARE COMING AGAIN, AND THEY'RE BRINGING GREAT ARMIES FROM THE EAST.

LIKE GRASSHOPPERS, THE ENEMY SWARMS OVER THE ISRAELITE FIELDS, STEALING GRAIN, CATTLE, AND SHEEP.

ONE DAY A YOUNG ISRAELITE IS SECRETLY THRESHING HIS GRAIN WHEN A STRANGER APPEARS BEFORE HIM.

WHO ARE YOU? WHAT DO YOU WANT?

YOU ARE A MIGHTY WARRIOR, GIDEON. GOD HAS CHOSEN YOU TO SAVE HIS PEOPLE.

ME? MY FAMILY IS THE WEAKEST OF THE WHOLE TRIBE, AND I'M THE WEAKEST ONE IN MY FAMILY. IF YOU'RE REALLY AN ANGEL OF THE LORD, THEN GIVE ME A SIGN.

GIDEON PREPARES SOME FOOD AND BRINGS IT TO THE STRANGER.

PUT THE FOOD ON THE ROCK.

THE STRANGER TOUCHES THE FOOD WITH HIS STAFF. INSTANTLY, A FIRE BURSTS FORTH AND CONSUMES IT.

I HAVE SEEN THE ANGEL OF THE LORD FACE-TO-FACE!

WHEN THE ANGEL DISAPPEARS, GOD SPEAKS TO GIDEON AND TELLS HIM TO DESTROY THE ALTAR OF BAAL.

BUT GIDEON IS AFRAID OF THE TOWNSPEOPLE, SO HE WAITS UNTIL DARK TO OBEY.

WON'T THE PEOPLE KILL US IF THEY FIND OUT?

THAT'S WHY WE'RE DOING THIS AT NIGHT.

BUT GIDEON STILL HOPES THAT GOD HASN'T REALLY CALLED HIM. HE ASKS FOR A SIGN ...

OKAY, GOD, TOMORROW MORNING IF THIS WOOL IS WET WITH DEW AND THE GROUND IS DRY, THEN I'LL KNOW THAT YOU HAVE TRULY CHOSEN ME.

THE NEXT MORNING, GIDEON HAS HIS SIGN.

THE GROUND IS DRY—BUT THERE'S ENOUGH DEW ON THIS WOOL TO FILL A WHOLE BOWL.

BUT GIDEON IS STILL AFRAID.

OH GOD, PLEASE DON'T BE ANGRY, BUT GIVE ME JUST ONE MORE SIGN. THIS TIME MAKE THE WOOL DRY AND THE GROUND WET. THEN I'LL REALLY TRUST IN YOU.

THE NEXT MORNING ...

THE WOOL IS DRY—AND THE GROUND IS WET! ALL RIGHT, GOD, I BELIEVE! NOW I KNOW THAT I AM THE ONE CALLED TO SAVE MY PEOPLE.

ONLY 300 MEN ARE LEFT OUT OF GIDEON'S ORIGINAL ARMY OF 32,000. NOW THE ISRAELITES KNOW BEYOND ALL DOUBT THAT ONLY WITH GOD'S HELP CAN THEY DEFEAT THE ENEMY.

HIDE YOUR TORCHES IN THESE PITCHERS. SPREAD OUT ON THREE SIDES OF THE CAMP. WAIT UNTIL NIGHTFALL, THEN LISTEN FOR MY SIGNAL ON THE TRUMPET.

WE'RE READY!

AT GIDEON'S SIGNAL, THE MEN BLOW THEIR TRUMPETS, SMASH THEIR PITCHERS, WAVE THEIR TORCHES, AND GIVE THE BATTLE CRY ...

THE SWORD OF THE LORD AND OF GIDEON!

THE STILLNESS OF THE NIGHT IS SUDDENLY BROKEN BY THE BLARE OF 300 TRUMPETS AND THE CRASH OF BROKEN PITCHERS. STARTLED FROM THEIR SLEEP, THE MIDIANITES RUSH OUT TO FIND THEIR CAMP ABLAZE WITH FLAMING TORCHES.

THOUGH THEY ARE ONLY 300, THE ISRAELITES' TORCHES, HORNS, AND SHOUTING THROW THE MIDIANITES INTO A PANIC. THEY LASH OUT WITH THEIR SWORDS, STRIKING EACH OTHER DOWN. WITHIN MINUTES THEY'VE KILLED MORE OF THEIR OWN MEN THAN GIDEON EVER COULD WITH HIS ORIGINAL ARMY. THE LORD HAS DEMONSTRATED HIS MIGHT ONCE AGAIN.

God's Enforcer
BASED ON JUDGES 13–14

AFTER GIDEON'S DEATH, NEW ENEMIES COME AGAINST ISRAEL. NOW PHILISTINE RAIDERS STRIKE TIME AND AGAIN AT THE ISRAELITE VILLAGES, CARRYING OFF GRAIN, CATTLE—AND EVEN CHILDREN TO WORK AS SLAVES. ONE ISRAELITE WOMAN RECEIVES A PROMISE FROM THE LORD.

YOU ARE GOING TO HAVE A BOY. SO KEEP YOURSELF PURE BECAUSE YOUR SON WILL HELP SAVE ISRAEL FROM THE PHILISTINES. AS A SIGN THAT HE IS SET APART FOR THE LORD, NO RAZOR OR SCISSORS MUST EVER TOUCH HIS HEAD.

A MAN CAME AND TOLD ME THAT WE'RE GOING TO HAVE A BOY AND HE WILL BE A HERO FOR GOD!

YOU'RE FEVERISH! EVEN IF WE DID HAVE A KID, THERE'S NO REASON GOD WOULD BLESS HIM WITH SUCH A GREAT DESTINY.

IT IS TRUE. YOUR SON WILL BE A NAZIRITE—SET APART FOR GOD FROM BIRTH. AND HE MUST NEVER CUT HIS HAIR, FOR THAT WILL BE THE SYMBOL OF HIS HOLINESS.

MY NAME DOESN'T MATTER—ONLY THE NAME OF OUR AWESOME LORD.

WHAT IS YOUR NAME, GREAT ONE?

THEN WE SHALL SACRIFICE A GOAT AS THANKS TO THE LORD.

AS THEY LIGHT A SMALL FIRE FOR THEIR SACRIFICE ...

BUT TO HIS PARENTS' DISMAY, AS THEIR SON, SAMSON, GROWS UP, HE DOESN'T ACT LIKE SOMEONE DESTINED TO BE GOD'S HERO. AN IRRESPONSIBLE YOUNG MAN, HE DISOBEYS MANY OF THE LORD'S COMMANDS, EXCEPT FOR THE ONE ABOUT CUTTING HIS HAIR.

MAY I GIVE YOU A DRINK OF WATER?

WE HAVE SEEN GOD!

THE LORD WILL SURELY FULFILL HIS PROMISE TO US.

YES, THANK YOU.

SHE'S THE MOST BEAUTIFUL GIRL I'VE EVER SEEN. I DON'T CARE IF SHE'S A PHILISTINE, THE ENEMY OF MY PEOPLE.

BACK HOME, SAMSON LOSES NO TIME TELLING HIS PARENTS WHAT HE WANTS.

I HAVE FALLEN IN LOVE WITH A PHILISTINE GIRL. MAKE ARRANGEMENTS WITH HER PARENTS FOR US TO GET MARRIED.

BUT YOU'RE SUPPOSED TO BE GOD'S DELIVERER!

HOW CAN YOU LOVE ONE OF OUR ENEMIES? SHE DOESN'T BELIEVE IN OUR GOD.

I DON'T CARE. MAKE IT HAPPEN.

223

IN TIMNAH, SEVERAL PHILISTINES GREET SAMSON ...

I AM YOUR BEST MAN, AND I HAVE BROUGHT 29 OF MY FRIENDS TO BE YOUR GUESTS.

UMM ... THANKS? HEY, I'VE GOT AN IDEA! IF ANY OF YOU CAN GUESS MY RIDDLE, I'LL GIVE EACH OF YOU A SHIRT AND A NICE ROBE. IF YOU CAN'T, EACH OF YOU HAS TO GIVE ME A SHIRT AND A ROBE.

AT LEAST ONE OF US SHOULD BE ABLE TO FIGURE OUT THIS STUPID ISRAELITE'S RIDDLE.

IT'S A BET!

"OUT OF THE EATER, SOMETHING TO EAT. OUT OF THE STRONG, SOMETHING SWEET." YOU MUST GUESS THE ANSWER WITHIN THE SEVEN DAYS OF MY WEDDING FEAST.

BUT AS THE WEEK GOES BY, NEITHER THE BEST MAN NOR ANY OF HIS FRIENDS CAN GUESS SAMSON'S RIDDLE.

WHAT WILL WE DO? I CAN'T AFFORD TO GIVE HIM A SHIRT AND A ROBE.

NEITHER CAN I. WE'LL HAVE TO GET THE ANSWER FROM HIS BRIDE. AFTER ALL, SHE IS A PHILISTINE.

WE DIDN'T COME HERE TO GET ROBBED BY YOUR FUTURE HUSBAND. GET THE ANSWER FROM SAMSON, OR WE'LL SET FIRE TO YOUR FATHER'S HOUSE WITH YOU IN IT!

I WILL! JUST GIVE ME TIME.

THAT EVENING ...

IF I'M GOING TO BE YOUR WIFE, WE SHOULDN'T HAVE SECRETS. TELL ME THE ANSWER TO YOUR RIDDLE.

NOT EVEN MY FATHER AND MOTHER KNOW THE ANSWER. WHY SHOULD I TELL YOU?

BUT SHE CRIES EVERY DAY, AND ON THE LAST DAY OF THE FEAST ...

YOU HATE ME! IF YOU LOVED ME, YOU'D TELL ME THE ANSWER.

FINE! THE ANSWER IS "A LION AND HONEY."

225

Defying the Philistines

BASED ON JUDGES 15

WITHOUT A THOUGHT FOR HIS BRIDE OR HIS WEDDING, SAMSON RETURNS TO HIS PARENTS' HOUSE. BUT AS HIS ANGER COOLS, HE THINKS OF HIS WIFE WAITING FOR HIM.

I GUESS IT REALLY WASN'T HER FAULT. THEY FORCED HER TO TELL THE ANSWER. I'LL GO TALK TO HER.

IN THE PHILISTINE CITY, HE GOES STRAIGHT TO THE HOME OF HIS WIFE'S FATHER.

I'VE COME TO SEE MY WIFE.

YOUR WIFE? WE THOUGHT YOU HATED HER. SHE MARRIED YOUR BEST MAN.

HERE IS HER YOUNGER SISTER. SHE'S EVEN MORE BEAUTIFUL. DO YOU WANT TO MARRY HER?

NO! I SHOULD HAVE KNOWN BETTER THAN TO TRUST A PHILISTINE. WHATEVER I DO NOW, IT'S YOUR FAULT.

ON THE WAY HOME, SAMSON GOES THROUGH FIELDS RICH WITH RIPENED GRAIN.

FIELDS AND VINEYARDS STOLEN FROM MY PEOPLE! I KNOW HOW I CAN MAKE THE PHILISTINES SORRY FOR STEALING MY WIFE!

IN NO TIME, SAMSON SETS FOXES RACING THROUGH THE FIELDS AND VINEYARDS WITH FLAMING TORCHES TIED TO THEIR TAILS. IN A MATTER OF MINUTES, THE WHOLE COUNTRYSIDE IS ABLAZE.

IN THE CITY, THE PHILISTINES WATCH WITH TERROR AS THE SKY GLOWS RED.

SAMSON DID THIS! HE'S GETTING EVEN WITH HIS WIFE'S FATHER FOR LETTING HER MARRY SOMEONE ELSE.

HER FATHER SHOULD HAVE KNOWN BETTER THAN TO TRICK SAMSON. COME ON, LET'S GIVE OUR COUNTRYMAN A TASTE OF HIS OWN MEDICINE.

THE ANGRY PHILISTINES SET FIRE TO THE HOME OF SAMSON'S FATHER-IN-LAW. BUT THEY DON'T COUNT ON SAMSON'S RETURN.

YOU KILLED MY WIFE? SHE WAS ONE OF YOUR OWN PEOPLE!

SOMEONE HAD TO BE PUNISHED.

THEN IT WILL BE YOU! NONE OF YOU PHILISTINES DESERVES TO LIVE!

AFTER KILLING THE PHILISTINES, SAMSON HIDES IN A CAVE IN JUDAH. THE PHILISTINE ARMY FOLLOWS HIM AND DEMANDS THAT THE TRIBE OF JUDAH TURN SAMSON OVER TO THEM. THE TRIBAL LEADERS ARE POWERLESS TO REFUSE. "IT'S YOU," THEY TELL SAMSON; "OR EVERY MAN, WOMAN, AND CHILD IN JUDAH." SO SAMSON LETS THEM TIE HIM UP.

THAT SHOULD DO IT. THE ROPES ARE NEW, AND THE KNOTS ARE TIGHT. YOUR CAPTURE WILL SPARE US THE PHILISTINES' WRATH, SAMSON. LET'S GO.

O GOD, DO NOT LET YOUR ENEMY DEFEAT ME.

WHEN THE PHILISTINES SEE SAMSON BOUND BEFORE THEM, THEY SHOUT IN RAGE AND CHARGE TO KILL HIM.

I'M SORRY, SAMSON. BUT THIS IS THE ONLY WAY TO PROTECT ISRAEL.

SUDDENLY, THE SPIRIT OF THE LORD GIVES SAMSON GREAT POWER AGAIN. HE BURSTS HIS ROPES AND GRABS THE JAWBONE OF A DONKEY LYING NEARBY ON THE GROUND.

I'VE THOUGHT OF ANOTHER WAY.

WITH DEADLY AIM, SAMSON STRIKES DOWN ONE PHILISTINE SOLDIER AFTER ANOTHER. THOSE WHO CAN ESCAPE RUN FOR THEIR LIVES.

WHEN HE IS DONE, A THOUSAND PHILISTINES LIE DEAD AROUND HIM.

THEN, WEARY AND THIRSTY, SAMSON PRAYS TO GOD.

LORD, YOU GAVE ME THE VICTORY. DON'T LET ME DIE OF THIRST NOW.

GOD PROVIDES A STREAM OF WATER TO STRENGTHEN SAMSON. AFTER THIS EVENT, SAMSON SERVES AS A LEADER AND PROTECTOR OF ISRAEL FOR 20 YEARS.

A Bad Haircut

BASED ON JUDGES 16:1-20

ONE EVENING, SAMSON VISITS THE PHILISTINE CITY OF GAZA.

WHAT IS YOUR BUSINESS IN GAZA?

I HAVE COME TO SEE A FRIEND.

I JUST SAW SAMSON ENTERING A HOUSE DOWN THE STREET. HOW DID HE GET IN?

SAMSON? I DIDN'T RECOGNIZE HIM.

NEVER MIND. CLOSE THE GATE AND WE'LL TRAP HIM IN THE CITY. CALL OUT ALL THE GUARDS! SAMSON WILL NEVER LEAVE GAZA ALIVE.

DO YOU THINK HE'S GOING TO TELL *US* WHAT IT IS?

NO, BUT HE'LL TELL THE RIGHT PERSON. I HEAR HE'S IN LOVE WITH DELILAH ...

DELILAH? SHE'S A PHILISTINE.

RIGHT. SHE'LL GET SAMSON TO TELL HER HIS SECRET. THEN SHE'LL TELL US.

WILL SHE? WHAT IF SHE'S IN LOVE WITH SAMSON?

SHE'S ALSO IN LOVE WITH MONEY. COME ON. LET'S GO SEE HER.

SO THE PHILISTINE RULERS VISIT DELILAH.

IF YOU FIND OUT SAMSON'S SECRET FOR US, WE'LL GIVE YOU 1,100 PIECES OF SILVER. EACH.

PAYABLE WHEN YOU DELIVER SAMSON INTO OUR HANDS.

HMM ... 1,100 TIMES FIVE EQUALS ... UMM, A LOT OF MONEY. HOW CAN I REFUSE?

THIS AMOUNT OF MONEY IS A SMALL FORTUNE. IF SHE CAN FIND OUT SAMSON'S WEAKNESS, DELILAH WILL BE AS RICH AS A MODERN MILLIONAIRE.

236

SAMSON WAKES UP READY TO DEFEND HIMSELF, BUT ...

MY HAIR! IT'S GONE! I HAVE BROKEN MY PROMISE, AND NOW GOD HAS TAKEN AWAY MY STRENGTH.

YOU BROKE THE LEATHER STRAPS, BUT LET'S SEE IF YOU CAN BREAK OUR CHAINS NOW.

SAMSON'S STRENGTH IS GONE! CHAINED AND UNDER HEAVY GUARD, HE IS TAKEN AWAY.

WHAT WILL THEY DO TO HIM?

PUT OUT HIS EYES AND THROW HIM INTO PRISON. OUR TROUBLES WITH SAMSON ARE OVER.

HERE'S YOUR MONEY, DELILAH. YOU'VE EARNED IT.

5,500 PIECES OF SILVER—ALL MINE!

WHILE DELILAH COUNTS HER MONEY, SAMSON IS LED THROUGH THE STREETS OF GAZA—A CAPTIVE IN CHAINS.

HA! THE MIGHTY JUDGE OF ISRAEL IS A WEAKLING NOW!

SO SAMSON IS BROUGHT OUT OF THE PRISON AND LED UP THE TEMPLE STEPS.

BRING HIM UP HERE SO EVERYONE CAN SEE WHAT THE MIGHTY JUDGE OF ISRAEL LOOKS LIKE NOW.

SHOW US HOW YOU CARRIED OFF THE GATES OF GAZA!

LET'S SEE YOU TEAR APART A LION WITH YOUR BARE HANDS NOW!

NOW THAT SAMSON'S HAIR HAS GROWN BACK, HE HOPES THAT GOD WILL RESTORE HIS STRENGTH.

WHERE ARE THE PILLARS? I WANT TO LEAN AGAINST THEM.

HERE, I'LL PUT YOUR HANDS ON THEM.

RUN, BOY, AND DON'T STOP UNTIL YOU'RE OUTSIDE THE TEMPLE.

O GOD, YOU BLESSED ME WITH GREAT STRENGTH ONCE. I IGNORED YOUR COMMANDS AND LOST YOUR BLESSING. I DESERVE TO DIE. BUT JUST LET ME TAKE SOME PHILISTINES WITH ME.

USING ALL HIS STRENGTH, SAMSON PUSHES AGAINST THE PILLARS—AND THE GIANT TEMPLE TO THE HEATHEN GOD DAGON CRASHES TO THE GROUND. CRUSHED BENEATH IT ARE THOUSANDS OF PHILISTINES WHO HAD MADE SLAVES OF SAMSON'S PEOPLE.

KHA-BOOM

SAMSON HAD GREAT STRENGTH, BUT A WEAK CHARACTER. YET GOD USED HIM TO HELP ISRAEL ANYWAY. NOW GOD WANTS TO SHOW THAT HE CAN ALSO USE SOMEONE WHO IS PHYSICALLY HELPLESS, BUT NOBLE AND FAITHFUL ...

Ruth's Redeemer

BASED ON RUTH

TWO WOMEN LIVE IN A FOREIGN LAND—NAOMI, A JEW, AND HER DAUGHTER-IN-LAW, RUTH, A MOABITE. ALL THE MEN IN THEIR FAMILY HAVE DIED, AND THEY ARE LEFT PENNILESS AND IN NEED.

LEAVE ME, RUTH. I HAVE NOTHING LEFT. I AM OLD. YOUR BEST HOPE IS TO FIND A HUSBAND WHO CAN TAKE CARE OF YOU.

NO, YOU ARE MY MOTHER. WHERE YOU GO, I WILL GO. YOUR PEOPLE WILL BE MY PEOPLE. AND YOUR GOD WILL BE MY GOD. HE WILL TAKE CARE OF US BETTER THAN ANY HUSBAND.

HE DIDN'T TAKE CARE OF MY HUSBAND. MY NAME MEANS "SWEET," AND FOR A WHILE MY LIFE WAS SWEET. BUT NOW THAT GOD HAS ABANDONED ME, THE NAME "BITTER" WOULD BETTER DESCRIBE ME.

COME, WE WILL GO BACK TO ISRAEL, WHERE I HAVE RELATIVES WHO MAY HELP TAKE CARE OF US.

BACK IN ISRAEL ...

THERE IS A LAW HERE THAT POOR WOMEN CAN GO TO THE FIELDS AND PICK UP ANY EXTRA GRAIN THAT THE WORKERS DROP. I AM TOO OLD TO WORK IN A FIELD ALL DAY. WILL YOU GO SO THAT WE MAY HAVE FOOD?

OF COURSE, MOTHER.

RUTH GOES TO A FIELD OWNED BY BOAZ, A DISTANT RELATIVE OF NAOMI'S. SHE WORKS HARD THERE, GATHERING THE UNUSED GRAIN.

ONE DAY, THE OWNER ARRIVES ...

HOW ARE THE BEST WORKERS IN ALL ISRAEL DOING? THE LORD BLESS YOU AND KEEP YOU!

WHAT A GODLY OWNER.

AND THE LORD BE WITH YOU!

BOAZ QUESTIONS HIS FOREMAN ABOUT PROGRESS ON HIS FIELDS.

... AND ARE YOU TAKING CARE OF THE POOR WOMEN?

YES, AND THERE IS A NEW WIDOW, RUTH FROM MOAB. SHE HAS BEEN LABORING HARD FOR WEEKS TO SUPPORT HER MOTHER-IN-LAW, NAOMI.

NAOMI IS ONE OF MY RELATIVES!

I HAVE HEARD HOW KIND YOU ARE TO YOUR MOTHER-IN-LAW. GLEAN IN MY FIELDS AS MUCH AS YOU LIKE, AND MAY GOD REWARD AND PROTECT YOU.

HE DOES. THANK YOU FOR YOUR KINDNESS.

AT LUNCHTIME, BOAZ IS IMPRESSED WITH RUTH'S FAITH AND WIT.

WHEN THE MEAL IS OVER AND RUTH HAS GONE BACK TO WORK ...

DROP SOME GRAIN ON PURPOSE FOR HER TO PICK UP. MAKE SURE NO HARM COMES TO HER.

DON'T WORRY, BOAZ. SHE WILL BE SAFE, AND SHE'LL FIND ALL THE GRAIN SHE NEEDS.

THAT EVENING ...

LOOK AT ALL THE GRAIN I GOT! NAOMI, YOUR GOD IS GOOD TO US!

WHEN MY HUSBAND AND SONS DIED, I THOUGHT GOD HAD FORGOTTEN ME. NOW I KNOW HOW MUCH HE LOVES ME, BECAUSE HE GAVE ME A DAUGHTER-IN-LAW WHO CARES FOR ME LIKE A DAUGHTER.

I MET THE OWNER OF THE FIELD TODAY. HIS NAME IS BOAZ— AND HE WAS VERY KIND.

BOAZ? HE IS A RELATIVE OF MY HUSBAND'S FAMILY. GOD BLESS HIM FOR BEING KIND TO YOU.

ALL THROUGH THE HARVEST SEASON, RUTH GLEANS IN BOAZ'S FIELD AND TAKES CARE OF NAOMI. ONE EVENING ...

BOAZ HAS SHOWN THAT HE IS KIND TO YOU. AS A KINSMAN, HE HAS THE RIGHT TO MARRY YOU. THE HARVEST CELEBRATION IS TONIGHT. YOU SHOULD WEAR YOUR NICEST DRESS TO THE PARTY, AND THEN YOU SHOULD ASK HIM IF HE—AS YOUR RELATIVE AND REDEEMER— WOULD WANT TO MARRY AND TAKE CARE OF YOU.

BOAZ IS A GODLY MAN, AND I'LL DO WHAT YOU TELL ME.

RUTH DOES EVERYTHING EXACTLY AS NAOMI DESCRIBED. AND BOAZ NOTICES.

RUTH CAME!

NAOMI TOLD ME TO ASK YOU—SINCE YOU ARE A KINSMAN, WOULD YOU BE MY REDEEMER? WOULD YOU ... MARRY ME?

IS THERE NO ONE TO TAKE CARE OF YOU?

NO.

THEN I WILL.

THE NEWS OF RUTH AND BOAZ'S COMING MARRIAGE SPREADS RAPIDLY THROUGHOUT ALL BETHLEHEM. AT THE WEDDING THERE IS FEASTING, MUSIC, AND LAUGHTER.

ARE YOU HAPPY, MY DEAR?

HAPPIER THAN I EVER DREAMED I COULD BE. GOD HAS BEEN GOOD TO ME.

AFTER THE WEDDING, RUTH AND NAOMI MOVE INTO BOAZ'S BIG HOUSE. LATER, WHEN A SON IS BORN TO RUTH, NAOMI PROUDLY CARES FOR THE CHILD.

I THANK GOD FOR THE DAY YOU LEFT MOAB TO COME WITH ME TO BETHLEHEM. HE HAS TAKEN MY BITTER LIFE AND MADE IT SWEET AGAIN.

I THANK GOD TOO, NAOMI. HE HAS MADE GOOD COME OUT OF OUR SADNESS. HE HONORED US WITH A MAN WHO HONORS HIM. AND NOW I HAVE A BEAUTIFUL BABY.

MY SON IS NAMED OBED, WHICH MEANS "SERVANT." AND MY PRAYER IS THAT OBED WILL SERVE GOD AND HIS PEOPLE.

RUTH'S PRAYER COMES TRUE— FOR HER SON WILL BECOME THE GRANDFATHER OF DAVID, ISRAEL'S GREATEST KING, WHO WILL FREE HIS PEOPLE FROM THEIR ENEMIES.

247

I AM SORRY FOR MY HASTY JUDGMENT. GO IN PEACE, HANNAH, AND MAY GOD GRANT YOU WHAT YOU'VE PRAYED FOR.

GOD DOES ANSWER HANNAH'S PRAYER. WHEN HER LITTLE BOY IS OLD ENOUGH, SHE BRINGS HIM TO ELI.

WHEN I ASKED GOD FOR A SON, I PROMISED THAT HE WOULD SERVE THE LORD ALL HIS LIFE. SO I HAVE BROUGHT HIM HERE TO BE TRAINED IN GOD'S HOUSE. HIS NAME IS SAMUEL.

GOD BLESS YOU, HANNAH. I WILL TEACH YOUR SON TO BE A SERVANT OF THE LORD.

SAMUEL STAYS WITH ELI AND EAGERLY LEARNS HOW TO SERVE GOD. EACH YEAR WHEN HANNAH AND HER HUSBAND COME TO WORSHIP, SHE BRINGS SAMUEL A NEW COAT.

IT'S JUST LIKE A PRIEST'S ROBE. THANK YOU, MOTHER.

OH, LORD ALMIGHTY, IF YOU WILL HAVE PITY ON MY MISERY AND GIVE ME A SON, I WILL DEDICATE HIM TO YOU FOR ALL HIS DAYS.

OLD ELI IS PROUD OF SAMUEL. AS SAMUEL WORKS IN THE TEMPLE, HE SHOWS HIS DEVOTION TO GOD, UNLIKE ELI'S TWO SONS, WHO SIN AGAINST GOD AND CHEAT THE PEOPLE—EVEN THOUGH THEY'RE PRIESTS! ONE NIGHT, SAMUEL HEARS A VOICE.

SAMUEL!

SAMUEL RUSHES TO FIND OUT WHAT ELI WANTS. BUT ELI HADN'T CALLED HIM. HE GOES BACK TO BED.

AGAIN, A VOICE CALLS HIM.

SAMUEL!

SAMUEL GOES RUNNING TO ELI'S ROOM AGAIN. EVENTUALLY, ELI REALIZES THAT GOD IS SPEAKING TO SAMUEL. HE INSTRUCTS SAMUEL TO ANSWER THE LORD, AND LISTEN TO WHATEVER MESSAGE GOD HAS FOR HIM.

THE NEXT MORNING, ELI ASKS SAMUEL WHAT GOD HAS TOLD HIM. SAMUEL DOESN'T WANT TO REPEAT THE MESSAGE, BUT ELI INSISTS ...

GOD SAID, "ELI'S SONS ARE WICKED AND ELI HAS NOT TRIED TO STOP THEM. THEY WILL BE PUNISHED FOR THE EVIL THEY HAVE DONE."

IT IS TRUE. HE IS THE LORD, AND HE WILL DO WHAT HE KNOWS IS RIGHT.

WORD SPREADS THAT GOD HAS SPOKEN TO SAMUEL. AS SAMUEL GROWS UP, ALL OF ISRAEL KNOWS THAT HE IS A TRUE PROPHET OF GOD.

IF ONLY OUR PRIESTS WERE MEN OF GOD LIKE SAMUEL. HOW LONG MUST WE SUFFER UNDER THE LYING AND CHEATING OF ELI'S SONS?

MARK MY WORDS, THEY WILL BRING ABOUT THEIR OWN DESTRUCTION.

Pass the Ark

BASED ON 1 SAMUEL 4–6

THE PHILISTINES HAVE CONTINUED TO TROUBLE THE ISRAELITES EVER SINCE THE DAYS OF SAMSON. THE ISRAELITE SOLDIERS GO OUT TO FIGHT AGAINST THE PHILISTINES, BUT THE BATTLE DOES NOT GO WELL.

WE'VE LOST 4,000 MEN.

WHAT CAN WE DO?

I HAVE IT! MOSES AND JOSHUA USED TO ALWAYS BRING THE ARK OF THE COVENANT WITH THEM INTO BATTLE. IF WE BRING THE SACRED ARK HERE, MAYBE IT WILL WIN THE BATTLE FOR US.

YES! SEND FOR THE ARK RIGHT AWAY!

EVEN THOUGH IT IS FORBIDDEN, ELI'S TWO SONS GO INTO THE HOLY OF HOLIES. THERE THEY TAKE THE SACRED ARK FROM THE LORD'S HOUSE. WHEN THEY BRING IT TO CAMP, THE ISRAELITES SHOUT WITH SO MUCH JOY ...

THE PHILISTINES ATTACK! BUT THE ISRAELITES, BELIEVING IN THE POWER OF THE ARK, COUNTERATTACK WITH SUDDEN FURY.

CAPTURE THE ARK, AND THEY'LL GIVE UP!

THE PHILISTINES CAPTURE THE ARK, AND THE ISRAELITES FLEE IN TERROR. THEIR FAITH IN GOD HAD BECOME A SUPERSTITIOUS BELIEF IN THE ARK. A MESSENGER TAKES THE NEWS TO ELI.

THE BATTLE IS LOST! YOUR SONS ARE DEAD! AND THE PHILISTINES HAVE CAPTURED THE ARK.

THE ARK IS CAPTURED?

AT THE NEWS, ELI FALLS AND BREAKS HIS NECK. MEANWHILE, THE PHILISTINES TRIUMPHANTLY CARRY THE ARK HOME TO THE CITY OF ASHDOD AND PLACE IT IN THE TEMPLE OF THEIR GOD, DAGON.

LET THIS BE A SIGN THAT OUR GOD DAGON HAS CONQUERED THE GOD OF ISRAEL.

BUT IN THE MORNING ...

LOOK! OUR GREAT GOD DAGON LIES BROKEN BEFORE THE ARK OF THE ISRAELITES!

NOT ONLY IS THEIR IDOL DESTROYED, BUT A PLAGUE BREAKS OUT IN ASHDOD. SO THE PHILISTINES CARRY THE ARK FROM ONE CITY TO ANOTHER. IN EACH CITY A PLAGUE BREAKS OUT.

OUR FIELDS ARE OVERRUN WITH MICE. I TELL YOU, A CURSE HAS BEEN PUT ON OUR CITIES.

NOT A SINGLE FAMILY HAS ESCAPED THIS MYSTERY DISEASE.

THE PHILISTINES SOON REALIZE THAT THEIR TROUBLES BEGAN WHEN THEY CAPTURED THE ARK OF ISRAEL. FINALLY, THEY RETURN THE ARK. BUT NOW ISRAEL IS WORSHIPPING IDOLS. SOME MEN TAKE THE ARK TO A HOUSE IN KIRIATH JEARIM, WHERE IT LIES FORGOTTEN FOR MANY YEARS ...

A Miracle at Mizpah

YOUNG SAMUEL GROWS UP TO BE A GODLY MAN. AND AFTER YEARS OF STRUGGLE UNDER THE PHILISTINES, THE ISRAELITES ARE FINALLY READY TO LISTEN WHEN SAMUEL SPEAKS ...

RETURN TO THE LORD! WORSHIP HIM WITH ALL YOUR HEARTS, AND GOD WILL DELIVER YOU FROM THE PHILISTINES.

SAMUEL IS RIGHT! LET'S THROW AWAY OUR IDOLS AND WORSHIP GOD.

LET'S ALL GO TO THE CITY OF MIZPAH, WHERE WE CAN REPENT AND PRAY TOGETHER!

EAGERLY, THE PEOPLE FOLLOW THIS MAN WHO SPEAKS BOLDLY FOR GOD. BY THE THOUSANDS THEY SET OUT ...

BUT THE PHILISTINES DISCOVER THE GREAT MARCH TO MIZPAH.

IF THOUSANDS OF ISRAELITES ARE MASSING AT MIZPAH, IT CAN MEAN ONLY ONE THING—THEY PLAN TO ATTACK US.

WE'LL STRIKE BEFORE THEY DO, AND THIS TIME WE'LL CRUSH THEM SO BADLY THEY'LL NEVER FIGHT AGAIN.

Search for a King

BASED ON 1 SAMUEL 8—10

FOR YEARS, SAMUEL JUDGES THE PEOPLE OF ISRAEL AND THERE IS PEACE. BUT AS HE GROWS OLD, THE TRIBAL LEADERS BECOME WORRIED ...

SAMUEL, YOU'RE GETTING OLDER. GIVE US A KING TO BE A LEADER. LET US BE LIKE THE OTHER NATIONS.

WHY WOULD YOU WANT TO BE LIKE OTHER NATIONS? WE'VE BEEN CONQUERING THOSE OTHER NATIONS! BUT VERY WELL, I WILL ASK GOD.

LATER ...

GOD WANTS ME TO WARN YOU WHAT A KING WILL DO. HE'LL SEND YOUR SONS TO BATTLE. HE WILL MAKE YOUR DAUGHTERS BECOME HIS SERVANTS. HE'LL TAKE YOUR CROPS AWAY FROM YOU AND USE THEM TO FEED HIS ROYAL COURT.

MAYBE SO, BUT WE STILL WANT A KING!

AGAIN, SAMUEL PRAYS TO GOD; THEN ...

FINE. GOD WILL GIVE YOU EXACTLY WHAT YOU'VE ASKED FOR. GO HOME, AND I WILL SEND WORD WHEN I HAVE FOUND A KING FOR YOU.

A FEW DAYS LATER SAMUEL SETS OUT EAGERLY FOR THE GATE OF THE CITY. GOD HAS TOLD HIM THAT ON THIS DAY HE WOULD MEET THE MAN WHO WILL BE THE KING OF ISRAEL.

MAYBE THE PROPHET OF THIS TOWN CAN TELL ME WHERE MY FATHER'S DONKEYS ARE.

THAT MUST BE HIM!

SAMUEL DOESN'T EXPLAIN ANYTHING TO THE GUESTS AT THE FEAST. BUT EARLY THE NEXT MORNING, HE LEAVES THE CITY WITH SAUL AND HIS SERVANT.

SEND YOUR SERVANT ON AHEAD, SAUL. I HAVE A MESSAGE FOR YOU FROM GOD.

THE LORD HAS ANOINTED YOU TO RULE OVER HIS PEOPLE. CALL ON THE LORD, AND HE WILL BE WITH YOU.

AND THESE WILL BE THE SIGNS SO YOU KNOW I SPEAK THE TRUTH: ON YOUR WAY HOME, SOMEONE WILL CONFIRM THAT YOUR DONKEYS HAVE BEEN FOUND. AS YOU APPROACH THE GATES OF GIBEAH, YOU WILL MEET A PROCESSION OF PROPHETS PLAYING MUSICAL INSTRUMENTS AND SPEAKING IN TONGUES. YOU WILL PROPHESY JUST LIKE THEM.

STILL BEWILDERED AT EVERYTHING THAT'S HAPPENING TO HIM, SAUL SETS OUT FOR HOME. EVERYTHING HAPPENS AS SAMUEL PREDICTED, INCLUDING SAUL BEING CAUGHT UP IN THE SPIRIT AND PROPHESYING. SAUL'S NEIGHBORS ARE VERY SURPRISED TO WITNESS THIS PUBLIC DISPLAY.

IS SAUL A PROPHET NOW?

A FEW DAYS LATER, SAMUEL CALLS ALL THE TRIBES TOGETHER.

TODAY, GOD WILL REVEAL TO YOU YOUR KING!

WHO IS HE?

THE PEOPLE CAST LOTS, KNOWING THAT GOD'S SPIRIT WILL DECIDE THE OUTCOME. SLOWLY BUT SURELY, THE CHOICE FOR THEIR NEW KING GETS NARROWED DOWN.

OUR KING WILL COME FROM THE TRIBE OF BENJAMIN ...

... AND THE CLAN OF MATRI ...

... AND THE FAMILY OF KISH ...

OUT OF ALL THE PEOPLE AND TRIBES, SAUL'S NAME IS CHOSEN, JUST AS GOD FORETOLD. BUT SAUL IS NOWHERE TO BE FOUND. SAMUEL TELLS THE PEOPLE WHERE TO SEARCH, AND SAUL IS SOON FOUND—HIDING AMONG THE LUGGAGE!

WHAT ARE YOU DOING HIDING IN THE BAGS AND BASKETS??

I WAS SCARED TO BE CHOSEN KING.

HIDING IN THE LUGGAGE? NOT A GREAT START FOR A NEW KING!

SOON AFTERWARD, SAUL GETS ANOTHER CHANCE TO PROVE HIMSELF. THE AMMONITE KING OFFERS SOME ISRAELITES THE CHANCE TO BE HIS SLAVES—AS LONG AS THEY EACH GOUGE ONE OF THEIR OWN EYES OUT. SAUL FACES HIS FIRST TEST AS KING. THE SPIRIT FILLS HIM AND HE IS READY TO FIGHT! BUT TO HIS AMAZEMENT—AND ANGER—HE DISCOVERS THAT SOME OF HIS PEOPLE ARE AFRAID TO FIGHT! HE ACTS AT ONCE.

THE KING ORDERS US TO KILL THE OXEN OF ANY MAN WHO REFUSES TO DEFEND HIS COUNTRYMEN.

ER ... I'LL JOIN THE ARMY RIGHT NOW!

WITH SUCH AN EFFECTIVE RECRUITING METHOD, AN ARMY FORMS QUICKLY, AND SAUL ATTACKS AT DAWN. CATCHING THE AMMONITES BY SURPRISE, THE ISRAELITES SWIFTLY DEFEAT THEM.

PROUD OF THEIR VICTORY, THE ISRAELITES SHOUT THEIR PRAISES TO SAUL.

SURE, THEY'RE ALL FOR YOU TODAY. BUT WHAT ABOUT THE MEN WHO DIDN'T WANT YOU TO BE KING? THEY SHOULD BE KILLED.

NO! NO MAN WILL BE PUT TO DEATH FOR THAT.

NOW THAT ISRAEL HAS A KING, SAMUEL PREPARES TO WITHDRAW FROM HIS POSITION AS JUDGE. BUT BEFORE HE DOES, HE CALLS THE PEOPLE TOGETHER AND SPEAKS TO THEM AS THE PROPHET OF GOD.

OBEY THE LORD AND SERVE YOUR KING. THEN ALL WILL BE WELL WITH YOU. BUT IF YOU RETURN TO ANY OF YOUR WICKED WAYS, YOU WILL BE DESTROYED—BOTH YOU AND YOUR KING!

SPURRED ON BY HIS VICTORY OVER THE AMMONITES, SAUL FORMS A STANDING ARMY AND PREPARES TO WIN HIS PEOPLE'S FREEDOM FROM THE PHILISTINES. HIS SON JONATHAN STARTS BY SUCCESSFULLY CONQUERING A PHILISTINE GARRISON—AND AGAIN ISRAEL CHEERS.

263

Honeycomb Argument

THE PHILISTINES IMMEDIATELY PLAN THEIR COUNTERATTACK AGAINST THIS UPSTART KING AND HIS BRAVE SON.

TAKE 3,000 CHARIOTS, 6,000 HORSEMEN, AND ALL OUR INFANTRY. SET UP A CAMP AT MICMASH. FROM THERE WE CAN SEND OUT RAIDING PARTIES THAT WILL DRAW SAUL FROM HIS STRONGHOLD AT GILGAL.

DESPITE THEIR VICTORIES, MANY OF THE ISRAELITES LOSE COURAGE WHEN THEY SEE THE SIZE OF THE ENEMY FORCES.

THE PHILISTINES OUTNUMBER US BY THOUSANDS. I'M HIDING OUT UNTIL THIS IS OVER.

THERE'S A PIT DOWN THE VALLEY— I'LL HIDE THERE.

EVEN IN THE CAMP OF KING SAUL, THE SOLDIERS ARE AFRAID.

A RAID ON THE PHILISTINE GARRISON IS ONE THING. FIGHTING THE WHOLE PHILISTINE ARMY IS SOMETHING ELSE.

THESE MEN ARE LOSING THEIR NERVE. SAMUEL SAID HE WOULD BE HERE BY NOW TO OFFER A SACRIFICE TO GOD. WE CAN'T WAIT MUCH LONGER FOR HIM TO COME, OR THERE WON'T BE AN ARMY LEFT TO FIGHT.

YOU'RE RIGHT. WE WON'T WAIT. I WILL MAKE THE OFFERING MYSELF.

SECRETLY, JONATHAN AND HIS ARMOR-BEARER LEAVE CAMP. WHEN THEY REACH THE FOOT OF THE CLIFF THAT LEADS TO THE PHILISTINE GARRISON, THE ENEMY DARES THEM TO COME UP AND FIGHT. BOLDLY, JONATHAN AND HIS FRIEND SCALE THE CLIFF ...

FOLLOW ME. SINCE THE LORD IS WITH US, WE DON'T NEED A LOT OF SOLDIERS.

AT THE TOP OF THE CLIFF, THEY ATTACK WITH SUCH DARING THAT THE PHILISTINES FLEE IN PANIC. IN THEIR CONFUSION, THE PHILISTINES EVEN ATTACK ONE ANOTHER.

FROM HIS CAMP, SAUL SEES THE PHILISTINES RETREATING. WHEN HE DISCOVERS THAT JONATHAN IS MISSING, HE KNOWS WHO MUST BE RESPONSIBLE FOR THIS MIRACLE. SAUL'S SOLDIERS RUN TO CATCH UP TO JONATHAN AND JOIN IN THE ATTACK.

JONATHAN'S PURSUIT OF THE FLEEING PHILISTINES TAKES HIM THROUGH THE WOODS. THERE HE SEES HONEY OOZING OUT OF A FALLEN BEEHIVE.

PRAISE THE LORD, I HAVEN'T EATEN ALL DAY.

HE GRABS A HONEYCOMB. AS SOON AS HE'S EATEN IT, HE GETS ALL OF HIS ENERGY BACK.

COME ON! LET'S TEACH THESE PAGAN DOGS A LESSON!

BUT THE SOLDIERS DON'T FOLLOW HIM.

WHY IS EVERYONE SO TIRED? GOD HAS DELIVERED THESE PHILISTINES INTO OUR HANDS, IF WE CAN JUST KEEP CHASING THEM!

WHILE YOU WERE GONE, YOUR FATHER SWORE AN OATH THAT NO SOLDIER COULD EAT ANYTHING UNTIL NIGHTFALL.

THE HUNGRY SOLDIERS GIVE UP THEIR PURSUIT AND GO BACK TO KING SAUL'S CAMP. SAUL IS FURIOUS WHEN HE FINDS OUT THAT JONATHAN ATE SOME FOOD.

YOU DISHONORED MY OATH! SO HELP ME GOD; I WILL HAVE YOU EXECUTED FOR THIS!

YOU WILL KILL ME BECAUSE I DIDN'T KNOW ABOUT YOUR FOOLISH OATH?? IF OUR SOLDIERS HAD BEEN ALLOWED TO EAT, WE COULD HAVE CONQUERED ALL THE PHILISTINES ON THIS DAY. YOUR STUPID DECISION COST US THE VICTORY THAT GOD TRIED TO GIVE US!

YOUR SON IS A HERO! HE DELIVERED US FROM THE PHILISTINES! GOD HAS SHOWN HIM FAVOR; WE WILL NOT LET HIM BE KILLED!

SAUL BACKS DOWN, BUT THIS IS NOT THE LAST TIME HIS TEMPER WILL GET HIM IN TROUBLE ...

The Final Strike

BASED ON 1 SAMUEL 15

EVEN THOUGH THE PHILISTINES ARE NOT COMPLETELY DEFEATED, THEY STOP BOTHERING ISRAEL FOR A WHILE. BUT OTHER ENEMIES CONTINUE TO TROUBLE THE PEOPLE. ONE DAY SAMUEL CALLS SAUL TO HIM ...

THE LORD WANTS YOU TO DESTROY THE AMALEKITES. THEY HAVE BEEN ENEMIES OF ISRAEL EVER SINCE OUR PEOPLE LEFT EGYPT. DESTROY EVERYTHING! DON'T BRING ANYTHING HOME WITH YOU, FOR THIS IS NOT A WAR TO GET RICH.

SAUL ATTACKS THE AMALEKITES AND DRIVES THEM BACK TOWARD EGYPT. BUT INSTEAD OF KILLING EVERYTHING, HE BRINGS THE BEST OF THE SHEEP AND OXEN HOME WITH HIM.

AT GILGAL, SAUL COMES FACE-TO-FACE WITH SAMUEL ...

I HAVE OBEYED GOD'S COMMAND AND DESTROYED THE AMALEKITES AND EVERYTHING THEY POSSESS.

God's New King

GOD SENDS HIS PROPHET SAMUEL TO BETHLEHEM, WHERE HE IS GREETED BY JESSE, THE GRANDSON OF RUTH AND BOAZ.

SAMUEL! OH NO, WHAT HAVE WE DONE WRONG?

DON'T WORRY, I HAVEN'T COME TO JUDGE YOU. I'VE COME TO GIVE AN OFFERING TO GOD.

JESSE, GOD WANTS ME TO CHOOSE ONE OF YOUR SONS FOR A SPECIAL SERVICE. WILL YOU BRING YOUR SONS TO ME?

OF COURSE.

THIS IS MY OLDEST SON, ELIAB.

HE IS SO TALL AND STRONG! SURELY THIS IS THE ONE GOD HAS CHOSEN.

BUT SAMUEL HEARS GOD'S VOICE: "YOU CAN ONLY SEE HOW TALL AND HANDSOME HE IS. I CAN SEE HIS HEART. HE IS NOT THE ONE."

I'M SORRY. ELIAB IS NOT THE ONE. CALL ANOTHER.

ABINADAB!

SEVEN OF JESSE'S SONS APPEAR BEFORE SAMUEL— BUT NOT ONE OF THEM IS CHOSEN.

HAVE I SEEN ALL YOUR SONS?

NO, THE YOUNGEST ONE, DAVID, IS TENDING THE SHEEP. I'LL SEND ONE OF MY SONS AND A SERVANT FOR HIM.

I WONDER WHY SAMUEL INSISTS ON SEEING DAVID?

THIS WHOLE THING IS A MYSTERY.

JESSE'S SON FINDS HIS BROTHER IN THE FIELDS OUTSIDE BETHLEHEM.

THERE'S DAVID.

LOOK— A LION! AND DAVID DOESN'T SEE IT!

A Psalming Influence

DAVID DOESN'T KNOW WHEN HE WILL BECOME KING. BUT AS HE GOES BACK TO HIS SHEEP, HE HAS A SPECIAL FEELING OF GOD'S PRESENCE WITH HIM.

THE LORD IS MY SHEPHERD; MY NEEDS ARE SUPPLIED. HE SHOWS ME SAFE PASTURES WHERE WE WALK SIDE BY SIDE.

THAT'S A BEAUTIFUL SONG. BUT I'VE NEVER HEARD IT BEFORE.

I JUST MADE IT UP. IT GETS LONELY OUT HERE, SO I WRITE SONGS AND SING THEM TO THE LORD.

BACK AT THE PALACE, THE MEN GO TO SEE KING SAUL—BUT THEY FIND HIM STARING WILDLY INTO SPACE.

SOMETIMES I THINK THE KING IS GOING MAD. MUSIC SEEMS TO BE THE ONLY THING THAT HELPS.

I KNOW—THE SHEPHERD BOY!

O KING, WE KNOW A YOUNG SHEPHERD WHO PLAYS THE HARP AND SINGS BEAUTIFUL SONGS. IT'S PLAIN THAT GOD IS WITH THE BOY. WOULD YOU LIKE TO HEAR HIM?

SEND FOR HIM.

GOD USES DAVID'S MUSICAL TALENT TO INTRODUCE HIM TO THE ROYAL COURT—THE FIRST STEP TOWARD MAKING HIM KING OF ISRAEL ONE DAY. HERE DAVID CAN LEARN ABOUT KINGSHIP AND GOVERNMENT. HE CAN ALSO WITNESS WHAT LIFE IS LIKE FOR KING SAUL, WHO DOESN'T RELY ON THE LORD.

THE KING IS VERY ILL TODAY, SO HE MAY BE DANGEROUS. DON'T TAKE YOUR EYES OFF OF HIM FOR A SECOND.

QUIETLY, DAVID ENTERS THE KING'S ROOM AND BEGINS TO PLAY. SAUL STARES AT HIM WILDLY, BUT DAVID CONTINUES TO PLAY AND SING OF HIS FAITH IN GOD.

AT LAST KING SAUL RELAXES AND FALLS ASLEEP. AFTER THAT, DAVID IS OFTEN CALLED TO THE PALACE. HIS MUSIC QUIETS SAUL'S TORTURED MIND, AND EVENTUALLY THE KING SEEMS WELL AGAIN—FOR A TIME.

A Giant Challenge

BASED ON 1 SAMUEL 17

A FEW YEARS LATER, THE PHILISTINES COLLECT THEIR FORCES FOR AN ATTACK AGAINST ISRAEL. SAUL MASSES HIS ARMY AGAINST THEM, AND DAVID'S THREE OLDEST BROTHERS JOIN THE KING'S FORCES.

ONE EVENING DAVID COMES IN FROM THE FIELDS TO FIND HIS FATHER BUSY PACKING FOOD.

THIS IS FOR YOUR BROTHERS. I WANT YOU TO TAKE IT TO THEM.

NOT GOOD, AND I'M WORRIED.

I'LL LEAVE RIGHT AWAY. WHAT'S THE LATEST NEWS FROM THE BATTLEFRONT?

THE "NOT GOOD" NEWS IS THIS—A GIANT IS FIGHTING FOR THE PHILISTINES. ALL THE ISRAELITES ARE SCARED OF HIM, INCLUDING KING SAUL.

WHAT'S GOING ON?

ELIAB, DAVID'S OLDEST BROTHER, OVERHEARS DAVID ASKING ABOUT GOLIATH.

WHAT ARE YOU DOING HERE, MOUTHING OFF? WHY AREN'T YOU HOME WHERE YOU BELONG—TAKING CARE OF THE SHEEP?

FATHER SENT ME HERE WITH FOOD FOR YOU. AND I'M NOT THE ONE MOUTHING OFF; THIS PHILISTINE IS INSULTING OUR GOD!

EVER SINCE THE PROPHET SAMUEL CHOSE DAVID INSTEAD OF HIM, ELIAB HAS BEEN FILLED WITH JEALOUSY. NOW HIS SHAME BURSTS INTO THE OPEN.

YOU'RE JUST A SPOILED KID WHO WANTS TO WATCH A BATTLE FOR YOUR OWN FUN.

NO, I JUST HATE TO SEE OUR GOD DISRESPECTED. I'LL FIGHT THE GIANT.

DAVID'S WORDS SPREAD THROUGH THE CAMP.

O KING, THERE IS ONE PERSON WHO WILL FIGHT, BUT ...

BRING HIM HERE AT ONCE!

The Jealous King
BASED ON 1 SAMUEL 18—19

WHEN THE ARMY RETURNS, SAUL'S GENERAL, ABNER, TAKES DAVID TO SEE THE KING.

YOU SAVED ISRAEL, DAVID. FROM NOW ON, YOU WILL LIVE IN THE PALACE. PRINCE JONATHAN WILL TAKE YOU BACK WITH HIM.

JONATHAN HAS JUST RETURNED FROM THE PALACE. HE IMMEDIATELY RECOGNIZES A KINDRED SPIRIT IN DAVID.

DAVID, I'M PROUD TO BE THE FRIEND OF THE BRAVEST MAN IN ISRAEL. I WANT TO GIVE YOU MY ROBE AND ARMOR AS A SIGN THAT I WILL BE LOYAL TO YOU FOREVER.

THANK YOU, JONATHAN. GOD IS MY WITNESS THAT I WILL BE YOUR FRIEND UNTIL DEATH.

FOR THE REST OF THE MILITARY CAMPAIGN, SAUL GIVES DAVID LOTS OF RESPONSIBILITIES. DAVID EXCELS AT EVERYTHING HE'S ASKED TO DO, AND SAUL PROMOTES HIM TO A HIGH-RANKING OFFICER.

DAVID'S REPUTATION SPREADS, SO BY THE TIME THE ARMY RETURNS HOME, HE IS A HERO.

SAUL HAS SLAIN HIS THOUSANDS—AND DAVID HIS TEN THOUSANDS!

TRIUMPHANTLY, KING SAUL AND HIS VICTORIOUS SOLDIERS PARADE THROUGH THE STREETS. THE WOMEN RUSH OUT OF THE CITIES TO GREET THEM AND SING THEIR PRAISES.

THE PEOPLE'S PRAISE OF DAVID TURNS SAUL'S APPRECIATION TO RAGE. HE THINKS OF WHAT THE PROPHET SAMUEL TOLD HIM. "THE LORD WILL TAKE YOUR KINGDOM FROM YOU."

THE PEOPLE KNOW DAVID IS A GREATER WARRIOR THAN I AM. MAYBE HE'S THE ONE WHO WILL TAKE MY KINGDOM FROM ME!

THAT NIGHT, SAUL CANNOT SLEEP.

MY SOLDIERS ALREADY LOVE HIM, AND NOW MY PEOPLE LOVE HIM.

ONE DAY, WHILE DAVID PLAYS THE HARP TO SOOTHE SAUL'S SPIRIT ...

DAVID! HE'S THE HERO NOW! BUT HE CAN'T TAKE MY KINGDOM FROM ME IF HE'S DEAD.

IN A BURST OF RAGE, SAUL GRABS A SPEAR.

THUNK

I MISSED!

I'M SORRY, DAVID. I DON'T KNOW WHAT CAME OVER ME. IT MUST BE THIS EVIL SPIRIT THAT TORMENTS ME.

IT MUST HAVE BEEN AN ACCIDENT. WHY WOULD HE HAVE PROMOTED ME ONLY TO KILL ME?

BUT SAUL'S JEALOUSY CONTINUES TO GROW BECAUSE HE KNOWS DAVID HAS THE LORD'S FAVOR.

NOT ONLY DOES THE LORD FAVOR DAVID, SO DOES SAUL'S DAUGHTER, MICHAL.

THAT GIVES ME AN IDEA.

DAVID, IT SEEMS MY DAUGHTER IS IN LOVE WITH YOU. AND WHO CAN BLAME HER? YOU ARE THE MOST POPULAR MAN IN THE KINGDOM. BUT SINCE YOU ARE A POOR COMMONER, YOU CANNOT AFFORD THE CUSTOMARY BRIDE PRICE FOR A KING'S DAUGHTER. SO I WILL WAIVE THAT FEE. HOWEVER, TO PROVE YOUR VALOR, YOU MUST KILL 100 PHILISTINES.

THANK YOU, MY KING. I AM HIGHLY HONORED.

YOU MAY BE ABLE TO BEAT ONE GIANT PHILISTINE, BUT 100 OF THEM SHOULD BE ABLE TO KILL YOU.

ONE MONTH LATER ...

WELL? DID YOU KILL 100 PHILISTINES?

NO.

I KILLED 200.

AFTER DAVID AND MICHAL'S WEDDING, SAUL TURNS TO HIS FAITHFUL SON.

JONATHAN, I KNOW HE'S YOUR FRIEND, BUT DAVID HAS BECOME A THREAT TO THE KINGDOM. HE WANTS TO TAKE THE CROWN FROM ME. WILL YOU HELP ME KILL HIM?

HOW CAN YOU SAY THAT? HE'S NEVER DONE ANYTHING TO WRONG YOU. AND WITH HIS BATTLES, HE'S INCREASED YOUR HONOR AND POWER.

YOU'RE RIGHT, JONATHAN. I PROMISE NOT TO HARM DAVID.

EVEN MY OWN SON LOVES DAVID MORE THAN HE LOVES ME.

FEELING BETRAYED BY HIS OWN FAMILY, SAUL RESORTS TO CONSPIRACY.

WAIT UNTIL EVERYONE IS ASLEEP, THEN GO TO DAVID'S HOUSE AND TELL HIM I NEED TO SEE HIM. WHEN HE GETS HERE, WE CAN KILL HIM WITH NO WITNESSES.

OH NO! I MUST TELL MICHAL.

MICHAL, WHY ARE YOU PACKING UP MY CLOTHES?

MY FATHER PLANS TO KILL YOU TONIGHT. YOU MUST RUN FOR YOUR LIFE! I'LL DELAY HIS GUARDS WHILE YOU MAKE YOUR ESCAPE.

MICHAL LETS DAVID OUT A BACK WINDOW, THEN PREPARES THE NEXT PART OF HER PLAN.

285

LET US IN! KING SAUL NEEDS TO SEE DAVID ON A MATTER OF HIGH IMPORTANCE!

AS YOU CAN SEE, HE'S SICK IN BED. I THINK IT'S CONTAGIOUS. I'D LET YOU IN, BUT THEN YOU'D BE CEREMONIALLY UNCLEAN FOR BEING NEAR A SICK PERSON. I'M SO SORRY.

MICHAL'S BOLD LIE CONFUSES THE GUARDS, WHO BRING THIS NEW DEVELOPMENT TO SAUL. AT FIRST, HE SEEMS TO TAKE THE NEWS CALMLY.

OH, I DIDN'T REALIZE HE WAS SICK. WE'LL WAIT UNTIL HE'S HEALTHY BEFORE WE KILL HIM.

YOU FOOLS!

BRING HIM HERE NOW IF YOU HAVE TO CARRY HIM IN HIS BED TO DO IT!

BUT WHEN THE MEN BARGE INTO DAVID'S ROOM, THEY FIND ONLY A STATUE WITH A GOAT HAIR WIG IN HIS BED.

HOW COULD MY OWN DAUGHTER LIE TO ME TO PROTECT MY ENEMY?

HE'S NOT YOUR ENEMY, FATHER!

I WILL THINK OF A SUITABLE PUNISHMENT FOR YOU.

ON THE SECOND DAY OF THE KING'S FEAST, SAUL'S TEMPER EXPLODES WHEN JONATHAN TELLS HIM OF DAVID'S ABSENCE.

YOU SON OF A STUBBORN CONCUBINE! DON'T YOU KNOW THAT AS LONG AS DAVID LIVES YOU WILL NEVER BE KING? BRING HIM HERE IMMEDIATELY. HE MUST DIE!

WHY SHOULD HE BE KILLED? WHAT HAS HE DONE BUT SERVE YOU WELL IN BATTLE?

MY OWN SON IS A TRAITOR.

I'LL KILL YOU, TOO!

I AM ASHAMED TO CALL YOU FATHER!

SAUL DOESN'T KILL HIS SON. BUT THE NEXT MORNING, JONATHAN GOES OUT TO THE FIELDS AND GIVES DAVID THE SIGNAL.

GO GET MY ARROWS. I OVER-SHOT THE TARGET, SO YOU'LL HAVE TO *RUN FAR AWAY* TO FIND THEM.

THANK YOU, JONATHAN. I WILL FLEE FROM SAUL AND LET THE LORD TELL ME WHEN I CAN COME BACK.

The Outlaws of Judah

BASED ON 1 SAMUEL 21–24

WITHOUT EVEN TAKING THE TIME TO PACK PROVISIONS, DAVID FLEES FOR JUDAH, HIS HOME COUNTRY. FAMISHED AND TIRED, HE STOPS FOR A REST AT NOB. THERE HE SEEKS THE HELP OF AHIMELECH, THE HIGH PRIEST.

DAVID! YOU LOOK TERRIBLE. WHAT ARE YOU DOING HERE THIS LATE AT NIGHT? AND ALONE?

DAVID LIES TO PROTECT THE PRIEST.

DON'T BE ALARMED. I'M ON A SECRET MISSION FOR KING SAUL. BUT I NEED BREAD, FOOD—ANYTHING YOU HAVE!

ALL I HAVE IS THE HOLY BREAD IN THE TABERNACLE. BUT IF IT'S A MATTER OF STARVING TO DEATH, I CAN LET YOU HAVE IT.

ALSO, I LEFT IN SUCH A HURRY THAT I FORGOT TO BRING A WEAPON. DO YOU HAVE A SWORD OR SPEAR?

WE ARE PRIESTS. WE DON'T FIGHT OR KEEP WEAPONS. THE ONLY THING WE HAVE IS THE SWORD OF GOLIATH. WE'VE KEPT IT HERE AS A TROPHY OF YOUR VICTORY.

ONCE YOU WERE USED TO FIGHT AGAINST THE LORD— BUT NOW I WILL WIELD YOU IN THE LORD'S SERVICE!

UNFORTUNATELY, ONE OF SAUL'S SPIES SEES DAVID LEAVE THE PRIESTS AT NOB. HE GOES TO REPORT TO HIS MASTER...

DAVID GOES INTO HIDING IN JUDAH.

LORD, YOU SAID I WOULD BE KING. NOW HERE I AM, AN OUTLAW, ALL ALONE IN A CAVE. I TRUST YOU, BUT I DON'T SEE THAT I'M MUCH OF A KING. A REAL KING HAS AN ARMY, PROPHETS, AND PRIESTS.

I ONLY HAVE A SWORD THAT'S TOO BIG FOR ME.

NEWS OF DAVID'S WHEREABOUTS SPREADS QUICKLY. 400 MEN—REFUGEES, HOMELESS, AND HIS RELATIVES—JOIN HIM IN EXILE.

KING SAUL HAS DECLARED YOU AN OUTLAW. BUT WE WANT TO FIGHT FOR YOU!

THEN FIGHT FOR ME YOU SHALL. WE WILL PROTECT THE POOR PEOPLE OF JUDAH IN THE NAME OF THE LORD.

AND SO, OUT OF REJECTS AND RELATIVES, DAVID GETS HIS FIRST ARMY.

AMONG HIS RELATIVES, THREE OF DAVID'S NEPHEWS WILL BECOME INDISPENSABLE TO HIM. JOAB WILL BE DAVID'S COMMANDER. ABISHAI WILL GROW INTO A MIGHTY WARRIOR AND BODYGUARD. AND ASAHEL, FAST AS A GAZELLE, WILL CHASE DOWN DAVID'S ENEMIES.

ONE DAY ...

I AM GAD, ONE OF KING SAUL'S PROPHETS. BUT THE LORD HAS TOLD ME THAT YOU ARE HIS ANOINTED KING. SO I AM HERE TO SERVE YOU. AND AS MY FIRST DUTY, I MUST WARN YOU TO MOVE YOUR CAMP INTO THE FOREST OF HERETH.

AND SO, DAVID GETS HIS FIRST PROPHET.

MEANWHILE, SAUL HAS SUMMONED AHIMELECH AND ALL THE PRIESTS OF NOB. HE ACCUSES THEM OF TREASON FOR HELPING DAVID.

HOW IS IT TREASON TO HELP ONE OF YOUR MOST LOYAL SOLDIERS? HE'S YOUR SON-IN-LAW! OF COURSE I HELPED HIM.

YOU HELPED MY ENEMY—AND FOR THIS YOU WILL DIE!

IN HIS INSANE DESIRE FOR REVENGE, SAUL ORDERS THE DEATH OF NOT ONLY THE PRIESTS OF NOB, BUT EVERY MAN, WOMAN, AND CHILD IN THEIR CITY. ONLY ONE MAN ESCAPES, ABIATHAR, THE SON OF AHIMELECH THE HIGH PRIEST.

HE CARRIES THE TRAGIC NEWS TO DAVID.

I AM THE ONLY PRIEST LEFT. BUT I SAVED THE HIGH PRIEST'S EPHOD AND BROUGHT IT WITH ME.

GOD FORGIVE ME. I AM PARTLY TO BLAME. I ASKED FOR HELP, AND YOUR FATHER GAVE IT. STAY WITH ME, FOR NOW SAUL WANTS YOUR LIFE AS WELL AS MINE.

SAUL HAS BROKEN HIS FAITH WITH THE LORD. I WILL SERVE YOU.

AND SO, DAVID GETS HIS FIRST PRIEST. GOD HAS NOW GIVEN HIM THE FULL ENTOURAGE OF A KING.

ENCOURAGED BY DAVID'S WORDS, HIS MEN SHAKE OFF THEIR FEAR AND MARCH TO FIGHT. THEY INFLICT HEAVY LOSSES ON THE PHILISTINES, TAKING THEIR PLUNDER AND SHARING IT WITH THE PEOPLE OF KEILAH.

BUT WHILE THEY ARE CELEBRATING THEIR FIRST VICTORY, DAVID'S PROPHET AND PRIEST BRING HIM TROUBLING NEWS.

DAVID, GOD WARNED ME THAT SAUL IS ON HIS WAY HERE TO CAPTURE YOU.

ABIATHAR, USE THE EPHOD TO ASK THE LORD IF THE PEOPLE OF KEILAH WILL DEFEND ME OR HAND ME OVER TO SAUL.

THE LORD SAYS THEY WILL BETRAY YOU TO SAUL.

THEN LET'S GO.

EVEN THOUGH HE HAS JUST RESCUED THEIR TOWN, DAVID IS FORCED TO FLEE FROM THE FICKLE CITIZENS OF KEILAH AND HIDE IN NEARBY CAVES. HOWEVER, 200 MEN ARE IMPRESSED BY HIS BRAVERY AND JOIN HIS ARMY. HE NOW HAS 600 SOLDIERS.

KING SAUL AND HIS ARMY ARRIVE TOO LATE TO CAPTURE DAVID AT KEILAH. AS SAUL HUNTS FOR DAVID IN THE DESERT, HE STOPS TO REST IN A CAVE—UNAWARE THAT DAVID AND SOME OF HIS MEN ARE HIDING IN THE BACK OF IT.

WHY DOESN'T DAVID KILL HIM?

THIS IS IT, UNCLE DAVID. THE LORD PROMISED YOU WOULD BE KING, AND NOW THE LORD HAS DELIVERED THE OLD KING, HELPLESS, INTO YOUR HANDS.

DAVID LOOKS DOWN AT THE KING—AND THINKS OF ALL THE TIMES SAUL HAS TRIED TO KILL HIM. NOW THE JEALOUS KING IS AT HIS MERCY—BUT DAVID ONLY BENDS DOWN AND CAREFULLY CUTS OFF A PIECE OF THE ROYAL ROBE.

I UNDERSTAND. HE'S YOUR FATHER-IN-LAW. IF YOU DON'T WANT TO KILL HIM, I'LL DO IT FOR YOU.

NO! HE WAS CHOSEN BY GOD TO BE OUR KING. IT'S NOT FOR US TO DECIDE WHEN HE WILL DIE.

DAVID AND HIS ARMY SET OUT JUST AS ABIGAIL ARRIVES WITH HER PROVISIONS. WHEN ABIGAIL SEES DAVID SUDDENLY APPEAR WITH FURY IN HIS EYES, SHE FALLS TO HER KNEES.

MY LORD AND FUTURE KING!

LISTEN TO ME, PLEASE! IGNORE THE INSULTS OF MY STUPID HUSBAND, NABAL. HIS NAME MEANS "FOOL" FOR A REASON. PLEASE, MY MASTER, DON'T SINK TO HIS LEVEL. DON'T BLOODY YOUR HANDS FOR THE SAKE OF REVENGE. LET THE LORD JUDGE NABAL FOR HIS WICKEDNESS. WHEN YOU ARE KING, YOU WILL NOT WANT YOUR PEOPLE TO SAY YOU MURDERED ONE OF YOUR OWN SUBJECTS.

DAVID'S ANGER HAS COOLED DURING THIS FAITHFUL WOMAN'S BRAVE SPEECH.

PRAISE THE LORD FOR SENDING YOU! YOU HAVE SAVED BOTH MY HONOR AND INNOCENT LIVES. THANK YOU FOR THIS GIFT. TAKE YOUR DONKEYS AND GO IN PEACE.

THE NEXT MORNING, WHEN ABIGAIL TELLS NABAL ABOUT HIS NARROW ESCAPE, HE IS STRUCK DEAD WITH FRIGHT.

WHEN DAVID HEARS THE NEWS, HE REALIZES HOW RIGHT ABIGAIL HAD BEEN; THE LORD PUNISHED NABAL SO THAT HE WOULD NOT HAVE TO FIGHT A FELLOW ISRAELITE.

YOU KNOW, NOW THAT SAUL HAS GIVEN MICHAL TO ANOTHER MAN IN MARRIAGE, YOU COULD USE AN INTELLIGENT AND RESOURCEFUL WOMAN AROUND HERE.

YOU'RE RIGHT! ABIGAIL HAS PROVEN HER WISDOM. AND SHE BELIEVES IN ME. I WANT TO BE THE HONORABLE, GOD-FEARING KING SHE THINKS I CAN BE. I WILL ASK HER TO BE MY WIFE.

AS DAVID'S NEW WIFE, ABIGAIL CONTINUES TO PROVE HER WISDOM AND RESOURCEFULNESS IN HELPING DAVID RUN HIS CAMP. UNDER HER INFLUENCE, HIS MEN BEGIN TO ACT LESS LIKE A BAND OF RENEGADES AND MORE LIKE A KING'S ARMY.

DAVID LEADS HIS MEN WISELY AND WELL FOR SEVERAL YEARS. BUT HE IS ALWAYS UNDER THE SHADOW OF SAUL'S JEALOUSY ...

THE NEXT MORNING, DAVID CALLS DOWN TO SAUL'S CAMP.

KING SAUL! DO THESE LOOK FAMILIAR?

YOU TOOK THEM WHILE I SLEPT! AGAIN YOU COULD HAVE KILLED ME—AND YOU DIDN'T. I HAVE BEEN A FOOL. I'LL NEVER TRY TO HURT YOU AGAIN.

LOOK! THEY'RE LEAVING. YOU'RE SAFE.

NO. SAUL MADE THE SAME PROMISE BEFORE. I'LL NEVER BE SAFE AS LONG AS THE KING LIVES.

BUT SAUL IS NOT SAFE EITHER. HIS ARMY IS CONFRONTED BY THE UNIFIED PHILISTINE FORCES. WHEN SAUL SEES THE POWERFUL PHILISTINE ARMY, HE IS AFRAID. FRANTICALLY, HE CALLS UPON GOD FOR HELP—BUT BECAUSE HE'D KILLED GOD'S PRIESTS AND DISOBEYED GOD'S COMMANDS, GOD WOULD NO LONGER SPEAK TO HIM. TERRIFIED, HE RESORTS TO A DARK POWER.

THE WOMAN CALLS FOR THE SPIRIT OF SAMUEL. FOR A MOMENT ALL IS STILL. THEN A HUMAN SHAPE SLOWLY APPEARS IN THE SMOKE ...

PLEASE DON'T HURT ME FOR DOING WHAT YOU ASKED. I AM SORRY THAT SAMUEL HAD SUCH BAD NEWS FOR YOU. PLEASE JUST TAKE THIS FOOD AND LEAVE ME IN PEACE.

SAUL DOESN'T WANT ANY FOOD, BUT THE WITCH AND HIS GUARDS ENCOURAGE HIM TO EAT. AFTER HE HAS TIME TO REGAIN SOME STRENGTH, HE RETURNS TO HIS CAMP.

THE NEXT MORNING, THE PHILISTINES ATTACK. UNDER A WEAK AND FRIGHTENED KING, ISRAEL RETREATS IN PANIC.

THE ENEMY IS EVERYWHERE! WE CAN'T STOP THEM!

MY SONS— WHERE ARE THEY?

DEAD, SIR.

DEAD! AND I AM BADLY WOUNDED.

DRAW YOUR SWORD AND KILL ME. I WOULD RATHER DIE BY YOUR HAND THAN BE CAPTURED BY THE PHILISTINES.

KILL MY KING? I CAN'T! I CAN'T!

SO SAUL DRAWS HIS OWN SWORD—AND FALLS ON IT, KILLING HIMSELF. SAMUEL'S PROPHECY IS FULFILLED. THE REIGN OF KING SAUL COMES TO A TRAGIC END.

305

Just Rewards

BASED ON
2 SAMUEL 1:1—2:7

THE BOOKS OF
2 SAMUEL AND
1 CHRONICLES RECORD
THE SAME PERIOD OF
HISTORY—THE REIGN
OF DAVID, ISRAEL'S
GREATEST KING.
2 SAMUEL IS THE
ORIGINAL HISTORY, AS
WRITTEN DOWN BY
THE PROPHETS, WHILE
1 CHRONICLES FILLS
IN GAPS FROM THE
PERSPECTIVE OF THE
PRIESTS.

STILL IN EXILE, DAVID ALWAYS THINKS
ABOUT SAUL AND JONATHAN. HE WONDERS
HOW THEIR BATTLE WITH THE PHILISTINES
TURNED OUT. A THIEF WHO HAD LOOTED THE
BATTLEFIELD TRIES TO WIN DAVID'S FAVOR.

WHO ARE
YOU, AND
WHAT BRINGS
YOU HERE?

I COME FROM
THE BATTLE BETWEEN
THE PHILISTINES AND
ISRAEL. I HAVE GREAT
NEWS! YOUR OLD ENEMY,
KING SAUL, IS DEAD—
AND SO IS PRINCE
JONATHAN!

HOW DO
YOU KNOW
THIS?

I DON'T KNOW
HOW JONATHAN
DIED, BUT I FOUND
THE KING ON THE
BATTLEFIELD. HE
WAS INJURED AND
ASKED ME TO KILL
HIM. I DID—AND
HERE ARE HIS
CROWN AND
ARMBAND TO
PROVE IT!

WHAT!

EVEN IF THE KING ASKED YOU TO KILL HIM, YOU HAD NO RIGHT TO TAKE THE LIFE OF THE MAN GOD CHOSE TO BE KING OF ISRAEL. FOR THIS CRIME YOU WILL PAY WITH YOUR OWN LIFE.

SO THE MAN WHO LIED TO GET A REWARD RECEIVED A DIFFERENT REWARD—THE ONE HE DESERVED.

EVEN THOUGH SAUL HAD TREATED HIM UNFAIRLY, DAVID MOURNS THE DEATHS OF HIS KING AND HIS BEST FRIEND. IN HIS GRIEF, DAVID WRITES A LAMENT, A MOURNFUL SONG PRAISING SAUL AND JONATHAN. HE TEACHES IT TO ALL HIS FOLLOWERS, AND THEY SING IT TOGETHER. IT'S CALLED THE SONG OF THE BOW.

THE GLORY OF ISRAEL LIES SLAIN IN THE HILLS.

DO NOT SPREAD THIS EVIL NEWS,

THE BOW OF JONATHAN DID NOT TURN BACK.

SAUL AND JONATHAN—LOVED IN LIFE, TOGETHER IN DEATH.

HOW THE MIGHTY HAVE FALLEN!

DO NOT GIVE OUR ENEMIES A REASON TO REJOICE.

THE SWORD OF SAUL DID NOT RETREAT.

THEY WERE FASTER THAN EAGLES AND STRONGER THAN LIONS.

I GRIEVE BECAUSE JONATHAN, MY BROTHER, IS DEAD.

WE WEEP BECAUSE SAUL, OUR FATHER, IS DEAD.

HOW THE MIGHTY HAVE FALLEN!

ISRAEL'S HEROES LIE SLAIN IN THE HILLS.

LORD, SHALL I RETURN NOW TO MY OWN PEOPLE IN JUDAH?

EVENTUALLY, DAVID THINKS OF HIS OWN FUTURE. NOW THAT SAUL IS DEAD, DAVID KNOWS THAT HE CAN RETURN FROM EXILE. BUT BEFORE HE MAKES ANY PLANS, HE PRAYS TO GOD.

GOD TELLS DAVID TO GO HOME—AND WHEN HE DOES, THE PEOPLE OF JUDAH WELCOME THEIR HERO AND MAKE HIM KING OF THEIR TRIBE.

GOD BLESS KING DAVID!

LONG LIVE THE KING!

FOR HIS FIRST ACT AS KING, DAVID COMMENDS THE MEN FROM JABESH GILEAD, WHO HAD SNUCK PAST THE PHILISTINES TO MAKE SURE THAT SAUL AND JONATHAN RECEIVED AN HONORABLE BURIAL. HE PROMISES THAT HE AND GOD WILL SHOW THEM FAVOR FOR THEIR BRAVERY.

Royal Rivals

BASED ON 2 SAMUEL 2:8—3:21

NOW THAT KING SAUL IS DEAD, DAVID IS MADE KING OF HIS OWN TRIBE OF JUDAH. BUT TROUBLE BREWS ACROSS THE JORDAN RIVER. SAUL'S MOST POWERFUL GENERAL, ABNER, DECLARES THAT SAUL'S YOUNGEST SON, ISH-BOSHETH, IS KING OVER ALL THE OTHER TRIBES OF ISRAEL. BUT THE CRAFTY GENERAL KNOWS THAT ISH-BOSHETH IS SO WEAK THAT ABNER HIMSELF WILL ALWAYS BE THE REAL POWER BEHIND THE THRONE.

BUT WILL THE PEOPLE SUPPORT ME, ABNER? DAVID HAS MANY LOYAL FOLLOWERS.

THAT'S WHY WE MUST WIPE HIM OUT RIGHT NOW. IF WE WAIT, HE WILL BE STRONG ENOUGH TO TAKE YOUR KINGDOM FROM YOU.

WITHOUT WASTING ANY TIME, ABNER MARSHALS WHAT IS LEFT OF SAUL'S ARMY AND RIDES AGAINST JOAB AND DAVID'S FORCES.

IN TURN, JOAB RALLIES DAVID'S MEN AND MEETS ABNER'S ARMY AT THE POOL OF GIBEON. FOR A MOMENT, THE TWO ARMIES FACE EACH OTHER, UNCERTAIN WHAT TO DO AGAINST THEIR OWN COUNTRYMEN. THE FIRST BLOW IN THIS BATTLE WILL MARK THE BEGINNING OF A CIVIL WAR.

309

DAVID'S NEPHEW FOCUSES HIS PURSUIT ON ABNER.

GO BACK, ASAHEL! I KNOW YOUR BROTHER JOAB. I DON'T WANT TO HAVE TO KILL YOU.

NO, I WILL NOT LET YOU GET AWAY!

KNOWING HE CAN'T OUTRUN THE YOUNGER MAN, ABNER STOPS SUDDENLY AND PLANTS HIS SPEAR IN THE GROUND. ASAHEL IS RUNNING SO QUICKLY THAT HE CAN'T STOP IN TIME—AND IS KILLED.

THE BATTLE IS A VICTORY FOR DAVID'S MEN. THEY KILL 360 OF ABNER'S FORCES AND LOSE ONLY 20 SOLDIERS THEMSELVES— INCLUDING ASAHEL. BUT WHEN JOAB LEARNS OF HIS BROTHER'S DEATH, HE IS FILLED WITH GRIEF AND THE NEED FOR REVENGE.

WITH EACH BATTLE, DAVID GROWS STRONGER. ISH-BOSHETH GROWS MORE FEARFUL BY THE DAY. NOT ONLY DOES HE FEAR DAVID, BUT HE ALSO STARTS TO DISTRUST ABNER'S MOTIVES. ONE DAY, HE ACCUSES ABNER.

HOW DARE YOU QUESTION ME! JUST FOR THAT, I WILL TRANSFER MY ALLEGIANCE TO DAVID. BY LOSING ME, YOU JUST LOST YOUR KINGDOM.

ABNER HAD REALIZED THAT DAVID WOULD EVENTUALLY DEFEAT ISH-BOSHETH. HE WANTED TO SWITCH HIS LOYALTIES ANYWAY, AND THIS GIVES HIM JUST THE EXCUSE. ABNER CARRIES OUT HIS THREAT AND OFFERS TO HELP DAVID ADD THE REST OF ISRAEL TO HIS KINGDOM.

I'VE SPOKEN WITH THE OTHER TRIBES. THEY WILL BOW TO YOU IF I SAY THE WORD.

DAVID REPLIES WITH AN INVITATION TO A FEAST.

THANK YOU FOR YOUR KINDNESS. I'LL JOIN FORCES WITH YOU. YOU, MY LORD, WILL REIGN OVER ALL ISRAEL!

Assassinations

BASED ON
2 SAMUEL 3:22—5:5

AFTER GIVING HIS SUPPORT TO KING DAVID, ABNER GOES TO RALLY THE ELDERS OF ISRAEL. BUT ABNER IS SCARCELY OUT OF THE CITY WHEN JOAB RETURNS ...

ABNER JUST LEFT! DAVID HAD A BIG FEAST FOR HIM.

ABNER WAS HERE! AND DAVID LET HIM GO?

ANGRILY, JOAB RUSHES TO SEE DAVID ...

DON'T YOU KNOW THAT ABNER CAME HERE AS A SPY— TO FIND OUT YOUR STRENGTH? AND HE KILLED MY BROTHER, YOUR OWN NEPHEW!

DAVID REFUSES TO LISTEN—AND IN A RAGE JOAB STORMS OUT.

DAVID MAY HAVE MADE HIS PEACE WITH YOU, BUT I NEVER WILL.

JOAB IS FURIOUS! THIS COULD MEAN TROUBLE.

HE WOULDN'T DARE DEFY THE KING!

THAT NIGHT JOAB AND SOME OF HIS MEN FIND THE WATERWAY THAT LEADS OUT OF THE BACK OF THE CITY.

YUCK! CRAWLING THROUGH THE SEWERS. WE'LL BE UNCLEAN FOR A MONTH AFTER THIS.

WE HAVE NO CHOICE. THE OUTSIDE DEFENSES ARE IMPREGNABLE— JERUSALEM MUST BE TAKEN FROM WITHIN.

SURPRISED BY THE SUDDEN APPEARANCE OF DAVID'S MEN, THE GUARDS ARE QUICKLY OVERCOME.

GIVE THE ORDER TO OPEN THE GATES—OR DIE!

THE TERRIFIED OFFICER SHOUTS THE ORDER. THE HUGE GATES SWING OPEN ...

... AND DAVID'S ARMY CHARGES THROUGH—JERUSALEM IS NOW HIS, AND ALMOST WITHOUT A FIGHT.

Temple Dreams

BASED ON 2 SAMUEL 6—7;
1 CHRONICLES 13; 15—17;
PSALMS 24; 96; 105; 106

JERUSALEM IS NOW THE CAPITAL CITY OF ISRAEL. BUT DAVID WANTS A SPIRITUAL CAPITAL AS WELL. IT IS TIME TO GIVE THE ARK OF THE COVENANT A PERMANENT HOME. EVER SINCE THE PHILISTINES TRIED TO CAPTURE THE ARK, IT HAS BEEN KEPT IN KIRIATH JEARIM. DAVID WANTS IT BROUGHT TO JERUSALEM.

UNFORTUNATELY, THE ISRAELITES HAVE FORGOTTEN GOD'S INSTRUCTIONS FOR MOVING THE ARK. AS THEY TRANSPORT IT IN AN OXCART, THE OXEN STUMBLE. ONE OF THE GUARDS REACHES OUT TO KEEP THE ARK FROM FALLING—AND TOUCHES IT.

AHHH!

HE IS KILLED INSTANTLY BECAUSE GOD'S LAW ALLOWS ONLY A LEVITE TO TOUCH THE ARK. DAVID LEAVES THE ARK NEARBY UNTIL GOD GIVES HIM PERMISSION TO BRING IT TO JERUSALEM.

WHEN DAVID TRIES AGAIN TO BRING THE ARK TO JERUSALEM, HE PAYS ATTENTION TO THE LORD'S INSTRUCTIONS. HE ASSEMBLES ALL THE PRIESTS OF ISRAEL, WITH INSTRUCTIONS THAT ONLY THE LEVITES MAY TOUCH THE ARK. THE PROCESSION IS ACCOMPANIED BY THE FINEST MUSICIANS IN THE LAND, WHO PLAY AND SING SONGS OF PRAISE TO THE LORD.

LET THE HEAVENS REJOICE; MAY THE EARTH BE GLAD. SING FOR JOY TO THE LORD BECAUSE HE RULES IN RIGHTEOUSNESS!

GIVE THANKS TO THE LORD, FOR HE IS GOOD. HIS LOVE ENDURES FOREVER!!

GIVE THANKS TO THE LORD, CALL ON HIS NAME, LET ALL COUNTRIES KNOW WHAT HE HAS DONE. SING HIS PRAISE, SEEK HIS FACE, AND NEVER FORGET HIS WONDERS!

WHEN THEY REACH JERUSALEM, DAVID IS SO OVERJOYED THAT HE DANCES AND SINGS AT THE FRONT OF THE PARADE.

LIFT UP YOUR HEADS, YOU MIGHTY GATES! OPEN SO THE KING OF GLORY MAY ENTER!

THE LEVITES PUT THE ARK IN A TENT IN THE CENTER OF THE CITY. BUT THAT DOESN'T FEEL PROPER TO DAVID. HE CALLS THE PROPHET NATHAN IN FOR A DISCUSSION.

IT DOESN'T FEEL RIGHT FOR GOD'S HOUSE TO BE IN A TENT WHILE I LIVE IN A PALACE. I'D LIKE TO BUILD A TEMPLE TO GOD.

THAT SOUNDS LIKE A GREAT IDEA. I'M SURE GOD WOULD BE PLEASED.

BUT THE NEXT DAY ...

DAVID, WAIT! GOD SPOKE TO ME LAST NIGHT. HE SAID THAT HIS TEMPLE MUST BE A HOUSE OF PEACE, AND YOU HAVE BEEN FORCED TO BE A MAN OF WAR. YOU CANNOT BUILD A NEW HOUSE FOR HIM. BUT DON'T WORRY. ONE OF YOUR SONS WILL BE A MAN OF PEACE, AND HE WILL BUILD A HOUSE FOR GOD SOMEDAY.

GREAT IS THE SOVEREIGN LORD FOR GIVING ME SUCH A PROMISE. THANK YOU, O GOD. AND WITH YOUR BLESSING MY HOUSE WILL BE BLESSED FOREVER.

David's Sin
BASED ON 2 SAMUEL 11

WORD HAS COME THAT THE ARAMEANS AND AMMONITES ARE JOINING FORCES AGAINST US.

I DON'T FEEL LIKE LEAVING JERUSALEM RIGHT NOW, JOAB. YOU TAKE THE ARMY AND GO FIGHT THEM.

UNDER DAVID'S LEADERSHIP, ISRAEL GROWS STRONGER EVERY DAY. AFTER MANY YEARS OF VICTORIES AGAINST THE PHILISTINES, RULERS OF THE COUNTRIES AROUND THEM DECIDE THAT ISRAEL MUST BE DEFEATED. BUT DAVID IS TIRED OF THE CONSTANT WARFARE.

JOAB TAKES CHARGE OF THE WAR. AS THE FIGHTING DRAGS ON WITHOUT HIM, DAVID GETS BORED SITTING IN JERUSALEM. ONE EVENING, AS DAVID STROLLS ON THE ROOF OF HIS PALACE ...

WHO IS THAT BEAUTIFUL WOMAN?

HER NAME IS BATHSHEBA. HER HUSBAND IS URIAH, A SOLDIER IN YOUR ARMY.

NOT KNOWING THAT HIS OWN KING HAS BETRAYED HIM, LOYAL URIAH RIDES FURIOUSLY BACK TO CAMP.

WELCOME BACK, URIAH. DID YOU SEE THE KING?

YES, HE ASKED ME ABOUT OUR MILITARY CAMPAIGN. I TOLD HIM OF YOUR PLANS TO FORCE THE ENEMY TO SURRENDER. HE SENT YOU THIS MESSAGE.

JOAB BREAKS THE KING'S SEAL AND READS ...

SEND URIAH INTO THE THICK OF THE FIGHT SO HE WILL BE KILLED.
- DAVID

JOAB DOESN'T KNOW WHY DAVID DESIRES URIAH'S DEATH, BUT HE IS ALWAYS WILLING TO OBEY.

HMM ... DAVID WANTS US TO ATTACK AT ONCE. URIAH, I NEED YOU TO LEAD AN ASSAULT AGAINST THE MAIN GATE OF THE CITY.

ATTACK THE MAIN GATE? THAT'S THE BEST-DEFENDED PART OF THE CITY. WHAT ABOUT OUR PLANS FOR THE SIEGE?

YOUR KING HAS COMMANDED YOU.

FOLLOW ME, MEN WE HAVE PLEDGE THE KING OUR LOYA AND TODAY HE ASK FOR OUR STRENGT WE WILL FIGHT FC THE HONOR OF OL KING AND OUR GO

322

URIAH BOLDLY ATTACKS THE GATE, BUT THE ARCHERS PROTECTING THE CITY WALL EASILY KILL HIM AND HIS MEN. THE REST OF THE ISRAELITES ARE FORCED TO FALL BACK.

AND SO, SEVERAL BRAVE SOLDIERS DIE TO COVER UP FOR DAVID'S SIN.

JOAB'S MESSENGER BRINGS THE NEWS TO DAVID, THINKING HE WILL BE UPSET AT THE DEATH OF HIS MEN.

WE FOUGHT BRAVELY, BUT THE ARCHERS ON THE CITY WALLS HAD THE ADVANTAGE. URIAH AND SEVERAL OTHERS WERE KILLED.

TELL JOAB NOT TO FEEL BAD. WAR ALWAYS TAKES SOME OF OUR BEST MEN. WAIT UNTIL THE DEFENDERS HAVE RUN OUT OF FOOD, AND THEN ATTACK AGAIN AND TAKE THE CITY.

WHEN BATHSHEBA'S TIME OF MOURNING IS OVER, DAVID CALLS HER TO THE PALACE, AND THEY GET MARRIED.

LONG LIVE THE KING! LONG LIVE THE QUEEN!

THE PEOPLE ARE HAPPY. BUT GOD IS NOT. INSTEAD OF BEING A SHEPHERD WHO PROTECTS GOD'S PEOPLE, DAVID HAS COMMITTED MURDER AND STOLEN A MAN'S WIFE. GOD CANNOT LET DAVID'S SECRET SIN GO UNPUNISHED.

INJUSTICE? IN MY KINGDOM? TELL ME ABOUT IT.

THERE WERE TWO MEN IN A CITY ...

ONE WAS RICH, THE OTHER POOR. THE RICH MAN HAD MANY SHEEP AND CATTLE, BUT THE POOR MAN HAD ONLY ONE LITTLE LAMB. HE RAISED IT WITH HIS CHILDREN. IT SHARED HIS FOOD AND SLEPT IN HIS ARMS. HE LOVED THAT LITTLE LAMB LIKE A DAUGHTER.

ONE DAY THE RICH MAN HAD A GUEST.

I DON'T WANT TO WASTE ANY OF MY WEALTH. GO KILL MY NEIGHBOR'S SHEEP FOR A FEAST FOR ME AND MY GUEST.

HIS SERVANTS SNUCK INTO THE POOR MAN'S YARD, WHERE THEY STOLE AND KILLED HIS PRECIOUS LITTLE LAMB.

325

WHEN NATHAN LEAVES, DAVID IS ALONE IN HIS SHAME. HE IS TRULY SORRY FOR THE CRIME HE HAS COMMITTED AND TURNS TO GOD IN PRAYER ...

CREATE IN ME A CLEAN HEART, O GOD. GIVE ME A NEW SPIRIT, FAITHFUL TO YOU.

FOR DAYS, DAVID NEITHER DRINKS NOR EATS. HE FASTS AND CRIES OUT TO THE LORD, ASKING GOD TO SPARE HIS CHILD.

HE HASN'T SPOKEN FOR DAYS.

EXCEPT TO GOD.

BUT HIS EFFORTS ARE IN VAIN. AFTER SEVEN DAYS, HIS BABY DIES.

IF HE WAS THAT SAD WHILE THE CHILD WAS STILL ALIVE, WHAT WILL HE DO WHEN WE TELL HIM IT'S DEAD?

I HOPE HE WON'T DO ANYTHING DESPERATE.

BUT WHEN HE HEARS THE NEWS, DAVID INSTANTLY GETS UP, TAKES A BATH, AND PUTS ON NEW CLOTHES. THEN HE ASKS FOR HIS FIRST FOOD IN A WEEK.

WHAT ARE YOU DOING? WHEN THE CHILD WAS ALIVE, YOU FASTED AND WEPT. BUT NOW THAT HE'S DEAD, YOU EAT? WHY AREN'T YOU SAD?

WHILE THE BABY WAS ALIVE, I THOUGHT THE LORD MIGHT ANSWER MY PRAYERS. BUT NOW THAT HE IS DEAD, NO AMOUNT OF GRIEVING WILL BRING HIM BACK. I WILL SEE MY BABY AGAIN ONE DAY.

IN THE MEANTIME, DAVID'S GENERAL, JOAB, CONTINUES THE SIEGE AGAINST THE CITY OF RABBAH. WHEN THE CITY IS READY TO GIVE UP, HE SENDS WORD FOR THE KING TO COME AND MAKE THE FINAL ATTACK. DAVID LEADS THE CHARGE—AND THE CITY SURRENDERS.

AS HE RETURNS VICTORIOUS TO JERUSALEM, THE CROWD GREETS DAVID WITH SHOUTS OF PRAISE. HE IS PLEASED AND PROUD. ISRAEL IS NOW SECURE FROM THE COUNTRIES AROUND IT. BUT IT IS A BITTERSWEET VICTORY FOR HIM ...

... DAVID MAY HAVE WON HIS BATTLE, BUT HE LOST HIS BABY.

BUT SOON GOD SHOWS HIS FORGIVENESS IN ANOTHER WAY. DAVID AND BATHSHEBA HAVE A LITTLE BOY.

WE SHALL NAME HIM SOLOMON BECAUSE WE HAVE HAD WAR FOR TOO LONG, AND HE WILL BE A MAN OF PEACE.

MORE GOOD NEWS COMES. NATHAN, WHO HAS ALSO FORGIVEN DAVID, BRINGS NEWS THAT GOD HAS GIVEN THEIR NEW BABY A SPECIAL NAME: JEDIDIAH. THE NAME MEANS "LOVED BY GOD" AND SHOWS THAT GOD HAS SPECIAL PLANS FOR DAVID AND BATHSHEBA'S SON.

Battling Brothers

FOR MANY YEARS, DAVID REIGNS OVER ISRAEL. UNFORTUNATELY, SIN AND VIOLENCE REIGN WITHIN HIS OWN FAMILY. HIS OLDEST SON, AMNON, IS THE HEIR TO HIS THRONE. BUT ANOTHER SON, ABSALOM, HATES AMNON AND WANTS THE CROWN FOR HIMSELF. KNOWING THAT HIS FATHER DOESN'T LIKE TO LEAVE JERUSALEM, HE ASKS A QUESTION ...

FATHER, IT IS SHEEPSHEARING TIME, AND I'M HAVING A BIG FEAST IN THE COUNTRY. WILL YOU HONOR MY GUESTS WITH YOUR PRESENCE?

WELL, SINCE YOU CAN'T COME, PRINCE AMNON CAN REPRESENT YOU.

THANK YOU, ABSALOM. BUT IF YOU ARE HAVING A BIG FEAST, I DON'T WANT TO ADD TO YOUR EXPENSES.

BUT HE HATES HIS HALF BROTHER. CAN I TRUST HIM?

VERY WELL. BUT I'M SURE *ALL* MY SONS WOULD ENJOY CELEBRATING THE SHEEPSHEARING FESTIVAL AT YOUR HOUSE. I WILL SEND ALL YOUR BROTHERS TO REPRESENT THE ROYAL INTERESTS AT YOUR FEAST.

HE WON'T DARE DO ANYTHING FOOLISH WITH ALL HIS BROTHERS AROUND. LORD, PROTECT MY SONS FROM EACH OTHER.

BUT ABSALOM HAS PLOTTED FOR TWO YEARS TO KILL HIS OLDER BROTHER. NOTHING WILL STOP HIM.

ALL MY BROTHERS WILL BE HERE, BUT IT WILL MAKE NO DIFFERENCE. BY THE END OF THE FEAST THEY WILL BE TOO DRUNK TO REACT. WHEN I GIVE THE WORD, KILL AMNON!

ABSALOM THROWS A MERRY FEAST, WITH PLENTY OF FOOD AND WINE. BEFORE LONG, HIS BROTHERS ARE IN HIGH SPIRITS, ENJOYING THEMSELVES WITHOUT ANY WORRIES. ABSALOM SIGNALS HIS SERVANTS.

ABSALOM'S SERVANTS COME FORWARD TO DO THEIR DIRTY WORK. THE OTHER BROTHERS AND THEIR SERVANTS FLEE IN TERROR.

ONE OF THE SERVANTS RACES TO JERUSALEM.

MY LORD! ABSALOM HAS MURDERED ALL OF YOUR SONS!

DAVID TEARS HIS CLOTHES IN GRIEF. HIS WORST FEARS HAVE COME TRUE!

BUT IN HIS FEAR, THE SERVANT HAD EXAGGERATED THE TRAGEDY. DAVID'S OTHER SONS SOON COME STUMBLING INTO THE PALACE.

WE'RE OKAY! ABSALOM ONLY MURDERED AMNON—THE REST OF US ESCAPED!

THANK GOD YOU ARE SAFE! BUT AMNON, MY FIRSTBORN SON, IS DEAD! ABSALOM MUST BE PUNISHED FOR THIS!

BUT ABSALOM HAS ALREADY FLED TO GESHUR, WHERE HIS GRANDFATHER IS KING.

The Scheming Prince
BASED ON 2 SAMUEL 14:1–15:13

FOR THREE YEARS, DAVID GRIEVES FOR HIS SONS—THE ONE WHO IS DEAD AND THE ONE WHO RAN AWAY. BUT HE DOES NOTHING. FINALLY, JOAB CONFRONTS HIM.

DAVID, YOU *MUST* DO SOMETHING. THE KINGDOM NEEDS AN HEIR TO THE THRONE, AND RIGHT NOW THAT HEIR IS HIDING OUT IN EXILE.

VERY WELL. BUT ON ONE CONDITION ...

YOUR FATHER MISSES YOU, ABSALOM. HE SENT ME TO BRING YOU BACK TO JERUSALEM.

I'M GLAD HE'S FINALLY FORGIVEN ME.

WELL, NOT ENTIRELY. HE SAYS YOU CAN'T LIVE IN THE PALACE OR COME TO SEE HIM.

IF THAT'S THE WAY HE WANTS IT, I WILL DO AS MY FATHER COMMANDS.

HE WON'T TREAT ME THAT WAY FOR LONG!

FOR TWO YEARS, ABSALOM LIVES IN JERUSALEM WITHOUT SEEING HIS FATHER. HE RESENTS THIS TREATMENT, AND HIS ANGER GROWS UNTIL AT LAST HE CAN'T STAND IT ANY LONGER. HE SENDS FOR JOAB, BUT JOAB REFUSES TO COME.

FINE. IF JOAB DOESN'T THINK I'M IMPORTANT ENOUGH TO TALK TO, THEN I'LL GIVE HIM SOMETHING IMPORTANT TO DEAL WITH.

JOAB HAS A BARLEY FIELD NEXT TO MINE. SET FIRE TO IT!

WHAT ON EARTH DOES HE THINK HE'S DOING? PRINCE OR NO PRINCE, I'M GOING TO—

AH, JOAB! I'M GLAD YOU COULD JOIN ME. I'VE DECIDED THAT I'M TIRED OF THIS ISOLATION. MY FATHER ASKED ME TO COME BACK TO JERUSALEM. IF HE WANTS TO PUNISH ME FOR WHAT I DID, LET HIM DO IT. BUT IF NOT, THEN HE NEEDS TO FORGIVE ME AND TREAT ME LIKE A SON AGAIN.

ONE DAY I'LL GET EVEN WITH YOU FOR THE WAY YOU'VE TREATED ME.

GRUDGINGLY, JOAB TAKES ABSALOM'S MESSAGE TO KING DAVID.

YOUR SON MISSES YOU. HE WANTS YOU TO FORGIVE HIM AND WELCOME HIM BACK INTO THE FAMILY.

HE MISSES ME? TRUTH BE TOLD, I MISS HIM TOO. ALL RIGHT. TELL HIM HE MAY COME SEE ME.

STAND UP, ABSALOM. I FORGIVE YOU. FROM NOW ON YOU WILL BE WELCOME AT THE PALACE AS A PRINCE OF ISRAEL.

ABSALOM PRETENDS TO BE HUMBLE AS HE BOWS BEFORE HIS FATHER, ASKING FORGIVENESS. BUT IN HIS HEART, HE HAS AN EVIL PLAN.

ABSALOM LOSES NO TIME IN LETTING THE PEOPLE OF JERUSALEM KNOW THAT HIS FATHER HAS FORGIVEN HIM.

ABSALOM IS THE MOST HANDSOME OF ALL THE PRINCES OF ISRAEL.

HIS CHARIOT AND HORSES ARE AS FINE AS THE KING'S.

ABSALOM IS A TRUE POLITICIAN. HE SPENDS MOST OF HIS DAYS AT THE CITY GATES, WINNING OVER THE AFFECTION OF TRAVELERS FROM ALL OVER ISRAEL AND ENCOURAGING MEN TO TELL HIM THEIR PROBLEMS.

THE TAX COLLECTOR HAS CHEATED ME. I'M GOING TO TAKE MY CASE TO THE KING.

UNFORTUNATELY, MY FATHER IS TOO BUSY TO WORRY ABOUT YOUR PROBLEMS. NOW, IF I WERE KING, I'D MAKE SURE YOU GOT YOUR MONEY BACK.

BUT I'M NOT KING. AND UNTIL I AM, I CAN'T DO ANYTHING FOR YOU.

I WISH YOU WERE KING!

SOON, MY FRIEND. VERY SOON.

AFTER SEVERAL YEARS SPENT WINNING THE AFFECTION OF THE PEOPLE, ABSALOM DECIDES HE HAS ENOUGH POPULAR SUPPORT TO TAKE THE THRONE FROM HIS FATHER. HE GOES TO HEBRON, HIS BIRTH-PLACE AND THE OLD CAPITAL OF ISRAEL, TO LAUNCH HIS REBELLION. HE INVITES SEVERAL IMPORTANT ISRAELITE LEADERS TO MEET HIM THERE AND GIVES INSTRUCTIONS TO HIS LOYAL MESSENGERS.

SPREAD OUT THROUGH ALL THE TRIBES OF ISRAEL. WHENEVER YOU COME TO A NEW TOWN, BLOW YOUR TRUMPETS AND SHOUT, "ABSALOM IS THE NEW KING IN HEBRON!"

IN HEBRON, ABSALOM WAITS UNTIL GREAT THRONGS OF HIS FOLLOWERS REACH THE CITY. THEN HE APPEARS BEFORE THE PEOPLE. THE TRUMPET SOUNDS ...

ABSALOM!

LONG LIVE THE KING!

ABSALOM IS THE RULER OF HEBRON!

ONE OF THE LEADERS CHEERING FOR ABSALOM IS AHITHOPHEL, HIS FATHER'S CHIEF ADVISER. AHITHOPHEL IS BATHSHEBA'S GRANDFATHER, AND HE HAS LONG HELD A SECRET GRUDGE AGAINST DAVID FOR KILLING BATHSHEBA'S FIRST HUSBAND.

WHAT DO WE DO NEXT?

WE MARCH ON JERUSALEM. DAVID HASN'T HAD TIME TO RALLY HIS ARMY. IF HE TRIES TO FIGHT BACK, HE WON'T HAVE A CHANCE— NOW THAT YOU HAVE *ME* TO ADVISE YOU!

335

MEANWHILE, MORE AND MORE PEOPLE RUSH TO HEBRON.

WHAT'S THE EXCITEMENT?

ABSALOM IS LEADING A REVOLT AGAINST KING DAVID. WE'RE GIVING OUR ALLEGIANCE TO ABSALOM.

ABSALOM IS FOR THE PEOPLE. THESE ARE GREAT DAYS FOR ISRAEL. COME JOIN US!

UMM ... I WILL. BUT MY SHEEP—I MUST TAKE CARE OF THEM FIRST.

INSTEAD OF JOINING THE CROWDS ON THE WAY TO HEBRON, THE FAITHFUL SHEPHERD RUNS NORTH—UNTIL HE REACHES THE GATES OF DAVID'S CAPITAL, JERUSALEM.

OPEN UP! THE KING'S LIFE IS IN DANGER!

THE PEOPLE HAVE REVOLTED! THEY ARE PROCLAIMING THAT ABSALOM IS KING IN HEBRON.

MY SON! WHY HAS HE DONE THIS TO ME?

THE LEVITES, LED BY TWO HIGH PRIESTS—ZADOK AND DAVID'S OLD FRIEND ABIATHAR—BRING GOD'S HOLY ARK AS THEY FOLLOW DAVID OUT OF THE CITY.

ABSALOM MAY TRY TO STEAL YOUR THRONE, BUT HE WILL NOT STEAL THE THRONE OF GOD!

THANK YOU FOR YOUR FAITHFULNESS, BUT NO. TAKE IT BACK TO THE CITY. I AM FORCED TO FLEE, BUT GOD'S HOUSE WILL REMAIN IN JERUSALEM. IF GOD SEES FIT, I WILL RETURN TO THE CITY AND WORSHIP AGAIN BEFORE HIS ARK.

BUT YOU CAN SERVE ME IN THIS WAY: BE MY EYES AND EARS IN JERUSALEM. BECAUSE YOU ARE PRIESTS, ABSALOM WILL NOT HARM YOU. USE YOUR SONS TO SEND ME ANY MESSAGES.

HUSHAI PRESENTS HIMSELF TO ABSALOM.

WHY ARE YOU HERE? I THOUGHT YOU WERE LOYAL TO MY FATHER.

WHY DID AHITHOPHEL CHOOSE TO SERVE YOU AND NOT YOUR FATHER? I WISH TO SERVE THE ONE CHOSEN BY THE LORD.

VERY WELL. NOW THAT I'VE TAKEN JERUSALEM WITHOUT A FIGHT, WHAT SHOULD MY NEXT STEP BE?

AHITHOPHEL HAS THOUGHT LONG AND HARD ABOUT THE DAY HE WOULD REBEL AGAINST DAVID. HE SPEAKS FIRST.

I WOULD TAKE 12,000 MEN AND SET OUT TONIGHT IN PURSUIT OF DAVID. THEN I WOULD ATTACK HIM WHILE HE IS WEARY AND WEAK FROM FLEEING JERUSALEM. I WOULD KILL ONLY THE KING. ONCE HE IS DEAD, ALL ISRAEL WILL CLAIM YOU AS THEIR KING. WE WON'T HAVE TO KILL ANY MORE CITIZENS.

THIS PLAN IS CLEARLY A GOOD ONE. ABSALOM'S BEST CHANCE IS TO STRIKE BEFORE DAVID CAN COLLECT HIS ARMY. BUT HUSHAI KNOWS THAT DAVID NEEDS MORE TIME TO ESCAPE AND ORGANIZE HIS COUNTERATTACK. HE ALSO KNOWS THAT ABSALOM IS A VAIN YOUNG MAN ...

AHITHOPHEL'S ADVICE IS GOOD—FOR AHITHOPHEL. OF COURSE HE WANTS TO TRY TO CAPTURE DAVID HIMSELF. IT'S HIS BEST CHANCE FOR GLORY. BUT HE FORGETS ONE THING: DAVID AND HIS MEN ARE ISRAEL'S BEST FIGHTERS. RIGHT NOW THEY ARE ANGRY AS BEARS WHO HAVE BEEN ROBBED OF THEIR CUBS. IF YOU ATTACK AND SUFFER ANY DEFEAT, THE PEOPLE WILL SAY THAT YOU ARE WEAK AND WILL TURN AGAINST YOU.

INSTEAD, O KING, YOU SHOULD WAIT UNTIL YOU CAN CALL ON THOUSANDS OF MEN FROM THE SURROUNDING TRIBES. THEN IF YOU, AS THEIR HEROIC LEADER, GO FORTH BEFORE YOUR ARMY, DAVID WILL NOT BE ABLE TO STAND AGAINST YOU.

YES, HUSHAI'S PLAN MAKES SURE THAT I GET ALL THE GLORY.

I HAVE CHOSEN THE WRONG MAN TO SUPPORT AS KING—A CONCEITED FOOL!

IF ABSALOM LISTENS TO ME, DAVID WILL HAVE TIME TO ESCAPE.

DAVID'S PRAYER HAS BEEN ANSWERED. ABSALOM FOOLISHLY REJECTS AHITHOPHEL'S ADVICE. BUT AHITHOPHEL KNOWS THAT HUSHAI'S ADVICE WILL HELP DAVID MORE THAN ABSALOM. MOREOVER, HE KNOWS THAT ABSALOM'S DEFEAT WILL MEAN HIS DEATH FOR SUPPORTING A TRAITOR AGAINST KING DAVID. SOLEMNLY, HE RIDES BACK HOME AND GETS HIS AFFAIRS IN ORDER.

ONCE HIS WILL AND BUSINESS MATTERS ARE ARRANGED, AHITHOPHEL HANGS HIMSELF. IT IS A SORRY END FOR A MAN WHO ONCE WAS ONE OF THE KING'S WISEST ADVISERS.

HUSHAI'S MESSENGERS BRING DAVID A WARNING. HE MUSTN'T REST UNTIL AFTER HE GETS HIS GROUP ACROSS THE JORDAN AND INTO FRIENDLY TERRITORY.

THAT NIGHT, DAVID AND HIS FOLLOWERS FORD THE JORDAN RIVER. ON THE OTHER SIDE, THEY SEEK REFUGE IN THE CITY OF MAHANAIM, WHOSE LEADERS ARE LOYAL TO DAVID.

HERE'S SOME FOOD AND BEDDING MY MASTER HAS SENT FOR KING DAVID AND HIS FRIENDS.

GOD BLESS YOU. TELL YOUR MASTER I WILL NOT FORGET HIS KINDNESS.

THIS WILL BE A GOOD PLACE TO MUSTER THE ROYAL ARMY AND WAIT FOR ABSALOM.

YES, WE WILL BATTLE AGAINST MY SON HERE. BUT NO MATTER WHICH SIDE WINS, I WILL LOSE.

THE TWO ARMIES MEET IN THE FOREST OF EPHRAIM. JOAB HAS CHOSEN THE BATTLEFIELD WELL—ABSALOM'S MEN CAN'T FIGHT WELL IN THE ROUGH TERRAIN. SUDDEN CLIFFS, THICK TREES, AND WILD BEASTS ARE JUST AS DANGEROUS TO THE REBELS AS THE SWORDS OF DAVID'S SOLDIERS.

ABSALOM TRIES TO RETREAT ON HIS HORSE.

BUT AS HE TAKES FLIGHT ...

... HIS HEAD GETS CAUGHT IN THE LOW-HANGING BRANCHES OF AN OAK TREE!

WHILE ABSALOM HANGS HELPLESS, JOAB FINDS HIM. THERE, IN DIRECT DEFIANCE OF DAVID'S ORDER, HE ENDS THE REBELLION IN THE SIMPLEST WAY HE KNOWS.

I'M SORRY, ABSALOM, BUT THIS IS THE BEST THING FOR THE KINGDOM.

SOUND THE TRUMPET. WE HAVE THE VICTORY.

MY KING, WE HAVE WON THE BATTLE!

FINE. FINE. WHAT ABOUT MY SON ABSALOM? IS HE ALL RIGHT?

AT THE NEWS THAT ABSALOM IS DEAD, DAVID CLIMBS TO THE LOOKOUT ABOVE THE CITY GATE. ALONE, HE MOURNS FOR HIS SON.

OH, ABSALOM! IF ONLY I HAD DIED INSTEAD OF YOU. MY SON! MY SON!

IN HIS GRIEF, DAVID TURNS HIS BACK ON THE MEN WHO WON THE VICTORY FOR HIM. FINALLY JOAB GOES TO SEE THE KING.

YOU ACT AS IF YOU WISH ABSALOM HAD WON THE BATTLE! HAVE YOU FORGOTTEN THE MEN WHO FOUGHT TO SAVE YOU— AND YOUR FAMILY AND YOUR KINGDOM? IF THIS KEEPS UP, ALL YOUR ALLIES WILL TURN AGAINST YOU.

DAVID SEES THE TRUTH OF JOAB'S WORDS. HE MAKES PEACE WITH THE TRIBES THAT SIDED WITH ABSALOM AND GOES BACK TO JERUSALEM.

BUT WHEN DAVID FINDS OUT THAT JOAB HAD DELIBERATELY KILLED ABSALOM, RAGE CONSUMES HIM. HE RELIEVES JOAB FROM COMMAND OF THE ARMY.

BUT I DID IT ALL FOR YOU.

HOWEVER, LIKE ALWAYS, DAVID IS UNABLE TO PUNISH HIS OWN RELATIVES. HE EVENTUALLY LETS JOAB TAKE CHARGE OF THE ARMY AGAIN.

IN THE MEANTIME, YOUNG SOLOMON—THE PRINCE WHOSE NAME MEANS "PEACE"—IS GROWING UP AND LEARNING FROM THE WISE MEN AROUND HIM.

HIS MOTHER NEVER FORGETS THE LORD'S SPECIAL BLESSING ON SOLOMON, AND HOPES HE WILL ONE DAY BE KING.

LORD, YOU WOULD NOT HAVE SHOWN HIM SPECIAL FAVOR UNLESS YOU HAD BIG PLANS FOR HIM. MAY THEY COME TO PASS.

YEARS PASS, AND DAVID GROWS OLD. FINALLY WORD SPREADS THROUGHOUT JERUSALEM THAT THE KING'S HEALTH IS FAILING FAST. THE PEOPLE KNOW THAT DAVID HAS CHOSEN SOLOMON TO BE KING AND TO BUILD THE TEMPLE OF GOD. BUT THERE ARE RUMORS ...

Family Plots

BASED ON 1 KINGS 1

THE BOOKS OF 1 AND 2 KINGS AND 2 CHRONICLES RECORD THE HISTORY OF THE HEBREW EMPIRE THROUGH THE YEARS OF SOLOMON'S REIGN, THE DIVISION OF THE KINGDOM INTO TWO SEPARATE NATIONS—JUDAH AND ISRAEL—AND THE FALL OF BOTH.

WITH HIS OLDER BROTHERS DEAD, ADONIJAH BELIEVES THAT FATE HAS LEFT HIM IN THE PERFECT POSITION.

MY FATHER IS GROWING WEAKER BY THE DAY. AS THE ELDEST REMAINING SON, I WILL SURELY BE NAMED KING IN HIS PLACE. BRING ALL THE KING'S SONS—EXCEPT MY HALF BROTHER SOLOMON— AND MEET ME AT THE SERPENT'S STONE.

EAT AND BE MERRY! ANY DAY NOW, MY FATHER WILL NAME ME THE NEXT KING OF ISRAEL. AND YOU, MY FRIENDS, WILL HAVE POSITIONS OF HIGH HONOR IN MY COURT.

ADONIJAH THINKS HE HAS ALL THE SUPPORT HE NEEDS WITH JOAB, THE HEAD OF THE ARMY, AND ABIATHAR, ONE OF THE TWO HIGH PRIESTS. BUT NOT ONLY HAS ADONIJAH LEFT SOLOMON OUT OF HIS PLANS, HE'S ALSO FORGOTTEN NATHAN, GOD'S PROPHET, AND BENAIAH, THE HEAD OF DAVID'S PERSONAL GUARD.

AND UNFORTUNATELY FOR ADONIJAH, NATHAN ALREADY KNOWS GOD'S WILL.

THAT PRIDEFUL PEACOCK IS SO CERTAIN HE WILL BE THE NEXT KING. BUT GOD HAS CHOSEN ANOTHER.

WHILE ADONIJAH IS FEASTING, NATHAN IS TALKING WITH QUEEN BATHSHEBA.

IF ADONIJAH BECOMES KING, HE WILL CERTAINLY HAVE YOU AND SOLOMON EXILED, IF NOT EXECUTED. IF YOU WANT TO SAVE YOURSELF AND YOUR SON, DO AS I SAY.

TELL ME WHAT TO DO AND I'LL DO IT.

FOLLOWING NATHAN'S ADVICE, SHE GOES AT ONCE TO DAVID.

MY LORD, YOU PROMISED THAT MY SON, SOLOMON, WOULD RULE AFTER YOU, BUT EVEN NOW HIS HALF BROTHER ADONIJAH HAS DECLARED HIMSELF YOUR SUCCESSOR.

SEND FOR NATHAN AND ZADOK THE PRIEST.

NATHAN CHOOSES THIS MOMENT TO ENTER.

IT IS TRUE WHAT SHE SAYS. ADONIJAH IS TRYING TO TAKE THE CHOICE OF THE NEXT KING AWAY FROM YOU.

ZADOK AND NATHAN ACT IMMEDIATELY. SOLOMON RIDES HIS FATHER'S MULE TO THE SPRING OF GIHON AND THERE SOLOMON IS ANOINTED KING OF ISRAEL. THE TRUMPET SOUNDS ...

BENAIAH LEADS HIS NEW KING TO THE CITY, WHERE THE PEOPLE GREET HIM WITH SHOUTS OF JOY.

THE NOISE OF THE CELEBRATION IS SO LOUD THAT IT REACHES ADONIJAH'S FEAST. A MESSENGER INTERRUPTS THEIR FEAST WITH THE NEWS THAT DAVID HAS JUST MADE SOLOMON THE KING. KNOWING THAT THEY MAY BE BRANDED AS TRAITORS, ADONIJAH'S GUESTS FLEE IN TERROR.

THERE'S ONLY ONE CHANCE TO SAVE MY LIFE!

PRINCE ADONIJAH FLEES TO THE TABERNACLE WHERE THE PEOPLE WORSHIP GOD. HE GRABS HOLD OF THE HORNS OF THE ALTAR OF SACRIFICE.

I CANNOT BE HARMED AT GOD'S ALTAR! I WON'T LET GO UNLESS SOLOMON PROMISES NOT TO KILL ME.

WHEN SOLOMON FINDS HIS BROTHER AT THE TABERNACLE, HE AGREES TO SPARE ADONIJAH'S LIFE—IF HE PROVES HIMSELF WORTHY OF THE NEW KING'S TRUST. THE COWARDLY ADONIJAH PROMISES ANYTHING THAT HE THINKS WILL SPARE HIM.

BUT LATER, SOLOMON IS FORCED TO EXECUTE BOTH ADONIJAH AND GENERAL JOAB WHEN THEY COMMIT SUSPECTED ACTS OF TREASON.

AS A SHEPHERD:

THE LORD IS MY LIGHT AND MY SALVATION—WHO SHOULD I FEAR?

WHEN EVIL MEN ATTACK ME, THEY WILL STUMBLE AND FALL.

WHEN A WARRIOR IN EXILE:

GOD IS MY HIDEOUT AND MY STRENGTH. THOUGH THE EARTH FALL APART, THE MOUNTAINS CRUMBLE, AND THE SEAS RISE UP, THE LORD IS MIGHTY TO SAVE: "BE STILL, AND KNOW THAT I AM GOD."

The Death of God's King

BASED ON PSALMS 27; 46; 84; 2 SAMUEL 23

AFTER RULING ISRAEL FOR 40 YEARS, KING DAVID DIES. HE IS BURIED IN A TOMB UNDERNEATH JERUSALEM. ALL ISRAEL MOURNS THE DEATH OF THE SHEPHERD BOY WHO BUILT ISRAEL INTO A MIGHTY EMPIRE. NO MATTER THE CIRCUMSTANCES IN HIS LIFE, HE ALWAYS GAVE HONOR TO GOD ...

AS A KING:

WHEN ONE RULES OVER MEN IN RIGHTEOUSNESS, WHEN HE RULES IN THE FEAR OF GOD, HE IS LIKE THE DAWNING LIGHT AT SUNRISE ON A CLOUDLESS MORNING, LIKE THE BRIGHTNESS AFTER RAIN THAT BRINGS THE GRASS FROM THE EARTH.

AND AT HIS DEATH:

HOW BEAUTIFUL IS YOUR HEAVENLY KINGDOM, O LORD. BETTER IS ONE DAY IN YOUR COURTS THAN A THOUSAND DAYS SPENT ANYWHERE ELSE.

Solomon's Wisdom

BASED ON 1 KINGS 3

SOLOMON, THE FIRST OF DAVID'S SONS TO HONOR HIS FATHER AND THE LORD, IS NOW THE HOLY ANOINTED KING OF ISRAEL. HE TAKES THREE IMMEDIATE ACTIONS TO SOLIDIFY THE STATUS OF HIS KINGDOM. THESE THREE STEPS WILL MARK THE REST OF HIS RULE.

FIRST, TO CEMENT AN ALLIANCE WITH EGYPT, SOLOMON TAKES PHARAOH'S DAUGHTER AS A WIFE.

THEN, SINCE HIS FATHER, DAVID, HAD NOT BEEN ALLOWED TO BUILD A TEMPLE FOR GOD, SOLOMON MAKES PLANS FOR A TEMPLE THAT WILL BE A FITTING HOUSE FOR THE CREATOR OF THE UNIVERSE.

FINALLY, HE GOES TO THE ALTAR AT GIBEON TO MAKE SACRIFICES AND SEEK GOD'S BLESSING. THERE HE PRAYS TO GOD AT THE ALTAR ALL NIGHT LONG.

THAT NIGHT SOLOMON HAS A DREAM ...

WHAT WOULD YOU ASK OF ME, SON OF MY SERVANT DAVID?

DIVINE KING, I WOULD ONLY ASK FOR A WISE HEART TO HELP ME GOVERN YOUR PEOPLE AND TO DISTINGUISH BETWEEN RIGHT AND WRONG.

YOU COULD HAVE ASKED FOR RICHES, LONG LIFE, OR THE DEATHS OF YOUR ENEMIES. INSTEAD, YOU ASKED FOR WISDOM. SO I WILL GIVE YOU WHAT YOU ASK FOR. YOU WILL HAVE WISDOM LIKE NO MAN BEFORE YOU. BUT I WILL ALSO GIVE YOU WHAT YOU DID NOT ASK FOR. YOU WILL HAVE RICHES AND HONOR LIKE NO KING BEFORE YOU. AND IF YOU FOLLOW MY COMMANDS, I WILL GRANT YOU LONG LIFE.

WHEN THE PEOPLE OF ISRAEL HEARD OF SOLOMON'S WISE STRATAGEM TO FIND THE TRUE MOTHER, THEY WERE IN AWE BECAUSE THEY KNEW HE SPOKE WITH GOD'S WISDOM.

דוגלאש מאוס

TRUST IN THE LORD,
NOT YOUR OWN ABILITIES.
FOLLOW HIM, AND HE WILL
MAKE YOUR PATH STRAIGHT.

שרגיו קאריעללו

THE MORE YOU ARE
CORRECTED, THE MORE YOU
LEARN; ONLY FOOLISH PEOPLE
THINK THEY'RE PERFECT.

קבין מוללינס

A SOFT ANSWER TURNS AWAY WRATH,
BUT A HARSH WORD STIRS UP ANGER.

Solomon's Proverbs

BASED ON PROVERBS

*WITH HIS GOD-GIVEN
WISDOM, SOLOMON
WROTE MANY SIMPLE
SAYINGS TO TEACH
PEOPLE HOW TO LIVE.*

יפפרי באֹרנס

A GOOD ATTITUDE
IS GOOD MEDICINE,
BUT A BROKEN SPIRIT
DRIES UP YOUR BONES.

יבא הותה

A TRUE FRIEND IS
ONE WHO STICKS BY
YOU, ESPECIALLY WHEN
TIMES ARE HARD.

אנדרע לע בלֹאנק

A GOOD REPUTATION IS
BETTER THAN GREAT RICHES;
TO BE RESPECTED IS BETTER
THAN SILVER OR GOLD.

Solomon's Seasons

BASED ON ECCLESIASTES 3

THERE IS A TIME FOR EVERYTHING,
AND A SEASON FOR EVERY
ACTIVITY UNDER HEAVEN:

A TIME TO BE BORN
AND A TIME TO DIE,
A TIME TO PLANT
AND A TIME TO UPROOT,
A TIME TO KILL
AND A TIME TO HEAL,
A TIME TO TEAR DOWN
AND A TIME TO BUILD,
A TIME TO WEEP
AND A TIME TO LAUGH,
A TIME TO MOURN
AND A TIME TO DANCE,
A TIME TO SCATTER STONES
AND A TIME TO GATHER THEM,
A TIME TO EMBRACE
AND A TIME TO REFRAIN;
A TIME TO SEARCH
AND A TIME TO GIVE UP,
A TIME TO KEEP
AND A TIME TO THROW AWAY,
A TIME TO TEAR
AND A TIME TO MEND;
A TIME TO BE SILENT
AND A TIME TO SPEAK,
A TIME TO LOVE
AND A TIME TO HATE,
A TIME FOR WAR
AND A TIME FOR PEACE.

HE HAS MADE EVERYTHING BEAUTIFUL
IN ITS TIME ... EVERYTHING GOD DOES
WILL ENDURE FOREVER.

Solomon's Temple

BASED ON 1 KINGS 5–9; 2 CHRONICLES 2–8

THE PEOPLE ARE HAPPY. ISRAEL IS AT PEACE. SOLOMON HAS ESTABLISHED GOOD RELATIONSHIPS WITH MANY NEIGHBORING COUNTRIES. RULERS OF THE COUNTRIES DAVID HAD CONQUERED PAY TRIBUTE MONEY TO SOLOMON'S TREASURY. SO BEGINS THE GOLDEN AGE OF ISRAEL.

TO LAUNCH HIS FIRST GREAT BUILDING PROJECT, SOLOMON SENDS A MESSENGER TO HIS FATHER'S OLD FRIEND, KING HIRAM OF TYRE.

KING SOLOMON SENDS HIS GREETINGS AND ASKS IF YOU WILL SEND HIM YOUR RENOWNED CEDAR AND CYPRESS TREES FOR LUMBER SO THAT HE CAN BUILD A TEMPLE TO GOD IN JERUSALEM.

BLESSED BE THE LORD FOR GIVING MY FRIEND DAVID SUCH A WISE SON. TELL YOUR KING I WILL GIVE HIM WHAT HE ASKS FOR IN EXCHANGE FOR WHEAT AND OIL, WHICH OUR COUNTRY NEEDS.

THE TWO KINGS MAKE A DEAL. SOON MEN BY THE THOUSANDS ARE WORKING IN THE FORESTS OF LEBANON, CUTTING CEDAR TREES FOR SOLOMON'S TEMPLE.

NEAR JERUSALEM, THOUSANDS OF MEN TOIL IN GREAT QUARRIES, CHISELING OUT THE HUGE STONE BLOCKS NEEDED FOR THE FOUNDATION AND WALLS OF GOD'S TEMPLE. THE FINEST MASONS WORK ON EACH PIECE, SO THAT EVERY STONE BLOCK WILL FIT TOGETHER PERFECTLY.

THE CEDARS OF LEBANON, THE FINEST WOOD KNOWN TO MAN, ARE SHIPPED FROM TYRE. SOME LOGS ARE CARVED INTO HUGE PILLARS, WHILE OTHERS ARE SET INTO PLACE FOR THE ROOF.

NEXT, BRONZE IS USED FOR THE METALWORK.

MEANWHILE, THE FINEST GOLD CRAFTSMEN IN THE LAND ARE WORKING ON ALL THE FURNITURE AND NECESSITIES FOR THE TEMPLE. SOLOMON'S WISH IS TO HAVE ALL OF GOD'S TEMPLE GLEAM WITH GOLD.

AFTER SEVEN LONG YEARS OF HARD WORK, THE MAGNIFICENT TEMPLE OF GOD IS COMPLETED. MEN, WOMEN, AND CHILDREN FROM ALL CORNERS OF ISRAEL CROWD INTO JERUSALEM TO WATCH THE PRIESTS CARRY THE SACRED ARK INTO THE TEMPLE. INSIDE, IN THE HOLY OF HOLIES—A DARK, WINDOWLESS, HEAVILY CURTAINED ROOM—THE ARK IS CAREFULLY PLACED BENEATH THE PROTECTING WINGS OF TWO 15-FOOT CHERUBIM.

THEN, BEFORE ALL THE PEOPLE IN ISRAEL, SOLOMON KNEELS IN PRAYER ...

LORD, THERE IS NO GOD LIKE YOU! FORGIVE AND GUIDE YOUR PEOPLE THE WAY YOU GUIDED MOSES, WHO BROUGHT US OUT OF SLAVERY IN EGYPT.

BUT SOLOMON'S BUILDING PROGRAM DOES NOT END WITH THE TEMPLE. SOON A LARGE PALACE IS UNDER CONSTRUCTION.

I MEAN TO MAKE JERUSALEM THE MOST BEAUTIFUL CITY IN THE WORLD.

SOLOMON, IT WILL BE BEAUTIFUL— CEDAR AND BRONZE AND GOLD!

AND RICHES KEEP POURING IN FROM MANY COUNTRIES. SHIPS FROM ARABIA AND AFRICA BRING RARE AND PRECIOUS GIFTS.

PEACOCKS AND IVORY! WHAT ARE THEY GOOD FOR?

WHEN YOU'RE AS RICH AS SOLOMON, THINGS DON'T HAVE TO BE USEFUL.

BUT NOT EVERYONE IN ISRAEL IS RICH. OUTSIDE THE CITY OF JERUSALEM, PEOPLE ARE BEGINNING TO COMPLAIN ...

THERE! THAT'S MY SHARE OF GRAIN FOR KING SOLOMON'S HORSES.

HORSES! BETWEEN FEEDING THE KING'S FOREIGN WIVES, HIS SERVANTS, AND HIS HORSES, THERE'S NOT MUCH LEFT FOR POOR PEOPLE LIKE US!

BUT SOLOMON HAS EVEN MORE EXPANSION IN MIND ...

OUR CARAVANS TRAVEL NORTH, SOUTH, EAST, AND WEST. BUT WE HAVE MISSED ONE VITAL TRADE ROUTE.

WHERE?

THE SEA! I HAVE DECIDED TO BUILD MERCHANT SHIPS TO SAIL BEYOND THE RED SEA.

THE FLEET IS BUILT. ITS SHIPS BRING TREASURES INTO JERUSALEM AND CARRY AWAY WITH THEM STORIES OF THE CITY'S BEAUTY AND THE RULER'S WISDOM. THE STORIES REACH FAR AND WIDE—EVEN TO DISTANT LANDS IN THE ARABIAN PENINSULA.

Foreign Fame

SOLOMON'S FAME SPREADS FAR AND WIDE, EVEN TO THE QUEEN OF SHEBA ...

SOLOMON! SOLOMON! ALL I HEAR ARE TALES OF HIS WEALTH AND WISDOM. I'M GOING TO JERUSALEM TO FIND OUT FOR MYSELF WHETHER THE STORIES ARE TRUE.

THE QUEEN SETS OUT IN A HUGE CARAVAN. SHE HAS MANY CAMELS LOADED WITH WEALTH—PRECIOUS SPICES, PILES OF GOLD AND MANY PRECIOUS STONES. FINALLY HER PROCESSION CATCHES SIGHT OF JERUSALEM.

WHAT A BEAUTIFUL CITY! IT SITS ON THE HILL LIKE A GLISTENING CROWN.

SOLOMON GIVES THE QUEEN A ROYAL WELCOME. SHE IS AWESTRUCK BY THE LUXURY OF THE KING'S PALACE. BUT SHE QUICKLY TRIES TO TEST HIS WISDOM WITH A RIDDLE.

WHAT IS THE MOST CERTAIN THING IN THE WORLD, AND THE MOST UNCERTAIN?

THE MOST CERTAIN THING IN THIS WORLD IS DEATH; BUT THE MOST UNCERTAIN IS OUR SHARE IN THE WORLD TO COME.

IMPRESSED WITH HIS ANSWER, THE QUEEN OF SHEBA CONTINUES TO ASK SOLOMON THE HARDEST RIDDLES IN HER LAND. HE SUCCESSFULLY ANSWERS ALL OF HER PUZZLES, THEN TAKES HER FOR A TOUR OF THE CITY. SOLOMON SHOWS HER THE BEAUTIFUL TEMPLE OF GOD AND THE GIANT MARBLE PALACES, AND HE DISPLAYS HIS THOUSANDS OF FINE HORSES AND CHARIOTS.

JERUSALEM HAS OUTGROWN ITS OLD WALLS OF DEFENSE. WE'RE BUILDING NEW ONES.

THAT FOREMAN SEEMS TO KNOW WHAT HE IS DOING.

YOU'RE VERY OBSERVANT! THAT IS JEROBOAM, MY CHIEF LABOR FOREMAN.

WHEN HER CURIOSITY IS SATISFIED, THE QUEEN OF SHEBA PRESENTS SOLOMON WITH GIFTS OF GOLD, RARE SPICES, AND PRECIOUS STONES. THEN SHE LEAVES FOR HOME, IMPRESSED WITH HIS WISDOM AND WEALTH. BUT WHEREAS SOLOMON HAD ONCE USED HIS WISDOM TO HELP GOD'S PEOPLE, NOW HE USES IT TO IMPRESS FOREIGN LEADERS AND GAIN EVEN MORE HONOR AND FAME.

SOLOMON CONTINUES TO BUILD—BUT NOW THE PEOPLE ARE WORRIED AND SHOCKED BY WHAT THEY SEE.

ANOTHER TEMPLE TO THE IDOL OF ONE OF THE KING'S FOREIGN WIVES. AND HE USES OUR TAXES TO BUILD IT!

THOSE HEATHEN TEMPLES PROVE THAT SOLOMON IS NO LONGER ASKING GOD FOR GUIDANCE. THERE'S TROUBLE AHEAD FOR ISRAEL.

AHIJAH TEARS THE ROBE INTO 12 STRIPS.

HERE, TAKE THESE TEN PIECES. THEY REPRESENT THE TEN TRIBES OF ISRAEL THAT YOU'LL RULE OVER WHEN SOLOMON DIES. THE OTHER TWO TRIBES WILL BE GIVEN TO SOLOMON'S SON SO THAT GOD'S PROMISE TO DAVID WILL STILL BE FULFILLED.

SOLOMON FLIES INTO A RAGE WHEN HE HEARS ABOUT AHIJAH'S PROPHECY.

I MADE JEROBOAM A LEADER—AND NOW HE IS USING HIS POSITION TO TURN PEOPLE AGAINST ME. FIND HIM AND KILL HIM!

BUT FRIENDS WARN JEROBOAM, AND HE ESCAPES INTO EGYPT.

I'LL STAY HERE UNTIL SOLOMON DIES. THEN WE'LL SEE IF AHIJAH SPOKE THE TRUTH ABOUT MY RULING THE NORTHERN TRIBES OF ISRAEL.

REPORTS OF YOUR PEOPLE'S COMPLAINTS HAVE BEEN REACHING US FOR SOME TIME.

BUT SOLOMON CONTINUES TO LIVE IN LUXURY—AND SO FAR REMOVED FROM HIS PEOPLE THAT THEIR COMPLAINTS DO NOT REACH HIM. HE EVEN IGNORES AHIJAH'S PROPHECY AND GOD'S WARNING THAT THE KINGDOM WILL BE DIVIDED BECAUSE HE WORSHIPS FALSE GODS.

AT LAST, SOLOMON EVEN JOINS HIS FOREIGN WIVES IN THEIR WORSHIP OF HEATHEN IDOLS.

PLEASE PRAY TO MY GOD WITH ME, SOLOMON. IT WOULD PLEASE ME SO MUCH!

IT CAN'T HURT ANYTHING. I STILL PRAY EVERY DAY TO THE GOD OF ISRAEL.

WHERE THE KING GOES, THE PEOPLE FOLLOW. MANY OF THE ISRAELITES START WORSHIPPING IDOLS. NO COUNTRY THAT TURNS AWAY FROM GOD CAN REMAIN STRONG AND FREE. ISRAEL IS DOOMED!

EVENTUALLY SOLOMON DIES. WITH GOD'S HELP, HE HAD BUILT ISRAEL INTO A STRONG NATION. BUT IN HIS GREED FOR MORE WEALTH AND POWER, HE TURNED AWAY FROM GOD—AND DAVID'S ONCE-MIGHTY KINGDOM WILL NOW CRUMBLE ...

A Kingdom Torn in Two

BASED ON 1 KINGS 12:1-27

NOW THAT KING SOLOMON HAS DIED, HIS SON REHOBOAM HAS GONE TO SHECHEM TO BE CROWNED KING OF ALL ISRAEL. THE NORTHERN TRIBES OF ISRAEL HAVE BROUGHT THEIR LEADER, JEROBOAM, BACK FROM HIS EXILE IN EGYPT TO PLEAD THEIR CASE BEFORE THE NEW KING.

YOUR FATHER FORCED US TO PAY HEAVY TAXES AND WORK HARD ON HIS BUILDING PROJECTS. WE CANNOT CONTINUE TO CARRY SUCH BURDENS! LIGHTEN OUR LOAD AND WE WILL SERVE YOU FAITHFULLY; BUT ...

COME BACK IN THREE DAYS AND I WILL GIVE YOU MY ANSWER.

REHOBOAM CONSULTS HIS ADVISERS. THE OLDER MEN TELL HIM TO HEED THE CRIES OF HIS PEOPLE; BUT HIS YOUNG FRIENDS ...

IF YOU GIVE IN TO THEIR DEMANDS, THEY WILL THINK YOU ARE WEAK. YOU NEED TO PROVE TO THEM THAT YOU'LL BE EVEN TOUGHER THAN YOUR FATHER.

THREE DAYS LATER, THE PEOPLE RETURN FOR THE KING'S ANSWER. BUT THEY ARE DISAPPOINTED.

MY FATHER MADE YOUR YOKE HEAVY? I'LL MAKE IT HEAVIER! MY FATHER WHIPPED YOU? I'LL WHIP YOU WITH SCORPIONS!

REHOBOAM'S ARROGANT WORDS SPARK THE REBELLION GOD PROMISED. JUST AS THE PROPHET AHIJAH HAD SAID, TEN TRIBES OF ISRAEL BREAK FROM THE KINGDOM AND MAKE JEROBOAM THEIR KING. IN FEAR FOR HIS LIFE, REHOBOAM RACES BACK TO JERUSALEM AND THE TRIBE OF JUDAH THAT REMAINS LOYAL TO HIM.

THIS IS A MESSAGE FROM GOD TO THE KING OF JUDAH AND ALL HIS PEOPLE.

WHY DIDN'T HE REFER TO ME AS THE KING OF ISRAEL?

IT IS GOD'S WILL THAT THE COUNTRY BE DIVIDED AT THIS TIME. YOU MEN OF JUDAH SHOULD NOT FIGHT YOUR BROTHERS OF ISRAEL. ALL OF YOU GO BACK TO YOUR OWN HOMES.

WHO IS THIS MAN TRYING TO GIVE US ORDERS?

HE'S SHEMAIAH, A PROPHET OF GOD. I, FOR ONE, WILL NOT DISOBEY ORDERS FROM GOD.

THE ARMY BREAKS UP AND GOES HOME. THE 12 TRIBES—WHICH HAD BEEN UNITED UNDER THE KINGSHIPS OF SAUL, DAVID, AND SOLOMON—ARE NOW SPLIT BETWEEN THE NORTHERN TRIBES OF ISRAEL AND THE SOUTHERN TRIBE OF JUDAH.

AS A FINAL EMBARRASSMENT TO REHOBOAM, THE EGYPTIAN PHARAOH SHISHAK (JEROBOAM'S ALLY) RAIDS SOLOMON'S BEAUTIFUL TEMPLE AND STEALS ALL THE FINE GOLD AND RICHES. IN SHAME, REHOBOAM REPLACES THE FIXTURES WITH BRONZE.

A Bad Start for Israel
BASED ON 1 KINGS 12:25–14:20

JEROBOAM HAS BEEN MADE KING OVER THE NORTHERN TRIBES KNOWN AS ISRAEL, AND KING REHOBOAM RULES THE SOUTHERN KINGDOM OF JUDAH. UNFORTUNATELY FOR JEROBOAM, THE HOLY TEMPLE OF HIS PEOPLE IS NOT IN ISRAEL—IT'S IN JUDAH.

KING JEROBOAM, DO YOU KNOW THAT ALL THE PEOPLE STILL GO TO JERUSALEM TO WORSHIP IN THE TEMPLE?

I KNOW! AS LONG AS THEY STILL GO TO JUDAH TO WORSHIP, THEY WILL STILL HAVE SOME ALLEGIANCE TO THE OTHER KINGDOM. I DON'T WANT MY SUBJECTS TO HAVE SPLIT LOYALTIES.

THEY ONLY GO TO JERUSALEM BECAUSE THERE IS NO TEMPLE HERE.

THAT GIVES ME AN IDEA ...

TO KEEP THE PEOPLE FROM WORSHIPPING IN JUDAH, JEROBOAM MAKES TWO GOLDEN CALVES.

WHEN OUR PEOPLE ESCAPED FROM EGYPT YEARS AGO, THEY WORSHIPPED THIS GOD. WORSHIP IT NOW AND YOU WON'T HAVE TO MAKE THE LONG, HARD TRIP TO JERUSALEM.

AFTER BEING HEALED, JEROBOAM RULES FOR MANY YEARS, UNEVENTFULLY. HE HOPES THAT MAYBE GOD'S ANGER HAS ABATED. BUT THEN ONE DAY ...

OUR SON IS VERY ILL, JEROBOAM. I'M WORRIED.

SO AM I. IF ONLY I KNEW ... BUT NONE OF GOD'S PROPHETS WILL SPEAK TO ME ANYMORE.

AHIJAH THE PROPHET! HE TOLD ME I WOULD BE KING. HE KNOWS WHAT WILL HAPPEN. DISGUISE YOURSELF SO THAT HE WON'T RECOGNIZE YOU AND SEE IF YOU CAN GET HIM TO PROPHESY ABOUT OUR SON.

IMMEDIATELY THE QUEEN DISGUISES HERSELF AND SETS OUT FOR AHIJAH'S HOUSE. BUT AS SHE STEPS THROUGH THE DOOR ...

I AM BLIND, BUT GOD HAS TOLD ME WHO YOU ARE AND WHY YOU'VE COME. GOD GAVE HIS FAVOR TO YOUR HUSBAND AND MADE HIM KING. JEROBOAM USED THAT POWER TO DO EVIL—AND EVIL WILL COME TO HIM.

HIS CHILD WILL DIE, AND ONE DAY THE PEOPLE OF ISRAEL WILL BE CONQUERED AND SCATTERED IN OTHER LANDS BECAUSE THEY HAVE WORSHIPPED IDOLS.

THE FIRST PART OF AHIJAH'S PROPHECY COMES TRUE RIGHT AWAY. WHEN THE QUEEN GETS HOME, SHE FINDS HER SON DEAD! BUT JEROBOAM IS NOT WISE ENOUGH TO HEED THIS WARNING. HE CONTINUES TO LEAD HIS PEOPLE IN IDOL WORSHIP, AND ISRAEL NEVER RETURNS TO A PURE WORSHIP OF THE LORD. AS A RESULT, THE KINGS OF ISRAEL ARE PLAGUED BY WAR, BLOODSHED, AND ASSASSINATION. FOR 40 YEARS, EACH KING IS MORE EVIL THAN THE ONE BEFORE HIM. THEN KING AHAB COMES TO THE THRONE, AND HE IS EVEN WORSE ...

BASED ON 1 KINGS 16:29—17:6

ABOUT 60 YEARS AFTER ISRAEL SPLIT INTO TWO KINGDOMS, AHAB COMES TO THE THRONE. EVENTUALLY, AHAB PROVES HIMSELF TO BE THE MOST EVIL IN A LONG LINE OF BAD KINGS. BUT HIS FIRST—AND MOST WICKED—ACT BEGINS WHEN HE MARRIES JEZEBEL, A FOREIGN PRINCESS WHO WORSHIPS A FOREIGN GOD.

IF I AM TO BE QUEEN OF ALL ISRAEL, THEN ALL OF ISRAEL MUST WORSHIP MY GOD, BAAL.

PLEASE, MY DEAR, BUILD ME A TEMPLE FOR BAAL.

ANYTHING YOU ASK FOR, MY QUEEN.

OH, GOOD. BECAUSE I'VE ALREADY INVITED SEVERAL HUNDRED PRIESTS FROM MY HOME COUNTRY TO SETTLE HERE.

MORE SACRIFICES TO BAAL, JEZEBEL'S GOD OF RAIN. HMMPH!

SHE DOESN'T RESPECT THE ONE TRUE GOD, THAT WICKED QUEEN.

WATCH YOUR TONGUE! OR YOU'LL LOSE IT. QUEEN JEZEBEL WON'T STAND FOR TALK LIKE THAT.

BUT ELIJAH DISAPPEARS BEFORE ANYONE CAN LAY HANDS ON HIM. OUTSIDE THE PALACE, THE WORD OF THE LORD COMES TO ELIJAH.

FOLLOWING THE LORD'S INSTRUCTIONS, ELIJAH GOES TO A TINY CREEK EAST OF THE JORDAN RIVER.

IT IS TIME TO HIDE.

THERE, RAVENS BRING HIM BREAD AND MEAT IN THE MORNING AND EVENING.

THE LORD HAS A SENSE OF HUMOR. HE COULD HAVE USED ANY KIND OF MIRACLE TO FEED ME, YET HE'S USING UNCLEAN BIRDS TO BRING ME FOOD.

I WILL WAIT HERE UNTIL GOD TELLS ME MY NEXT STEP. I MUST SAY, I'D RATHER PASS THE TIME WITH UNCLEAN ANIMALS THAN WITH BAAL-WORSHIPPING PEOPLE.

MEANWHILE, JEZEBEL IS FURIOUS.

OBADIAH, SINCE YOU ARE OUR CHIEF STEWARD, I ORDER YOU TO HUNT DOWN ANYONE WHO STILL WORSHIPS YAHWEH AND KILL THEM. ESPECIALLY THE PROPHETS. AND ESPECIALLY THIS ELIJAH.

BUT OBADIAH HIMSELF IS STILL FAITHFUL TO THE LORD. INSTEAD OF KILLING THE LORD'S PROPHETS, HE SECRETLY HIDES THEM IN CAVES.

AS THE MONTHS GO BY WITH NO RAIN, ISRAEL'S ONCE-GREEN LAND SLOWLY BUT STEADILY BECOMES A DESERT. THE STREAMS DRY UP AND THE CROPS DIE. A FAMINE OVERCOMES THE LAND.

THIS IS ALL ELIJAH'S FAULT!

Elijah's Flour Power

THE DROUGHT HAS AFFECTED ELIJAH'S CREEK AS WELL. AFTER A YEAR WITH NO RAIN, HIS WATER SOURCE DRIES UP.

I WILL TRUST IN THE LORD TO TELL ME WHAT TO DO NEXT. UNLESS YOU RAVENS CAN LEARN HOW TO CARRY WATER.

GO HIDE IN JEZEBEL'S HOMELAND. I HAVE CHOSEN A WIDOW WHO WILL PROVIDE FOR YOU.

GOD WANTS ME TO LEAVE ISRAEL AND LIVE AMONG BAAL WORSHIPPERS? AND HOW WILL A POOR WIDOW HAVE ANY FOOD DURING A FAMINE? WELL, I STAND BEFORE YOU, LORD. I TRUST AND OBEY.

WHEN ELIJAH ENTERS THE TOWN OF ZAREPHATH, HE SEES AN OLD WOMAN GATHERING STICKS.

MOTHER, COULD YOU PLEASE GIVE ME A DROP OF WATER, A CRUMB OF BREAD?

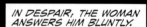

IN DESPAIR, THE WOMAN ANSWERS HIM BLUNTLY.

YOU ARE AN ISRAELITE. YOUR LORD MAY GRANT YOU LONG LIFE. BUT I AM NOT SO LUCKY. I HAVE BUT A HANDFUL OF FLOUR LEFT AND NO MONEY TO BUY MORE FOOD FOR ME AND MY SON. I AM GATHERING THESE STICKS TO COOK ONE LAST MEAL BEFORE WE DIE OF STARVATION.

AT LEAST WE WILL DIE TOGETHER.

MY LORD WILL PROVIDE A MIRACLE FOR US. GO BAKE YOUR BREAD ... AND HAVE HOPE.

TRUE TO ELIJAH'S WORD, EVERY TIME THE WIDOW COOKS, HER JAR OF FLOUR ALWAYS HAS A LITTLE EXTRA LEFT OVER. AND HER JAR OF OIL NEVER RUNS DRY. FOR TWO YEARS, THOSE TWO TINY JARS PROVIDE FOOD FOR HERSELF, HER SON, AND ELIJAH.

BUT TRAGEDY SEEMS NEVER FAR FROM HER HOUSEHOLD.

WHY DID YOU COME HERE? YOUR GOD NEVER NOTICED ME OR MY SINFUL WAYS BEFORE YOU CAME. NOW HE'S PUNISHED ME BY KILLING MY ONE AND ONLY SON.

HAVE PEACE, MOTHER. MY GOD DOES NOT WORK THAT WAY.

RIGHT? WHY WOULD YOU SAVE US JUST TO KILL HER SON?

THE LORD RESPONDS TO ELIJAH'S QUESTION WITH POWER AND BRINGS THE BOY BACK TO LIFE.

SEE, YOUR SON IS NOT DEAD, BUT ALIVE.

NOW I BELIEVE IN YOUR GOD AND TRUST THAT YOU SPEAK HIS TRUTH.

THROUGH THIS MIRACLE, GOD SHOWS THAT HE CARES FOR ALL PEOPLE, NOT JUST THE ISRAELITES.

Battle of the Gods

BASED ON 1 KINGS 18

ELIJAH HAS BEEN HIDING IN SIDON FROM THE ATTACKS OF QUEEN JEZEBEL. AFTER THREE YEARS OF DROUGHT, GOD TELLS ELIJAH TO RETURN TO ISRAEL SO THAT THE RAINS MAY COME AGAIN.

IT IS TIME TO BE SEEN.

THE FIRST PERSON HE MEETS ON THE ROAD IS OBADIAH, WHO IS LOYAL TO THE LORD EVEN THOUGH HE'S KING AHAB'S CHIEF COUNSELOR.

AFTER ALL THESE YEARS, ELIJAH, IS IT REALLY YOU?

TELL KING AHAB I AM HERE.

ARE YOU KIDDING? HE'LL KILL YOU. AND THEN HE'LL KILL ME.

WHICH LORD DO YOU SERVE? AHAB OR YAHWEH?

I'VE SPENT THREE YEARS PROTECTING THE LORD'S PROPHETS FROM AHAB AND JEZEBEL. I AM THE LORD'S SERVANT.

THEN TRUST IN ME. TRUST IN THE LORD. TELL AHAB WHERE I AM.

WHEN OBADIAH REPORTS BACK TO AHAB, THE KING WASTES NO TIME IN GALLOPING OFF TO CONFRONT ELIJAH.

TROUBLEMAKER!

YOU ARE THE ONE WHO HAS MADE THE TROUBLE, O KING! YOU BROKE GOD'S COMMANDMENTS AND WORSHIPPED BAAL. YOU WANT ME TO END THE DROUGHT? SEND FOR ALL THE PROPHETS OF BAAL, GATHER THE PEOPLE OF ISRAEL, AND THEN MEET ME ON MOUNT CARMEL.

AHAB IS HAPPY WITH THIS PROPOSITION, SINCE MOUNT CARMEL IS CONSIDERED THE SACRED DWELLING OF BAAL. HE BRINGS ALL THE PROPHETS OF BAAL—450 OF THEM—TO MEET ELIJAH, AND THOUSANDS OF ISRAELITES FOLLOW THEM TO SEE WHAT WILL HAPPEN. THE MORNING DAWNS ON A GREAT CROWD GATHERED ON THE MOUNTAIN BY THE SEA.

WE SHALL HAVE A CONTEST. BRING TWO BULLS. GIVE ONE TO BAAL'S PROPHETS AND ONE TO ME. LET THEM MAKE AN OFFERING AND CALL ON THE NAME OF THEIR GOD. I WILL CALL ON THE NAME OF THE LORD. THE GOD WHO ANSWERS—WITH FIRE—IS THE REAL GOD.

OH! AND I'LL LET THEM GO FIRST.

PEOPLE OF ISRAEL! HOW LONG WILL YOU LIMP BACK AND FORTH BETWEEN THE LORD AND BAAL? IF BAAL IS GOD, WORSHIP HIM. IF THE LORD IS GOD, WORSHIP HIM—AND HIM ONLY. TODAY, YOU MUST CHOOSE!

THE CROWD REACTS WITH AWE AT THIS TEST, KNOWING THAT IF ELIJAH LOSES, AHAB WILL CONDEMN HIM TO DEATH.

THE PROPHETS OF BAAL ARE FORCED TO ACCEPT THE CHALLENGE. WITH GREAT CEREMONY, THEY PREPARE THE ALTAR AND SACRIFICE AND BEGIN TO CHANT AND CALL UPON THEIR GOD.

THE PROPHETS CHANT PRAYERS TO BAAL FROM MORNING UNTIL NOON. BUT THERE IS NO VOICE; THERE IS NO ONE TO ANSWER.

CALL A LITTLE LOUDER! PERHAPS BAAL IS DEEP IN THOUGHT AND CAN'T HEAR YOU. OR MAYBE HE'S IN THE BATHROOM. OR SLEEPING!

IN RESPONSE, THE PROPHETS CHANT THEMSELVES INTO A FRENZY! FOR THREE MORE HOURS THEY DANCE AROUND THE ALTAR FRANTICALLY, EVEN CUTTING THEMSELVES, HOPING TO GET A REACTION FROM THEIR GOD. BUT THERE IS NO VOICE; THERE IS NO ONE TO ANSWER. THERE IS NO GOD PAYING ATTENTION TO THEM.

FINALLY, AFTER A FULL DAY OF TRYING, THE EXHAUSTED PROPHETS OF BAAL GIVE UP.

INSTANTLY, LIGHTNING STRIKES OUT OF THE CLOUDLESS SKY AND BURNS UP NOT ONLY THE SACRIFICE, BUT THE STONES OF THE ALTAR AND EVERY DROP OF WATER IN THE TRENCH.

KRA-KOOM

THE LORD IS GOD!!

WHEN THE PEOPLE SEE GOD'S POWER, THEY TURN ANGRILY AGAINST THE FRIGHTENED PROPHETS OF BAAL.

THE LORD—HE IS GOD!

THE PROPHETS OF BAAL ARE FALSE!

THEY KILLED THE PROPHETS OF GOD. THEY SHOULD BE PUT TO DEATH!

LOOK, JUST AS GOD HAS PROMISED, A CLOUD TO BRING THE RAIN!

THAT'S IT?

SUDDENLY THE TINY CLOUD GIVES WAY TO A HUGE DOWNPOUR! WITHIN MOMENTS, EVERYONE IS DRENCHED. KING AHAB FALLS TO THE GROUND IN SHOCK.

GET UP, KING AHAB. THE LORD HAS SHOWN HIMSELF AGAIN IN HIS LAND. THIS IS A RAIN OF REPENTANCE, TO RENEW AND PURIFY GOD'S LAND AND HIS PEOPLE.

NOW YOU HAD BETTER GET IN YOUR CHARIOT AND HEAD BACK TO JEZEBEL, BEFORE THE PARCHED GROUND BECOMES TOO MUDDY FOR YOUR WHEELS.

AS AHAB SPURS ON HIS HORSES, GOD GIVES ELIJAH THE STRENGTH TO OUTRUN EVEN THE KING'S CHARIOT. THIS LETS ELIJAH GET BACK TO TOWN FIRST, SO HE CAN GIVE CREDIT FOR THE RAINS TO THE LORD BEFORE AHAB HAS THE CHANCE TO SPREAD FALSE RUMORS ABOUT THE CONTEST.

The Sound of Silence

BASED ON 1 KINGS 19:1-18

ELIJAH BRINGS NEWS OF THE LORD'S OVERWHELMING VICTORY AT MOUNT CARMEL, AND THE END OF THE THREE-YEAR DROUGHT. IN THE HOMES OF ISRAEL, THERE IS JOY, THANKSGIVING, AND REPENTANCE.

RAIN AT LAST! PRAISE THE LORD!

YES, IT WAS THE LORD WHO ANSWERED WITH FIRE. WE SHOULD NEVER HAVE WORSHIPPED BAAL.

BUT IN THE PALACE, QUEEN JEZEBEL IS FURIOUS ...

WHEN THE PEOPLE SAW THE FIRE FROM GOD, THEY TURNED ON THE PROPHETS OF BAAL AND KILLED THEM. ELIJAH—

MY PROPHETS ARE DEAD? SO HELP ME, GODS, IF BY THIS TIME TOMORROW ELIJAH IS NOT THE SAME!

FOR YEARS, ELIJAH HAS TRUSTED THE LORD IN EVERY CIRCUMSTANCE. BUT WHEN HE HEARS OF JEZEBEL'S DEATH THREAT, FEAR AND DESPAIR OVERTAKE HIM.

I MUST FLEE FAR, FAR AWAY, INTO JUDAH. THE DESERT! EVEN JEZEBEL WON'T FIND ME THERE.

ELIJAH JOURNEYS SOUTH FOR WEEKS, CROSSING ALL OF ISRAEL AND JUDAH. THEN HE CONTINUES INTO THE WILDERNESS. BUT AFTER A DAY'S TRAVEL ...

I'VE HAD ENOUGH! LORD, JUST TAKE MY LIFE. I THOUGHT AHAB AND JEZEBEL AND ALL OF ISRAEL WOULD REPENT AND TURN BACK TO YOU WHEN THEY SAW MY MIRACLES, BUT THEY PERSIST IN THEIR WICKEDNESS. I AM JUST A MAN. MY EFFORTS ARE WASTED. LET ME DIE.

THEN, HUNGRY AND TIRED, ELIJAH FALLS ASLEEP. WHILE HE'S SLEEPING, A MESSENGER OF THE LORD APPEARS WITH BREAD AND WATER.

WAKE UP, ELIJAH, AND EAT.

WITHOUT QUESTIONING THIS LATEST MIRACLE, ELIJAH EATS AND FALLS BACK ASLEEP. WHEN HE WAKES AGAIN, THE MESSENGER IS STILL THERE, WITH MORE FOOD.

GOD IS NOT WILLING TO LET ELIJAH GIVE UP IN THE DESERT.

YOUR JOURNEY IS NOT YET DONE. EAT, OR ELSE THE WAY WILL BE TOO HARD FOR YOU.

BUT ELIJAH DOESN'T WANT TO BE A PROPHET ANYMORE. HE GOES TO CONFRONT GOD AT SINAI, THE SAME MOUNTAIN WHERE MOSES TALKED TO GOD. IT TAKES ELIJAH 40 DAYS TO GET THERE. AT THE MOUNTAIN, HE CLIMBS THE SLOPE TO A CAVE.

I WILL WAIT HERE UNTIL GOD SEES FIT TO ANSWER ME.

WHAT ARE YOU DOING HERE, ELIJAH?

I HAVE ZEALOUSLY DEFENDED YOU, LORD. BUT IT HASN'T MADE ANY DIFFERENCE.

COME SEE ME AT THE MOUTH OF THE CAVE.

THEN AN EARTHQUAKE SHAKES APART THE ROCKS!

THEN LIGHTNING SPLITS THE SKY INTO A THOUSAND PIECES!

A POWERFUL WIND TEARS APART THE MOUNTAINSIDE!

BUT GOD IS NOT IN THE EARTHQUAKE.

BUT GOD IS NOT IN THE LIGHTNING.

BUT GOD IS NOT IN THE WIND.

AND AFTER THE STORM SUBSIDES COMES THE SOUND OF SHEER SILENCE.

Passing the Mantle
BASED ON 1 KINGS 19:19–21

GOD HAS ENCOURAGED ELIJAH ON THE TOP OF MOUNT CARMEL. BUT ELIJAH NEEDS A SUCCESSOR. A YOUNG EARNEST MAN PLOWS HIS PARENTS' FIELDS.

WHEW! NOW THAT THE RAINS HAVE COME AGAIN, THE FIELDS ARE FERTILE AGAIN AND RIPE FOR PLOWING. A GOOD THING, TOO. OUR STORES WERE ABOUT USED UP. BUT THE LORD TAKES CARE OF HIS FAITHFUL.

ELIJAH! THE LORD'S PROPHET!

WITHOUT A WORD, ELIJAH TAKES OFF HIS MANTLE AND PLACES IT ON ELISHA'S SWEATY SHOULDERS.

DOES THIS MEAN ...?

THANK YOU FOR CALLING ME, ELIJAH! LET ME JUST SAY GOOD-BYE TO MY PARENTS.

WELL, DO WHAT YOU MUST. BUT GOD'S WORK WON'T WAIT VERY LONG.

The Grapes of Envy

BASED ON 1 KINGS 21

WHILE ELIJAH AND ELISHA DO GOD'S WORK IN THE COUNTRYSIDE, KING AHAB MAKES A SURPRISE VISIT TO ONE OF HIS SUBJECTS.

NABOTH, I WANT TO BUY THIS VINEYARD. OR, IF YOU LIKE, I'LL GIVE YOU ANOTHER ONE IN EXCHANGE FOR IT.

I'M SORRY, O KING, BUT OUR FAMILY HAS OWNED THIS VINEYARD FOR MANY YEARS. IT WOULD NOT BE RIGHT TO SELL IT TO SOMEONE OUTSIDE THE FAMILY.

YOU MAY ALSO FIND THAT IT IS NOT RIGHT TO DISPLEASE YOUR KING!

LIKE A SPOILED CHILD WHO CAN'T HAVE HIS OWN WAY, AHAB RETURNS TO THE PALACE.

WHAT'S THE MATTER? ARE YOU ILL?

NO. I WANT NABOTH'S VINEYARD, BUT HE WON'T SELL IT TO ME.

WHAT DO YOU MEAN? WHO'S THE KING HERE? DON'T WORRY, I WILL GIVE YOU THE VINEYARD.

QUICKLY, JEZEBEL WRITES A LETTER TO THE CITY LEADERS, BUT SHE SIGNS THE KING'S NAME TO IT.

FIND TWO SCOUNDRELS AND HAVE THEM ACCUSE NABOTH OF BLASPHEMING AGAINST GOD. THEN STONE NABOTH TO DEATH.

WHEN THE ELDERS RECEIVE THE LETTER ...

BUT NABOTH IS A GOOD MAN! THIS LETTER MAY SAY AHAB, BUT IT'S THE WORK OF JEZEBEL.

DO WE DARE DISOBEY THESE ORDERS IF THEY CAME FROM THE QUEEN?

NOT IF WE VALUE OUR LIVES. NO ONE CAN SAVE NABOTH IF JEZEBEL IS OUT TO GET HIM.

THE ELDERS CARRY OUT JEZEBEL'S INSTRUCTIONS EXACTLY AS SHE HAS COMMANDED. AT THEIR HANDS AND HER ORDERS, AN HONORABLE MAN IS WRONGLY EXECUTED. NABOTH IS STONED TO DEATH IN THE STREETS, AND STRAY DOGS LICK HIS BLOOD OFF THE STONES.

WHEN JEZEBEL GETS THE REPORT OF NABOTH'S DEATH, SHE HURRIES TO THE KING.

IT'S YOUR LUCKY DAY! NABOTH IS DEAD. I'M GIVING YOU HIS VINEYARD.

GOOD! I'LL TAKE IT AT ONCE.

I LOVE GETTING WHAT I WANT. AND I DIDN'T EVEN HAVE TO PAY FOR IT.

BUT AS KING AHAB IS GLOATING OVER HIS NEW VINEYARD, ELIJAH, THE PROPHET OF GOD, SUDDENLY APPEARS ...

IF IT ISN'T MY OLD ENEMY!

YES, AND I HAVE A MESSAGE FROM GOD. DID YOU KILL TO GET YOUR WILL? THEN YOU WILL SUFFER AS NABOTH SUFFERED—AND SO WILL YOUR WIFE, JEZEBEL!

UNWILLINGLY SUMMONED, THE PROPHET MICAIAH DULY APPEARS BEFORE THE KINGS.

I WAS SURE HE MEANT ELIJAH!

OH, MOST SINCERELY, MY HONORED KING, YOU WILL *DEFINITELY* WIN THIS BATTLE. ATTACK AND BE VICTORIOUS!

DON'T BE SARCASTIC. TELL THE THE TRUTH!

YOU WANT THE TRUTH? ALL THESE PROPHETS ARE LIARS, AND THE ARAMEANS WILL CERTAINLY KILL YOU. MAY I GO NOW?

SEE? I TOLD YOU HE HATES ME.

TAKE HIM AWAY. LOCK HIM UP. YOU'LL GET OUT OF PRISON WHEN I RETURN SAFELY.

IF YOU RETURN SAFELY, THEN I'M NOT A PROPHET OF THE LORD. I MEAN IT.

AS KING AHAB PREPARES FOR BATTLE AGAINST THE ARAMEAN INVADERS, HE WORRIES ABOUT MICAIAH'S PROPHECY.

I'LL DISGUISE MYSELF SO THE ENEMY WON'T RECOGNIZE ME!

AHAB IS RIGHT—THE ENEMY DOESN'T RECOGNIZE HIM. THE ARAMEAN SOLDIERS FOCUS THEIR ATTACK ON KING JEHOSHAPHAT. BUT IN THE HEAT OF BATTLE, A STRAY ARROW STRIKES AHAB.

DRIVE ME OUT OF THE FIGHTING! I'VE BEEN WOUNDED.

BUT THE BATTLE IS SO FIERCE AROUND THEM THAT HIS DRIVER IS UNABLE TO RETREAT. AHAB FAINTS, PROPPED UP FOR HOURS AS HE SLOWLY BLEEDS TO DEATH IN HIS OWN CHARIOT. WHEN THE BATTLE FINALLY ENDS FOR THE DAY ...

LOOK! THE KING IS DEAD!

WITHOUT THEIR KING, THE ISRAELITES RETREAT, AND THE CAMPAIGN FAILS. KING AHAB'S BODY IS TAKEN BACK TO HIS CAPITAL FOR BURIAL, AND HIS CHARIOT IS TAKEN OUTSIDE THE CITY TO BE WASHED. MICAIAH'S PROPHECY AND THE FIRST PART OF ELIJAH'S PROPHECY HAS COME TRUE.

Chariots of Fire BASED ON 2 KINGS 2:1-18

AHAB'S KINGDOM PASSES TO HIS SONS, BUT QUEEN JEZEBEL REMAINS THE POWER BEHIND THE THRONE. DURING THE REIGN OF HER SECOND SON, JORAM, ELIJAH RECEIVES A MESSAGE FROM GOD.

THE LORD HAS TOLD ME TO GO TO THE JORDAN. STAY HERE, ELISHA.

NO. AS LONG AS YOU LIVE, I WILL FOLLOW YOU, ELIJAH.

SO THEY SET OUT TOGETHER. GOD HAS REVEALED TO BOTH OF THEM THAT THIS IS ELIJAH'S LAST JOURNEY, BUT THEY SAY NOTHING. WHEN THEY REACH THE JORDAN RIVER, ELIJAH STRIKES IT WITH HIS CLOAK—AND THE WATERS PART. THEY WALK ACROSS ON DRY LAND.

ON THE OTHER SIDE OF THE RIVER, ELIJAH STOPS, AS IF HE HAS REACHED THE END OF HIS JOURNEY.

IS THERE ANYTHING YOU WANT TO ASK BEFORE GOD TAKES ME AWAY?

YES. LET ME INHERIT YOUR SPIRITUAL POWER.

ONLY GOD CAN GRANT THAT. IF YOU ARE ABLE TO SEE WHAT GOD DOES NEXT, THEN YOUR REQUEST WILL BE ANSWERED.

WHEN ELIJAH'S MANTLE DROPS FROM HEAVEN, IT CONFIRMS THAT THE MIRACLE ELISHA WITNESSED MEANS HE IS TO CARRY ON ELIJAH'S WORK BY HIMSELF.

WHEN ELISHA GOES BACK TO THE JORDAN RIVER, HE STRIKES THE WATER WITH ELIJAH'S MANTLE—AND THE WATERS PART.

GOD'S POWER HAS COME TO ME. THANK YOU, MY LORD.

A GROUP OF YOUNG PROPHETS ARE WAITING ON THE OTHER SIDE OF THE RIVER, AND THEY WITNESS ELISHA'S PARTING OF THE WATERS.

WE KNOW GOD HAS TAKEN ELIJAH'S SPIRIT, AND NOW WE KNOW THAT YOU ARE TRULY HIS HEIR.

SHOULD WE LOOK FOR ELIJAH'S BODY SO WE CAN GIVE HIM A PROPER BURIAL?

LOOK ALL YOU LIKE, THERE WILL BE NOTHING FOR YOU TO FIND.

THE PROPHETS SPREAD THE NEWS THROUGHOUT ISRAEL THAT ELIJAH HAS BEEN TAKEN UP TO HEAVEN, AND ELISHA HAS TAKEN HIS PLACE.

A Rash of Miracles

NEWS THAT ELIJAH IS GONE SPREADS QUICKLY. IN THE PALACE OF SAMARIA, QUEEN JEZEBEL GLADLY PASSES THE NEWS ON TO HER SON.

WITH ELIJAH OUT OF THE WAY, WE CAN RULE ISRAEL AS WE PLEASE.

UNDER THE QUEEN'S EVIL INFLUENCE, MEN FEEL FREE TO TAKE ADVANTAGE OF THOSE WHO HAVE OPPOSED THE QUEEN.

YOUR HUSBAND OWED ME MONEY WHEN HE WAS ALIVE. PAY ME WHAT HE OWED, OR I'LL TAKE YOUR SONS AS SLAVES!

SLAVES! NO! O GOD, WHAT CAN I DO?

SADLY, THERE'S ONLY ONE THING YOU CAN DO. LUCKILY, YOUR BOYS WILL MAKE WONDERFUL SLAVES. REMEMBER, THE LAW IS ON MY SIDE.

IN DESPERATION, THE WOMAN RUNS TO ELISHA.

MY SONS! THE MONEYLENDER WILL TAKE THEM AS SLAVES—TOMORROW—UNLESS I GIVE HIM THE MONEY MY HUSBAND OWED HIM. AND I HAVE NO MONEY! I'M DOWN TO MY LAST JAR OF OIL.

DON'T WORRY. I PROMISE YOU WILL HAVE A SURPRISE FOR THE MONEYLENDER WHEN HE COMES.

ELISHA PERFORMS MANY MIRACLES TO PROTECT GOD'S PEOPLE AND GOD'S NAME. TO SAVE A VILLAGE, HE PURIFIES A POLLUTED WELL.

JUST LIKE ELIJAH BEFORE HIM, HE RAISES A YOUNG BOY FROM THE DEAD.

AND WHEN A GANG OF YOUNG MEN THREATEN HIM ...

WE'LL SEND YOU UP TO HEAVEN LIKE YOUR MASTER, BALDY!

ELISHA CALLS DOWN THE CURSE OF GOD—AND TWO BEARS COME TO HIS DEFENSE, MAULING 42 OF THEM.

WHEN THE COMPANY OF PROPHETS IS BUILDING A SETTLEMENT FOR ELISHA TO LIVE IN, AN ACCIDENT HAPPENS.

OH NO! IT WAS BORROWED. I'D HAVE TO BE A SLAVE FOR A LIFETIME TO PAY IT BACK!

ELISHA MIRACULOUSLY MAKES THE HEAVY IRON AXHEAD FLOAT.

A Miracle for a Rash

BASED ON 2 KINGS 5

IN THE NEIGHBORING LAND OF ARAM, THE BEST GENERAL IN THE ARMY IS A MAN NAMED NAAMAN. HE IS NOBLE AND HONORABLE AND HAS WON MANY BATTLES FOR HIS KING. BUT ONE DAY HE COMES DOWN WITH A DISEASE THAT WILL CHANGE HIS LIFE FOREVER.

WHAT IS THAT ON YOUR ARM, NAAMAN? DID YOU HURT YOURSELF?

I DON'T THINK SO. IT'S A RASH.

OH NO! IT'S LEPROSY!

WHAT WILL I DO? THIS DISEASE WILL SLOWLY KILL ME. MY FAMILY, MY CAREER—ALL GONE!

BUT GOD HAS SET THE STAGE TO SHOW HIS POWER ONCE AGAIN. NAAMAN'S HOUSEHOLD HAS SEVERAL ISRAELITE SLAVES. HE HAS ALWAYS TREATED THEM WELL, AND ONE SERVANT GIRL WISHES TO HELP HER MASTER IN RETURN.

THERE'S NO CURE!

THERE IS A PROPHET IN ISRAEL WHO CAN DO MIRACULOUS THINGS.

IF MY MASTER WOULD GO TO HIM, HE WOULD SURELY BE CURED.

ALTHOUGH NORMALLY NAAMAN WOULD NEVER SEEK HELP FROM FOREIGNERS, HE FEELS HE HAS NO CHOICE. NAAMAN GOES TO ASK HIS KING FOR PERMISSION TO VISIT ISRAEL, AN ENEMY COUNTRY.

I'M AFRAID IT IS A FOOL'S ERRAND, NAAMAN, BUT IF THERE'S ANY CHANCE OF A CURE, I WANT YOU TO FIND IT. I'LL GIVE YOU A LETTER TO TAKE TO THE KING OF ISRAEL.

NAAMAN SENDS THE LETTER TO KING JORAM IN SAMARIA, THE CAPITAL OF ISRAEL. THE LETTER DOES NOT MENTION ELISHA BY NAME, SO THE KING DOESN'T UNDERSTAND IT.

WHAT'S THIS? THE KING OF ARAM IS ASKING ME TO CURE HIS GENERAL OF LEPROSY?

ARAM HAS BEEN FIGHTING WITH ISRAEL ON AND OFF FOR SEVERAL YEARS, INCLUDING THE BATTLE THAT KILLED JORAM'S FATHER, KING AHAB. JORAM SUSPECTS THIS IS AN EXCUSE FOR ARAM TO WAGE WAR AGAINST ISRAEL AGAIN.

AM I A GOD THAT I CAN CURE AN INCURABLE DISEASE? IS THE KING OF ARAM TRYING TO PICK A FIGHT WITH ME IF I DON'T DO THIS IMPOSSIBLE REQUEST?

WHEN ELISHA HEARS OF KING JORAM'S DISTRESS, HE SENDS HIS SERVANT TO THE KING.

DON'T PANIC. ELISHA SAYS THAT IF YOU SEND NAAMAN TO HIM, THE GENERAL WILL LEARN THE POWER OF GOD IN ISRAEL.

IN THE MEANTIME, NAAMAN'S LEPROSY HAS GROWN WORSE. HE LOSES NO TIME IN GOING TO ELISHA'S HOUSE, BUT THE PROPHET IS NOT THERE TO MEET HIM.

GREETINGS, GENERAL NAAMAN. ELISHA SAYS THAT IF YOU WILL WASH SEVEN TIMES IN THE JORDAN RIVER, YOU WILL BE CURED.

MY LORD, THINK ABOUT IT. IF ELISHA HAD ASKED YOU TO DO SOMETHING HARD, YOU WOULD HAVE DONE IT EAGERLY. WHY NOT DO THIS EASY THING? DON'T LET YOUR PRIDE STAND IN THE WAY OF A POSSIBLE CURE.

WHAT? ELISHA WON'T EVEN MEET ME? I'VE ALREADY HUMBLED MYSELF TO COME TO THIS BACKWATER TOWN, AND NOW HE INSTRUCTS ME TO WASH IN A BACKWATER RIVER? WE HAVE BETTER RIVERS IN DAMASCUS—I COULD HAVE WASHED IN ANY OF THOSE.

THE GENERAL TAKES HIS SERVANT'S ADVICE AND GOES TO THE JORDAN RIVER. BUT HE'S STILL GRUMPY ABOUT IT.

I DON'T SEE HOW THIS MUDDY WATER WILL CURE LEPROSY.

I'VE HAD ENOUGH HUMILIATION. IF YOU'RE GOING TO MAKE A FOOL OF ME, THEN I'M LEAVING.

408

Invisible Army
BASED ON 2 KINGS 6:8-23

BUT THE HEALING OF NAAMAN DOES NOT KEEP THE KING OF ARAM FROM PLOTTING AGAINST ISRAEL. HE HAS HIS SOLDIERS SET UP AN AMBUSH TO CAPTURE THE KING OF ISRAEL. BUT AS KING JORAM IS ABOUT TO RIDE INTO THE TRAP ...

STOP! ELISHA SENDS WORD FOR YOU TO TAKE ANOTHER ROAD THE ARAMEANS ARE WAITING ON THIS ROAD TO CAPTURE YOU.

FOR DAYS, THE ARAMEAN SOLDIERS WAIT FOR THE ISRAELITE KING—BUT HE DOESN'T COME. TIME AND TIME AGAIN, THE ARAMEAN KING SETS UP A TRAP, AND ELISHA WARNS THE ISRAELITE KING TO ESCAPE. FINALLY, IN FRUSTRATION ...

I'VE HAD ENOUGH! WHICH OF YOU IS A TRAITOR??

NONE OF US, O KING. IT'S ELISHA, THE PROPHET IN ISRAEL. HE KNOWS EVERYTHING YOU DO.

ELISHA, IS IT? FIND OUT WHERE HE IS, AND I'LL SEND AN ARMY TO KILL HIM.

THE ARAMEANS QUIETLY SNEAK IN AND SET UP THEIR CAMP BY NIGHT. THE NEXT MORNING, ELISHA'S SERVANT RISES EARLY AND SEES THE ARMY.

ELISHA! WE'RE SURROUNDED BY THE WHOLE ARAMEAN ARMY! WE'RE OUTNUMBERED.

NO, THEY ARE.

ELISHA PRAYS, AND THE SERVANT'S EYES ARE SUDDENLY OPENED. HE LOOKS OUT OVER THE SURROUNDING ARAMEAN ARMY, BUT NOW HE SEES ...

... AN ARMY OF FIERY HORSES AND WARRIORS SURROUNDING THEM!

IT'S THE ARMY OF HEAVEN!

LIKE I SAID—WE'RE PROTECTED. O LORD, STRIKE THE ARAMEANS BLIND SO THAT THEY MAY SEE YOUR POWER.

I CAN'T SEE! WHAT HAPPENED?

I'M BLIND!

I'LL HELP YOU. YOU'RE LOOKING FOR ELISHA; I'LL TAKE YOU WHERE YOU CAN SEE HIM.

ELISHA LEADS THE ENEMY SOLDIERS TEN MILES SOUTH AND INTO THE CAPITAL CITY OF ISRAEL.

O LORD, OPEN THEIR EYES SO THEY CAN SEE YOU.

INSTANTLY, SIGHT RETURNS TO THE ARAMEANS.

WE'RE IN SAMARIA!

WE'RE TRAPPED! THEY'LL KILL US!

SHALL WE KILL THEM, ELISHA?

NO! THEY'RE MY GUESTS. FEED THEM AND SEND THEM HOME.

TO THEIR AMAZEMENT, THE ARAMEAN SOLDIERS ARE TREATED TO A FEAST AND RELEASED TO GO HOME.

I CAN'T BELIEVE IT! WE TRIED TO KILL BOTH THE KING AND ELISHA—AND THEY TREAT US LIKE FRIENDS!

BACK HOME, THE ARAMEANS TELL ABOUT THE KINDNESS OF THE ISRAELITES AND THE POWER OF THEIR GOD, AND FOR A TIME THE TWO NATIONS HAVE PEACE.

Lepers Under Siege! BASED ON 2 KINGS 6:24—7:16

WE'LL CUT OFF THE FOOD SUPPLY TO SAMARIA. THEN WE'LL SURROUND IT AND STARVE THE PEOPLE INTO SURRENDER.

EXCELLENT! THE LONGER THEY HOLD OUT, THE EASIER IT WILL BE TO CONQUER THEM.

ISRAEL AND ARAM HAVE LONG ALTERNATED BETWEEN OUTRIGHT WAR AND UNEASY PEACE. THE WARMONGERING KING OF ARAM CHAFES AT THE CURRENT TRUCE WITH ISRAEL.

SO THE ARAMEAN ARMY PITCHES ITS TENTS AROUND THE WALLS OF SAMARIA AND WAITS ...

I WONDER HOW LONG THEY CAN HOLD OUT.

THE CITY MAKES A BRAVE STAND TO HOLD OUT, BUT AS THE MONTHS PASS AND NO FOOD IS ALLOWED THROUGH THE GATES, THE ISRAELITES ARE REDUCED TO EATING DONKEY HEADS AND BIRD DROPPINGS—AND WORSE! THE PEOPLE PLEAD FOR THE KING TO TAKE ACTION.

OUR CHILDREN ARE DYING! WE MUST HAVE FOOD.

I'D RATHER TAKE MY CHANCES FIGHTING THE ENEMY THAN STARVING TO DEATH.

WE'RE SO WEAK NOW, THEY'D DEFEAT US EASILY.

413

THIS IS THE MOMENT THE QUEEN MOTHER, JEZEBEL, HAS BEEN WAITING FOR.

YOUR PEOPLE ARE STARVING—AND WHAT IS ELISHA'S GOD DOING ABOUT IT? NOTHING! GET RID OF ELISHA AND CALL ON MY GOD, BAAL.

YOU'RE RIGHT, MOTHER. I'LL ORDER HIM PUT TO DEATH IMMEDIATELY.

BUT ELISHA HAS NO FEAR OF THE WEAK KING WHO WAVERS BETWEEN GOD AND BAAL.

THIS SIEGE IS NOT THE LORD'S FAULT. IT IS ISRAEL'S OWN PUNISHMENT FOR NOT STAYING FAITHFUL TO GOD. NEVERTHELESS, THE LORD SAYS THERE WILL BE ENOUGH FOOD FOR EVERYONE TOMORROW.

THAT'S IMPOSSIBLE! WHAT, WILL YOU MAKE THE WHOLE ARMY DISAPPEAR? EVEN THEN, IT WOULD TAKE DAYS FOR FOOD TO GET HERE.

MEANWHILE FOUR LEPERS EXILED OUTSIDE THE CITY PONDER THEIR FATE.

I'M STARVING.

WHAT CAN YOU DO? THERE'S NO FOOD IN THE CITY. THE ARAMEAN SOLDIERS ARE THE ONLY ONES WITH FOOD AROUND HERE.

THEN LET'S GO OVER TO THE ARAMEAN CAMP. MAYBE THEY'LL GIVE US SOMETHING TO EAT. IF WE STAY HERE, WE'LL DEFINITELY DIE.

IF WE SURRENDER TO THE ARAMEAN SOLDIERS WE MIGHT DIE—BUT THEY ALSO MIGHT HAVE MERCY ON US AND FEED US. EITHER WAY, WE HAVE NOTHING TO LOSE.

I WANT TO SURRENDER FIRST! MAYBE THEY'LL GIVE ME FIRST CHOICE OF FOOD.

IN DESPERATION,
THE FOUR HUNGRY
LEPERS APPROACH
THE ARAMEAN CAMP.

SOMETHING STRANGE IS GOING ON. THERE'S NOT A GUARD IN SIGHT. MAYBE IT'S A TRAP ...

MAYBE IT IS— BUT IT'S THIS OR STARVE TO DEATH. I'D RATHER DIE QUICKLY THAN SLOWLY.

HOW CAN I SURRENDER WITHOUT A GUARD TO SURRENDER TO?

THERE'S NOBODY HERE!

BUT THEY LEFT ALL THEIR FOOD.

AND THEIR STUFF. LOOK, GOLD! WE'RE RICH!

FOR A WHILE,
THE LEPERS REVEL IN
THEIR GOOD FORTUNE.
BUT THEN ...

YOU KNOW, IT'S PROBABLY NOT RIGHT TO KEEP ALL OF THIS FOOD FROM THE STARVING PEOPLE IN THE CITY.

IF WE DON'T SHARE THE GOOD NEWS, PEOPLE MIGHT BLAME US.

WELL, OKAY, BUT FIRST LET'S HIDE SOME TREASURE FOR OURSELVES.

THE LEPERS GO BACK TO THE CITY AND POUND ON THE GATES UNTIL A GUARD ANSWERS.

THE ARAMEANS ARE GONE.

GONE? WHERE?

WE DON'T KNOW—WE JUST ATE THEIR FOOD.

ROUSED FROM HIS BED, KING JORAM RECEIVES THE NEWS AND CALLS FOR HIS ADVISERS.

IT MUST BE A TRAP. THE ARAMEANS ARE WAITING IN AMBUSH TO CAPTURE US IF WE LEAVE THE CITY.

MAYBE, BUT LET'S SEND OUT A FEW MEN TO SEE WHAT'S GOING ON.

THE KING'S MEN CONFIRM THAT THE ENEMY CAMP IS EMPTY, THEN QUICKLY PICK UP THE ARAMEAN TRAIL BY FOLLOWING THE CLOTHING, WEAPONS, AND VESSELS DROPPED ALONG THE WAY.

LOOK, MORE SHIELDS. THE ARAMEANS WERE RUNNING AWAY SO FAST THEY DIDN'T WANT ANYTHING TO SLOW THEM DOWN.

WHAT COULD HAVE HAPPENED TO MAKE TRAINED SOLDIERS THROW AWAY THEIR WEAPONS AND RUN FOR THEIR LIVES?

416

THE ISRAELITE SCOUTS FOLLOW THE FLEEING ARAMEAN ARMY TO THE JORDAN RIVER. ALONG THE WAY THEY OVERTAKE ONE OF THE ENEMY SOLDIERS.

PULL UP— HERE'S ONE WHO DROPPED BEHIND. MAYBE HE CAN TELL US WHAT HAPPENED.

WHY DID YOU ARAMEANS DESERT CAMP IN THE MIDDLE OF THE NIGHT?

WE WERE GOING TO BE ATTACKED! WE THOUGHT THE HITTITES WERE COMING FROM THE NORTH—AND THE EGYPTIANS FROM THE SOUTH—TO TRAP US.

THERE WERE NO SIGNS OF ANY OTHER ARMIES.

YOU SAW THEM?

WE HEARD THEM.

AND THAT WAS ENOUGH.

BACK IN SAMARIA, THE STARVING ISRAELITES RUSH OUT TO THE ARAMEAN CAMP, EAT THEIR FILL, AND HAUL THE REST OF THE FOOD BACK TO THE CITY.

YOU SAID THERE WOULD BE FOOD, ELISHA, BUT I DIDN'T BELIEVE YOU.

IT WAS THE LORD WHO PROMISED THE FOOD—AND YOU CAN ALWAYS COUNT ON THE PROMISES OF GOD.

Anointed Jehu, Painted Jezebel

BASED ON 2 KINGS 9

IN SPITE OF THE FACT THAT GOD HAD SAVED ISRAEL, KING JORAM AND HIS MOTHER KEEP ON WORSHIPPING BAAL. IN ANOTHER BATTLE AGAINST ARAM, JORAM IS WOUNDED. HE LEAVES CAPTAIN JEHU IN CHARGE AND RETURNS HOME TO RECUPERATE. THE TIME HAS COME FOR THE LORD'S PROPHECY TO ELIJAH TO BE FULFILLED. ELISHA CALLS FOR A YOUNG PROPHET TO MAKE A QUICK JOURNEY FOR HIM.

TAKE THIS OIL. GO TO JEHU, CAPTAIN OF THE ARMY, AND ANOINT HIM THE NEXT KING OF ISRAEL, AS THE LORD TOLD MY MASTER, ELIJAH, TO DO. WHEN YOU'VE DONE THAT, RUN! YOU DON'T WANT TO BE CAUGHT IN THE BLOODSHED THAT FOLLOWS.

AT THE CAMP, THE YOUNG PROPHET GOES STRAIGHT TO THE OFFICERS' TENTS.

CAPTAIN JEHU! THERE'S SOMETHING I MUST TELL YOU ...

... ALONE.

THE LORD SAYS, "I ANOINT YOU KING OF MY PEOPLE ISRAEL, TO FIGHT FOR THOSE WHO WORSHIP ME AND DESTROY THE HOUSE OF AHAB AND ALL THOSE WHO WORSHIP BAAL."

THEN THE YOUNG PROPHET IMMEDIATELY RUNS FROM THE CAMP.

WHAT DID THAT MADMAN WANT?

HE WAS A MESSENGER FROM GOD—AND HE ANOINTED ME TO BE KING OF ISRAEL!

BUT KING JORAM IS STILL KING.

IT IS A TENSE MOMENT. WILL THE ARMY SUPPORT JEHU OR JORAM?

FOR SEVERAL SECONDS, NO ONE SAYS A WORD. THEN ...

JEHU IS KING!

LONG LIVE THE KING!

HIS MEN GO WILD WITH JOY! THEY BLOW THEIR TRUMPETS AND THROW DOWN THEIR GARMENTS TO MAKE A THRONE.

THANK YOU FOR SUPPORTING ME, MY FRIENDS. BUT WE MUST TAKE CARE OF JORAM AND HIS WICKED MOTHER, JEZEBEL. QUICKLY, BEFORE WORD CAN SPREAD.

JEHU AND A COMPANY OF MEN SET OUT AT ONCE—AND AS THEY APPROACH JEZREEL ...

CHARIOTS! A WHOLE LINE OF THEM. THE LEADER DRIVES LIKE A MADMAN!

IT MUST BE JEHU.

JORAM THINKS JEHU IS BRINGING NEWS OF THE WAR. SO WITH HIS NEPHEW—KING AHAZIAH OF JUDAH—HE RIDES OUT TO MEET JEHU.

DO YOU BRING NEWS OF PEACE?

HOW CAN THERE BE PEACE IN ISRAEL WHILE YOU AND YOUR MOTHER, JEZEBEL, WORSHIP BAAL?

TREACHERY, AHAZIAH! FLEE FOR YOUR LIFE!

KREEEK

THAT'S THE FIRST BLOW STRUCK FOR ISRAEL.

BUT NOT THE LAST! YOU, FOLLOW AHAZIAH AND KILL HIM. I GO TO MAKE JEZEBEL PAY FOR HER SINS!

IS IT RIGHT FOR JEHU TO ORDER AHAZIAH'S DEATH? HE'S A DESCENDANT OF DAVID!

BUT ALSO A DESCENDANT OF AHAB. HE AND HIS MOTHER, ATHALIAH, WORSHIP BAAL IN JUDAH. WE MUST FOLLOW JEHU'S ORDERS, RIGHT OR NOT.

MEANWHILE, NEWS OF JEHU'S REBELLION REACHES THE PALACE IN JEZREEL BEFORE HE DOES.

QUEEN JEZEBEL! JEHU HAS KILLED YOUR SON!

JEHU! HE'LL BE HERE NEXT!

WITHOUT PANICKING, JEZEBEL CALMLY SITS AT HER MIRROR AND PUTS ON HER FINEST MAKEUP.

HE WILL NOT SEE ME CRY. AND I WILL NOT BEG FOR MY LIFE.

JEZEBEL! IT IS FINALLY TIME FOR YOU TO PAY FOR YOUR SINS.

THAT'S WHAT ALL REBELLIOUS SERVANTS SAY. YOU WILL NOT LAST A WEEK AS KING.

JEHU ORDERS THE PALACE SERVANTS TO SHOW THEIR ALLEGIANCE TO HIM BY PUSHING QUEEN JEZEBEL FROM THE WINDOW TO HER DEATH IN THE STREET BELOW. HER BODY IS LEFT UNBURIED, AND THE WILD ANIMALS EAT HER REMAINS. SO JEZEBEL PAYS WITH HER LIFE FOR THE EVIL SHE HAS DONE—AND THE FINAL PART OF ELIJAH'S PROPHECY COMES TRUE.

JEHU LOSES NO TIME CELEBRATING HIS NEW KINGSHIP.

FIND ANY OTHER RELATIVES, FRIENDS, AND SERVANTS OF AHAB AND JEZEBEL. KILL THEM ALL FOR THEIR WICKEDNESS.

DESTROY THE IDOLS OF BAAL!

JEHU WIPES OUT THE WORSHIP OF BAAL IN ISRAEL. BUT EVEN THOUGH HE COMMITS GOOD ACTS FOR THE LORD, HE IS MOSTLY REMEMBERED FOR HIS EAGERNESS TO KILL ANYONE HE THOUGHT MIGHT CHALLENGE HIS RULE.

PRIDE GOES BEFORE THE FALL.

A Queen's Plot

BASED ON 2 KINGS 11:1-3;
2 CHRONICLES 22:10-12

ELISHA HAS ANOINTED JEHU TO BE THE NEXT KING OF ISRAEL. JEHU ASSURES HIS CLAIM TO THE THRONE BY KILLING ANYONE RELATED TO THE WICKED AHAB AND JEZEBEL. TO THE SOUTH, IN THE KINGDOM OF JUDAH, AHAZIAH'S MOTHER, ATHALIAH, RECEIVES THE NEWS ...

I BRING BAD NEWS. YOUR MOTHER, QUEEN JEZEBEL, AND BROTHER, KING JORAM, ARE DEAD. AND YOUR SON, KING AHAZIAH, IS DEAD TOO. ISRAEL'S NEW KING—JEHU—HAS KILLED THEM ALL.

POOR LITTLE PRINCE JOASH! YOUR FATHER, AHAZIAH, IS DEAD, AND YOUR GRANDMOTHER HATES YOU.

STOP HOVERING! TAKE MY GRANDSON AWAY AND LEAVE ME ALONE IN MY TERRIBLE GRIEF.

BUT ATHALIAH'S GRIEF IS ONLY A COVER FOR HER PLAN.

THE GOD OF ISRAEL HAS KILLED ALL MY FAMILY. VERY WELL. I WILL KILL ALL OF HIS FAMILY. NO DESCENDANT OF DAVID WILL BE LEFT ALIVE TO RULE IN JUDAH. THEN I CAN BE QUEEN AND WORSHIP BAAL LIKE MY MOTHER TAUGHT ME.

SHE ACTS AT ONCE TO CARRY OUT HER BOLD PLOT.

ORDER YOUR SOLDIERS TO KILL ALL OF THE KING'S MALE RELATIVES. DON'T LET EVEN ONE OF THEM ESCAPE—NOT ONE.

BUT NEWS OF THE PLOT REACHES JEHOSHEBA, THE WIFE OF THE HIGH PRIEST AND SISTER TO THE DEAD KING AHAZIAH.

THE QUEEN MOTHER HAS GONE MAD. SHE HAS ORDERED SOLDIERS TO KILL THE KING'S SONS. HIDE JOASH IN A STOREROOM UNTIL WE HAVE A CHANCE TO GET HIM OUT OF THE PALACE.

THAT NIGHT ...

IT'S A ROTTEN BUSINESS— KILLING BABIES.

IT WAS QUEEN ATHALIAH'S WISH, NOT OURS.

THAT WAS CLOSE!

YES, THE SLIGHTEST CRY COULD HAVE COST JOASH HIS LIFE. WE MUST HURRY TO BRING HIM TO MY HUSBAND.

UNDER COVER OF DARKNESS, THE TWO WOMEN HURRY TO THE TEMPLE OF GOD. THEY MEET JEHOIADA AT THE SUR GATE.

WE HAVE BABY JOASH. HELP US SAVE HIM FROM THE QUEEN.

COME IN! WE CAN HIDE HIM IN THE TEMPLE.

ONLY THE PRIESTS USE THIS ROOM. JOASH WILL BE SAFE HERE AS LONG AS IT IS NECESSARY TO HIDE HIM.

A FEW HOURS LATER, THE QUEEN'S OFFICER REPORTS THAT ALL MALE DESCENDANTS TO THE THRONE ARE DEAD—NOT REALIZING THAT THEY HAVE MISSED ONE.

NOW THERE IS NO ONE TO SAY I CANNOT RULE JUDAH.

ONCE THE IMMEDIATE DANGER IS OVER, JEHOSHEBA REJOINS JEHOIADA IN THE TEMPLE. FOR SIX YEARS, ATHALIAH RULES JUDAH WITH A CRUEL HAND UNTIL AT LAST THE PEOPLE BEGIN TO COMPLAIN. UNKNOWN TO THEM—IN A SECRET ROOM OF THE TEMPLE—YOUNG PRINCE JOASH SPENDS THOSE SIX YEARS BEING RAISED BY THE HIGH PRIEST AND HIS WIFE.

THE NEXT SABBATH IN THE TEMPLE, JEHOIADA HANDS OUT THE SPEARS AND SHIELDS IN THE TEMPLE, WEAPONS THAT USED TO BELONG TO KING DAVID.

GOD PROTECT US, AND DAVID'S WEAPONS DEFEND US.

MEANWHILE, IN THE PALACE ...

THE SOUND OF CHEERING—IT'S COMING FROM THE TEMPLE. I WONDER WHAT IT MEANS!

QUEEN ATHALIAH HEARS THE SOUND OF SHOUTING AND RUSHES TO THE TEMPLE—TO FIND A SMALL BOY BEING CROWNED KING.

LONG LIVE THE KING OF JUDAH!

GOD SAVE THE KING!

GOD SAVE THE KING!

CONSPIRACY! CONSPIRACY! STOP THIS AT ONCE!

Dagger in the Night

BASED ON 2 CHRONICLES 24:17-27; 2 KINGS 12

UNDER THE GUIDANCE OF JEHOIADA, THE HIGH PRIEST, JOASH DESTROYS THE TEMPLE OF BAAL AND LEADS HIS PEOPLE BACK TO THE WORSHIP OF GOD. THE HOUSE OF GOD IS REPAIRED, AND FOR YEARS JUDAH PROSPERS. BUT WHEN JEHOIADA DIES, JOASH IS TOO WEAK TO STAND UP UNDER THE PRESSURE OF THOSE WHO WANT TO TURN HIM AWAY FROM GOD. FINALLY, JEHOIADA'S SON, ZECHARIAH, GOES TO THE KING.

KING JOASH, I SPEAK TO YOU AS MY FATHER WOULD SPEAK. YOU AND YOUR PEOPLE ARE FORSAKING GOD. JUDAH WILL BE DESTROYED UNLESS YOU STOP THEM!

AS SOON AS ZECHARIAH LEAVES, JOASH'S ADVISERS GIVE THEIR ADVICE.

ZECHARIAH IS A TROUBLEMAKER.

HE SHOULD BE PUT TO DEATH BEFORE HE TURNS ALL OF JUDAH AGAINST YOU.

YOU'RE RIGHT. STIR UP THE PEOPLE SO THEY WILL GET RID OF HIM.

AND SO JOASH, WHO WAS ONCE A GOOD KING, LISTENS TO EVIL ADVICE. ZECHARIAH—SON OF THE MAN WHO HAD SAVED JOASH'S LIFE—IS STONED TO DEATH BY A MOB. AND SOON HIS PROPHECY OF DISASTER COMES TRUE ...

ZECHARIAH'S PREDICTED DISASTER COMES SOON—IN AN ATTACK BY THE KING OF ARAM. DURING THE ATTACK, JOASH IS WOUNDED AND HIS EVIL ADVISERS ARE KILLED. IN AN ATTEMPT TO SAVE JERUSALEM, JOASH TRIES TO BUY OFF THE ENEMY. HIS WOUND IS TOO SERIOUS FOR HIM TO LEAVE THE PALACE, SO HE SENDS A MESSENGER.

GIFTS FROM MY LORD, KING JOASH OF JUDAH. THESE ARE ALL THE RICHES WE HAVE IN OUR TEMPLE. HE ASKS THAT YOU ACCEPT THEM AND LEAVE JERUSALEM IN PEACE.

TELL YOUR KING I ACCEPT HIS OFFER.

HOW IS THE KING TODAY?

NO BETTER, NO WORSE. TOO BAD THE ARAMEANS DIDN'T KILL THE KING ALONG WITH THE MEN WHO ADVISED HIM TO MURDER ZECHARIAH. WITH THEM GONE, WE COULD SAVE JUDAH—IF IT WEREN'T FOR ...

THAT NIGHT, WHEN ALL THE PALACE IS ASLEEP ...

REMEMBER, WE'RE DOING THIS TO SAVE OUR COUNTRY.

SO KING JOASH IS MURDERED BY HIS OWN MEN.

FOR ALMOST 100 YEARS, JUDAH IS RULED BY KINGS WHO WAVER BETWEEN WORSHIPPING GOD AND HEATHEN IDOLS. DURING THIS PERIOD, GOD SENDS PROPHET AFTER PROPHET TO WARN THE PEOPLE OF THEIR WICKED WAYS. SOME PROPHETS DO BETTER THAN OTHERS ...

A Fishy Story
BASED ON JONAH

GOD SENDS A MESSAGE TO JONAH, A PROPHET OF ISRAEL.

GO TO THE CORRUPT CITY OF NINEVEH AND TELL THE PEOPLE IF THEY DON'T TURN AWAY FROM THEIR SINS I WILL DESTROY THEM.

JONAH IMMEDIATELY MAKES HIS WAY TO JOPPA, A BUSY SEAPORT TOWN WITH SHIPS GOING TO ALL CORNERS OF CIVILIZATION. THERE HE INQUIRES OF A SHIP'S CAPTAIN ...

WHERE'S THIS SHIP GOING?

TO TARSUS.

IS THAT CLOSE TO NINEVEH?

OH, I'M SORRY. IT'S THE OPPOSITE DIRECTION FROM NINEVEH.

PERFECT.

HAVING PAID FOR HIS JOURNEY OF DISOBEDIENCE, JONAH BOARDS THE SHIP.

I'M SORRY, GOD. I CAN'T GO TO SUCH A FILTHY, DESPICABLE PLACE AS NINEVEH.

THE MOMENT THE SEA MONSTER SWALLOWS JONAH, THE STORM CALMS. AT THIS, THE SAILORS GIVE PRAISE TO GOD, WHO THEY NOW KNOW COMMANDS ALL OF NATURE.

BUT JONAH IS NOT DEAD. GOD KEEPS HIM ALIVE INSIDE THE GIANT FISH FOR THREE DAYS AND THREE NIGHTS. THIS GIVES HIM LOTS OF TIME TO THINK AND PRAY ... AND MAYBE REALIZE HOW ARROGANT IT WAS TO DISOBEY HIS LORD.

LORD, I CALLED OUT TO YOU AND YOU SAVED ME. THE WATERS WERE ALL AROUND ME, BUT YOU KEPT ME SAFE. YOU ARE THE ONE WHO SAVES!

GOD HEARS JONAH'S PRAYER AND MAKES THE FISH SPIT HIM UP ON DRY GROUND—JUST OUTSIDE NINEVEH.

NOW DO WHAT I HAVE COMMANDED!

AND WHEN GOD DOES PUNISH YOU LIKE YOU DESERVE, DON'T SAY I DIDN'T WARN YOU.

ONCE AGAIN, GOD TELLS JONAH TO GO TO NINEVEH. THIS TIME JONAH OBEYS.

TURN AWAY FROM YOUR SIN, OR THE WHOLE CITY WILL BE DESTROYED. THIS IS WHAT GOD SAYS.

BUT TO JONAH'S SHOCK AND DISMAY, THE PEOPLE ACTUALLY LISTEN TO HIM. TO SHOW HOW SORRY THEY ARE, THEY PUT ON BLACK CLOTHES—EVEN THE KING!

THIS IS A ROYAL ORDER. CALL OUT TO GOD WITH ALL YOUR HEARTS. STOP DOING EVIL. THEN GOD MIGHT TAKE PITY ON US.

GOD SEES THAT THE PEOPLE OF NINEVEH HAVE TURNED AWAY FROM THEIR SIN. THEN, TRUE TO HIS HOLY WORD, HE DOES NOT DESTROY THEM AFTER ALL.

JONAH DOES NOT TAKE GOD'S CHANGE OF HEART VERY WELL.

I SHOULD HAVE KNOWN! EVEN WHEN PEOPLE ARE SCUM AND DESERVE TO DIE, YOU SHOW THEM MERCY, LORD. JUST KILL ME, IF THIS IS THE KIND OF WORK YOU'RE GOING TO ASK ME TO DO.

BUT GOD SCOLDS JONAH FOR HIS ATTITUDE.

YOU'RE ALWAYS SO WILLING TO DIE, YOU AND YOUR PRIDE. BUT THERE ARE 120,000 PEOPLE IN THE CITY OF NINEVEH, AND I DESIRE THAT THEY HAVE THE CHANCE TO LIVE.

HOSEA

HOSEA LOVES HIS WIFE, GOMER, VERY MUCH. BUT ONE DAY SHE LEAVES HIM. THE LAW SAYS HOSEA CAN DIVORCE HIS WIFE, BUT HE CHOOSES TO STAY MARRIED TO HER. HE TELLS THE PEOPLE OF ISRAEL THAT THEY HAVE TREATED GOD THE SAME WAY. GOD LOVES HIS PEOPLE, BUT THEY HAVE RUN AWAY TO WORSHIP IDOLS.

DON'T YOU SEE HOW MUCH GOD LOVES YOU, EVEN THOUGH YOU DON'T LOVE HIM BACK? IF GOD CAN LOVE AN UNFAITHFUL PEOPLE, THEN I CAN LOVE AN UNFAITHFUL WIFE.

AMOS

AMOS, A SHEPHERD AND FIG-PICKER, IS WATCHING HIS SHEEP WHEN GOD CALLS HIM TO A DANGEROUS JOB. AMOS GOES TO THE CITY OF BETHEL IN ISRAEL AND GIVES GOD'S MESSAGE.

YOU ARE LIKE A CROOKED WALL THAT MUST BE DESTROYED BEFORE A NEW ONE CAN BE BUILT.

JOEL

LIKE A MIGHTY ARMY DESTROYING EVERYTHING IN ITS PATH, MILLIONS OF LOCUSTS SWARM OVER JUDAH. THEY EAT ALL THE CROPS AND LEAVE EMPTY FIELDS BEHIND.

WHAT THE BIG LOCUSTS MISS, THE YOUNG LOCUSTS WILL EAT. BUT IF YOU WILL TURN BACK TO GOD, HE WILL REPAY YOU FOR WHAT THE LOCUSTS HAVE EATEN.

AND IN THE LATER DAYS, GOD'S SPIRIT WILL BE WITH YOU. YOUR CHILDREN WILL PROPHESY; THE ELDERLY WILL DREAM DREAMS, AND THE YOUNG WILL SEE VISIONS.

MICAH

MICAH, A SMALL-TOWN PROPHET, WANTS LIFE TO BE BETTER FOR THE POOR. HE DARES TO TELL THE WEALTHY LEADERS OF JUDAH AND ISRAEL WHAT THEY ARE DOING WRONG.

YOU HATE JUSTICE, AND YOU HOLD DOWN THE POOR. YOU KNOW WHAT GOD WANTS YOU TO DO! BE FAIR, BE FORGIVING, AND BE FRIENDS WITH GOD.

ONE DAY, IN THE LITTLE TOWN OF BETHLEHEM, A SAVIOR WILL BE BORN AND HIS KINGDOM WILL LAST FOREVER.

A Burning Coal

BASED ON ISAIAH 6

ONE DAY A YOUNG MAN NAMED ISAIAH IS PRAYING IN THE TEMPLE, WHEN HE SEES A VISION. THE LORD IS SEATED ON A THRONE. FLYING AROUND HIM ARE SERAPHIM, HEAVENLY CREATURES WITH SIX WINGS. WHEN THEY SPEAK, THE WALLS SHAKE AND THE TEMPLE FILLS WITH SMOKE.

HOLY, HOLY, HOLY IS THE LORD ALMIGHTY. THE WHOLE EARTH IS FULL OF HIS GLORY!

Hezekiah's Healing

BASED ON 2 KINGS 17:1–18:16; 20;
2 CHRONICLES 29–30; ISAIAH 38–39

THROUGH THE INFLUENCE OF PROPHETS LIKE ISAIAH, HEZEKIAH IS A RIGHTEOUS KING.

OUR FATHERS DISOBEYED GOD, AND JUDAH HAS BECOME WEAK. WE WILL SERVE THE LORD, AND WITH HIS HELP MAKE OUR NATION STRONG AGAIN.

BUT BEFORE HEZEKIAH CAN BEGIN TO REFORM THE RELIGION OF JUDAH, A CATASTROPHE STRIKES. OFF TO THE NORTH, THE PEOPLE SEE SMOKE AND FEAR THE WORST.

BEFORE LONG, SHOCKING NEWS FILLS THE STREETS OF JERUSALEM WITH GRIEF AND ALARM.

THE KING OF ASSYRIA HAS DESTROYED THE CITY OF SAMARIA AND TAKEN THE PEOPLE OF ISRAEL AWAY AS CAPTIVES.

OUR BROTHERS MURDERED! OUR SISTERS TAKEN FROM THE LAND GOD GAVE US!

WITH THE FALL OF SAMARIA, THE NORTHERN KINGDOM OF ISRAEL COMES TO AN END. GREAT MASSES OF PEOPLE ARE CARRIED AWAY, NEVER TO RETURN. THE FEW ISRAELITES LEFT IN THE LAND MIX WITH THE OTHER NATIONS THAT THE CONQUERORS BRING IN.

WITH ISRAEL CONQUERED, WE ARE ALL THAT REMAINS OF GOD'S PEOPLE. AND SENNACHERIB, THE KING OF ASSYRIA, WILL NOT BE CONTENT WITH JUST ISRAEL. HIS NEXT MOVE WILL BE AGAINST JERUSALEM. WE MUST PREPARE TO DEFEND THE CITY—BOTH SPIRITUALLY AND PHYSICALLY.

AT HEZEKIAH'S ORDERS, THE TEMPLE IS REPAIRED, AND THE KING LEADS HIS PEOPLE BACK TO THE WORSHIP OF GOD.

GOD'S HOLY TEMPLE HAS BEEN REBUILT IN JERUSALEM. KING HEZEKIAH INVITES ALL ISRAELITES EVERYWHERE TO COME AND WORSHIP IN THE HOUSE OF THE LORD. ESPECIALLY THOSE SCATTERED IN EXILE BY THE ASSYRIANS—WE WELCOME YOU HOME TO GOD'S TEMPLE.

AT HEZEKIAH'S DIRECTION, WORKERS BUILD A TUNNEL BETWEEN A SPRING OUTSIDE THE WALLS AND A POOL INSIDE THE CITY.

THIS WILL PROTECT THE FLOW OF WATER TO US AND CUT OFF THE WATER SUPPLY FOR THE ASSYRIANS.

MY BROTHERS ARE HELPING TO BUILD UP THE WALLS. THANK GOD WE HAVE A KING WHO WILL DEFEND US.

THEN HEZEKIAH CALLS THE PEOPLE TOGETHER ...

DON'T BE AFRAID. WE HAVE MORE POWER ON OUR SIDE THAN ASSYRIA HAS, BECAUSE THE LORD GOD IS WITH US.

HEZEKIAH FIGHTS OFF ASSYRIA. BUT TEN YEARS LATER THE ASSYRIANS ATTACK AGAIN. THIS TIME HE PAYS ASSYRIA A RANSOM OF SILVER AND GOLD TO LEAVE JUDAH ALONE—AND HE IS FORCED TO TAKE SOME OF IT FROM GOD'S TEMPLE. SOON AFTERWARD, HE BECOMES DEATHLY ILL. THE PROPHET ISAIAH VISITS HIM AT HIS SICKBED.

I AM SORRY, MY KING. THE LORD HAS SPOKEN: "GET YOUR WILL READY AND CHOOSE YOUR HEIR TO THE THRONE. YOU WILL NOT RECOVER FROM THIS SICKNESS."

AFTER ISAIAH LEAVES, HEZEKIAH CRIES OUT TO THE LORD.

LORD! HAVEN'T I BEEN YOUR FAITHFUL SERVANT? I'VE SERVED YOU WITH MY WHOLE HEART AND TRIED TO DO WHAT YOU THINK IS GOOD.

AT THAT MOMENT, ISAIAH COMES BACK INTO THE ROOM.

VERY WELL, GOD HAS HEARD YOUR PRAYERS. HE WILL GIVE YOU ANOTHER 15 YEARS TO LEAD HIS PEOPLE. BUT DON'T RULE IN FEAR! MAKE SURE YOU LEAD THEM IN HOLINESS AND FAITH.

THANK YOU, LORD! AS PROOF OF YOUR PROMISE, WILL YOU MAKE THE SHADOW ON THE SUNDIAL OF AHAZ GO BACKWARD TEN DEGREES?

HEZEKIAH LOOKS OUT THE WINDOW AT THE STEPS OF THE SUNDIAL ...

GOD MIRACULOUSLY MAKES THE SUN MOVE BACKWARD IN THE SKY TO SHOW HE WILL KEEP HIS PROMISE TO HEZEKIAH.

AFTER HEZEKIAH GETS BETTER, AMBASSADORS VISIT HIM FROM A DISTANT COUNTRY CALLED BABYLON.

OUR KING HEARD YOU WERE SICK, AND SENT US WITH THESE LETTERS AND A GIFT.

WELL, THANK YOUR KING FOR ME. MAY I SHOW YOU AROUND?

HEZEKIAH SHOWS OFF HIS ARMY AND ALL THE RICHES HE HAS STORED UP IN THE TEMPLE AND HIS VARIOUS WAREHOUSES.

AFTER THEY'VE SEEN EVERY PIECE OF WEALTH IN THE CITY, THE AMBASSADORS HEAD BACK TO BABYLON. AS THEY'RE LEAVING, THE PROPHET ISAIAH COMES TO SEE HIS KING.

WHO WERE THOSE MEN, AND WHERE DID THEY COME FROM?

THEY WERE AMBASSADORS FROM SOME FAR-OFF COUNTRY YOU'VE NEVER HEARD OF—I FORGET THE NAME ... BABEL? ... BABILU? ... BABYLON! VERY NICE FELLOWS. I SHOWED THEM ALL MY TREASURES.

YOU PRIDEFUL KING! YOU MAY DEFEAT THE ASSYRIANS, BUT BABYLON WILL ONE DAY BE THE DESTRUCTION OF JUDAH! YOUR DESCENDANTS WILL BE TAKEN AWAY FROM JERUSALEM AND SERVE AS SLAVES TO THE BABYLONIAN KING.

OH! WELL, AT LEAST IT WON'T HAPPEN IN MY LIFETIME.

WHEN NEWS OF THE PEOPLE'S FEAR REACHES KING HEZEKIAH, HE TEARS HIS CLOTHES IN ANGUISH.

IN DIRE CIRCUMSTANCES LIKE THESE, ONLY GOD CAN SAVE US. SEND FOR ISAIAH! ASK HIM IF GOD HAS ANY COMFORT.

ISAIAH BRINGS AN ENCOURAGING WORD FROM THE LORD.

DO NOT LISTEN TO THE INSULTS OF THIS ARROGANT KING. THE LORD WILL DEFEND HIS CITY—THE CITY OF HIS SERVANT DAVID. HAVE FAITH! GOD WILL NOT DESERT US.

THAT NIGHT, THE LORD SENDS AN ANGEL WHO ANNIHILATES THE ASSYRIAN ARMY.

THE NEXT MORNING, WHEN THEY SEE THAT THE ENEMY SOLDIERS ARE ALL DEAD, THE PEOPLE OF JERUSALEM GO WILD WITH JOY.

ISAIAH SAID GOD WAS ON OUR SIDE!

AND GOD DOESN'T ABANDON PEOPLE WHO TRUST IN HIM.

NEVER AGAIN WHILE HEZEKIAH IS KING DO THE ASSYRIANS TRY TO TAKE JERUSALEM. HEZEKIAH LEADS HIS PEOPLE IN THE WORSHIP OF THE TRUE GOD, AND FOR YEARS THEY ARE HAPPY AND AT PEACE.

NAHUM

MEANWHILE, SENNACHERIB RETREATS BACK TO NINEVEH IN DISGRACE. THERE HIS OWN SON ASSASSINATES HIM. OVER A CENTURY BEFORE, ALL OF NINEVEH HAD REPENTED WHEN THE PROPHET JONAH BROUGHT THEM GOD'S WARNING. NOW THEY SEEK WORLD DOMINATION THROUGH WAR AND CRUELTY. SO THE PROPHET NAHUM GOES TO ASSYRIA'S CAPITAL TO SHARE ONE FINAL WARNING. THEIR EVIL WAYS WILL EVENTUALLY CATCH UP WITH THEM, AND THEY WILL BE DESTROYED.

THE LORD PROTECTS THOSE WHO TRUST IN HIM, BUT HE WILL DROWN NINEVEH IN ITS OWN ARROGANCE.

UNDER HEZEKIAH'S REIGN, JUDAH TRUSTS IN THE LORD, BUT WHEN HEZEKIAH EVENTUALLY DIES, HIS SON LEADS JUDAH INTO IDOLATRY. ISAIAH SPENDS HIS REMAINING YEARS PLEADING WITH HIS PEOPLE TO DESTROY THEIR IDOLS AND RETURN TO GOD. BUT ONLY A FEW LISTEN. HE WARNS THE KINGS OF WHAT WILL HAPPEN IF THEY DISOBEY GOD, BUT THE KINGS IGNORE HIS WARNINGS. AT LAST ISAIAH PROPHESIES DESTRUCTION ...

BECAUSE JUDAH HAS TURNED AWAY FROM THE HOLY ONE OF ISRAEL, IT WILL BE DESTROYED. THE PEOPLE OF JERUSALEM WILL BE CARRIED AWAY AS CAPTIVES.

IS THERE NO HOPE FOR GOD'S PEOPLE?

YES. GOD WILL SEND A DELIVERER TO SAVE ALL WHO BELIEVE IN HIM. AND HIS NAME SHALL BE CALLED WONDERFUL COUNSELOR, MIGHTY GOD, AND THE PRINCE OF PEACE.

GOD'S SERVANT WILL SUFFER FOR US. HE WILL BE DESPISED AND REJECTED BY MEN. BUT EVEN THOUGH WE REJECT HIM, HE WILL BE SPEARED AND TORTURED FOR OUR SINS.

AND BY HIS WOUNDS ... WE WILL BE HEALED!

THE PEOPLE DON'T UNDERSTAND AT THE TIME, BUT ISAIAH IS PREDICTING THE COMING OF JESUS CHRIST.

A Righteous King and a Reluctant Prophet

BASED ON 2 KINGS 22—23;
2 CHRONICLES 34—35;
JEREMIAH 1

JOSIAH BECOMES THE KING OF JUDAH WHEN HE IS ONLY EIGHT YEARS OLD. THE HIGH PRIEST HILKIAH HELPS RAISE HIM, TEACHING THE YOUNG KING TO REMAIN TRUE TO GOD.

HIS FAITH AND RIGHTEOUSNESS ARE LIKE THAT OF A YOUNG DAVID.

BUT GOD ISN'T ONLY RAISING UP A RIGHTEOUS KING—HE IS ALSO RAISING UP A RELUCTANT PROPHET.

WHAT DO YOU SEE?

INVADERS COMING DOWN FROM THE NORTH TO DESTROY JUDAH! WILL ANYONE BELIEVE ME?

THIRTEEN YEARS LATER, GOD SPEAKS TO A YOUNG MAN NAMED JEREMIAH.

BEFORE I FORMED YOU IN THE WOMB I KNEW YOU. AND I SET YOU APART TO BE A PROPHET TO THE NATIONS.

BUT I AM JUST A CHILD. NO ONE WILL LISTEN TO ME.

NO, THEY WILL FEAR YOU AND TRY TO KILL YOU. BUT DO NOT BE AFRAID, FOR I AM WITH YOU.

BUT AS HE READS THE SCROLL TO KING JOSIAH, HILKIAH'S JOY TURNS TO DESPAIR.

GOD'S LAWS ARE CLEARLY STATED—AND SO IS THE PUNISHMENT FOR ANYONE WHO DISOBEYS THEM.

THEN JUDAH IS DOOMED! WE HAVE BROKEN GOD'S LAWS MANY TIMES. I HAD NO IDEA.

CAN WE JUST PRETEND WE DIDN'T FIND THIS SCROLL?

NO! WE CANNOT IGNORE GOD'S WORD.

JOSIAH IS SO UPSET THAT HE QUICKLY SENDS SEVERAL HIGH-RANKING OFFICIALS TO THE PROPHETESS HULDAH.

IS THERE ANYTHING THAT CAN BE DONE?

THIS IS WHAT GOD SAYS: "BECAUSE JUDAH DISOBEYED ME, JUDAH WILL BE DESTROYED. BUT BECAUSE JOSIAH'S HEART IS HUMBLE BEFORE THE LORD, THE DESTRUCTION WILL NOT HAPPEN WHILE JOSIAH IS KING."

HOPING TO WIN GOD'S FORGIVENESS FOR HIS NATION, JOSIAH READS THE SCROLL OF GOD'S LAWS TO THE PEOPLE. HE ASKS THEM TO COMMIT TO FOLLOWING GOD'S COMMANDS, AND HE REESTABLISHES THE CELEBRATION OF PASSOVER.

WHY IS THIS NIGHT DIFFERENT FROM ALL OTHER NIGHTS? ...

Why Do Bad Things Happen to Good People?

BASED ON 2 KINGS 23:29—24:4; HABAKKUK

FOR SEVERAL YEARS, JEREMIAH AND THE KING WORK TOGETHER TO DESTROY IDOL WORSHIP. NEVER BEFORE OR SINCE HAS THERE BEEN A KING LIKE JOSIAH. HE SERVES THE LORD WITH ALL HIS HEART, SOUL, AND STRENGTH. THEN ONE DAY, A MILITARY COMMANDER BRINGS SOME FRIGHTENING NEWS.

THE ASSYRIAN EMPIRE IS FALLING APART, JUST LIKE NAHUM PREDICTED. EGYPT'S ARMY IS MARCHING NORTH. I THINK PHARAOH NECO HOPES TO GRAB WHAT'S LEFT.

IF EGYPT BECOMES THE NEXT SUPERPOWER, THEY WILL WANT TO CONTROL JUDAH AS WELL. I MUST STOP THEM.

STOP EGYPT? BUT IT'S ONE OF THE STRONGEST COUNTRIES IN THE WORLD. AND GOD HAS WARNED ME THAT BABYLON IS THE COUNTRY THAT WILL ONE DAY DESTROY JERUSALEM, NOT EGYPT.

IGNORING JEREMIAH'S ADVICE, KING JOSIAH LEADS HIS SOLDIERS OUT TO DEFEND THE PASS OF MEGIDDO—AND INTO THE PATH OF THE ONCOMING EGYPTIAN ARMY.

IN THE BATTLE, PHARAOH NECO FACES OFF AGAINST KING JOSIAH AND KILLS HIM.

WHEN SOLDIERS BRING JOSIAH'S BODY BACK IN HIS CHARIOT, JEREMIAH IS OVERCOME WITH GRIEF AT THE DEATH OF HIS GODLY KING. HE KNOWS THAT JOSIAH'S DEATH MARKS THE BEGINNING OF THE END FOR JERUSALEM. NOW JEHOIAKIM SITS ON THE THRONE OF JUDAH AS A PUPPET RULER FOR EGYPT. BUT HE DOES EVIL AND LEADS HIS PEOPLE AWAY FROM THE LORD—AND DISREGARDS JEREMIAH'S WARNINGS.

HABAKKUK

AT THIS TIME, THE PROPHET HABAKKUK ASKS GOD SOME TOUGH QUESTIONS. WHY IS THE WORLD SO UNFAIR? WHY WOULD GOD LET A GOOD KING DIE, WHILE WICKED PEOPLE LEAD RICH AND HAPPY LIVES?

WATCH AND WAIT! I PROMISE THAT IN THE END, EVERYONE WILL GET WHAT HE DESERVES. BUT FOR NOW, THE RIGHTEOUS MUST TRUST IN ME AND LIVE BY FAITH.

I WILL TRUST IN THE SOVEREIGN LORD, WHO GIVES ME SURE FOOTING ON TREACHEROUS GROUND.

HOW LONG, O LORD, MUST THE RIGHTEOUS CALL FOR YOUR HELP? WHY DO CRIMES GO UNPUNISHED? ANSWER ME, PLEASE!

IN THE MEANTIME, MORE BAD THINGS HAPPEN TO JUDAH. BABYLON COMES TO POWER JUST LIKE JEREMIAH PREDICTED. THE BABYLONIAN KING, NEBUCHADNEZZAR, CONQUERS EGYPT AND FORCES JUDAH TO SURRENDER. TO ENSURE JEHOIAKIM'S LOYALTY, NEBUCHADNEZZAR TAKES MANY OF THE PRINCES AND JERUSALEM'S FINEST YOUNG MEN AS HOSTAGES.

ALL JERUSALEM SADLY WATCHES ITS FINEST YOUNG MEN BEING MARCHED AWAY. AMONG THE HOSTAGES ARE A YOUNG MAN NAMED DANIEL AND HIS THREE FRIENDS. GOD WILL SOON SHOW HOW HE CAN WORK GOOD OUT OF THIS SAD EVENT.

Unpopular Prophecies

BASED ON JEREMIAH; 2 KINGS 23:36—24:1

THE NEW YOUNG KING JEHOIAKIM CONTINUES HIS ANCESTORS' TRADITION OF DISHONORING GOD.

MY FATHER ORDERED US NOT TO WORSHIP ANY GOD BUT JEHOVAH, AND LOOK WHAT HAPPENED! JUDAH IS NO LONGER A FREE COUNTRY. CLEARLY GOD CANNOT SAVE US. IT SHOULD BE ALLOWED TO WORSHIP ANY GOD ANYBODY THINKS MIGHT HELP US. MAYBE THE BABYLONIANS' GODS ...

TO JEREMIAH'S DISMAY, THE PEOPLE HAD NOT REALLY BELIEVED IN JOSIAH'S REFORMS. IN THEIR HEARTS, THEY ARE HAPPY TO FOLLOW JEHOIAKIM IN HIS IDOL WORSHIP. SO JEREMIAH PREACHES AT THE ENTRANCE TO GOD'S TEMPLE.

YOU THINK GOD IS SATISFIED WITH YOU BECAUSE YOU ARE CIRCUMCISED. BUT YOU MUST ALSO CIRCUMCISE YOUR HEARTS!

THE PEOPLE DON'T LISTEN, SO JEREMIAH COMES BACK TO PROPHESY AT THE TEMPLE AGAIN.

BECAUSE YOUR HEARTS ARE FALSE, YOUR WORSHIP DOES YOU NO GOOD. YOUR PRAYERS DO YOU NO GOOD. YOUR SACRIFICES DO YOU NO GOOD.

AND AGAIN ...

GOD HAS *TRIED* TO DISCIPLINE AND CORRECT YOU, BUT IT DOES YOU NO GOOD. SO NOW GOD WILL DESTROY JERUSALEM AND EXILE YOU TO BABYLON! BECAUSE YOU SERVE FOREIGN GODS IN YOUR OWN LAND, YOU WILL NOW SERVE FOREIGNERS IN A FOREIGN LAND.

AND AGAIN ...

IF YOU REALLY KNOW EVERYTHING, WHEN IS THIS SUPPOSED "EXILE" GOING TO HAPPEN?

YOU SHOULD START PACKING.

AT THESE WORDS, THE CROWD FLIES INTO A RAGE. THEY DRAG JEREMIAH TO THE CITY OFFICIALS.

HE IS SPEAKING AGAINST US AND AGAINST GOD'S CITY OF JERUSALEM! HE SHOULD BE STONED TO DEATH.

WHAT DO YOU HAVE TO SAY FOR YOURSELF?

I AM ONLY SAYING WHAT THE LORD HIMSELF TOLD ME TO SAY. "YOUR OWN BEHAVIOR AND ACTIONS HAVE BROUGHT THIS PUNISHMENT UPON YOU." AND IF YOU KILL ME TODAY, THE LORD WILL ADD IT TO YOUR LIST OF SINS FOR SHEDDING INNOCENT BLOOD.

THANKFULLY, ONE OF KING JOSIAH'S OLD OFFICIALS IS AT THE TEMPLE. AHIKAM HAD BEEN AN HONEST AND RIGHTEOUS MAN IN THE SERVICE OF JOSIAH, AND HE BELIEVES IN THE MINISTRY OF THE LORD THROUGH JEREMIAH.

PEOPLE, WHAT JEREMIAH SAYS IS NOT NEW. THE PROPHET MICAH PREDICTED THE SAME THING ABOUT JERUSALEM A CENTURY AGO, AND KING HEZEKIAH DID NOT PUT HIM TO DEATH. WE MUST NOT KILL THIS MAN FOR SPEAKING SIMILAR WORDS.

THE PEOPLE ARE STILL INFURIATED AT JEREMIAH, BUT THEY CANNOT STONE HIM WITHOUT AHIKAM'S PERMISSION. SULKILY THEY RETREAT ... FOR NOW. AS JEREMIAH BRUSHES HIMSELF OFF, A YOUNG SCRIBE, BARUCH, COMES FORWARD.

I BELIEVE YOU, JEREMIAH! IS THERE ANYTHING I CAN DO TO HELP YOU?

I NEED SOMEONE TO WRITE DOWN MY PROPHECIES. THESE PEOPLE MAY ACTUALLY KILL ME SOMEDAY, AND GOD'S WORD MUST LIVE ON.

SOON GOD GIVES JEREMIAH AND BARUCH ANOTHER MESSAGE TO SHARE WITH THE PEOPLE—WHETHER THEY WANT IT OR NOT.

THIS WILL DO NICELY.

I'D LIKE TO BUY THIS POT, PLEASE.

PEOPLE! ISN'T THIS A FINE POT? THE POTTER CLEARLY TOOK HIS TIME AND CRAFTED A BEAUTIFUL PIECE OF ART.

SUDDENLY, HE SMASHES THE POT TO THE GROUND.

SMASH

AND EVEN THOUGH GOD SET OUR PEOPLE AND OUR CITY APART, YOU HAVE TURNED YOUR BACKS ON HIM. SO HE WILL SMASH THIS CITY TO PIECES JUST LIKE I SMASHED THIS POT. YOU HAVE BEEN WARNED!

A PRIEST NAMED PASHHUR HEARS THE COMMOTION. HE COMES OVER AND SEES THE SHATTERED REMAINS OF THE POT AND THE PEOPLE MURMURING AMONG THEMSELVES.

HELLO, JEREMIAH. WHAT'S THE BAD NEWS FROM THE LORD TODAY?

YOU ARE. THAT'S WHY GOD IS GETTING RID OF YOU.

AT THIS INSOLENCE, PASHHUR HAS JEREMIAH BEATEN AND THROWN INTO STOCKS FOR THE NIGHT. IN HUMILIATION AND PAIN, JEREMIAH CRIES OUT TO THE LORD.

CURSE THE DAY I WAS BORN! WHY DIDN'T YOU LEAVE ME IN THE WOMB, LORD? WHY DID YOU FORCE ME INTO BEING YOUR PROPHET? YOUR WORDS ARE NOTHING BUT DOOM AND DESTRUCTION, AND THE PEOPLE HATE ME FOR IT. BUT IF I TRY TO IGNORE YOUR PROPHECIES, YOUR WORD BURNS IN MY HEART AND SETS FIRE TO MY BONES.

BUT YOU ARE MY PROTECTOR. IF THE ALMIGHTY LORD CANNOT SAVE ME, NO ONE CAN. I PUT ALL MY HOPE IN YOU.

JEREMIAH IS RELEASED THE NEXT MORNING, BUT TROUBLE BREWS IN THE PALACE.

WHY SHOULD WE PAY TRIBUTE TO BABYLON? I SAY LET'S STOP AND USE THE MONEY TO BUILD UP OUR OWN ARMY. THEN WE'LL BE READY IF BABYLON ATTACKS AGAIN.

YOU'RE RIGHT—THOSE HOSTAGES IN BABYLON ARE NOT AS IMPORTANT AS ALL OF US HERE IN JUDAH.

WORD LEAKS OUT THAT KING JEHOIAKIM IS BREAKING HIS AGREEMENT WITH BABYLON. BUT JEREMIAH KNOWS THE KING'S DECISION IS AGAINST THE WILL OF GOD, AND NO ONE CAN DEFY GOD!

Ezekiel's Exile

BASED ON EZEKIEL; JEREMIAH 29:1-14

KING JEHOIAKIM'S REVOLT AGAINST BABYLON IS WELL UNDER WAY WHEN—SUDDENLY—HE DIES. BABYLON EASILY OVERWHELMS JUDAH'S ARMY. YOUNG KING JEHOIACHIN, WHO HAS RULED THREE MONTHS, IS FORCED TO SURRENDER TO KING NEBUCHADNEZZAR.

THIS TIME I WILL TAKE YOUR TREASURES, YOUR NOBLES, YOUR SKILLED WORKERS, AND YOUR KING! LET THIS BE A LESSON TO THE ONES WHO ARE LEFT.

SO JEREMIAH'S PROPHECY COMES TRUE! THE TEMPLE TREASURES ARE LOOTED; THE KING AND 10,000 OF JUDAH'S STRONGEST MEN ARE LED AWAY. PRINCE ZEDEKIAH IS MADE KING—AFTER HE PROMISES LOYALTY TO BABYLON.

FRIGHTENED AND WEARY FROM THE 900-MILE MARCH, THE 10,000 CAPTIVES FROM JUDAH REACH THE GATES OF BABYLON, THE GIANT CITY OF THEIR CONQUERORS. EZEKIEL, A YOUNG PRIEST, AND HIS WIFE ARE AMONG THE CAPTIVES WONDERING WHERE THEY WILL LIVE.

YOU ISRAELITES CAN GO TO TEL-ABIB ON THE KEBAR RIVER. THERE'S UNCLAIMED LAND THERE WHERE YOU CAN FARM AND BUILD YOUR HOMES.

I SPENT MY WHOLE LIFE PREPARING TO BE A PRIEST IN JERUSALEM. BUT GOD IS STRONG, EVEN WHEN JUDAH IS WEAK. HE IS GOD, EVEN IN THIS FOREIGN LAND.

IN THE MONTHS THAT FOLLOW, EZEKIEL WORKS HARD TO MAKE A LIVING IN THE NEW LAND.

IT IS NOT AS BAD AS I THOUGHT IT WOULD BE. WE'RE TOGETHER, AND THEY TREAT US WELL.

BUT GOD HAS MORE IN STORE FOR EZEKIEL THAN BEING A FARMER IN A FOREIGN LAND ...

AS EZEKIEL PROPHESIES, THE BONES FORM BACK INTO HUMAN BEINGS—BUT THERE IS STILL NO LIFE IN THEM.

TELL THEM I WILL FILL THEM WITH MY BREATH, MY SPIRIT.

EZEKIEL CONTINUES TO PREACH, AND THE BODIES START BREATHING AGAIN. THEY COME TO LIFE AND STAND UP, THOUSANDS OF THEM!

EZEKIEL IS TRANSPORTED BACK TO HIS FELLOW JEWS IN BABYLON, WHERE HE TELLS THEM THIS STORY.

... AND THOSE BONES REPRESENT ISRAEL! IF GOD CAN BRING DEAD BONES TO LIFE, HE CAN BRING THE PEOPLE OF ISRAEL BACK TO JERUSALEM SOMEDAY. AND WHEN HE DOES, HE WILL FILL US WITH HIS SPIRIT.

GOD SAYS: "I WILL GATHER YOU FROM ALL THE COUNTRIES IN THE WORLD AND BRING YOU BACK INTO YOUR OWN LAND."

"I WILL CLEANSE YOU FROM ALL YOUR FILTH AND IDOLS."

"AND I WILL PUT MY SPIRIT IN YOU AND MOVE YOU TO FOLLOW MY DECREES AND KEEP MY LAWS. YOU WILL LIVE IN THE LAND I PROMISED YOU; YOU WILL BE MY PEOPLE, AND I WILL BE YOUR GOD."

"I WILL GIVE YOU A NEW HEART AND PUT A NEW SPIRIT IN YOU; I WILL REMOVE FROM YOU YOUR HEART OF STONE AND GIVE YOU A HEART OF FLESH."

"THERE WILL BE A NEW TEMPLE AND A NEW JERUSALEM, BUT JERUSALEM WILL HAVE A NEW NAME THAT MEANS ...

... THE LORD IS THERE!"

The Yoke's on Jeremiah

BASED ON JEREMIAH 27; 37—38

BACK IN JERUSALEM, KING ZEDEKIAH STILL RULES—AS LONG AS HE REMAINS LOYAL TO NEBUCHADNEZZAR. FOR A FEW YEARS ZEDEKIAH PAYS HIS TRIBUTE TO BABYLON. THEN, IN SPITE OF JEREMIAH'S WARNINGS, HE BEGINS TO THINK ABOUT REBELLING. HE CALLS TOGETHER THE OTHER FOREIGN KINGS WHO ARE RULED BY BABYLON.

WHAT DO WE GET FROM THE MONEY WE PAY TO BABYLON?

WE GET PEACE!

PEACE—BUT NOT FREEDOM! MAYBE THE EGYPTIANS WILL JOIN US. THEY HATE BABYLON TOO.

WHEN JEREMIAH LEARNS THAT THERE IS TALK OF ANOTHER REVOLT, HE PUTS AN OX YOKE ON HIS SHOULDERS AND BURSTS INTO THE KINGS' CONFERENCE—UNINVITED.

WHAT ARE YOU DOING?

GOD HAS RAISED UP BABYLON FOR A PURPOSE. EVERYTHING ON EARTH—INCLUDING THE WILD ANIMALS—WILL SERVE BABYLON'S KING. IF YOU TRY TO THROW OFF THE YOKE OF BABYLON, YOU WILL BE CRUSHED LIKE LEAVES UNDERFOOT. SERVE UNDER THE YOKE OF BABYLON AND YOU WILL LIVE. ANY PROPHET WHO TELLS YOU OTHERWISE IS LYING.

BUT ONE OF THE PROPHETS IN ATTENDANCE—HANANIAH—DOESN'T APPRECIATE JEREMIAH'S INTERRUPTION.

OH, REALLY? BECAUSE GOD TOLD ME EXACTLY WHAT TO DO WITH THE YOKE OF BABYLON. BREAK IT!

I PREDICT THAT IN TWO YEARS, BABYLON WILL BE DESTROYED AND WE'LL GET ALL OUR TEMPLE TREASURES BACK.

THAT'S GREAT NEWS! IF ONLY IT WERE TRUE. UNFORTUNATELY, YOU WILL BE PROVEN WRONG. YOU MAY BREAK A WOODEN YOKE, BUT THE YOKE OF BABYLON IS MADE OF IRON.

GOD IS TIRED OF YOUR LIES IN HIS NAME. YOU'LL BE DEAD WITHIN THE YEAR.

KRAK

ZEDEKIAH KNOWS JEREMIAH IS A TRUE MAN OF GOD, BUT HE DOESN'T WANT TO LISTEN. EVEN WHEN HANANIAH DIES A FEW MONTHS LATER, ZEDEKIAH STILL DOESN'T WANT TO BELIEVE JEREMIAH. DURING ALL OF THIS TIME, EGYPT HAS KEPT AN ANXIOUS EYE ON THE GROWING TENSIONS IN JUDAH. AT THE RIGHT MOMENT, IT SENDS AN AMBASSADOR TO KING ZEDEKIAH.

BABYLON IS YOUR ENEMY AS WELL AS OURS. ALONE, NEITHER OF US CAN DEFEAT THEM, BUT ...

TOGETHER, WE CAN DO IT!

AS JEREMIAH PROPHESIED, BABYLON ANSWERS THIS LATEST REVOLT WITH A SWIFT ATTACK. FOR WEEKS THE SOLDIERS OF JUDAH FIGHT TO DEFEND JERUSALEM'S WALLS.

WHERE ARE THE EGYPTIANS? THEY PROMISED THEY WOULD COME.

SUDDENLY, THE ATTACK STOPS ...

THE BABYLONIANS ARE BREAKING CAMP. THEY'VE GIVEN UP THE SIEGE!

WE'VE WON! JUDAH IS FREE!

WHAT DOES GOD HAVE TO SAY NOW, HUH?

THE PEOPLE THINK THEY'VE WON. BUT GOD HAS REVEALED THE TRUTH TO JEREMIAH.

NO! THE BABYLONIANS HAVE NOT QUIT. THEY'VE GONE TO STOP THE EGYPTIANS WHO WERE COMING TO HELP US. THEY'LL BE BACK.

HOW DOES HE KNOW SO MUCH ABOUT WHAT THE BABYLONIANS ARE DOING?

A FEW DAYS LATER, JEREMIAH STARTS ON A TRIP TO HIS HOMETOWN A FEW MILES FROM JERUSALEM. BEFORE HE GETS OUT OF THE GATE, SOLDIERS STOP HIM.

YOU'RE THE ONE WHO PROPHESIED THAT BABYLON WOULD CONQUER US. THIS IS ALL YOUR FAULT!

SINCE YOU DON'T SUPPORT US IN THE WAR, YOU'RE A TRAITOR TO JUDAH.

WHAT? I'VE ONLY SPOKEN GOD'S TRUTH.

IN SPITE OF HIS INNOCENCE, JEREMIAH IS THROWN INTO PRISON. WITHIN A FEW WEEKS, THE BABYLONIANS DEFEAT THE EGYPTIANS AND RETURN TO THE GATES OF JERUSALEM. JEREMIAH'S ENEMIES BRING HIM BEFORE THE KING AND ACCUSE HIM OF BEING A TRAITOR.

I REPEAT THE WARNING GOD GAVE ME. INVADERS FROM THE NORTH WILL CONQUER JUDAH. GOD CHOSE THE BABYLONIANS TO DESTROY OUR NATION BECAUSE OF THE SINS OF OUR PEOPLE.

IT'S THIS KIND OF TALK THAT MAKES OUR SOLDIERS LOSE COURAGE. PUT THIS TRAITOR TO DEATH, OR THE CITY WILL FALL.

HE'S IN YOUR HANDS. DO WHAT YOU WANT WITH HIM.

QUICKLY—BEFORE THE KING CAN CHANGE HIS MIND—JEREMIAH'S ACCUSERS PUT HIM IN AN OLD EMPTY WELL BENEATH THE PRISON FLOOR.

LET HIM STARVE TO DEATH!

THE OLD WELL DOESN'T HAVE WATER IN IT ANYMORE—BUT IT DOES STILL HAVE MUD AND SLIME. JEREMIAH GAGS TO BE TRAPPED IN SUCH FILTH AND WONDERS HOW LONG HE CAN SURVIVE. BUT EBED-MELECH, A SERVANT IN THE PALACE, GETS PERMISSION FROM THE KING TO PUT JEREMIAH IN THE PRISON YARD.

THANK GOD FOR YOUR HELP. I WOULD HAVE DIED IN THAT AWFUL HOLE.

AS THE SIEGE CONTINUES, PEOPLE IN JERUSALEM ARE STARVING AND BEG FOR FOOD. AT LAST THE FRIGHTENED KING CALLS FOR JEREMIAH.

WHAT WILL HAPPEN TO US?

IT'S SIMPLE. IF YOU SURRENDER, JERUSALEM WILL BE SAVED. IF YOU DON'T, IT WILL BE BURNED, AND THE BABYLONIANS WILL TORTURE AND KILL YOU.

SURRENDER? I DON'T DARE. MY OWN PEOPLE WOULD TURN AGAINST ME.

YOU SHOULD BE MORE CONCERNED THAT GOD HAS TURNED AGAINST YOU.

ZEDEKIAH IS UNHAPPY WITH THIS ANSWER. HE KEEPS JEREMIAH UNDER HOUSE ARREST. THE SIEGE GOES ON, BUT AFTER 30 MORE MONTHS ...

465

Jerusalem Falls!

BASED ON JEREMIAH 39—44; 2 KINGS 25; 2 CHRONICLES 36:15-23; LAMENTATIONS; OBADIAH

FOR TWO AND A HALF YEARS, FORCES FROM THE GREAT BABYLONIAN ARMY ATTACK THE CITY OF JERUSALEM. AT LAST THEY BREAK THROUGH THE WALL. AS BABYLONIAN SOLDIERS POUR THROUGH THE BROKEN WALLS, KING ZEDEKIAH TRIES TO ESCAPE WITH HIS FAMILY.

THE BABYLONIANS CAPTURE ZEDEKIAH BEFORE HE CAN REACH THE RIVER. THEY PUT OUT HIS EYES AND BRING HIM TO THE CAPTAIN OF THE GUARD.

SINCE YOU COULDN'T SEE YOUR DUTY TO KING NEBUCHADNEZZAR, NOW YOU WILL SEE NOTHING EVER AGAIN.

TAKE HIM TO BABYLON!

BUT KING NEBUCHADNEZZAR HAS HEARD OF JEREMIAH'S PROPHECIES ALL THE WAY FROM BABYLON. HIS CAPTAIN HAS SPECIAL INSTRUCTIONS.

JEREMIAH, WE KNOW THAT YOU ARE FAITHFUL TO YOUR GOD. BECAUSE YOU TRIED TO KEEP YOUR COUNTRY FROM REBELLING AGAINST US, YOU ARE FREE! GO WHEREVER YOU WANT AND LIVE WHEREVER YOU WANT. IF YOU COME BACK WITH ME TO BABYLON, I WILL MAKE SURE THAT YOU HAVE WEALTH AND COMFORT FOR THE REST OF YOUR LIFE.

THANK YOU, BUT NO. I MUST STAY HERE TO HELP GOD'S PEOPLE WHO HAVE BEEN LEFT IN ISRAEL WITHOUT A LEADER.

THEN THE BABYLONIANS STRIP THE SILVER, GOLD, AND VALUABLE OBJECTS FROM THE TEMPLE AND PALACE BUILDINGS.

SET FIRE TO EVERY CORNER OF THE CITY. DON'T LET ANYTHING SURVIVE THAT WOULD GIVE ANYONE IDEAS ABOUT REBUILDING JERUSALEM.

FOR DAYS, THE FIRE RAGES—UNTIL ALL THAT IS LEFT OF THE BEAUTIFUL CITY OF JERUSALEM IS A HEAP OF ASHES AND BLACKENED STONES.

TO LAMENT MEANS TO EXPRESS SORROW. IN THE BOOK OF LAMENTATIONS, JEREMIAH SHARES THE GRIEF THE JEWS FEEL OVER THE DESTRUCTION OF JERUSALEM.

AND NOW THE STREETS OF JERUSALEM LIE EMPTY.
BITTERLY OUR CITY WEEPS TONIGHT—
COMFORT IS FAR FROM HER.
DESTRUCTION HAS COME FROM BABYLON,
ENEMIES HAVE TAKEN HER TREASURES,
FOR THE LORD HAS REJECTED HER. BUT REMEMBER,

GOD'S GREAT LOVE WILL NOT LET US BE BURNED UP FOREVER.
HIS LOVE WILL NEVER FAIL BECAUSE
IT IS NEW EVERY MORNING. GREAT IS GOD'S FAITHFULNESS!

JERUSALEM, DAUGHTER OF ZION, YOU WILL RETURN.
KEEP YOUR HEART STRONG AND YOUR EYES FOCUSED ON THE LORD.
LORD, YOUR THRONE WILL LAST FOREVER.
MAY YOU RESTORE US AND BRING US BACK TO YOU!

ISRAEL'S ANCESTOR, JACOB, SPENT A LIFETIME FIGHTING WITH HIS BROTHER ESAU. NOW ESAU'S DESCENDANTS, THE EDOMITES, CELEBRATE THAT THEIR COUSINS IN JERUSALEM HAVE BEEN CONQUERED. THE PROPHET OBADIAH SCOLDS THEM FOR THEIR HEARTLESS ATTITUDE.

YOU SHOULD NOT KICK YOUR BROTHER WHEN HE IS DOWN. DO NOT TAKE JOY OVER THE PEOPLE OF JUDAH IN THE DAY OF THEIR DESTRUCTION, AND DO NOT MOCK THEIR TROUBLES, FOR THESE SAME TROUBLES WILL COME TO YOU SOMEDAY.

OBADIAH

THE BABYLONIANS SET UP HEADQUARTERS AT MIZPAH AND APPOINT GEDALIAH AS GOVERNOR. GEDALIAH HAS ALWAYS BEEN FAITHFUL TO THE LORD AND BELIEVED THE WORDS OF JEREMIAH. PLEASED TO HAVE A GODLY GOVERNOR, JEREMIAH JOINS HIM AND BECOMES HIS ADVISER.

TOGETHER WE'LL ENCOURAGE THE PEOPLE TO BUILD UP THEIR HOMES AND REPLANT THEIR VINEYARDS AND FIELDS.

SOMEDAY THE CAPTIVES WILL RETURN—AND JUDAH WILL BECOME A NATION AGAIN.

GOD HASN'T DONE SUCH A GOOD JOB KEEPING US SAFE IN JERUSALEM. WE'RE GOING TO EGYPT.

EVEN AFTER EVERYTHING THAT'S HAPPENED, YOU STILL DON'T BELIEVE IN GOD'S WORD. YOU JUST HOPED I'D GIVE YOU PERMISSION FOR WHAT YOU'D ALREADY DECIDED TO DO.

BUT GOOD NEWS IS ALWAYS TEMPORARY FOR JEREMIAH. BEFORE THE GOVERNOR'S DREAM CAN COME TRUE, HE IS MURDERED. FEARFUL THAT BABYLON WILL BLAME ALL ISRAEL FOR THE MURDER, A GROUP OF PEOPLE GO TO SEE JEREMIAH ...

WE WANT TO GO TO EGYPT, WHERE THERE IS PEACE AND PLENTY TO EAT. WILL YOU ASK OF THE LORD IF THAT'S OKAY?

THE LORD HAS WARNED ME THAT YOU WILL FIND NEITHER PEACE NOR FOOD IN EGYPT. STAY HERE. THE BABYLONIANS WILL NOT HURT YOU.

BUT THE PEOPLE DO NOT CARE. THEY FLEE TO EGYPT, FORCING JEREMIAH TO GO WITH THEM. THEY THINK THEY WILL BE SAFE, BUT NEBUCHADNEZZAR CONQUERS EGYPT NEXT, KILLING EVERYONE WHO FLED FROM JERUSALEM. THE FUTURE HOPE FOR GOD'S PEOPLE NOW LIES WITH THE EXILES IN BABYLON ...

Eat Your Vegetables

BASED ON DANIEL 1

THE STORY OF WHAT HAPPENS TO A ROYAL CAPTIVE FROM JUDAH BEGINS WHEN DANIEL AND HIS THREE FRIENDS—SHADRACH, MESHACH, AND ABEDNEGO—ENTER THE CITY OF BABYLON AT THE END OF THEIR 900-MILE MARCH FROM JERUSALEM.

WHAT DO YOU THINK THEY'LL DO TO US, DANIEL?

I DON'T KNOW, SHADRACH. BUT I'M SURE GOD IS WITH US.

SOON AFTER THE PRISONERS REACH THE CITY, DANIEL AND SEVERAL OTHERS ARE BROUGHT BEFORE AN OFFICER OF KING NEBUCHADNEZZAR.

AS NOBLES FROM JERUSALEM, YOU WILL BE GIVEN A CHANCE TO TRY OUT FOR POSITIONS IN THE KING'S COURT. BUT I WARN YOU—YOU MUST BE STRONG, SMART, AND HANDSOME.

THE CHIEF OFFICIAL MOVES THROUGH THE RANKS OF EXILES. HE STOPS IN FRONT OF DANIEL.

IF YOUR GOD IS SO POWERFUL, WHY DID HE LET YOU HEBREWS BE CONQUERED?

DOESN'T A FATHER SOMETIMES NEED TO PUNISH HIS OWN CHILDREN?

HMMPH. GOOD ANSWER.

470

THE NEXT DAY ...

YOU HAVE BEEN CHOSEN! NOW YOU'LL BE GIVEN THREE YEARS TO STUDY UNDER OUR WISE MEN. AFTER THAT, THE KING HIMSELF WILL CHOOSE THOSE BEST QUALIFIED TO BE HIS ADVISERS. AS A BONUS, YOU WILL GET TO EAT THE EXTRA FOOD FROM THE KING'S TABLE!

THE YOUNG MEN ARE ASSIGNED A ROOM AT THE PALACE TO BEGIN THEIR STUDIES. EVEN THOUGH THEY ARE TECHNICALLY CAPTIVES, THEY RECEIVE THE BEST OF EVERYTHING—INCLUDING THE KING'S FOOD.

HERE YOU GO, THE BEST FOOD IN THE KINGDOM. IT'S EVEN BEEN BLESSED BY OUR GOD MARDUK.

WE CAN'T EAT THIS! IT'S BEEN DEDICATED TO THE BABYLONIAN IDOLS.

THANK YOU FOR THE HONOR YOU HAVE SHOWN US, BUT OUR HEBREW LAWS FORBID US FROM EATING YOUR MEAT AND WINE. PLEASE JUST GIVE US PLAIN VEGETABLES AND WATER.

VEGETABLES AND WATER? THAT'S NOT ENOUGH FOOD FOR GROWING YOUNG MEN. I NEED YOU LOOKING STRONG AND WELL-FED, OR THE KING WILL HAVE MY HEAD.

HOW ABOUT THIS? TEST US FOR A FEW DAYS. LET US EAT OUR PLAIN FOOD AND THEN SEE HOW WE COMPARE TO THE OTHERS.

FOR TEN DAYS, THE OTHER TRAINEES EAT THEIR STEAK AND FINE WINE TAKEN FROM THE TEMPLE OF MARDUK. DANIEL AND HIS THREE FRIENDS EAT NOTHING BUT BOILED VEGETABLES AND WATER.

AT THE END OF TEN DAYS, THERE'S NO DOUBT—DANIEL AND HIS FRIENDS NOT ONLY LOOK BETTER, BUT THEY ARE CLEARLY STRONGER AND FASTER THAN THEIR PEERS.

FINE! EAT WHATEVER YOU WANT.

AFTER THIS, THE FOUR YOUNG HEBREWS BUSY THEMSELVES WITH THEIR STUDIES, LEARNING EVERYTHING THEIR BABYLONIAN TEACHERS CAN TEACH.

BUT EVEN THOUGH THEY'RE KEEPING THEMSELVES PURE FROM UNGODLY FOOD, THEY WORRY ABOUT THEIR UNGODLY STUDIES AS WELL.

WHY ARE WE STUDYING THE BABYLONIAN HISTORY, AND THEIR GODS AND ASTROLOGY? WE DON'T BELIEVE IN ANY OF IT.

FOR BETTER OR FOR WORSE, THIS IS THE CULTURE WE LIVE IN. IT'S GOOD TO UNDERSTAND THEIR WAYS, JUST NOT TO FOLLOW THEM.

THE FOUR YOUNG MEN CONSISTENTLY PRAY TO GOD THREE TIMES A DAY. IN ANSWER TO THEIR FAITHFULNESS, GOD GIVES THEM KNOWLEDGE AND WISDOM. TO DANIEL, GOD EVEN GIVES AN UNDERSTANDING OF DREAMS. AT THE END OF THE THREE YEARS, THE YOUNG MEN ARE TAKEN BEFORE THE KING. HE TALKS WITH EACH ONE, THEN MAKES HIS DECISION.

I HAVE CHOSEN THESE FOUR—DANIEL, SHADRACH, MESHACH, AND ABEDNEGO—TO SERVE IN MY GOVERNMENT. THEY ARE TEN TIMES BETTER THAN ALL MY MAGICIANS, ENCHANTERS, AND ADVISERS!

A Deadly Dream

BASED ON DANIEL 2

DANIEL AND HIS FRIENDS BECOME POPULAR MEMBERS OF THE KING'S COURT. BUT ONE DAY, THE KING HAS AN UNUSUALLY DIFFICULT PROBLEM AND HE CALLS FOR HIS OLDER, MORE EXPERIENCED ADVISERS.

I HAD A STRANGE DREAM THAT IS BOTHERING ME. I WANT TO KNOW WHAT IT MEANS.

OF COURSE, YOUR HIGHNESS. TELL US WHAT YOU DREAMED AND WE WILL INTERPRET IT FOR YOU.

NO. THIS IS WHAT I'VE DECIDED TO DO: IF ONE OF YOU CAN TELL ME WHAT IT WAS AND WHAT IT MEANS, I WILL REWARD YOU GREATLY. BUT IF YOU GET IT WRONG, I'LL CUT YOU INTO LITTLE PIECES AND BURN YOUR HOUSE DOWN.

WE CAN TELL YOU WHAT A DREAM MEANS, OH KING, BUT NO ONE CAN TELL YOU WHAT YOU ACTUALLY DREAMED. ONLY THE GODS THEMSELVES COULD DO WHAT YOU ASK.

JUST WHAT I THOUGHT! YOU ARE DECEIVERS AND LIARS, ALL OF YOU. YOU DO NOT TRULY UNDERSTAND THE SUPERNATURAL. PUT THESE MEN TO DEATH—AND EVERY WISE MAN IN MY KINGDOM!

THE CAPTAIN OF THE KING'S GUARD IS FORCED TO CARRY OUT HIS UGLY TASK.

I'M SORRY, DANIEL, YOU AND YOUR FRIENDS ARE UNDER ARREST. THE KING HAS ORDERED ALL OF HIS WISE MEN PUT TO DEATH!

PUT TO DEATH? WHY? WHAT HAVE WE DONE?

473

WHEN THE GUARD EXPLAINS NEBUCHADNEZZAR'S ANGER, DANIEL REACTS CALMLY AND WISELY. HE ASKS FOR PERMISSION TO SPEAK TO THE KING.

O KING, GIVE ME TIME, AND I WILL TELL YOU WHAT YOU DREAMED.

YOU HAVE UNTIL TOMORROW AT THIS TIME—BUT NOT ONE MINUTE MORE!

DANIEL RUSHES BACK TO HIS FRIENDS WITH THE NEWS.

BUT, DANIEL, NO ONE ON EARTH CAN DO WHAT YOU PROMISED TO DO. IT'S IMPOSSIBLE!

YOU'RE RIGHT—BUT WHAT IS IMPOSSIBLE FOR US IS POSSIBLE FOR GOD. WE MUST PRAY—ALL NIGHT IF NECESSARY—AND ASK GOD TO GIVE US THE ANSWER SO WE WON'T BE EXECUTED.

AS THE FOUR YOUNG HEBREWS PRAY, GOD SHOWS DANIEL THE DREAM AND ITS MEANING.

PRAISE BE TO GOD! YOU GIVE WISDOM TO THE WISE. YOU REVEAL MYSTERIES THAT ARE HIDDEN AND BRING LIGHT TO WHAT WAS DARK! THANK YOU FOR REVEALING NEBUCHADNEZZAR'S DREAM.

THE NEXT DAY ...

HAVE YOU COME TO ASK FOR MORE TIME—OR CAN YOU TELL ME MY DREAM?

NO MAN CAN DO WHAT YOU HAVE ASKED. BUT THERE IS A GOD IN HEAVEN WHO HAS SHOWN YOUR DREAM TO ME.

YOU SAW A MIGHTY STATUE. ITS HEAD WAS MADE OF GOLD, ITS SHOULDERS OF SILVER, AND ITS LEGS OF BRONZE AND IRON. BUT ITS FEET WERE MADE OF CLAY. THEN YOU SAW A LARGE STONE STRIKE AT THE FEET OF THE STATUE AND BREAK IT INTO MANY PIECES.

YES! THAT'S RIGHT! BUT WHAT DOES IT MEAN?

THE HEAD OF GOLD STANDS FOR YOU AND YOUR GREAT KINGDOM. OTHER LESSER KINGDOMS WILL FOLLOW, BUT AFTER THEY FALL, GOD WILL SET UP A KINGDOM THAT WILL NEVER BE DESTROYED.

YOUR GOD IS A GOD ABOVE ALL GODS. AND YOU SHALL BE RULER OF THE PROVINCE OF BABYLON OVER ALL THE WISE MEN WHOSE LIVES YOU SAVED TODAY.

AT KING NEBUCHADNEZZAR'S COMMAND, A GIANT STATUE—90 FEET HIGH—HAS BEEN BUILT ON THE PLAINS OF DURA. ALL OF THE OFFICIALS OF BABYLON ARE ORDERED TO WORSHIP IT. THE HOUR OF WORSHIP COMES—THE MOMENT THE KING'S JEALOUS ADVISERS HAVE BEEN WAITING FOR ...

THE MUSICIANS HAVE TAKEN THEIR PLACES. THE SIGNAL WILL COME SOON—THE ONE THAT MEANS DEATH TO DANIEL'S FRIENDS.

MUSIC FILLS THE AIR. THE OFFICIALS OF BABYLON BOW DOWN AND WORSHIP THE GOLDEN STATUE—ALL BUT SHADRACH, MESHACH, AND ABEDNEGO.

SEE? THEY REFUSE TO BOW DOWN!

The Four Beasts from Below

BASED ON DANIEL 7

ONE NIGHT, DANIEL HAS A DREAM. FOUR BEASTS RISE OUT OF THE SURGING SEA ...

THEN, A FEROCIOUS BEAR COMES FORTH.

THIRD, A BEAST LIKE A LEOPARD WITH FOUR HEADS AND FOUR WINGS.

FIRST, A LION WITH EAGLE'S WINGS.

FINALLY, A TERRIFYING AND POWERFUL BEAST WITH IRON TEETH RISES UP. IT CRUSHES AND DEVOURS ALL THE BEASTS THAT CAME BEFORE IT. NOTHING CAN STOP IT.

GOD GIVES HIM THE MEANING OF THIS DREAM. THE FOUR BEASTS, JUST LIKE THE FOUR METALS IN NEBUCHADNEZZAR'S STATUE, REPRESENT FOUR KINGDOMS—BABYLON, PERSIA, GREECE, AND ROME. BUT A DIFFERENT KIND OF KINGDOM—GOD'S KINGDOM—WILL COME AFTER ROME, AND IT WILL LAST FOREVER.

The Writing on the Wall

BASED ON DANIEL 5

AFTER NEBUCHADNEZZAR DIES, DANIEL CONTINUES TO GOVERN UNDER MANY DIFFERENT KINGS. BUT THE NEW RULER, BELSHAZZAR, IS YOUNG AND SPOILED. HE SPENDS ALL HIS TIME IN FEASTS AND PARTIES AND DOESN'T EVEN KNOW THAT DANIEL QUIETLY KEEPS THE KINGDOM RUNNING. HE LAUGHS AT TWO GREAT THREATS TO HIS KINGDOM: ANGRY PRIESTS WHO ARE TURNING AGAINST HIM AND THE APPROACH OF THE MIGHTY PERSIAN ARMY. INSTEAD HE PREPARES A GREAT FEAST AND INVITES A THOUSAND GUESTS.

HE GIVES NO THOUGHT TO THE ENEMY AT HIS GATES OR THE GOD HE HAS OFFENDED.

BRING THE GOBLETS AND PLATES THAT WE TOOK FROM THE HEBREW TEMPLE IN JERUSALEM!

I'D LIKE TO GIVE THANKS TO THE GOD OF GOLD FOR MAKING THIS CUP!

AND TO THE GOD OF SILVER FOR MAKING THIS PLATE.

AND TO THE GOD OF WOOD FOR MAKING THIS WALL ... OR ELSE I'D FALL DOWN.

BUT THEIR DRUNKENNESS AND BLASPHEMY IS CUT SHORT. SUDDENLY BELSHAZZAR STARES AT A PLACE HIGH ON THE BANQUET WALL. HE TURNS PALE AND HIS HANDS TREMBLE ...

LOOK! ON THE WALL! WHAT IS IT? WHAT DOES IT MEAN?

THE BANQUET HALL IS SO QUIET YOU CAN HEAR A PIN DROP UNTIL DANIEL APPEARS BEFORE THE KING.

DIVIDE

TELL ME WHAT THOSE WORDS MEAN AND YOU WILL BE THE THIRD HIGHEST RULEER IN BABYLON. I'LL GIVE YOU HALF MY WEALTH!

KEEP YOUR RICHES TO YOURSELF AND GIVE YOUR PROMOTION TO SOMEONE ELSE. YOUR ANCESTOR NEBUCHADNEZZAR MADE MISTAKES, BUT AT LEAST HE LEARNED FROM THEM AND GAVE HONOR TO GOD. BUT YOU ARE ARROGANT. YOU ATE AND DRANK OUT OF THE SACRED TREASURES OF GOD'S TEMPLE. YOU PRAISED THE GODS OF GOLD AND SILVER AND WOOD—WHICH DON'T EVEN EXIST! BUT YOU HAVE GIVEN NO HONOR TO GOD.

THESE WORDS ARE GOD'S PROMISE TO YOU. THEY MEAN THIS: YOUR DAYS ARE NUMBERED! YOU'VE BEEN MEASURED AND FOUND WANTING! AND YOUR KINGDOM WILL BE DIVIDED AMONG THE PERSIANS!

WELL, THAT SOUNDS A LITTLE FARFETCHED, BUT I'LL KEEP MY PROMISE. HERE, THIS CHAIN MAKES YOU NEXT TO ME IN ALL THE KINGDOM.

NOW, ON WITH THE FEAST!

AS BELSHAZZAR SPEAKS, PERSIAN SOLDIERS SUDDENLY FILL THE HALL AND TAKE HIM PRISONER.

SOLDIERS? WHERE DID THEY COME FROM? WHERE ARE MY GUARDS?

BEFORE MORNING, THE CITY IS IN THE HANDS OF THE ENEMY. BELSHAZZAR IS EXECUTED BY THE CONQUERING PERSIANS.

WHEN DARIUS'S NEW LAW IS ANNOUNCED, DANIEL IMMEDIATELY RECOGNIZES THE TRAP SET BY THE DISHONEST ADVISERS.

OH, LORD, HOW THE WICKED TRY TO DISHONOR YOUR NAME AND DISCREDIT YOUR SERVANTS. OH, WELL. I HAVE PRAYED TO YOU, AND NOBODY BUT YOU, FOR MY WHOLE LIFE. I'M NOT ABOUT TO STOP NOW.

DANIEL MAKES HIS WAY HOME ...

... AND GOES TO THE UPSTAIRS ROOM, WHERE THE WINDOWS FACE JERUSALEM. THERE, LIKE HE'S DONE EVERY DAY FOR THE PAST 70 YEARS, HE PRAYS.

SEE— DANIEL PRAYS TO HIS GOD JUST LIKE WE THOUGHT HE WOULD.

GOOD. NOW WE'LL TELL DARIUS.

HAVE YOU NOT SIGNED A LAW FOR A PERSON TO BE THROWN TO THE LIONS IF HE BOWS BEFORE ANYONE BUT YOU?

I HAVE—AND THE LAW OF THE PERSIANS CANNOT BE CHANGED.

DANIEL HAS BROKEN YOUR LAWS. THREE TIMES A DAY HE PRAYS TO HIS GOD—IN FRONT OF A WINDOW WHERE EVERYONE CAN SEE.

DANIEL, MY FRIEND!

I SEE IT NOW. MY ADVISERS TRICKED ME INTO SENDING DANIEL TO HIS DEATH.

KING DARIUS HAD NOT THOUGHT OF THIS POSSIBLE OUTCOME FROM HIS LAW. HE WORKS ALL DAY TO TRY TO SAVE HIS TRUSTED ADVISER.

COULDN'T YOU MAYBE HOLD OFF ON PRAYING FOR ANOTHER 29 DAYS? YOU DON'T EVEN HAVE TO PRAY TO ME. OR MAYBE JUST PRAY WHERE PEOPLE CAN'T SEE YOU FOR A FEW WEEKS?

YOU TRUST ME BECAUSE I DO NOT COMPROMISE MY PRINCIPLES. I CANNOT COMPROMISE TO MY GOD.

DANIEL REMAINS FIRM. AND AT THE END OF THE DAY, KING DARIUS CANNOT CHANGE THE LAW, EVEN ONE THAT HE HIMSELF SIGNED.

RELUCTANTLY, HE ORDERS HIS GUARDS TO TAKE DANIEL TO THE LIONS' DEN AND THROW HIM IN.

LOOK! DANIEL DOESN'T SEEM TO BE AFRAID.

HE WILL BE WHEN HE GETS TO THE LIONS' DEN. OUR PLAN TO GET RID OF HIM IS WORKING PERFECTLY.

A FEW MINUTES LATER, DANIEL, WHO BROKE THE KING'S LAW BY PRAYING TO GOD, IS THROWN IN WITH THE LIONS.

SEAL THE DEN WITH A STONE SO THAT EVERYONE WILL KNOW I AM ENFORCING THE LAW.

MY OWN PRIDE AND THIS STUPID LAW HAVE COST ME MY ONLY TRUSTED FRIEND.

MY ONLY HOPE NOW IS THAT YOUR GOD IS STRONG ENOUGH TO SAVE YOU!

THAT NIGHT THE KING CAN'T EAT OR SLEEP. HE PACES BACK AND FORTH THINKING ABOUT DANIEL.

AT DAYBREAK, THE KING RUSHES TO THE LIONS' DEN.

ROLL AWAY THAT STONE!

DANIEL! DID YOUR GOD PROTECT YOU?

O KING, MY GOD SENT AN ANGEL WHO SHUT THE MOUTHS OF THE LIONS! MY GOD FOUND ME FAITHFUL. JUST LIKE I HAVE ALWAYS BEEN FAITHFUL TO YOU, MY KING.

A Pair of Queens

IN THE YEARS SINCE THE PERSIANS CONQUERED BABYLON, THE PERSIAN EMPIRE HAS BECOME THE MOST POWERFUL IN ALL THE WORLD—REACHING FROM INDIA TO ETHIOPIA. KING XERXES NOW SITS ON THE THRONE AT SUSA. TO CELEBRATE HIS GREATNESS, HE THROWS A PARTY FOR HIS NOBLEMEN—A BIG, EXPENSIVE, AND *LONG* PARTY.

THE KING HAS BEEN ENTERTAINING HIGH-RANKING OFFICIALS FOR SIX MONTHS NOW! HOW MUCH LONGER WILL THIS FEASTING GO ON?

UNTIL HE THINKS HE HAS IMPRESSED ALL OF HIS SUBJECTS WITH HIS WEALTH AND POWER.

XERXES' HUGE PARTY FINALLY COMES TO AN END. TO CELEBRATE, HE THROWS *ANOTHER* PARTY; THIS ONE FOR HIS CLOSEST FRIENDS. AFTER SEVERAL DAYS OF DRINKING, THE KING BEGINS HIS BOASTING.

YOU KNOW, I'M NOT JUST THE RICHEST AND THE STRONGEST. I ALSO HAVE THE MOST BEAUTIFUL WIFE IN THE EMPIRE. YOU DON'T BELIEVE ME, DO YOU? NO, NO, THAT'S OKAY. I'LL PROVE IT TO YOU.

SEND FOR QUEEN VASHTI!

JUST YOU WAIT. SHE'S STUNNING.

UMM ... YOUR HIGHNESS? THE QUEEN REFUSES TO COME.

WHAT???

THIS IS HORRIBLE. MY WIFE DOESN'T OBEY MY COMMANDS. MY NOBLEMEN, YOU MUST HELP ME. ACCORDING TO PERSIAN LAW, WHAT CAN I DO TO UNDO WHAT SHE DIDN'T DO?

AFTER PUZZLING THROUGH THE KING'S QUESTION, ONE OF HIS ADVISERS STANDS UP AND POINTS OUT THAT THE CONSEQUENCES ARE MUCH WORSE THAN THEY EVEN REALIZE ...

SHE HAS NOT JUST OFFENDED YOU, O KING. SHE HAS BROUGHT DISASTER UPON ALL THE MEN IN THE KINGDOM! ONCE WOMEN HEAR THAT QUEEN VASHTI HAS DISOBEYED YOU, THEY WILL START DISOBEYING THEIR OWN HUSBANDS. THEY'LL DO WHATEVER THEY WANT. THEY MIGHT EVEN *TALK* TO US! IT WILL BE CHAOS!

NOW IF I UNDERSTAND THE KING RIGHTLY, AND I THINK I DO, THEN THE KING SHOULD DO WHAT I WOULD DO.

WHICH IS?

FIRST, ANNOUNCE THAT VASHTI IS NO LONGER THE QUEEN. THEN, SEARCH THE COUNTRYSIDE LOOKING FOR THE MOST BEAUTIFUL, YOUNG, AND *QUIET* WOMEN IN THE LAND. YOU CAN PICK OUT A NEW WIFE. A *BETTER* WIFE!

THEN WOMEN WILL KNOW NOT TO TALK BACK TO THEIR HUSBANDS. AND WE'LL HAVE PEACE.

BRILLIANT!

HE'S SO RIGHT.

WE'LL MAKE OUR WOMEN RESPECT US!

SO THE KING BANISHES HIS QUEEN AND SENDS OUT A DECREE. "VASHTI IS NO LONGER THE QUEEN, AND I THINK EVERY MAN SHOULD BE KING IN HIS OWN HOUSEHOLD!"

AFTER HIS RAGE—AND THE WINE—WEARS OFF, KING XERXES STARTS TO MISS VASHTI. THEN HE REMEMBERS WHAT SHE HAD DONE—AND WHAT HE HAD DONE.

I DON'T HAVE A BEAUTIFUL QUEEN ANYMORE! AND I CAN'T BRING VASHTI BACK BECAUSE I CANNOT UNDO THE NEW LAW.

I KNOW WHAT WILL MAKE YOU FEEL BETTER. WE'LL BRING YOU ALL THE MOST BEAUTIFUL WOMEN IN THE KINGDOM. YOU CAN PICK YOUR FAVORITE TO BE YOUR NEW QUEEN. AND THE ONE YOU PICK WILL BE EVEN MORE BEAUTIFUL THAN VASHTI.

THE SHALLOW KING AGREES.

NOW THERE IS A JEWISH MAN NAMED MORDECAI WHO WORKS IN THE COURTS OF THE CAPITAL CITY OF SUSA. HE HAS A COUSIN NAMED ESTHER. ESTHER'S PARENTS DIED WHEN SHE WAS VERY YOUNG, SO MORDECAI HAS RAISED HER LIKE HIS OWN DAUGHTER. NOW THAT SHE'S GROWN UP, ESTHER IS A BEAUTIFUL WOMAN WHO IMPRESSES EVERYONE SHE MEETS.

WHEN ALL THE BEAUTIFUL WOMEN IN THE LAND ARE BROUGHT TO THE KING'S PALACE, ESTHER IS AMONG THEM.

DON'T BE AFRAID, YOU WILL BE TREATED WELL IN THE PALACE. BUT DON'T LET ANYONE KNOW THAT YOU ARE JEWISH!

IN THE PALACE, THE YOUNG WOMEN ARE BROUGHT BEFORE HEGAI, THE HEAD SERVANT IN CHARGE OF MAKING SURE ALL THE CANDIDATES ARE AS BEAUTIFUL AS CAN BE.

YOU GIRLS MAY HAVE BEEN PRETTY ENOUGH FOR THE PIG HERDER IN YOUR TINY TOWN. BUT NONE OF YOU IS PRETTY ENOUGH FOR THE KING! AT LEAST, NOT YET. NOT UNTIL I'VE WORKED MY MAGIC. YOU WON'T EVEN GET TO SEE THE KING UNTIL I'VE POLISHED YOUR LOOKS LIKE A JEWELER POLISHING A BEAUTIFUL GEMSTONE.

FIRST, WE'RE GOING TO TAKE SIX MONTHS TO TREAT YOUR SKIN WITH THE FINEST LOTIONS AND OILS. KING XERXES CAN'T STAND THE SIGHT OF PIMPLES.

THEN WE'LL TAKE ANOTHER SIX MONTHS FINDING EXACTLY THE RIGHT SCENT OF PERFUME FOR YOU. WE'LL ALSO TEACH YOU HOW TO APPLY MAKEUP TO BEST SHOW OFF YOUR FACE. THEN, AND ONLY THEN, WILL YOU GET TO SEE THE KING. AT THAT POINT, IF THE KING LIKES YOU AND REMEMBERS YOUR NAME, YOU WILL BE OUR NEXT QUEEN.

BUT I MUST TELL YOU—EVEN AFTER ALL MY BEAUTY TREATMENTS, THE KING HAS NEVER REMEMBERED ANY OF THE CANDIDATES' NAMES.

IN SPITE OF HIS LOW OPINION OF THE YOUNG WOMEN, HEGAI IS IMMEDIATELY CHARMED BY ESTHER.

YOU HAVE GRACE AND INTELLIGENCE LIKE NONE OF THESE OTHER GIRLS. I'M GIVING YOU SEVEN MAIDS TO ATTEND TO YOU PERSONALLY. YOU WILL HAVE THE BEST ROOM IN THE PALACE.

MEANWHILE, MORDECAI HAS BEEN WORRIED ABOUT HIS ADOPTED DAUGHTER. EVERY DAY HE HANGS AROUND THE OUTSIDE WALLS OF THE HAREM HOPING TO HEAR NEWS OF ESTHER. THERE HE MAKES FRIENDS WITH THE GUARDS, WHO LET HIM HANG OUT NEAR THE WOMEN'S SECTION OF THE PALACE.

DON'T WORRY. EVERYONE IN THE PALACE LOVES ESTHER.

YOU'RE A GOOD FATHER TO CHECK ON HER, BUT SHE IS WELL TAKEN CARE OF.

FINALLY, AFTER 12 MONTHS OF BEAUTY TREATMENTS, HEGAI THINKS ESTHER IS READY TO BE PRESENTED TO THE KING.

IS THERE ANYTHING YOU WANT TO BRING WITH YOU, ESTHER?

WHATEVER YOU RECOMMEND, HEGAI. I TRUST YOU.

SWEET GIRL. JUST BE YOURSELF WITH THE KING. DON'T BE NERVOUS. EVERYONE IN THE PALACE IS ROOTING FOR YOU.

IF ANYONE CAN PLEASE THE KING AND WIN HIS FAVOR, IT WILL BE ESTHER.

THE NEXT DAY, HEGAI IS CALLED BEFORE THE THRONE.

IT'S BEEN THREE YEARS, HEGAI! THREE YEARS OF YOUR BEAUTY TREATMENTS AND HO-HUM VILLAGE GIRLS. AND IN ALL THAT TIME, I HAVEN'T FOUND ANYONE WHO COULD COMPARE TO VASHTI. YOUR JOB IS FINISHED! DON'T BOTHER BRINGING ME ANY MORE GIRLS.

YES, YOUR HIGHNESS.

INSTEAD, BRING ME BACK THAT GIRL ESTHER TO BE MY NEW QUEEN.

Persian Politics

BASED ON ESTHER 2:19—3:15

FOR MONTHS, ESTHER—ALONG WITH HUNDREDS OF BEAUTIFUL WOMEN OF PERSIA—HAS LIVED IN THE PALACE WAITING FOR THE KING TO CHOOSE ONE OF THEM TO BE HIS WIFE. THE KING HAS FINALLY MADE HIS CHOICE ...

ESTHER, YOU ARE NOW MY WIFE, QUEEN OF ALL PERSIA.

I AM HONORED, MY LORD.

BUT ESTHER HAS KEPT HER FAMILY A SECRET. SHE HASN'T TOLD ANYONE ABOUT HER ADOPTED FATHER, MORDECAI, A JEWISH CITY OFFICIAL. LATE THAT NIGHT, HE GOES TO THE WALLS OF THE HAREM TO CHECK ON ESTHER, THE NEW QUEEN.

I AM SO PROUD AND HAPPY FOR YOU! BUT REMEMBER, EVEN THOUGH YOU'RE THE QUEEN NOW, DON'T LET ANYONE KNOW THAT YOU'RE JEWISH.

AS HE'S LEAVING ESTHER'S GARDEN, MORDECAI OVERHEARS TWO OF THE KING'S SERVANTS ...

OUR PLAN CANNOT FAIL.

NO, BY THIS TIME TOMORROW, THE KING WILL BE DEAD. AND NO ONE WILL KNOW WHO KILLED HIM.

MORDECAI QUICKLY SENDS WORD OF THE PLOT TO ESTHER. THAT VERY NIGHT, THE KING CALLS FOR HER.

WHY DO YOU LOOK TROUBLED, MY LOVELY? IT GIVES YOU WRINKLES.

MY KING, TWO OF YOUR SERVANTS PLAN TO ASSASSINATE YOU!

ANGERED BECAUSE MORDECAI WILL NOT BOW BEFORE HIM, HAMAN PREPARES HIS REVENGE. BUT FIRST HE MUST TRICK HIS FOOLISH KING.

MY KING, THERE'S A RACE OF PEOPLE IN YOUR KINGDOM WHO DO NOT OBEY YOU. FOR YOUR SAFETY, THEY SHOULD BE DESTROYED. GIVE ME PERMISSION TO MAKE A LAW THAT WILL GET RID OF THEM IN PERSIA.

OH, WOW! I'M GLAD YOU BROUGHT THIS TO MY ATTENTION, HAMAN. DO WHAT YOU NEED TO DO TO PROTECT ME. USE MY RING TO SEAL THE NEW LAW. THEN EVERYONE WILL KNOW THAT YOUR LAW IS MY LAW.

HAMAN'S LAW IS QUICKLY DISTRIBUTED THROUGHOUT THE KINGDOM OF PERSIA.

Every Jew in Persia is to be destroyed on the 13th day of the 12th month. Anyone who kills the Jews may keep everything that belongs to the Jews they kill.

LET US CELEBRATE YOUR GOOD DECISION. TO MY LOYAL PRIME MINISTER!

WHY WOULD THE KING DO THIS TO US? WE HAVEN'T DONE ANYTHING WRONG!

If I Perish, I Perish

BASED ON ESTHER 4

WHAT ARE YOU DOING HERE IN SACKCLOTH? DON'T YOU KNOW IT'S AGAINST THE LAW TO SHOW MOURNING IN THE KING'S PALACE? YOU COULD BE KILLED!

I AM TO BE KILLED ANYWAY—ALONG WITH ALL OF OUR PEOPLE.

WHEN MORDECAI HEARS THE ORDERS, HE DRESSES IN SACKCLOTH AND POURS ASHES OVER HIS HEAD TO SHOW HIS GRIEF. THEN HE VISITS ESTHER, WHO HE HOPES WILL BE ABLE TO DO SOMETHING.

WHAT? WHY?

THE KING HAS PASSED A NEW LAW ORDERING THAT ALL JEWS ARE TO BE KILLED. IT MUST BE HAMAN'S DOING. HIS PEOPLE HAVE HATED OUR PEOPLE EVER SINCE THE TIME OF KING SAUL.

YOU MUST GO TO THE KING AND ASK HIM TO SPARE THE JEWS.

I SHOULD GO SEE THE KING? THE KING HAS ONE RULE ABOUT ANYONE WHO APPROACHES HIM WITHOUT BEING INVITED: DEATH! UNLESS HE DECIDES TO HOLD OUT HIS SCEPTER. AND THE KING HASN'T CALLED FOR ME IN A MONTH. IF I GO TO KING XERXES UNINVITED, I FACE THE DEATH PENALTY!

IF YOU DON'T GO, YOUR WHOLE PEOPLE FACE THE DEATH PENALTY.

WHO KNOWS? MAYBE YOU HAVE BEEN PUT INTO THIS ROYAL POSITION FOR A TIME JUST LIKE THIS.

TODAY, YOU MUST BE MORE THAN A QUEEN—YOU MUST BE A JEW. AND TO SAVE US, YOU MUST BE MORE THAN A JEW—YOU MUST BE A QUEEN.

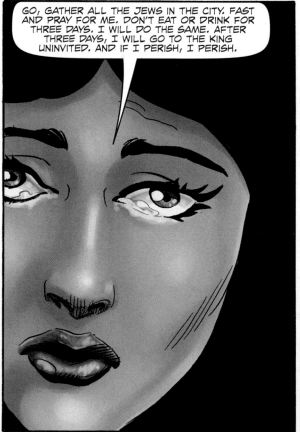

GO, GATHER ALL THE JEWS IN THE CITY. FAST AND PRAY FOR ME. DON'T EAT OR DRINK FOR THREE DAYS. I WILL DO THE SAME. AFTER THREE DAYS, I WILL GO TO THE KING UNINVITED. AND IF I PERISH, I PERISH.

BASED ON ESTHER 5—10

ESTHER! I DIDN'T INVITE HER TO COME BEFORE ME!

QUEEN ESTHER BREAKS A LAW BY APPEARING BEFORE THE KING WITHOUT AN INVITATION—SHE COULD BE PUNISHED BY DEATH. BUT THE LIVES OF HER PEOPLE, THE JEWS, ARE IN DANGER, AND SHE IS THE ONLY ONE WHO MAY BE ABLE TO SAVE THEM.

BUT AS XERXES LOOKS AT HIS BEAUTIFUL NEW QUEEN, HE DECIDES HE DOESN'T MIND THE INTRUSION. HE HOLDS OUT HIS SCEPTER TO SHOW HIS FORGIVENESS.

WHAT IS IT, MY BREATHTAKING BEAUTY? WHAT IS YOUR REQUEST? EVEN IF YOU WANTED HALF OF MY KINGDOM, I WOULD GIVE IT TO YOU.

THE MOMENT HAS COME WHEN ESTHER CAN ASK KING XERXES TO SPARE HER PEOPLE.

I ... REQUEST ... THAT YOU AND HAMAN ... COME TO A PRIVATE PARTY. JUST THE THREE OF US.

A PARTY WITH YOU? ABSOLUTELY! FIND HAMAN NOW!

ESTHER ENTERTAINS THE KING AND HAMAN IN HER OWN PRIVATE GARDEN. BUT SHE STILL DOESN'T TELL XERXES HER REAL REQUEST. INSTEAD, SHE INVITES HIM AND HAMAN TO COME TO ANOTHER PARTY TOMORROW. THEN, SHE PROMISES, SHE'LL TELL HIM HER TRUE REQUEST. THE KING ACCEPTS, AND SO DOES HAMAN, WHO IS OVERJOYED TO BE INCLUDED.

ANGRY AND HUMILIATED, HAMAN IS FORCED TO PERFORM FOR HIS ENEMY, MORDECAI, THE CEREMONY THAT HE PLANNED FOR HIMSELF.

THE KING RESPECTS THIS MAN ...

WHEN HE IS FINISHED, HE BARELY HAS TIME TO MAKE IT TO THE PALACE FOR HIS DATE WITH ESTHER AND THE KING. HE ARRIVES IN A FOUL MOOD.

AS DELIGHTFUL AS THESE PARTIES ARE, MY LUSCIOUS QUEEN, YOU MUST HAVE HAD A DIFFERENT REASON TO SEEK ME OUT. I PROMISE TO GIVE YOU ANYTHING YOU ASK FOR.

MY KING, IF YOU HAVE ANY LIKING FOR ME, SAVE MY LIFE! THAT IS MY REQUEST. AND SPARE THE LIVES OF MY PEOPLE. BY THE CRUEL PLAN OF A CERTAIN MAN, WE ARE TO BE PUT TO DEATH.

PUT *YOU* TO DEATH? WHO WOULD DARE DO SUCH A THING?

THE WICKED HAMAN!

BUT ESTHER KNOWS THIS IS NOT ENOUGH.

IF I HAVE PLEASED YOU, I BEG YOU TO TAKE BACK THE ORDER HAMAN SENT TO KILL ALL THE JEWS.

I WISH I COULD. BUT ACCORDING TO PERSIAN LAW, NO ONE—NOT EVEN THE KING—CAN CANCEL AN ORDER THAT HAS BEEN SEALED WITH THE KING'S RING.

BUT I CAN SEND A NEW ORDER!

THE ORDER IS WRITTEN AND RUSHED TO GOVERNORS THROUGHOUT THE EMPIRE.

LISTEN—THE KING SAYS THE JEWS MAY CARRY WEAPONS TO PROTECT THEMSELVES AND THAT MORDECAI, A JEW, HAS BEEN MADE PRIME MINISTER.

AH! THE KING IS ON THE SIDE OF THE JEWS! WE'D BETTER BE TOO.

MAYBE I SHOULD BECOME JEWISH.

HAMAN CAST LOTS—PURIM—TO DESTROY US, BUT INSTEAD WE HAVE BEEN SAVED FROM OUR ENEMY. I'VE WRITTEN AN ORDER THAT EVERY YEAR ALL JEWS MUST CELEBRATE THIS DAY. THERE SHOULD BE MUCH REJOICING AND GIVING OF GIFTS. IT WILL BE CALLED THE FEAST OF PURIM.

ON THE 13TH DAY OF THE 12TH MONTH, THE JEWS THROUGHOUT THE PERSIAN EMPIRE GATHER TOGETHER TO DEFEND THEMSELVES. WITH THE HELP OF THE KING'S GOVERNORS, THEY ARE SUCCESSFUL. AND AT THE PALACE ...

JEWISH PEOPLE THROUGHOUT THE WORLD STILL CELEBRATE THE FEAST OF PURIM.

505

ALTHOUGH THE CITY OF JERUSALEM IS IN RUINS, THE JEWS WHO HAVE RETURNED FROM CAPTIVITY IN BABYLON SET TO WORK TO REBUILD IT. JESHUA AND ZERUBBABEL START BY REBUILDING THE ALTAR ON ITS OLD SPOT IN FRONT OF THE TEMPLE.

IN THE MIDST OF THE RUINS, THE JEWISH PEOPLE CELEBRATE THE FEAST OF TABERNACLES FOR THE FIRST TIME IN MANY YEARS.

IT IS GOOD TO FINALLY BURN OFFERINGS TO THE LORD IN JERUSALEM, EVEN THOUGH THE TEMPLE IS NOT REBUILT YET.

NEXT THEY SET ABOUT REBUILDING THE TEMPLE. THEY APPOINT LEVITES TO SUPERVISE THE CONSTRUCTION. THEY SEND TO SIDON FOR THE BEST CEDAR LOGS, JUST LIKE SOLOMON USED WHEN HE BUILT THE TEMPLE ORIGINALLY.

WHEN THE FOUNDATION OF THE TEMPLE IS IN PLACE, THE HIGH PRIEST LEADS THE PEOPLE IN A SERVICE OF WORSHIP AND REJOICING.

GIVE THANKS TO THE LORD, FOR HE IS GOOD. HIS FAITHFUL LOVE LASTS FOREVER.

THE NOISE FROM THEIR CELEBRATION IS SO GREAT THAT IT CAN BE HEARD FROM MILES AWAY.

Temple Troubles

BASED ON EZRA 4–6;
HAGGAI; ZECHARIAH

BUT THE SOUND OF THE JEWS' REJOICING BRINGS TROUBLE. THE SAMARITANS WHO LIVE NEAR JERUSALEM COME WITH A REQUEST TO HELP BUILD THE TEMPLE.

WE'RE SORRY, BUT GOD PUNISHED US 70 YEARS AGO BECAUSE WE RELIED ON OTHER PEOPLE'S HELP, INSTEAD OF TRUSTING IN GOD ALONE. THIS IS SOMETHING WE MUST DO OURSELVES.

OH, I GET IT! YOU THINK YOU'RE TOO GOOD FOR US.

IF YOU WON'T LET US HELP BUILD THE TEMPLE, WE'LL MAKE SURE YOU DON'T BUILD IT AT ALL ...

THE SAMARITANS SEND A LETTER TO KING CYRUS.

DON'T YOU KNOW THAT JERUSALEM HAS ALWAYS BEEN A REBELLIOUS AND WICKED CITY? IF YOU LET THEM REBUILD THEIR CITY AND THEIR TEMPLE, THEY WILL EVENTUALLY REVOLT AGAINST YOU AND MAKE YOU LOOK WEAK.

CHECK THE HISTORY SCROLLS.

IT'S TRUE, SIRE. JERUSALEM HAS ALWAYS REBELLED AGAINST THE POWERFUL EMPIRES.

ORDER THEM TO STOP REBUILDING IMMEDIATELY! I WILL NOT LET THIS THREAT RISE FROM THE ASHES.

FORCED TO OBEY, THE JEWS TURN TO
WORK ON THEIR HOMES AND GARDENS.
SEVERAL YEARS PASS. CYRUS DIES,
AND NEW KINGS COME TO THE THRONE
OF PERSIA, BUT STILL THE TEMPLE IN
JERUSALEM IS NOT COMPLETED.

HAGGAI

ONE DAY, HAGGAI, ONE OF THE PROPHETS
IN JERUSALEM, RECEIVES A WORD FROM
THE LORD. HE IMMEDIATELY GOES TO
ZERUBBABEL AND JESHUA.

THE LORD WAS
WONDERING: WHY HAVE
YOU FINISHED BUILDING
YOUR HOUSES, WHILE
GOD'S HOUSE IS
STILL IN RUINS?

ZERUBBABEL TRIES TO DEFEND HIMSELF.

WE WERE FOLLOWING THE LAW
OF PERSIA. WE HAVE TOO MANY
ENEMIES WHO DON'T WANT US TO
REBUILD THE TEMPLE.

GOD SAYS,
"DO NOT BE AFRAID
OF YOUR ENEMIES.
FINISH MY TEMPLE,
FOR I AM WITH
YOU."

WITH HAGGAI'S PROPHETIC
ENCOURAGEMENT, THE JEWS
RESUME WORK ON THE TEMPLE.

BUT THE GOVERNORS IN THE AREA ARE
CONCERNED BY THE SUDDEN REBUILDING.

WHO GAVE YOU
PERMISSION
TO BUILD THIS
FORTRESS?

IT'S NOT A FORTRESS, IT'S THE TEMPLE TO OUR
GOD THAT WAS DESTROYED BY THE BABYLONIANS
MANY YEARS AGO. AND KING CYRUS HIMSELF GAVE US
PERMISSION TO REBUILD IT—HE EVEN PAID FOR IT
OUT OF THE ROYAL TREASURY.

WE'LL SEE IF
THAT'S TRUE.

EVERYONE
IS
AGAINST
US. WE'LL
NEVER
FINISH THE
TEMPLE.

Wall Warriors BASED ON NEHEMIAH

THE JEWISH EXILES WHO HAVE RETURNED FROM PERSIA TO JERUSALEM HAVE FINALLY SETTLED IN THEIR OLD CITY. THEY'VE BUILT HOUSES AND NEIGHBORHOODS FOR THEMSELVES, THEY'VE REBUILT THE TEMPLE TO MATCH ITS FORMER GLORY, AND UNDER THE LEADERSHIP OF EZRA, THEY'VE COMMITTED THEMSELVES TO FOLLOWING GOD'S WORD. BUT THEY HAVE NOT YET HAD THE CHANCE TO REBUILD THE OLD WALLS.

THAT NIGHT, WHILE THE CITY SLEEPS, A STRANGER AND HIS GUARDS RIDE AROUND JERUSALEM. THE STRANGER EXAMINES THE WALLS.

THE CITY COULD BE WIPED OUT IN ONE QUICK ATTACK.

YOU'RE RIGHT, NEHEMIAH. BUT IT MUST HAVE BEEN A GREAT FORTRESS AT ONE TIME. THESE WALLS ARE AS THICK AS ANY WE HAVE IN PERSIA.

THE NEXT DAY NEHEMIAH CALLS ON THE PRIESTS AND RULERS OF THE CITY.

I HAVE EXAMINED THE WALLS OF JERUSALEM. THEY ARE JUST HEAPS OF BROKEN STONE. THE CITY IS DEFENSELESS.

YOU'RE RIGHT, BUT WHY—

WHY HAVE I COME? BECAUSE I, TOO, AM A JEW. AND WHILE I WAS SERVING THE KING OF PERSIA AS HIS CUP-BEARER, I LEARNED THAT JERUSALEM WAS WITHOUT ANY DEFENSE. I PRAYED TO GOD, AND THE KING GAVE ME PERMISSION TO COME AND BUILD UP THE WALLS. ARE YOU WITH ME?

WE ARE! WE'LL GET STARTED RIGHT AWAY.

THE WORK BEGINS. EVERY ABLE-BODIED MAN AND BOY DOES HIS PART. THE WOMEN HELP ...

... AND SLOWLY THE WALLS BEGIN TO RISE.

BUT SOME OF THE NEIGHBORING COUNTRIES DO NOT WANT TO SEE JERUSALEM PROTECTED.

IF THE JEWS FINISH THOSE WALLS, THE CITY WILL BE TOO STRONG TO ATTACK.

WE MUST STOP IT NOW!

DOWN WITH THE WALLS!

BUT WHILE THE ENEMIES OF JERUSALEM PLAN TO TAKE THE CITY, NEHEMIAH PREPARES TO DEFEND IT.

WE DON'T HAVE AN ARMY—ONLY OURSELVES. FROM NOW ON, YOU MUST HOLD YOUR HAMMER IN ONE HAND AND A SWORD IN THE OTHER. AT A MOMENT'S NOTICE, WE MUST BE ABLE TO DEFEND OUR CITY. DON'T EVEN TAKE A WATER BREAK WITHOUT YOUR WEAPON.

THE ENEMY APPROACHES—BUT TO THEIR SURPRISE ARMED WORKERS RISE UP, THEIR SPEARS RAISED AND THEIR BOWS PULLED.

THEY'RE ARMED?

RUN AWAY!

THE WORKERS GO BACK TO THEIR JOBS, AND SOON STRONG WALLS AND HEAVY GATES AGAIN PROTECT THE CITY OF JERUSALEM. BUT INSIDE THERE IS AN EVEN STRONGER LINE OF DEFENSE—A NATION LED BY EZRA AND NEHEMIAH TO LOVE AND OBEY GOD!

MALACHI

THE FINAL PROPHET OF THE OLD TESTAMENT, TELLS THE PEOPLE HOW TO GIVE TRUE WORSHIP TO GOD.

DO YOU CALL THAT GOD'S SHARE OF GRAIN? HOW CAN YOU BE HAPPY WHEN YOU ROB GOD? GIVE GOD THE WHOLE OFFERING HE DESERVES, AND HE WILL FLOOD YOU WITH BLESSINGS!

Years of Waiting

BETWEEN THE OLD TESTAMENT AND THE NEW TESTAMENT

THE LAND OF JUDAH IS STILL UNDER THE RULE OF THE PERSIANS WHEN ALEXANDER, THE YOUNG KING OF MACEDONIA, SETS OUT TO CONQUER THE WORLD. RIDING HIS FAMOUS HORSE, BUCEPHALUS, HE LEADS HIS ARMY AGAINST THE COUNTRIES OF THE MIGHTY PERSIAN EMPIRE. ONE AFTER ANOTHER, THEY FALL. IN THE YEAR 332 BC ...

ON TO JERUSALEM!

WHEN THE HIGH PRIEST IN JERUSALEM HEARS THAT THEY ARE THE NEXT STOP IN ALEXANDER'S CONQUERING JOURNEY, HE PRAYS TO GOD IN DESPERATION. AND GOD GIVES HIM A DREAM.

PUT ON YOUR FORMAL ROBES. WE ARE TO MEET ALEXANDER OUTSIDE THE WALLS OF JERUSALEM.

BUT HE'LL BE ABLE TO KILL ALL OF US IF WE DON'T EVEN HIDE BEHIND THE CITY WALLS!

BUT EVERYONE OBEYS THE HIGH PRIEST. ON THE DAY ALEXANDER ARRIVES, ALL THE PRIESTS OF ISRAEL STAND TO GREET HIM. THE HIGH PRIEST WEARS HIS PURPLE ROBE AND OFFICIAL HAT.

ALEXANDER DISMOUNTS AND WALKS SLOWLY TOWARD THE HIGH PRIEST. EVERYONE WATCHES HIM IN TERROR ...

BUT ONCE AGAIN A CONQUEROR COMES FROM ACROSS THE MEDITERRANEAN SEA. ROMAN SHIPS AND ROMAN SOLDIERS CONQUER EVERYTHING IN THEIR PATH. AND IN 63 BC THE MIGHTY ROMAN ARMY TAKES JERUSALEM. AGAIN JUDAH IS DOWN—AND THIS TIME IT IS TOO WEAK TO RISE.

A FEW YEARS LATER, HEROD BECOMES A GOVERNOR IN THE ROMAN EMPIRE. A JEW BY BACKGROUND, HE'S ALWAYS WANTED TO RULE OVER HIS PEOPLE. HE GOES TO ROME TO APPEAL THEIR SENATE FOR A PROMOTION.

IF YOU MAKE ME RULER OF THE JEWS, I WILL ENSURE THAT THEY NEVER REVOLT AGAINST YOU.

THE ROMANS LIKE HIS PROMISES AND VOTE TO MAKE HEROD THE KING OF THE JEWS.

THOUGH HE'S A CRUEL MAN BY NATURE, HEROD IS ALSO A CRAFTY POLITICIAN. HE TRIES TO WIN THE JEWISH PEOPLE'S FAVOR BY BUILDING THEM A NEW AND MORE BEAUTIFUL TEMPLE. BUT THEY DESPISE HIM. BITTERLY, THE JEWS CRY OUT: "WHEN WILL GOD SEND THE DELIVERER THE PROPHETS PROMISED WOULD COME?"

BUT GOD WAS SILENT UNTIL ...

THE NEW TESTAMENT

The Life of Jesus

BASED ON MATTHEW; MARK; LUKE; AND JOHN

THOUGH MANY PEOPLE WITNESSED THE LIFE AND MIRACLES OF JESUS, ONLY FOUR WROTE AUTHENTIC STORIES ABOUT HIS TIME ON EARTH. THOSE MEN'S WRITINGS MAKE UP THE FIRST FOUR BOOKS OF THE NEW TESTAMENT—CALLED GOSPELS BECAUSE THEY SHARE THE "GOOD NEWS" OF JESUS CHRIST. EACH BOOK IS SLIGHTLY DIFFERENT, BUT TOGETHER THEY TELL ONE COMPLETE STORY OF JESUS' LIFE ON EARTH.

When in Rome ...

BASED ON MATTHEW 5:41

HERE, OLD MAN! CARRY THIS FOR ME.

THE MIGHTY ROMAN EMPIRE RULES PALESTINE, THE HOME OF GOD'S PEOPLE, THE JEWS. THE ROMANS HAVE APPOINTED HEROD TO GOVERN PALESTINE FOR THEM. HEROD IS CLEVER, BUT HE IS ALSO CRUEL. THE JEWS HATE HIM AND THE ROMAN OFFICIALS WHO WORK FOR HIM.

THAT CHEST IS TOO HEAVY FOR THAT OLD MAN TO CARRY. HE MIGHT HAVE A HEART ATTACK!

THE ROMANS DON'T CARE.

HOURS LATER, THE OLD MAN REACHES HOME.

GRANDFATHER! WHAT'S THE MATTER?

A ROMAN SOLDIER MADE HIM CARRY A HEAVY CHEST TO HEROD'S PALACE.

Angel Promises

BASED ON LUKE 1:5-56

AS JEWS IN JERUSALEM GATHER IN THE TEMPLE FOR PRAYER, AN OLD PRIEST NAMED ZECHARIAH ENTERS THE HOLY PLACE TO MAKE AN OFFERING OF INCENSE.

THIS IS THE GREATEST DAY OF MY LIFE! AFTER ALL THESE YEARS, IT'S FINALLY MY TURN TO OFFER INCENSE ON GOD'S HOLY ALTAR.

BUT ZECHARIAH STAYS SO LONG IN THE HOLY PLACE THAT THE PRIESTS BEGIN TO WONDER.

WHY IS ZECHARIAH PRAYING SO LONG?

I HOPE HE HASN'T DIED IN THERE. NO ONE ELSE IS ALLOWED IN THE HOLY PLACE.

MEANWHILE, THE FEARSOME ANGEL GABRIEL HAS APPEARED TO ZECHARIAH IN THE TEMPLE.

DO NOT BE AFRAID. YOU AND ELIZABETH WILL HAVE A SON. GOD WILL MAKE HIM MIGHTY AND FILLED WITH THE SPIRIT.

HIS NAME WILL BE JOHN, AND HE WILL PREPARE THE PEOPLE FOR GOD'S DELIVERER.

BUT WE'RE TOO OLD TO HAVE A BABY!

BECAUSE YOU DON'T BELIEVE, YOU WILL NOT BE ABLE TO TALK UNTIL THE BABY IS BORN.

AT LAST ZECHARIAH COMES OUT AND FACES THE PEOPLE. BUT HE CANNOT SPEAK! NO WORDS COME FROM HIS MOUTH.

WHAT HAPPENED IN THE HOLY PLACE OF GOD?

ZECHARIAH! WHAT'S WRONG? WHY DON'T YOU SPEAK TO ME?

ZECHARIAH CAN'T TELL ELIZABETH WHAT HAPPENED, SO HE WRITES DOWN EVERYTHING THE ANGEL TOLD HIM.

MARY CHERISHES THIS SECRET IN HER HEART, BUT SHE DOESN'T DARE TELL ANYONE ABOUT THE ANGEL'S PROMISE. JOSEPH IS A GOOD MAN, BUT IF PEOPLE FIND OUT SHE IS PREGNANT, SHE COULD BE KILLED.

I KNOW JOSEPH LOVES ME. BUT WOULD HE BELIEVE ME?

THE ANGEL HAD TOLD MARY THAT ELIZABETH WAS GOING TO HAVE A SON TOO. SO MARY GOES TO VISIT THE ONE PERSON SHE HOPES WILL UNDERSTAND. THE MOMENT ELIZABETH SEES MARY ...

MARY! YOU ARE BLESSED AMONG WOMEN! YOU ARE THE MOTHER OF OUR LORD!

MARY REALIZES THAT ELIZABETH KNOWS AND BELIEVES HER WONDERFUL SECRET. JOYFULLY SHE SINGS PRAISE TO GOD.

MY SOUL PRAISES THE LORD! AND MY SPIRIT REJOICES IN GOD, WHO SAVES ME! GOD IS MIGHTY, AND HE HAS DONE GREAT THINGS FOR ME. HIS NAME IS HOLY!

ZECHARIAH HAS BEEN SILENT FOR MONTHS. HE MOTIONS FOR A TABLET TO WRITE ON.

HIS NAME IS JOHN.

AT THAT VERY MOMENT, ZECHARIAH IS ABLE TO SPEAK AGAIN. HIS FIRST WORDS ARE A SONG OF WORSHIP TO THE LORD.

GIVE PRAISE TO THE LORD, THE GOD OF ISRAEL. HE HAS COME TO SET HIS PEOPLE FREE. HE HAS BEEN KIND TO HIS PEOPLE. AND YOU, MY CHILD, WILL BE CALLED A PROPHET OF THE MOST HIGH GOD.

BACK IN NAZARETH, JOSEPH HAS SECOND THOUGHTS ABOUT HIS ENGAGEMENT TO MARY BECAUSE HE DOESN'T KNOW ABOUT GOD'S PLAN FOR MARY AND HER BABY. SO ONE NIGHT, AN ANGEL COMES TO JOSEPH IN A DREAM.

DON'T BE AFRAID TO TAKE MARY AS YOUR WIFE. THE BABY INSIDE HER IS FROM THE HOLY SPIRIT. NAME HIM JESUS* BECAUSE HE WILL SAVE HIS PEOPLE FROM THEIR SINS.

* JESUS MEANS "GOD SAVES."

Birth of a Savior
BASED ON MATTHEW 1:18—2:11; LUKE 2:1-20

JOSEPH BELIEVES THE ANGEL AND MARRIES MARY, EVEN THOUGH HER PREGNANCY SEEMS SHAMEFUL TO OTHERS. ONE DAY THE NEWS COMES THAT THE ROMAN EMPEROR, CAESAR AUGUSTUS, WANTS TO HAVE A CENSUS. EVERYONE MUST GO TO HIS HOMETOWN TO BE COUNTED. EVEN THOUGH MARY'S BABY IS DUE ANY DAY NOW, JOSEPH AND MARY HAVE TO GO FROM NAZARETH TO BETHLEHEM.

WE'VE TRAVELED A LONG WAY. MY WIFE IS VERY TIRED. WE NEED A PLACE TO STAY.

I'M SORRY, BUT BETHLEHEM IS CROWDED BECAUSE OF THE CENSUS. WE DON'T HAVE ANY MORE EMPTY ROOMS.

EXHAUSTED, MARY AND JOSEPH HAVE NO CHOICE BUT TO STAY IN A STABLE. THERE, SURROUNDED BY ANIMALS, MARY GIVES BIRTH TO JESUS. SHE KEEPS HER BABY WARM IN A MANGER FILLED WITH HAY.

THAT SAME NIGHT, SOME SHEPHERDS ARE WATCHING THEIR SHEEP ON THE HILLS OUTSIDE BETHLEHEM. SUDDENLY, A GREAT LIGHT SPLITS THE NIGHT.

WHAT IS HAPPENING?

GOD SAVE US!

DON'T BE AFRAID. I BRING GOOD NEWS FOR YOU AND THE WHOLE WORLD.

TODAY IN THE CITY OF DAVID, A SAVIOR HAS BEEN BORN TO YOU. YOU WILL FIND THE BABY LYING IN A MANGER.

SUDDENLY THE SKY IS FILLED WITH A CHOIR OF ANGELS SINGING PRAISE TO GOD.

GLORY TO GOD IN THE HIGHEST, AND PEACE TO PEOPLE ON EARTH!

THE ANGELS LEAVE AND ONCE AGAIN DARKNESS FALLS UPON THE HILLS.

LET'S GO TO BETHLEHEM.

WE MUST SEE THE CHILD OF GOD FOR OURSELVES.

THE SHEPHERDS HURRY OFF TO BETHLEHEM.

536

Flight in the Night

BASED ON MATTHEW 2:12–18

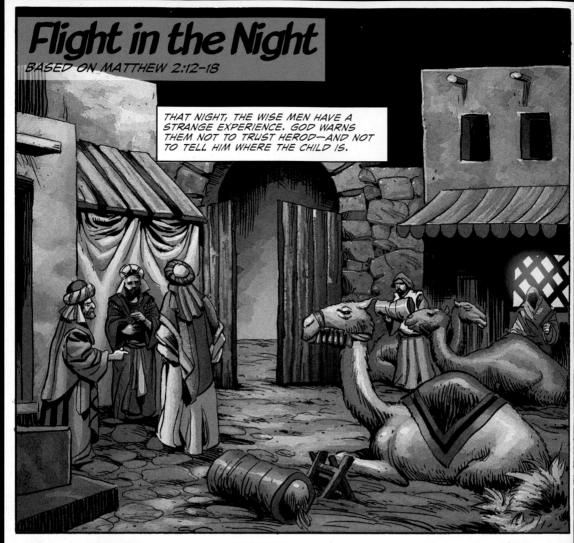

THAT NIGHT, THE WISE MEN HAVE A STRANGE EXPERIENCE. GOD WARNS THEM NOT TO TRUST HEROD—AND NOT TO TELL HIM WHERE THE CHILD IS.

I HAD A DREAM—

SO DID I! GOD WARNED US NOT TO GO BACK TO JERUSALEM.

I HAD THE SAME DREAM. WE MUST GO HOME ANOTHER WAY.

AFTER THE WISE MEN LEAVE, JOSEPH HAS ANOTHER DREAM.

ESCAPE TO EGYPT! STAY THERE UNTIL I TELL YOU TO COME BACK. HEROD WANTS TO KILL JESUS.

JOSEPH GETS UP QUICKLY AND PREPARES TO GO. IN THE MIDDLE OF THE NIGHT, JOSEPH, MARY, AND JESUS FLEE TO EGYPT.

THAT VERY NIGHT, HEROD'S SOLDIERS DESCEND ON BETHLEHEM AND BRUTALLY CARRY OUT THEIR EVIL ERRAND.

AND SO JEREMIAH'S PROPHECY IS FULFILLED: "THERE IS WEEPING AND GREAT MOURNING IN RAMAH. RACHEL WEEPS FOR HER CHILDREN AND WILL NOT BE COMFORTED, FOR THEY ARE NO MORE."

BUT JOSEPH AND MARY ARE ALREADY SAFELY ON THEIR WAY TO EGYPT, WHERE THEY'LL SPEND THE NEXT SEVERAL YEARS RAISING THEIR NEW BABY, THE SAVIOR OF THE WHOLE WORLD.

A Boy in the Temple

BASED ON MATTHEW 2:19–23; LUKE 2:39–52

WHEN KING HEROD DIES, AN ANGEL VISITS JOSEPH AGAIN IN A DREAM.

GET UP! TAKE THE CHILD AND HIS MOTHER AND GO BACK HOME TO ISRAEL. THE ONES WHO WERE TRYING TO KILL THE CHILD ARE DEAD.

JOSEPH TAKES THE FAMILY BACK TO NAZARETH, WHERE HE SETS UP HIS CARPENTER SHOP. JESUS GROWS UP STRONG AND WISE AND FILLED WITH GOD'S GRACE. EACH SPRING, MARY AND JOSEPH TRAVEL TO JERUSALEM TO ATTEND THE PASSOVER FEAST. THEY THANK GOD FOR DELIVERING HIS PEOPLE FROM SLAVERY IN EGYPT HUNDREDS OF YEARS AGO.

ONE YEAR, WHEN JESUS IS 12, THE FAMILY GOES TO THE FEAST AS USUAL.

IN JERUSALEM, JESUS SPENDS HIS TIME IN THE TEMPLE WITH THE WISE MEN AND TEACHERS.

AFTER THE FEAST IS OVER, MARY AND JOSEPH SET OUT FOR HOME. THAT NIGHT WHEN THEY MAKE CAMP ...

JOSEPH, WHERE IS JESUS?

HE MUST BE WITH HIS FRIENDS. I'LL FIND HIM.

BUT NO ONE HAS SEEN JESUS. FRANTIC, MARY AND JOSEPH GO BACK TO JERUSALEM. THEY LOOK FOR JESUS NEARLY EVERYWHERE IN THE CITY.

FINALLY, THEY FIND HIM IN THE TEMPLE. JESUS IS SITTING WITH THE TEACHERS.

JESUS! WE'VE BEEN LOOKING EVERYWHERE FOR YOU. WE WERE SO WORRIED.

WHY WERE YOU LOOKING FOR ME? YOU KNOW THAT I NEED TO BE IN MY FATHER'S HOUSE.

543

Baptized

BASED ON LUKE 3;
MATTHEW 3

JOHN, THE SON OF ZECHARIAH AND ELIZABETH, GROWS UP WITH GOD'S CALL ON HIS HEART. AS AN ADULT, HE MEDITATES IN THE DESERT, AND THERE HE HEARS GOD CALLING HIM. HE BEGINS PREACHING FORCEFULLY ALL AROUND THE JORDAN RIVER.

STOP SINNING! BE BAPTIZED! GOD'S KINGDOM IS VERY NEAR.

DRESSED IN CAMEL HAIR AND EATING NOTHING BUT LOCUSTS AND WHATEVER HONEY HE CAN SCROUNGE FROM WILD BEES, JOHN DOESN'T HAVE A LOT OF PATIENCE FOR PEOPLE WHO LIVE IN LUXURY AND IGNORE GOD.

JOHN REMINDS PEOPLE WHAT THE SCRIPTURES SAY IN THE BOOK OF ISAIAH:

A MESSENGER IS CALLING OUT FROM THE DESERT, "PREPARE THE WAY OF THE LORD." SOON ALL OF YOU WILL SEE GOD'S SALVATION WITH YOUR OWN EYES.

JOHN DOESN'T KNOW IT, BUT THE SAVIOR IS IN THE CROWD ONE DAY. JESUS HAS COME DOWN FROM NAZARETH TO HEAR JOHN SPEAK, AND HE ASKS TO BE BAPTIZED.

WHY DO YOU COME TO ME TO BE BAPTIZED?

I'M THE ONE WHO NEEDS TO BE BAPTIZED BY YOU!

JOHN, GOD CHOSE YOU TO INTRODUCE ME TO THE WORLD.

SO JOHN BAPTIZES JESUS. AND WHEN JESUS COMES UP OUT OF THE WATER, THE SPIRIT OF GOD DESCENDS IN THE SHAPE OF A DOVE.

YOU ARE MY BELOVED SON. I AM SO PROUD OF YOU!

GOD HAS SHOWN HIS APPROVAL OF JESUS. THE HOLY SPIRIT'S PRESENCE AT HIS BAPTISM MEANS GOD THE FATHER WILL HELP JESUS WITH HIS HOLY WORK. JESUS GOES INTO THE DESERT ALONE TO THINK ABOUT GOD'S PLAN FOR ESTABLISHING HIS KINGDOM.

FOR WEEKS, JESUS FASTS AND PRAYS. AT THE END OF 40 DAYS IN THE WILDERNESS, JESUS IS VERY HUNGRY.

IT IS THEN THAT HE HEARS THE VOICE OF THE DEVIL SPEAKING TO HIM ...

FINALLY, THE DEVIL GIVES UP AND LEAVES JESUS ALONE. ANGELS COME TO FEED AND TAKE CARE OF HIM, NOW THAT HE HAS RESISTED THE DEVIL'S TEMPTATIONS. REFRESHED, JESUS LEAVES THE WILDERNESS AND GOES TO BETHANY BEYOND THE JORDAN RIVER.

AS JESUS ENTERS BETHANY, JOHN THE BAPTIST SEES HIM. HE POINTS JESUS OUT TO TWO OF HIS FOLLOWERS, ANDREW AND JOHN.

THERE IS THE SAVIOR I HAVE BEEN TELLING YOU ABOUT. HE IS THE LAMB OF GOD WHO TAKES AWAY THE SIN OF THE WORLD.

ANDREW AND JOHN QUICKLY FOLLOW JESUS.

WHAT DO YOU WANT?

ONLY TO HEAR YOU SPEAK.

ANDREW STAYS WITH JESUS THE REST OF THE DAY. HOURS GO BY.

I CAN'T WAIT TO TELL MY BROTHER ABOUT YOU, JESUS.

ANDREW RUNS TO FIND HIS BROTHER, SIMON.

SIMON, I JUST MET THE SAVIOR OF THE WORLD!

SIMON FOLLOWS ANDREW BACK THROUGH THE STREETS OF BETHANY.

THIS IS SIMON, MY BROTHER.

YES, YOU ARE SIMON, BUT FROM NOW ON YOUR NICKNAME IS "PETER,"* BECAUSE YOU WILL BE THE ROCK I BUILD MY CHURCH ON.

* PETER MEANS "ROCK" IN GREEK.

THE NEXT DAY JESUS GOES NORTH TO GALILEE. HE INVITES ANOTHER YOUNG MAN, PHILIP, TO BE HIS DISCIPLE.

PHILIP ACCEPTS JESUS' INVITATION. LIKE ANDREW, HE WANTS TO SHARE HIS GOOD NEWS, SO HE HURRIES TO TELL A FRIEND.

NATHANAEL, COME WITH ME! I HAVE FOUND THE SAVIOR! HE IS JESUS OF NAZARETH.

NAZARETH? CAN ANYTHING GOOD COME FROM THAT TOWN?

IF WHAT YOU SAY IS TRUE, PEOPLE WOULD GIVE UP EVERYTHING THEY HAVE TO FOLLOW HIM.

COME AND SEE FOR YOURSELF.

NATHANAEL SEES JESUS, BUT HE STILL DOESN'T BELIEVE. THEN JESUS SPEAKS ...

The Wedding Saver
BASED ON JOHN 2:1-13, 23-25

IN CANA, JESUS ATTENDS A WEDDING FEAST. HIS MOTHER AND DISCIPLES ARE THERE TOO.

FOR DAYS, THE CELEBRATION IS LOUD AND JOYOUS. BUT THEN THEY RUN OUT OF WINE. BEFORE THE GUESTS CAN NOTICE, MARY TURNS TO HER SON TO FIX THE PROBLEM. AND BEFORE JESUS CAN SAY NO, MARY INSTRUCTS THE SERVANTS:

DO WHATEVER JESUS TELLS YOU TO DO.

FILL THESE JARS WITH WATER.

WHAT GOOD IS WATER? WE NEED MORE *WINE.*

THEN JESUS ORDERS THE SERVANTS TO POUR SOME FOR THE HEAD WAITER TO TASTE. CONFUSED, THEY OBEY.

WAIT! THIS IS ... TERRIFIC! THE BEST WINE OF THE WHOLE PARTY.

YOU CAN'T SEE THE WIND, BUT YOU CAN SEE WHAT IT DOES. YOU CAN'T SEE THE SPIRIT OF GOD, BUT YOU CAN TELL BY THE WAY PEOPLE LIVE IF THEY HAVE BEEN BORN AGAIN.

YOU'LL SEE FROM THEIR LIVES IF THEY HAVE THE SPIRIT OF GOD IN THEIR HEARTS.

JUST LIKE MOSES LIFTED UP A BRONZE SNAKE IN THE DESERT, THE SON OF MAN MUST BE LIFTED UP SO THAT EVERYONE MAY LIVE FOREVER.

DON'T YOU SEE? GOD LOVES THE WORLD SO MUCH THAT HE SENT ME. ANYONE WHO BELIEVES IN ME WILL NEVER DIE. I HAVE COME TO SAVE THE WORLD!

NICODEMUS GOES BACK OUT INTO THE NIGHT ... WITH MORE QUESTIONS THAN HE STARTED WITH.

JESUS AND HIS DISCIPLES LEAVE JERUSALEM AND GO OUT INTO THE COUNTRYSIDE OF JUDEA. THERE HE TELLS PEOPLE ABOUT GOD'S KINGDOM AND HOW THEY CAN ENTER IT. SOON PEOPLE COME FROM ALL OVER JUDEA TO BE BAPTIZED.

SOME OF JOHN THE BAPTIST'S DISCIPLES ARE JEALOUS.

EVERYONE IS LISTENING TO JESUS NOW. HE'S BECOMING MORE POPULAR THAN YOU.

THAT'S THE WAY IT SHOULD BE! JESUS MUST BECOME MORE IMPORTANT, AND I MUST BECOME LESS.

Living Water

BASED ON JOHN 4; LUKE 4:14-28

JESUS DECIDES TO GO FROM JUDEA TO GALILEE. ON THE WAY, HE PASSES THROUGH SAMARIA. AS HE AND HIS DISCIPLES APPROACH A WELL, JESUS SITS DOWN TO REST. HIS DISCIPLES GO INTO TOWN TO FIND FOOD.

I HOPE NONE OF THESE SAMARITANS CAUSES ANY TROUBLE!

WILL YOU GIVE ME A DRINK?

HE'S A JEW, AND I'M A SAMARITAN. DOESN'T HE KNOW HE IS NOT SUPPOSED TO TALK TO ME?

JEWS AND SAMARITANS HAVE BEEN BITTER ENEMIES FOR MORE THAN 500 YEARS. WHEN JESUS ASKS A SAMARITAN WOMAN FOR A DRINK OF WATER, SHE IS SHOCKED.

WHEN JESUS TELLS HER THAT HE IS THE SAVIOR FROM GOD, SHE BELIEVES HIM AND RUNS TO TOWN TO TELL THE GOOD NEWS.

COME! SEE A MAN WHO HAS TOLD ME THINGS ABOUT MY LIFE THAT NO STRANGER COULD KNOW. HE'S THE SAVIOR GOD PROMISED TO SEND!

WHILE THE WOMAN IS IN TOWN, JESUS' DISCIPLES RETURN WITH FOOD FOR HIM TO EAT.

THANK YOU, BUT NOT NOW. I HAVE FOOD TO EAT THAT YOU DON'T KNOW ANYTHING ABOUT.

SO WE WENT INTO TOWN FOR NOTHING?

MY FOOD IS TO DO WHAT GOD SENT ME TO DO. I AM FED BY FINISHING GOD'S WORK.

ALTHOUGH SAMARITANS HATE JEWS, MANY OF THEM BELIEVE IN JESUS BECAUSE OF WHAT THE WOMAN TELLS THEM. THEY ASK JESUS TO STAY AND TEACH THEM ABOUT GOD. HE STAYS TWO DAYS AND THEN GOES TO GALILEE.

THE PARALYZED MAN PICKS UP HIS MAT AND WALKS OUT. EVERYONE CAN SEE HIM.

MY SINS ARE FORGIVEN! I'M HEALED! PRAISE GOD!

I'VE NEVER SEEN ANYTHING LIKE THIS!

IT'S AMAZING!

JESUS LEAVES THE HOUSE. BUT AS HE PASSES BY THE TOLL HOUSE AT THE CITY GATE...

YOU TAX COLLECTORS ARE ALL ROBBERS. I CAN'T PAY THAT MUCH TAX, AND YOU KNOW IT.

YOU'D BETTER PAY IT! I CAN HAVE THE ROMANS THROW YOU IN JAIL IF YOU DON'T.

Dinner with Sinners

BASED ON MATTHEW 9:9-13; 12:9-14

THE JEWS HATE THE TAX COLLECTORS. ALTHOUGH THEY ARE ALSO JEWS, TAX COLLECTORS WORK FOR THE ROMANS, AND THEY CHEAT THEIR FELLOW JEWS OUT OF MONEY. BUT JESUS DOESN'T CARE WHAT THE PEOPLE THINK. HE LOVES EVEN THE TAX COLLECTORS. ONE DAY IN CAPERNAUM, JESUS LOOKS INTO THE EYES OF A HATED TAX COLLECTOR ...

MATTHEW, COME AND FOLLOW ME.

IMMEDIATELY MATTHEW GIVES UP HIS PROSPEROUS—BUT CORRUPT—JOB AND FOLLOWS JESUS.

NO GOOD JEW EVER WANTED MATTHEW FOR A FRIEND.

MATTHEW THROWS A DINNER PARTY TO HONOR JESUS. OTHER TAX COLLECTORS COME TO DINNER TOO. THE PHARISEES SEETHE WITH DISAPPROVAL.

WHY DOES YOUR TEACHER EAT WITH TAX COLLECTORS AND OTHER SINNERS?

PEOPLE WHO ARE HEALTHY DON'T NEED A DOCTOR. SICK PEOPLE DO. THE SINNERS ARE THE ONES WHO NEED ME.

THE PHARISEES DON'T KNOW WHAT TO SAY. BUT THEY GET EVEN ANGRIER AT JESUS AND START LOOKING FOR WAYS TO CRITICIZE HIM IN FRONT OF THE PEOPLE. ONE SABBATH DAY IN THE SYNAGOGUE ...

LOOK, JESUS IS TALKING TO THAT MAN WITH THE TWISTED HAND. LET'S SEE IF WE CAN TRICK HIM INTO BREAKING GOD'S LAW.

Sermon on a Mountain

BASED ON LUKE 6:12-16;
MATTHEW 5—8; 13;
MARK 4:1-20

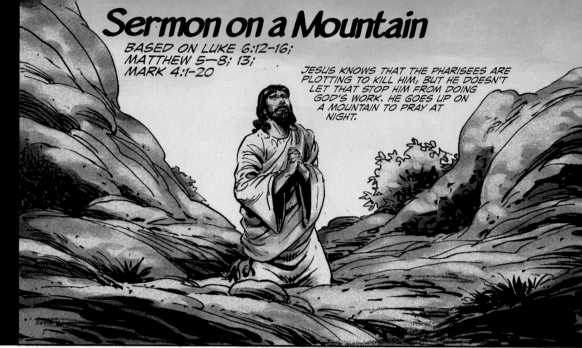

JESUS KNOWS THAT THE PHARISEES ARE PLOTTING TO KILL HIM, BUT HE DOESN'T LET THAT STOP HIM FROM DOING GOD'S WORK. HE GOES UP ON A MOUNTAIN TO PRAY AT NIGHT.

IN THE MORNING, JESUS NAMES 12 MEN TO BE FULL-TIME HELPERS IN GOD'S WORK: SIMON PETER, ANDREW, JAMES, JOHN, PHILIP, NATHANAEL BARTHOLOMEW, MATTHEW, THOMAS, JAMES THE SON OF ALPHAEUS, THADDEUS, SIMON THE ZEALOT, AND JUDAS ISCARIOT.

YOU WHO BELIEVE IN ME ARE LIKE SALT THAT GIVES FOOD ITS FLAVOR. YOU ARE A LIGHT IN THE DARKNESS, HELPING OTHERS TO SEE OUR HEAVENLY FATHER.

DON'T WORRY ABOUT WHAT YOU WILL EAT OR DRINK. LOOK AT THE BIRDS; THEY DON'T PLANT CROPS OR SHOP FOR FOOD, BUT YOUR HEAVENLY FATHER STILL FEEDS THEM. YOU ARE WORTH SO MUCH MORE THAN SPARROWS! GOD WILL TAKE CARE OF YOUR NEEDS. DON'T WORRY ABOUT TOMORROW; TOMORROW CAN WORRY ABOUT ITSELF.

IF YOU HEAR MY WORDS AND FOLLOW THEM, YOU'LL BE LIKE THE WISE MAN WHO BUILT HIS HOUSE ON THE ROCK.

A STORM CAME, BEATING AT HIS HOUSE WITH RAIN, FLOODS, AND WIND. BUT HIS HOUSE DID NOT FALL BECAUSE IT HAD A SOLID FOUNDATION BUILT ON A ROCK.

ANYONE WHO HEARS MY WORDS BUT DOESN'T FOLLOW THEM IS LIKE A FOOLISH MAN, WHO BUILT HIS HOUSE ON THE SAND. THAT SAME STORM LEFT HIS HOUSE IN RUINS.

AFTER THE SERMON, JESUS TAKES HIS DISCIPLES BACK TO CAPERNAUM. AN OFFICER IN THE ROMAN ARMY STOPS THEM IN THE STREET.

JESUS! MY SERVANT IS SICK. I DON'T DESERVE TO HAVE YOU COME TO MY HOUSE, BUT I KNOW THAT IF YOU SAY THE WORD, MY SERVANT WILL BE HEALED.

I HAVE NOT FOUND ANYONE IN ISRAEL WHOSE FAITH IS SO STRONG! GO, AND WHAT YOU BELIEVE WILL BE TRUE.

NEWS COMES THAT THE SERVANT WAS HEALED AT THE EXACT MOMENT THAT JESUS SAYS THIS.

ONE DAY THE CROWD THAT COMES TO HEAR JESUS IS SO LARGE THAT HE GETS IN A BOAT TO TEACH THEM. THE PEOPLE LISTEN FROM THE SHORE.

A MAN ONCE FOUND A VALUABLE PEARL. HE SOLD EVERYTHING HE HAD TO BUY IT. THE KINGDOM OF GOD IS LIKE THAT PEARL—IT'S WORTH EVERYTHING YOU OWN.

JESUS TELLS
ANOTHER STORY:

A FARMER
WENT OUT TO
PLANT HIS
SEEDS ...

SOME OF THE
SEEDS FELL ON
ROCKY SOIL. THEY
GREW FOR A LITTLE
BIT, BUT THEN THEY
WITHERED BECAUSE
THEY DIDN'T HAVE
STRONG ROOTS.

OTHER SEEDS
LANDED IN THE
MIDDLE OF WEEDS,
AND THE WEEDS
EVENTUALLY
CHOKED THE
PLANTS.

BUT SOME
SEEDS ... SOME
SEEDS FELL ON
GOOD SOIL. THEY
PRODUCED A CROP
A HUNDRED TIMES
GREATER THAN
WHAT HAD BEEN
PLANTED.

AS HE WAS
SCATTERING HIS
SEEDS, SOME FELL
ON THE PATH. BIRDS
QUICKLY CAME AND
ATE IT UP.

JESUS ENDS HIS PARABLE AND SITS
IN SILENCE, LETTING THE POINT OF HIS
STORY SINK IN WITH THE CROWD.

WE
DON'T GET
IT.

IF YOU
HAVE EARS,
LISTEN!

THE SEEDS ARE MY MESSAGE ABOUT THE KINGDOM OF GOD.
IF PEOPLE DON'T UNDERSTAND MY MESSAGE, THE DEVIL SWOOPS DOWN
LIKE THE BIRD AND DEVOURS MY WORDS BEFORE THEY CAN GROW. THE ROCKY
SOIL IS THOSE PEOPLE WHO HEAR MY WORDS BUT STOP FOLLOWING ME
BECAUSE IT IS TOO HARD. THE THORNS AND WEEDS ARE LIKE THE WORRIES
OF THIS LIFE THAT CHOKE OFF PEOPLE'S HOPE IN ME. BUT THE GOOD SOIL
REPRESENTS PEOPLE WHO HEAR MY WORDS, UNDERSTAND THEM, AND
FOLLOW MY WAYS.

AT THE END OF A DAY OF TEACHING, JESUS TELLS HIS DISCIPLES THAT THEY SHOULD CROSS TO THE OTHER SIDE OF THE SEA OF GALILEE. JESUS FALLS ASLEEP IN THE BACK OF THE BOAT. THE WEATHER SEEMS CALM ...

I DON'T LIKE THE LOOKS OF THOSE CLOUDS.

Storm at Sea

BASED ON MARK 4:35—5:24

SUDDENLY, A VIOLENT STORM SWEEPS ACROSS THE SEA! JESUS KEEPS ON SLEEPING, BUT THE DISCIPLES ARE TERRIFIED.

HURRY! LOWER THE SAIL!

WHERE'S THE ANCHOR?

GIANT WAVES POUR OVER THE SIDES OF THE BOAT. THE DISCIPLES CAN'T DO ANYTHING TO STOP THE WATER.

HELP! WE'RE BEING SWAMPED!

WE'RE GOING TO SINK!

SOMEHOW, JESUS HAS REMAINED ASLEEP THROUGH THE COMMOTION.

MASTER! DON'T YOU CARE THAT WE'RE GOING TO DROWN?

WITHOUT A WORD TO THE DISCIPLES, JESUS STANDS UP AND REACHES HIS HAND OUT TO THE STORM.

QUIET! BE STILL!

INSTANTLY THE WIND DIES DOWN AND THE SEA IS COMPLETELY CALM.

WHY ARE YOU SO AFRAID?

IS YOUR FAITH IN ME STILL SO WEAK?

EVEN THE WIND AND THE WAVES OBEY HIM!

WHEN THE BOAT REACHES SHORE, A MAN POSSESSED BY THOUSANDS OF EVIL SPIRITS RUNS OUT TO MEET JESUS.

BE CAREFUL!

NO ONE CAN KEEP HIM TIED UP ANYMORE, NOT EVEN WITH CHAINS.

WHAT DO YOU WANT WITH ME, SON OF THE MOST HIGH GOD?

COME OUT OF THIS MAN, YOU EVIL SPIRIT!

THE DEMONS ARE CAST OUT INTO A NEARBY HERD OF PIGS. THE NEWLY POSSESSED PIGS RUN OFF A CLIFF AND DROWN.

THE MAN IS CURED! IN THANKS, HE ASKS TO GO WITH JESUS, BUT JESUS TELLS HIM TO SHARE THE STORY OF THE LORD'S MERCY.

BACK IN GALILEE, AS JESUS IS TEACHING, JAIRUS, A SYNAGOGUE RULER, FALLS AT JESUS' FEET.

MY LITTLE GIRL IS DYING. IF YOU PLACE YOUR HANDS ON HER, SHE WILL LIVE. PLEASE COME!

JESUS GOES WITH JAIRUS. ON THE WAY, A SERVANT FROM JAIRUS'S HOUSE MEETS THEM.

IT'S TOO LATE! YOUR DAUGHTER IS DEAD!

A Death in the Family

BASED ON MARK 5:38–6:29; MATTHEW 10; 14:1-12

WHEN JESUS GETS TO JAIRUS'S HOUSE, HE FINDS A CROWD OF PEOPLE WEEPING BECAUSE THE LITTLE GIRL IS DEAD.

WHY ARE YOU CRYING? THE LITTLE GIRL IS JUST ASLEEP.

ASLEEP! ARE YOU JOKING—OR JUST STUPID? THE CHILD IS DEAD.

JESUS MAKES EVERYONE GO OUTSIDE EXCEPT FOR THE GIRL'S PARENTS AND HIS DISCIPLES. THEN HE TAKES THE GIRL'S HAND.

LITTLE GIRL, GET UP!

THE GIRL IMMEDIATELY COMES BACK TO LIFE. JESUS TELLS HER PARENTS TO GIVE HER SOMETHING TO EAT.

[J]AIRUS IS AN IMPORTANT MAN, SO NEWS [A]BOUT HIS DAUGHTER SPREADS QUICKLY. AS [J]ESUS TRAVELS AROUND PREACHING AND [H]EALING, HE BECOMES EVEN MORE FAMOUS [A]ND POPULAR. BUT JESUS IS CONCERNED [A]BOUT THE MANY PEOPLE WHO STILL HAVE [N]OT HEARD HIS MESSAGE.

THE PEOPLE ARE LIKE SHEEP WITHOUT A SHEPHERD.

I WANT YOU TO GO OUT IN PAIRS TO PREACH GOOD NEWS AND HEAL THE SICK.

IT'S DANGEROUS OUT THERE, SO YOU'LL NEED TO BE AS SMART AS SNAKES, BUT AS INNOCENT AS DOVES.

AND DON'T WORRY ABOUT WHAT TO SAY. THE SPIRIT OF GOD WILL SPEAK THROUGH YOU.

WHILE JESUS' DISCIPLES ARE OUT SPREADING HIS MESSAGE, JOHN THE BAPTIST IS BUSY ACCUSING THE KING OF BREAKING GOD'S LAW. AS USUAL, JOHN DOESN'T WORRY ABOUT BEING POLITE.

YOU SON OF A SNAKE! IT'S BAD ENOUGH THAT YOUR BROTHER DIVORCED HIS OWN WIFE. BUT NOW YOU'VE GONE AND MARRIED HER! TWO SINS DO NOT MAKE A RIGHT.

HEROD DOESN'T WANT TO KILL JOHN—IN FACT, HE THINKS JOHN'S SPEECHES ARE AMUSING, EVEN THOUGH HE DOESN'T UNDERSTAND HALF OF THEM. BUT HEROD'S WIFE IS FURIOUS, AND SHE FORCES HEROD TO PUT JOHN IN PRISON FOR HIS DISRESPECT.

THIS IS STILL NOT ENOUGH FOR HEROD'S NEW WIFE. SHE AND HER DAUGHTER SALOME HATCH AN EVIL PLAN. ONE NIGHT, WHEN ALL OF HEROD'S OFFICIALS AND GENERALS COME FOR A FEAST, SALOME PROVIDES THE ENTERTAINMENT.

HEROD'S STEPDAUGHTER IS A WONDERFUL DANCER!

AND SHE'S SMART, TOO.

SALOME! THANK YOU FOR ADDING TO OUR FESTIVITIES. ASK ME FOR ANYTHING YOU WANT, AND I WILL GIVE IT TO YOU, NO MATTER WHAT IT IS.

THANK YOU, MY LORD. WHAT I WOULD LIKE MOST IS ... THE HEAD OF JOHN THE BAPTIST, SERVED TO ME ON A PLATTER.

ALTHOUGH IT UPSETS HEROD TO EXECUTE JOHN, HE CAN'T BACK DOWN FROM HIS OATH IN FRONT OF ALL HIS ADVISERS. HE ORDERS JOHN THE BAPTIST TO BE EXECUTED IMMEDIATELY, AND HIS HEAD DELIVERED TO SALOME AND HER WICKED MOTHER.

A Hungry Crowd

BASED ON JOHN 6:1-14; MARK 6:30-44

THE DISCIPLES PREACH ALL AROUND GALILEE. WHEN THEY RETURN FROM THEIR TRIP, JESUS WANTS TO TAKE THEM TO A QUIET PLACE TO REST. BUT THE CROWDS FOLLOW HIM ONCE AGAIN. AFTER A FULL DAY OF PREACHING, THE CROWD STARTS TO GET HUNGRY ...

PHILIP, WHERE CAN WE BUY FOOD FOR ALL THESE PEOPLE?

THERE MUST BE 5,000 PEOPLE HERE. EVEN IF WE WORKED FOR EIGHT MONTHS, WE WOULDN'T HAVE ENOUGH MONEY TO FEED ALL THESE PEOPLE!

HERE'S A BOY WITH FIVE LOAVES OF BREAD AND TWO FISH. BUT HOW FAR WILL THAT GO IN THIS HUGE CROWD?

HAVE THE PEOPLE SIT DOWN.

THE CROWD IS HUNGRY, BUT THE PEOPLE SIT DOWN ON THE GRASS AND WAIT TO SEE WHAT JESUS WILL DO.

FATHER, THANK YOU FOR THIS BREAD AND FISH.

JESUS TELLS HIS DISCIPLES TO START PASSING OUT THE BREAD AND FISH.

LOOK! THE FOOD ISN'T RUNNING OUT! EVERYONE HAS ENOUGH.

IT'S A MIRACLE!

Walking on Water

BASED ON MATTHEW 14:22-33; JOHN 6:15-21; MARK 6:45-52

BUT GOD SENT JESUS TO BE THE SAVIOR OF THE WORLD—NOT THE CONQUEROR OF ARMIES. WHEN JESUS SEES THAT THE CROWD WANTS TO FORCE HIM TO BE A KING, HE QUICKLY CALLS HIS DISCIPLES AWAY FROM THE CROWD.

WE SHOULD LEAVE BEFORE THIS CROWD STARTS A RIOT. LAUNCH THE BOAT AND CROSS TO THE OTHER SIDE OF THE SEA. I WILL JOIN YOU LATER.

AS THE DISCIPLES ROW ACROSS THE SEA, JESUS GOES UP ON A MOUNTAIN TO PRAY. THAT NIGHT, ON THE SEA OF GALILEE ...

HOW WILL JESUS CATCH UP TO US WITHOUT A BOAT?

GUYS, LOOK! WHAT'S THAT?

YOU ARE THE CHRIST, THE SON OF THE LIVING GOD.

YOU ARE BLESSED, PETER. MY FATHER IN HEAVEN SHOWED YOU THIS IS TRUE.

NOW THAT THE DISCIPLES REALLY UNDERSTAND THAT JESUS IS THE MESSIAH, THE SAVIOR THAT GOD PROMISED TO SEND, JESUS TELLS THEM WHAT WILL HAPPEN WHEN HE GOES TO JERUSALEM.

THE PHARISEES AND PRIESTS DON'T BELIEVE I AM THE MESSIAH. THEY WILL HAVE ME KILLED. BUT IN THREE DAYS I WILL RISE TO LIFE AGAIN.

KILLED? NEVER!

PETER, YOU DON'T UNDERSTAND GOD'S PLAN FOR ME. IF ANY OF YOU WANTS TO FOLLOW ME, YOU MUST BE READY TO SUFFER THE WAY I WILL SUFFER.

BUT THE DISCIPLES STILL DO NOT UNDERSTAND ...

Mountain Vision

BASED ON MATTHEW 17:1-21; MARK 9:2-29

EVEN THOUGH JESUS CLAIMS THAT HE WILL BE KILLED, HIS DISCIPLES ARE SURE THAT HE CAN JUST USE HIS POWER TO SAVE HIMSELF. BUT JESUS WANTS THEM TO UNDERSTAND HIS TRUE MISSION. SO, A FEW DAYS LATER, JESUS SPEAKS TO PETER, JAMES, AND JOHN.

COME WITH ME UP ON THE MOUNTAIN.

WHY JUST US?

SUDDENLY, JESUS' FACE SHINES LIKE THE SUN, AND HIS CLOTHES BEGIN TO GLOW. AND STANDING WITH JESUS ARE ELIJAH AND MOSES, TWO OF GOD'S GREATEST PROPHETS.

IN SHOCK, PETER FALLS TO HIS KNEES AND CRIES OUT:

IT'S LUCKY WE'RE HERE! WE CAN PITCH TENTS FOR THE THREE OF YOU!

PETER'S MOUTH HAD ALWAYS MOVED FASTER THAN HIS BRAIN. BUT BEFORE ANYONE CAN REPLY, GOD SPEAKS OUT OF THE BRIGHT MIST AROUND THEM.

THIS IS MY BELOVED SON! DO AS HE SAYS.

TERRIFIED, PETER, JAMES, AND JOHN FALL FACEDOWN TO THE GROUND. WHEN JESUS TOUCHES THEM COMFORTINGLY, THEY LOOK UP AGAIN. JESUS IS NOW THE ONLY ONE THERE.

GET UP. DON'T BE AFRAID.

JESUS WARNS THE DISCIPLES NOT TO TELL ANYONE ABOUT WHAT THEY HAVE SEEN UNTIL HE HAS BEEN RAISED FROM THE DEAD.

AT THE BOTTOM OF THE MOUNTAIN, A CROWD WAITS.

TEACHER, A SPIRIT IS CONTROLLING MY SON. I ASKED YOUR DISCIPLES TO HELP, BUT THEY COULDN'T HEAL HIM.

BRING YOUR SON TO ME.

THE FATHER OBEYS JESUS, BUT THE SPIRIT TAKES CONTROL AND THROWS THE BOY TO THE GROUND.

IF YOU CAN DO ANYTHING, PLEASE HELP US!

EVERYTHING IS POSSIBLE FOR THE PERSON WHO BELIEVES.

I DO BELIEVE! HELP ME WITH MY UNBELIEF!

EVIL SPIRIT THAT TAKES OVER THIS BOY, I ORDER YOU TO COME OUT IMMEDIATELY!

585

Tough Lessons

BASED ON MATTHEW 18; JOHN 7:11—8:59

JESUS OVERHEARS THE DISCIPLES' QUARRELING AND REALIZES THAT THEY THINK HEAVEN WORKS THE SAME WAY AS EARTH. HE DECIDES THAT IT'S TIME FOR AN OBJECT LESSON. TO HELP HIS DISCIPLES UNDERSTAND MORE ABOUT THE KINGDOM OF GOD, JESUS CALLS A YOUNG BOY.

YOU NEED TO BECOME LIKE LITTLE CHILDREN. IF YOU DON'T, YOU WON'T ENTER THE KINGDOM OF HEAVEN.

YOU MUST BECOME AS TRUSTING AND INNOCENT AS THIS CHILD IS. WELCOME A LITTLE CHILD LIKE THIS IN MY NAME.

IF A PERSON SINS AGAINST YOU, DON'T WAIT FOR HIM TO APOLOGIZE. GO TALK TO THE PERSON. IF HE LISTENS, YOU WILL HAVE MADE A FRIEND.

HOW MANY TIMES SHOULD I FORGIVE SOMEONE WHO HURTS ME? SEVEN TIMES?

NO, NOT SEVEN TIMES, BUT 77 TIMES! DON'T EVEN KEEP TRACK. JUST KEEP FORGIVING.

FROM CAPERNAUM, JESUS GOES SOUTH TO JUDEA AND FINALLY REACHES JERUSALEM. HE KNOWS THAT HIS ARREST WILL HAPPEN SOON. PEOPLE ARE WONDERING ABOUT HIM ...

HE IS A GOOD MAN.

NO, HE'S A FAKE!

HOW DID HE LEARN SO MUCH WITHOUT STUDYING?

589

FOR A MOMENT, JESUS IGNORES THE PHARISEES' INTERRUPTION AND WRITES IN THE DIRT WITH HIS FINGER.

WELL??? WHAT'S YOUR ANSWER?

WHICHEVER OF YOU HAS NEVER SINNED, YOU MAY THROW THE FIRST STONE AT HER.

JESUS HAS CAUGHT THEM IN THEIR OWN TRAP—NONE OF THEM CAN PRETEND THEY'VE NEVER SINNED. ONE BY ONE, THE PHARISEES DROP THEIR STONES AND SLINK AWAY FROM THE CROWD.

WOMAN, WHO ACCUSES YOU OF A CRIME?

WELL ... NOBODY, I GUESS.

I DON'T ACCUSE YOU EITHER. GO IN PEACE, BUT SIN NO MORE.

NOW THE PHARISEES AND PRIESTS WANT TO STOP JESUS EVEN MORE.

ANYONE WHO BELIEVES JESUS IS THE MESSIAH SHOULD BE KICKED OUT OF THE SYNAGOGUE.

WE HAVE TO ARREST JESUS SOON, BEFORE MORE PEOPLE DECIDE HE'S THE SAVIOR.

JESUS IS TOO POPULAR TO ARREST. THE PRIESTS ARE AFRAID TO STIR UP TROUBLE WHILE THE CITY IS FILLED WITH PEOPLE ATTENDING THE FEAST. UNTIL ONE DAY ...

I COME TO BRING GLORY TO GOD. I WAS WITH GOD EVEN BEFORE THE DAYS OF ABRAHAM.

HOW DARE HE CLAIM TO KNOW GOD LIKE THAT!

STONE HIM! STONE HIM!

THE PHARISEES PICK UP STONES TO THROW AT JESUS, BUT HE SLIPS AWAY.

Faith at First Sight

BASED ON JOHN 9:1—10:21

LATER, JESUS MEETS A BLIND MAN BEGGING AT THE TEMPLE GATE. JESUS USES SPIT TO MAKE SOME MUD AND GENTLY PUTS IT ON THE MAN'S EYES.

GO AND WASH OFF THE MUD. TRUST ME.

THE BLIND MAN OBEYS JESUS AND FOR THE FIRST TIME IN HIS LIFE, HE CAN SEE! EVEN PEOPLE WHO KNOW HIM HAVE A HARD TIME BELIEVING HE IS THE SAME MAN WHO WAS BLIND.

IS THIS THE SAME MAN WHO USED TO BEG OUTSIDE THE TEMPLE?

IT CAN'T BE. IT ONLY LOOKS LIKE HIM.

I AM THE GOOD SHEPHERD.

THE GOOD SHEPHERD GIVES HIS LIFE FOR HIS SHEEP.

NO ONE CAN TAKE MY LIFE FROM ME, BUT I GIVE IT MYSELF.

I CAN GIVE AWAY MY LIFE AND THEN TAKE IT BACK AGAIN.

MY FATHER GAVE ME THIS POWER.

THIS MAN IS CRAZY—OR POSSESSED BY A DEMON. WHY SHOULD WE LISTEN TO HIM?

BUT CAN AN EVIL SPIRIT GIVE SIGHT TO THE BLIND?

THE PHARISEES AND PRIESTS CAN'T STOP ARGUING. SOME OF THEM THINK JESUS IS WORKING WITH THE DEVIL. OTHERS SAY HE ISN'T, BUT THEY STILL REFUSE TO BELIEVE HE IS THE SON OF GOD. A FEW DAYS LATER, JESUS LEAVES JERUSALEM TO TEACH IN THE AREA AROUND THE CITY.

IN ONE TOWN, A LAWYER IN THE CROWD WAITS FOR A CHANCE TO TEST JESUS.

I'LL FIND OUT FOR MYSELF HOW THIS YOUNG TEACHER ANSWERS A HARD QUESTION ...

BUT WHEN A SAMARITAN SEES THE WOUNDED MAN, HE STOPS. EVEN THOUGH SAMARITANS AND JEWS ARE BITTER ENEMIES, HE TAKES CARE OF THE MAN'S WOUNDS. THEN HE TAKES HIM TO AN INN AND PAYS SOMEONE TO LOOK AFTER HIM WHILE HE GETS WELL.

WHEN JESUS FINISHES THE STORY OF THE GOOD SAMARITAN, HE ASKS:

WHICH OF THESE TRAVELERS WAS A NEIGHBOR TO THE MAN WHO WAS ROBBED?

THE MAN WHO HELPED HIM.

GO AND DO THE SAME.

Praying Lessons

BASED ON
LUKE 10:38–11:4;
MATTHEW 6:9-13;
JOHN 10:22-39

JESUS CONTINUES ON HIS PREACHING TRIP. IN BETHANY, HE STOPS TO VISIT HIS FRIENDS MARY, MARTHA, AND LAZARUS. MARY DROPS EVERYTHING SHE'S DOING TO LISTEN TO JESUS. BUT MARTHA ...

IT ISN'T FAIR THAT I'M DOING ALL THE WORK!

597

FINALLY, MARTHA BECOMES SO UPSET THAT SHE COMPLAINS TO JESUS.

LORD, DON'T YOU CARE THAT MARY HAS LEFT ME TO DO ALL THE WORK? TELL HER TO HELP ME!

MARTHA, MARTHA. YOU'RE WORRIED ABOUT TOO MANY THINGS. MARY HAS CHOSEN THE IMPORTANT THING—TO SEEK GOD. I WON'T TAKE THAT AWAY FROM HER.

MARTHA TAKES JESUS' WORDS TO HEART. SOON HE JOINS HIS DISCIPLES FOR A TEACHING TRIP IN JUDEA.

I FEEL CLOSER TO GOD THAN EVER BEFORE.

DURING HIS TRAVELS, JESUS OFTEN STOPS TO PRAY. HIS DISCIPLES WITNESS THE POWER OF HIS PRAYERS AND WANT TO LEARN MORE.

LORD, TEACH US TO PRAY.

WHEN YOU PRAY, SAY, "OUR FATHER IN HEAVEN, YOUR NAME IS HOLY.

LET YOUR KINGDOM COME.

HELP US FOLLOW YOUR PLAN ON EARTH, LIKE IT HAPPENS IN HEAVEN.

GIVE US THE FOOD WE NEED FOR TODAY.

FORGIVE OUR SINS, LIKE WE SHOULD FORGIVE PEOPLE WHO SIN AGAINST US.

PROTECT US FROM TEMPTATION.

AND KEEP US SAFE FROM THE DEVIL."

FOR A MOMENT, NO ONE SPEAKS. THEN SOFTLY THE DISCIPLES SAY "AMEN" TO THIS SIMPLE PRAYER. AFTER THIS, JESUS AND HIS FOLLOWERS CONTINUE TRAVELING THROUGH JUDEA PREACHING AND HEALING. BY THE TIME JESUS RETURNS TO JERUSALEM FOR A RELIGIOUS FEAST, THE CITY IS FILLED WITH PEOPLE, TALKING AND WONDERING ABOUT JESUS.

AS JESUS WALKS ALONG SOLOMON'S PORCH AT THE TEMPLE, THE PEOPLE SURROUND HIM.

HOW LONG WILL YOU KEEP US WAITING? IF YOU ARE THE MESSIAH, TELL US!

I DID TELL YOU. BUT YOU DON'T BELIEVE THE THINGS I HAVE DONE IN MY FATHER'S NAME.

DID YOU HEAR THAT? HE CLAIMS TO BE GOD!

STONE HIM! ARREST HIM!

BUT JESUS CALMLY WALKS AWAY, AND STRANGELY, NO ONE TRIES TO STOP HIM.

A Loving Father

BASED ON LUKE 15:11-32

JESUS LEAVES JERUSALEM AND CONTINUES TO PREACH. THE PHARISEES COMPLAIN BECAUSE HE SPENDS TIME WITH SINNERS. SO JESUS TELLS THEM A STORY ABOUT A MAN WITH TWO SONS. ONE DAY THE YOUNGER SON COMES TO THE FATHER ...

FATHER, I WANT TO RUN MY OWN LIFE. GIVE ME MY SHARE OF YOUR MONEY NOW. I DON'T WANT TO WAIT FOR YOU TO DIE.

IF YOU WANT THE MONEY, YOU MAY HAVE IT. I'LL DIVIDE MY PROPERTY BETWEEN YOU AND YOUR BROTHER.

THE YOUNGER SON MOVES FAR AWAY TO ANOTHER COUNTRY ...

BRING MY SON THE BEST ROBE IN THE HOUSE! PREPARE A FEAST! MY SON WAS LOST AND NOW HE'S FOUND!

OUT IN THE FIELD, THE OLDER SON WORKS HARD.

IF MY BROTHER WERE HERE, I WOULDN'T HAVE TO WORK SO MUCH.

AT THE END OF THE DAY, THE OLDER SON COMES IN FROM THE FIELD. WHEN HE GETS CLOSE TO THE HOUSE, HE HEARS MUSIC AND DANCING.

WHAT'S GOING ON?

YOUR BROTHER HAS COME HOME SAFE AND SOUND. YOUR FATHER IS GIVING A FEAST FOR HIM.

IN ANGER, THE OLDER SON REFUSES TO GO INTO THE HOUSE AND JOIN THE PARTY. SO HIS FATHER COMES OUT TO TALK TO HIM.

I HAVE ALWAYS OBEYED EVERYTHING YOU WANTED ME TO DO, AND YOU'VE NEVER LET ME HAVE A PARTY WITH MY FRIENDS. BUT FOR HIM, YOU THROW THE BEST PARTY EVER.

EVERYTHING I HAVE IS YOURS. BUT WE HAVE TO CELEBRATE. YOUR BROTHER WAS THE SAME AS DEAD, AND NOW HE'S ALIVE AND SAFE.

TWO STRONG MEN HELP ROLL THE STONE AWAY FROM THE TOMB. IN A POWERFUL VOICE, JESUS PRAYS ALOUD TO GOD, THEN SPEAKS COMMANDINGLY:

LAZARUS, COME OUT!

LAZARUS IS ALIVE AGAIN! THEY QUICKLY TAKE THE FUNERAL CLOTHS OFF HIM.

THIS IS JESUS' GREATEST MIRACLE YET!

UNBELIEVABLE!

THE PHARISEES CALL AN EMERGENCY MEETING.

IF HE KEEPS DOING MIRACLES, THE PEOPLE WILL TRY TO MAKE HIM A KING.

IF JESUS STIRS UP A REBELLION, THE ROMANS WILL BLAME US. WE'LL LOSE OUR POSITIONS AND OUR NATION WILL BE DESTROYED.

DON'T YOU SEE? IT'S BETTER TO KILL JESUS THAN TO GET THE WHOLE COUNTRY IN TROUBLE. FOR THE SAKE OF THE NATION, THIS JESUS MUST DIE.

WHEN JESUS HEARS ABOUT THE JEWISH RULERS' INTENTIONS, HE GOES TO A QUIET PLACE TO WAIT FOR THE TIME TO COME TO FACE HIS ENEMIES. AS THE TIME FOR THE PASSOVER FEAST GETS CLOSER, PEOPLE FROM ALL OVER ARRIVE IN JERUSALEM, AND JESUS JOINS THEM.

PEOPLE BRING SMALL CHILDREN TO JESUS SO HE CAN BLESS THEM.

I WANT JESUS TO BLESS MY SON!

NO, TAKE THE CHILDREN AWAY. STOP BOTHERING JESUS.

BUT JESUS WELCOMES THE CHILDREN.

LET THE LITTLE ONES COME TO ME. DON'T KEEP THEM AWAY. GOD'S KINGDOM IS MADE UP OF PEOPLE LIKE THESE CHILDREN.

LATER, A YOUNG MAN STOPS JESUS TO ASK A QUESTION.

TEACHER, WHAT SHOULD I DO TO RECEIVE ETERNAL LIFE?

KEEP GOD'S COMMANDMENTS.

I ALREADY DO THAT—EVER SINCE I WAS A LITTLE BOY.

YOU ARE STILL MISSING ONE THING. SELL EVERYTHING YOU HAVE AND GIVE THE MONEY TO THE POOR, THEN FOLLOW ME.

BUT THE YOUNG MAN GOES AWAY SAD, BECAUSE HE IS QUITE WEALTHY. THE TRAVELERS KEEP MOVING TOWARD JERUSALEM. IN JERICHO ...

PLEASE, LET ME THROUGH!

HA! ZACCHAEUS, THE CROOKED LITTLE TAX COLLECTOR, WANTS TO SEE JESUS.

Man in a Tree

BASED ON LUKE 19:1-35; JOHN 12:1-8

ZACCHAEUS IMMEDIATELY COMES DOWN OUT OF THE TREE AND SHOWS JESUS THE WAY TO HIS HOUSE.

JESUS IS GOING TO STAY AT A SINNER'S HOUSE. WHY WOULD HE DO THAT?

BEING WITH JESUS HELPS ZACCHAEUS KNOW THAT HE HAS DONE A LOT OF WRONG THINGS. HE WANTS TO CHANGE.

I'M GOING TO GIVE HALF OF WHAT I OWN TO THE POOR FOUR TIMES WHAT I OWE TO ANYONE I'VE CHEATED.

SALVATION HAS COME TO YOUR HOUSE TODAY. YOU WERE LOST, AND I CAME TO SAVE YOU.

FROM JERICHO, THE CROWD CONTINUES THE TRIP TO JERUSALEM FOR THE GREAT PASSOVER FEAST. THE FESTIVAL IS STILL SIX DAYS AWAY, SO JESUS STOPS IN BETHANY TO VISIT HIS FRIENDS MARY, MARTHA, AND LAZARUS. AT A SUPPER IN THE HOME OF SIMON THE LEPER, MARY KNEELS AND POURS EXPENSIVE OIL OVER JESUS' FEET. THEN SHE WIPES HIS FEET WITH HER HAIR.

JUDAS ISCARIOT, TREASURER OF THE DISCIPLES, THINKS THIS IS A WASTE OF MONEY.

WE COULD HAVE SOLD THAT PERFUME AND GIVEN A YEAR'S WORTH OF MONEY TO THE POOR.

LEAVE HER ALONE. THE POOR WILL ALWAYS BE HERE FOR YOU TO HELP, BUT I WON'T ALWAYS BE HERE. SHE'S SHOWING HER LOVE.

JUDAS DOESN'T REALLY CARE ABOUT THE POOR. HE IS THINKING ABOUT THE MONEY BECAUSE ...

THE LESS MONEY THEY WASTE, THE MORE I CAN TAKE FOR MYSELF. NO ONE WILL EVER KNOW.

THE NEXT DAY, JESUS JOINS THE CROWD GOING TO JERUSALEM TO PREPARE FOR THE PASSOVER FEAST. ON THE WAY ...

GO TO THAT VILLAGE. WHEN YOU GET THERE, YOU WILL FIND A DONKEY'S COLT TIED UP. BRING IT TO ME. IF ANYONE ASKS, JUST TELL HIM, "THE LORD NEEDS IT."

TWO DISCIPLES FIND THE YOUNG DONKEY JUST AS JESUS SAID. WHEN THEY START TO UNTIE IT ...

WHY ARE YOU UNTYING THE COLT?

THE LORD NEEDS IT.

THE OWNER GIVES PERMISSION AND THE DISCIPLES TAKE THE COLT BACK TO JESUS.

I WONDER WHY JESUS WANTS MY COLT. NO ONE HAS EVER RIDDEN IT. IT'S NOT EVEN A VERY NOBLE BEAST FOR ANYONE AS IMPORTANT AS JESUS TO RIDE.

THAT EVENING, JESUS GOES BACK TO BETHANY. BUT ON MONDAY HE RETURNS TO THE TEMPLE IN JERUSALEM.

I'VE COME A LONG WAY TO OFFER A SACRIFICE TO GOD. BUT I CAN'T AFFORD THIS UNFAIR PRICE FOR A DOVE TO SACRIFICE.

THEN I'LL SELL IT TO SOMEONE ELSE. NOW MOVE YOU'RE BLOCKING MY TABLE.

IN RIGHTEOUS ANGER, JESUS DRIVES THE MERCHANTS OUT OF THE TEMPLE.

THE SCRIPTURES SAY, "MY HOUSE SHALL BE A HOUSE OF PRAYER." BUT YOU HAVE TURNED IT INTO A DEN OF THIEVES.

JESUS IS CRITICIZING HOW WE RUN THE TEMPLE. HE'S CHALLENGING OUR AUTHORITY!

WE NEED TO TRICK JESUS INTO MAKING A MISTAKE. THEN WE CAN TURN THE PEOPLE AWAY FROM HIM.

Money Troubles

BASED ON LUKE 20:20-26;
MARK 12:12-44;
MATTHEW 22:15-22

MASTER, WE KNOW YOU TEACH THE TRUTH. TELL US, IS IT RIGHT TO PAY TAXES TO CAESAR OR NOT?

THE PHARISEES PLOT THEIR STRATEGY. THEY DECIDE TO ASK A QUESTION THAT FORCES JESUS TO GIVE A WRONG ANSWER NO MATTER WHAT HE SAYS.

IF HE SAYS "YES," THE PEOPLE WILL TURN AGAINST HIM BECAUSE THEY HATE TO PAY TAXES.

AND IF HE SAYS "NO," THE ROMAN OFFICIALS WILL ARREST HIM FOR TREASON.

THEN JESUS WARNS THE PEOPLE AGAINST DOING GOOD DEEDS JUST SO OTHER PEOPLE CAN SEE THEM AND BE IMPRESSED. AS HE SPEAKS, HE SEES A PROUD MAN PUT A LOT OF MONEY IN THE TEMPLE OFFERING.

THEN A POOR WIDOW HUMBLY DROPS TWO SMALL COINS INTO THE OFFERING.

THE WIDOW HAS GIVEN MORE THAN ANYONE ELSE, BECAUSE SHE GAVE EVERYTHING SHE HAS TO GOD.

AFTER THIS, JESUS LEAVES THE TEMPLE—FOR THE LAST TIME. OUTSIDE JERUSALEM, ON THE QUIET SLOPES OF THE MOUNT OF OLIVES, SOME OF THE DISCIPLES ASK JESUS ABOUT THE FUTURE. JESUS EXPLAINS THAT THE GOSPEL WILL SPREAD THROUGH THE WHOLE WORLD, AND THEN HE WILL COME AGAIN TO JUDGE THE WORLD.

618

Passover Problems

BASED ON MATTHEW 26:14–25; LUKE 22:1–13; JOHN 13:1–30

JESUS AND HIS DISCIPLES RETURN TO BETHANY. LATER THAT NIGHT, JUDAS HURRIES TO JERUSALEM TO CARRY OUT AN IDEA HE'S BEEN PLANNING.

I WANT TO SEE THE CHIEF PRIEST.

A MAN NAMED JUDAS ISCARIOT WANTS TO SEE YOU. HE SAYS IT'S URGENT.

JUDAS ISCARIOT? HE'S ONE OF JESUS' DISCIPLES. SHOW HIM IN.

I KNOW HOW MUCH YOU WANT TO GET RID OF JESUS. WHAT WILL YOU GIVE TO HAVE HIM TURNED OVER TO YOU—AWAY FROM THE CROWDS WHO BELIEVE IN HIM?

THIRTY PIECES OF SILVER.

AFTER THIS, JUDAS WATCHES FOR THE RIGHT TIME TO TURN JESUS OVER TO THE JEWISH LEADERS.

WHILE JUDAS IS STRIKING A DEAL WITH THE CHIEF PRIEST, JESUS IS THINKING AHEAD TO PASSOVER. JESUS CALLS PETER AND JOHN ASIDE.

GO INTO JERUSALEM AND GET THINGS READY FOR THE PASSOVER FEAST.

WHERE CAN WE GO SO THAT YOUR ENEMIES WILL NOT SEE US?

WHEN YOU GO INTO THE CITY, YOU WILL SEE A MAN CARRYING A JUG OF WATER. FOLLOW HIM HOME. ASK THE OWNER OF THE HOUSE TO SHOW YOU THE ROOM WHERE WE CAN EAT THE PASSOVER.

PETER AND JOHN GO RIGHT AWAY. THEY FIND THE SERVANT CARRYING A JUG OF WATER AND FOLLOW HIM HOME.

WHERE IS THE ROOM WHERE JESUS AND HIS DISCIPLES CAN EAT THE PASSOVER MEAL?

COME WITH ME.

THE MAN WHO OWNS THE HOUSE SHOWS PETER AND JOHN A BIG UPPER ROOM. THERE THEY GET READY FOR THE PASSOVER MEAL.

AS THE DISCIPLES GET READY TO ENJOY THE MEAL, JESUS KNEELS LIKE A SERVANT TO WASH THEIR FEET.

NO, LORD, I'M NOT GOOD ENOUGH TO HAVE YOU BE A SERVANT TO ME.

UNLESS I WASH YOU, PETER, YOU CAN'T SHARE ETERNAL LIFE WITH ME.

621

AFTER JESUS WASHES ALL THE DISCIPLES' FEET, HE SITS DOWN AT THE TABLE AGAIN.

IF I, YOUR LORD AND MASTER, HAVE SERVED YOU, YOU SHOULD DO THE SAME FOR EACH OTHER. THE SERVANT IS NOT GREATER THAN THE MASTER.

JESUS TEACHES THE DISCIPLES, BUT THEY DON'T UNDERSTAND EVERYTHING HE SAYS. THEN HE MAKES A STARTLING STATEMENT.

ONE OF YOU IS GOING TO BETRAY ME.

LORD, IS IT I?

THE ONE I GIVE THIS BREAD TO WILL BETRAY ME.

IMMEDIATELY, JUDAS GETS UP FROM THE TABLE AND HURRIES OUT. BUT THE OTHER DISCIPLES DO NOT UNDERSTAND WHY ...

On Trial

BASED ON
MATTHEW 26:57—27:2;
JOHN 18:15-38;
LUKE 22:63—23:17

AFTER BEING ARRESTED, JESUS IS TAKEN TO THE PALACE OF THE HIGH PRIEST. FALSE WITNESSES ACCUSE HIM OF CRIMES HE DIDN'T COMMIT, BUT THEY CAN'T PROVE ANYTHING. FINALLY, CAIAPHAS, THE HIGH PRIEST, QUESTIONS JESUS HIMSELF.

TELL US ONCE AND FOR ALL IF YOU ARE THE SON OF GOD.

I AM.

THERE! YOU HEARD HIM! HE SPEAKS EVIL AGAINST GOD BY CLAIMING TO BE GOD'S SON.

HE MUST DIE!

INSTANTLY, THE MEN WHO ARE GUARDING JESUS BEGIN SPITTING ON HIM. THEY BLINDFOLD HIM AND HIT HIM IN THE FACE, DEMANDING THAT HE PROVE HIS POWER BY SAYING WHO STRUCK HIM.

THIS IS THE THIRD TIME PETER SAYS HE DOESN'T KNOW JESUS. JUST THEN, GUARDS LEAD JESUS THROUGH THE COURTYARD. JESUS TURNS AND LOOKS STRAIGHT AT PETER, AND AT THE SAME MOMENT, PETER HEARS A ROOSTER CROW, SIGNALING THE SUNRISE. HE REMEMBERS WHAT JESUS SAID.

SICK WITH SHAME, PETER RUSHES OUTSIDE AND WEEPS BITTERLY.

THREE TIMES I DENIED JESUS, JUST AS HE SAID I WOULD. GOD, FORGIVE ME!

THE JEWISH HIGH COURT IS NOT ALLOWED TO SENTENCE A PERSON TO DEATH. SO IN THE EARLY HOURS OF FRIDAY MORNING, THEY TAKE JESUS TO THE ROMAN GOVERNOR, PILATE. CLEVERLY, THEY DON'T CHARGE HIM WITH BREAKING JEWISH LAWS, BUT WITH TREASON AGAINST ROME. PILATE QUESTIONS JESUS PRIVATELY, THEN FACES THE RESTLESS MOB.

I DON'T FIND THIS MAN GUILTY OF ANY CRIME.

NOT GUILTY? HE TRIED TO START REVOLTS ALL OVER JUDEA AND GALILEE.

AT THE MENTION OF GALILEE, PILATE DECIDES TO SEND JESUS TO HEROD ANTIPAS, THE RULER OF GALILEE. HEROD IS IN JERUSALEM FOR THE PASSOVER FEAST. CURIOUS, HEROD HOPES THAT JESUS WILL PERFORM A MIRACLE. WHEN JESUS DOESN'T RESPOND TO HEROD, THE RULER BEGINS MAKING FUN OF HIM FOR THINKING HE IS A KING. WHEN HEROD TIRES OF HIS SPORT, HE SENDS JESUS BACK TO PILATE.

PILATE STILL DOES NOT WANT TO DECLARE JESUS GUILTY OF TREASON. BUT HE KNOWS THAT IF HE LETS JESUS GO, THE JEWISH LEADERS COULD CAUSE TROUBLE.

THE PEOPLE! I'LL LET THEM DECIDE! THEN, WHEN THEY RELEASE JESUS, I WON'T BE BLAMED.

Death Sentence

BASED ON JOHN 18:39—19:22; MATTHEW 27:3-10

PILATE IS AFRAID TO MAKE THE JEWS ANGRY BECAUSE HE DOES NOT WANT REPORTS OF TROUBLE TO REACH THE EMPEROR IN ROME. PILATE IS DESPERATE FOR AN IDEA THAT WILL MAKE THE JEWS HAPPY AND NOT MAKE HIM RESPONSIBLE FOR WHAT HAPPENS TO JESUS.

PILATE IS STUNNED. HE TRIES TO SATISFY THE CROWD WITH A LESSER PUNISHMENT.

WHIP HIM!

AFTER THE WHIPPING, SOLDIERS TWIST THORNS TOGETHER TO MAKE A CROWN AND THRUST IT ON JESUS' HEAD. THEY PUT A PURPLE ROBE ON HIM AND MAKE FUN OF HIM.

HA! SOME KING OF THE JEWS!

PILATE TRIES ONE MORE TIME TO SAVE JESUS, SHOWING THE CROWD THAT HE'S BEEN BRUTALLY BEATEN.

I FIND NO REASON TO CHARGE THIS MAN.

CRUCIFY HIM! CRUCIFY HIM!

PILATE IS MORE AND MORE AFRAID OF THE TROUBLE THE JEWISH LEADERS MIGHT CAUSE. FINALLY HE GIVES UP. BUT PILATE MAKES A SIGN TO PUT OVER JESUS' HEAD.

JESUS OF NAZARETH, THE KING OF THE JEWS

NO! DON'T WRITE THAT HE *IS* KING OF THE JEWS. WRITE THAT HE *SAID,* "I AM KING OF THE JEWS."

I'VE WRITTEN WHAT I'VE WRITTEN.

FOR JESUS, THE HOURS BETWEEN HIS ARREST AND BEING SENTENCED TO DIE HAVE BEEN FILLED WITH AGONY.

SOMETIME DURING THOSE DARK HOURS, THE TRAITOR, JUDAS, IS FILLED WITH REGRET. HE RUSHES TO THE CHIEF PRIESTS ...

Crucified!

BASED ON LUKE 23:26-52;
JOHN 19:23-28;
MATTHEW 27:32-58;
MARK 15:21-45

FOR DAYS, EXCITED JEWS FROM ALL OVER PALESTINE HAVE CROWDED INTO JERUSALEM FOR THE PASSOVER FEAST. BUT ON FRIDAY MORNING, THE CITY IS GREETED WITH STARTLING NEWS. JESUS OF NAZARETH IS GOING TO BE CRUCIFIED—FOR TREASON!

JESUS IS NOW IN THE HANDS OF THE ROMAN SOLDIERS, WHO FORCE HIM TO CARRY A HEAVY CROSS THROUGH THE STREETS TO A HILL CALLED GOLGOTHA, THE PLACE OF THE SKULL.

AS JESUS STUMBLES UNDER THE WEIGHT OF HIS CROSS, THE STREETS FILL WITH A STRANGE MIXTURE OF SPECTATORS AND MOURNERS: PRIESTS AND PHARISEES WHO DEMAND JESUS' DEATH; WOMEN WEEPING FOR THE MAN WHO FORGAVE SINS AND HEALED THE SICK; CURIOUS ONLOOKERS WHO WANT ONLY TO SEE THE CONDEMNED MAN CARRY HIS CROSS. TWO ROBBERS ARE SENTENCED TO CRUCIFIXION AS WELL.

ON THE WAY, JESUS FALLS UNDER THE WEIGHT OF THE HEAVY CROSS. TO KEEP THE UGLY PROCESSION MOVING, THE ROMAN OFFICERS SEIZE A BYSTANDER, SIMON OF CYRENE.

YOU! CARRY THE CROSS FOR HIM!

TO THE ROMAN SOLDIERS, JESUS IS JUST ANOTHER CRIMINAL. THEY NOTICE THAT JESUS HAS A NICE ROBE.

THIS ROBE IS SEAMLESS. HOW SHOULD WE DIVIDE IT?

IT'S TOO GOOD TO TEAR INTO PIECES. LET'S GAMBLE FOR IT.

AS JESUS' FRIENDS STAND WATCHING HIM SUFFER, CURIOUS CROWDS PASS BY. SOME WHO WANT HIM TO DIE TAUNT HIM.

IF YOU'RE THE KING OF THE JEWS, COME DOWN FROM THE CROSS. THEN WE'LL BELIEVE YOU.

ONE OF THE ROBBERS CRUCIFIED WITH JESUS HURLS INSULTS AT HIM TOO ...

IF YOU'RE THE MESSIAH, SAVE YOURSELF AND SAVE US!

HAVE SOME RESPECT FOR GOD! WE DESERVE TO DIE FOR OUR CRIMES, BUT THIS MAN HAS DONE NOTHING WRONG.

LORD, REMEMBER ME WHEN YOU COME INTO YOUR KINGDOM.

TODAY YOU WILL BE WITH ME IN HEAVEN.

JESUS LOOKS DOWN AND SEES HIS MOTHER, MARY, AND HIS FRIEND JOHN AT THE FOOT OF THE CROSS, WATCHING HIS AGONY.

JOHN, TAKE CARE OF MY MOTHER.

JOHN TAKES MARY TO HIS OWN HOME AND CARES FOR HER LIKE HIS OWN MOTHER.

IT IS NOW NOON. A STRANGE SHADOW COVERS THE LAND. JESUS SUFFERS FOR THREE HOURS UNDER THE DARK SKY AND THEN CRIES OUT TO GOD ...

FATHER, I PUT MY SPIRIT IN YOUR HANDS!

JESUS DIES. AT THAT MOMENT AN EARTHQUAKE SHAKES THE GROUND.

The Sealed Tomb

BASED ON MATTHEW 27:59—28:15; JOHN 19:38—20:18; LUKE 24:13-32

REVERENTLY, JOSEPH TAKES THE BODY OF JESUS FROM THE CROSS. NICODEMUS HELPS JOSEPH WRAP THE BODY IN LINEN CLOTH AND PLACE IT IN JOSEPH'S GARDEN TOMB.

THE NEXT DAY, THE CHIEF PRIESTS AND PHARISEES GO TO PILATE ...

JESUS SAID THAT AFTER THREE DAYS HE WOULD RISE FROM THE DEAD.

GIVE THE ORDER FOR YOUR SOLDIERS TO SEAL THE TOMB. WE DON'T WANT JESUS' DISCIPLES TO STEAL HIS BODY AND CLAIM THAT JESUS ROSE FROM THE DEAD.

TAKE THE SOLDIERS YOU NEED. SET UP A GUARD UNTIL AFTER THE THIRD DAY.

SO THE TOMB IS SEALED WITH A HEAVY STONE, AND ROMAN SOLDIERS STAND GUARD.

THAT'S THE LAST WE'LL HEAR ABOUT THIS MAN WHO CALLED HIMSELF THE SON OF GOD.

BUT BEFORE THE SUN CAN RISE ON SUNDAY MORNING, THE EARTH SUDDENLY SHUDDERS VIOLENTLY! AN ANGEL OF THE LORD ROLLS THE HEAVY STONE ASIDE. THE SOLDIERS FALL TO THE GROUND IN TERROR. WHEN THE EARTHQUAKE SUBSIDES, THEY FLEE BACK TO THE CITY.

AT DAWN THAT MORNING, MARY MAGDALENE AND OTHER FRIENDS OF JESUS HURRY TO THE TOMB. NOW THAT THE SABBATH IS OVER, THEY WANT TO PUT SPICES ON JESUS' BODY FOR A PROPER BURIAL. THEY WONDER WHO WILL HELP THEM MOVE THE STONE. BUT WHEN THEY REACH THE GARDEN ...

THE TOMB! IT'S OPEN!

MARY RUNS BACK TO JERUSALEM TO TELL PETER AND JOHN THAT SOMEONE HAS STOLEN JESUS' BODY. THE OTHER WOMEN GO IN THE TOMB—AND FIND AN ANGEL SEATED THERE!

DON'T BE FRIGHTENED. JESUS IS RISEN. GO AND TELL HIS DISCIPLES.

WHEN PETER AND JOHN HEAR MARY'S NEWS, THEY RACE TO THE TOMB TO SEE FOR THEMSELVES.

BY THE TIME MARY RETURNS TO THE GARDEN, THE OTHERS HAVE GONE. SHE STANDS OUTSIDE THE TOMB CRYING. SOMEONE SPEAKS TO HER ...

ONLY HIS BURIAL CLOTHS ARE HERE. WHAT DOES THAT MEAN?

WHY ARE YOU CRYING?

IF YOU HAVE TAKEN JESUS' BODY, PLEASE TELL ME WHERE YOU PUT IT.

HE ROSE FROM THE DEAD! HE SAID HE WOULD, BUT WE DIDN'T BELIEVE HIM.

TENDERLY, JESUS SPEAKS MARY'S NAME. SHE RECOGNIZES HIS VOICE NOW ...

MASTER!

JESUS' FRIENDS ARE NOT THE ONLY ONES TO HEAR THE NEWS. THE GUARDS FROM THE TOMB GO STRAIGHT TO THE PRIESTS TO TELL THEM WHAT HAPPENED. ALARMED, THE PRIESTS DON'T WANT ANYONE TO HEAR THE TRUTH, SO THEY COME UP WITH A DEVIOUS PLAN ...

HERE, TAKE THIS MONEY. TELL PEOPLE THAT JESUS' DISCIPLES STOLE HIS BODY WHILE ALL OF YOU WERE ASLEEP.

WHILE THE SOLDIERS SPREAD THIS LIE, JESUS JOINS TWO OF HIS FOLLOWERS AS THEY ARE TRAVELING. HE KEEPS THEM FROM RECOGNIZING HIM, AND HE EXPLAINS TO THEM WHAT THE SCRIPTURES SAY ABOUT HIS OWN DEATH.

THE PROPHETS *SAID* THAT THE CHRIST WOULD HAVE TO SUFFER BEFORE HE COULD BE THE SAVIOR OF THE WORLD.

HE EATS WITH THEM IN EMMAUS. WHEN JESUS BLESSES THE BREAD AND HANDS IT TO HIS FOLLOWERS, THEY SUDDENLY RECOGNIZE HIM.

JESUS!

AND JUST AS SUDDENLY JESUS VANISHES FROM THEIR SIGHT.

The Last Command

BASED ON LUKE 24:33-53; JOHN 20:19—21:17; MATTHEW 28:16-20

THROUGHOUT JERUSALEM LATE SUNDAY NIGHT, PEOPLE ARE MARVELING AT THE STRANGE REPORT OF THE ROMAN SOLDIERS.

THEY SAY JESUS' DISCIPLES STOLE HIS BODY TO MAKE US BELIEVE HE ROSE FROM THE DEAD.

WHAT WERE THOSE ROMAN SOLDIERS DOING WHILE THE TOMB WAS ROBBED?

JESUS' DISCIPLES HAVE ALSO HEARD THE SOLDIERS' REPORT. THEY ARE AFRAID THEY MAY BE ARRESTED, SO THEY LOCK THEMSELVES INTO A ROOM. ALL THE DISCIPLES EXCEPT THOMAS ARE THERE. THE TWO MEN WHO HAVE SEEN JESUS ON THE ROAD FIND THEM THERE.

JESUS IS ALIVE! WE WERE ON THE WAY TO EMMAUS WHEN A STRANGER JOINED US. WE ASKED HIM TO HAVE SUPPER WITH US.

WHEN HE BLESSED THE BREAD AND GAVE IT TO US, WE RECOGNIZED HIM. IT WAS JESUS! THEN HE DISAPPEARED, AND WE RACED BACK HERE TO TELL YOU.

A WEEK LATER, THOMAS IS WITH THE DISCIPLES WHEN THEY MEET AGAIN BEHIND LOCKED DOORS. ONCE AGAIN JESUS APPEARS TO THEM.

THOMAS, TOUCH MY HANDS AND MY SIDE.

MY LORD AND MY GOD!

YOU BELIEVE BECAUSE YOU'VE SEEN ME. BLESSED ARE THOSE WHO BELIEVE EVEN WITHOUT SEEING ME.

THE DISCIPLES LEAVE JERUSALEM AND GO BACK TO GALILEE. ONE EVENING THEY GO FISHING. THEY FISH ALL NIGHT BUT DON'T CATCH ANYTHING. AT DAYBREAK, THEY SEE SOMEONE STANDING ON THE SHORE.

CAST YOUR NET ON THE RIGHT SIDE OF THE BOAT!

THE DISCIPLES OBEY, AND SUDDENLY THE NET IS BURSTING WITH FISH ...

JOHN LOOKS UP AT THE MAN ON SHORE ...

IT'S THE LORD!

PETER IS SO EAGER TO REACH JESUS THAT HE LEAPS INTO THE WATER AND SWIMS TOWARD SHORE. THE OTHERS BRING THE BOAT IN. PETER HELPS DRAG THE NET TO SHORE. JESUS IS WAITING FOR THEM WITH SOME BREAD, AND FISH COOKING OVER A FIRE OF BURNING COALS.

COME AND HAVE BREAKFAST!

AFTER BREAKFAST, JESUS TALKS TO PETER PRIVATELY.

PETER, DO YOU LOVE ME?

YES, LORD, YOU KNOW I LOVE YOU.

TWO MORE TIMES JESUS ASKS PETER THE SAME QUESTION. EACH TIME, PETER DECLARES HIS LOYALTY. THEN JESUS GIVES PETER A JOB TO DO.

PETER, FEED MY SHEEP. TAKE CARE OF MY FOLLOWERS.

A FEW DAYS LATER, JESUS APPEARS TO 500 OF HIS FOLLOWERS GATHERED ON A MOUNTAIN NEAR THE SEA OF GALILEE. HE GIVES THEM ONE LAST COMMAND.

GO OUT AND SHARE THE GOOD NEWS WITH THE WHOLE WORLD.

BAPTIZE THE PEOPLE IN THE NAME OF THE FATHER AND OF THE SON AND OF THE HOLY SPIRIT.

TEACH THEM TO OBEY WHAT I HAVE COMMANDED. AND I WILL ALWAYS BE WITH YOU.

JESUS EXPLAINS HOW HE HAS COMPLETED GOD'S WORK. HE IS THE SAVIOR OF THE WORLD. NOW IT'S THEIR TURN TO CARRY ON GOD'S WORK. JESUS TELLS THEM TO WAIT IN JERUSALEM FOR THE HOLY SPIRIT TO COME.

THEN, WITH HIS FOLLOWERS GATHERED AROUND HIM ON THE MOUNT OF OLIVES NEAR BETHANY, JESUS ASCENDS INTO HEAVEN.

Waiting for the Spirit

BASED ON ACTS 1

IN AWE AND WONDER, JESUS' FOLLOWERS STAND AND LOOK UP INTO HEAVEN AS IF TO CATCH ONE MORE GLIMPSE OF THE MASTER THEY LOVE. SUDDENLY TWO ANGELS APPEAR ...

WHY DO YOU STAY HERE LOOKING AT THE SKY?

JESUS WAS TAKEN TO HEAVEN, BUT HE WILL COME BACK THE SAME WAY YOU SAW HIM GO.

THE DISCIPLES, WHO HAD ONCE FLED BECAUSE THEY WERE AFRAID OF BEING ARRESTED FOR BEING JESUS' FRIENDS, NOW RETURN TO JERUSALEM. THEY KNOW THAT JESUS IS DEPENDING ON THEM TO CARRY ON GOD'S WORK.

LET'S DO WHAT JESUS TOLD US—WAIT IN JERUSALEM FOR THE POWER HE PROMISED TO SEND US.

IN JERUSALEM, THE DISCIPLES GATHER TOGETHER. PETER TAKES CHARGE ...

JUDAS, WHO BETRAYED JESUS, IS DEAD. WE SHOULD APPOINT SOMEONE TO TAKE HIS PLACE.

I NOMINATE BARSABBAS.

I NOMINATE MATTHIAS.

THE DISCIPLES ASK GOD'S GUIDANCE FOR THEIR DECISION, AND MATTHIAS IS CHOSEN.

FOR THE NEXT TEN DAYS, THE DISCIPLES MEET TOGETHER IN PRAYER. THEY ARE WAITING FOR THE HOLY SPIRIT TO COME, AS JESUS PROMISED. AT THE SAME TIME, JEWS FROM ALL OVER PALESTINE—AND EVEN DISTANT COUNTRIES—ONCE AGAIN FILL THE STREETS OF JERUSALEM. THEY COME TO CELEBRATE THE FEAST OF THANKSGIVING CALLED PENTECOST.

THESE PILGRIMS COME WITH LOTS OF QUESTIONS AFTER THE RECENT EVENTS. "WAS JESUS RAISED FROM THE DEAD?" "OR DID HIS DISCIPLES STEAL HIS BODY FROM THE TOMB AND CLAIM THAT HE WAS ALIVE?" THESE QUESTIONS LINGER IN THE AIR AS JEWS FLOOD INTO JERUSALEM FOR THE PENTECOST FEAST. JESUS' DISCIPLES KNOW THE TRUTH, BUT THERE ARE ONLY A FEW OF THEM.

Tongues of Fire!

BASED ON ACTS 2

EARLY ON THE DAY OF PENTECOST, 120 FOLLOWERS OF JESUS GATHER TO PRAY. SUDDENLY A SOUND LIKE A MIGHTY RUSHING WIND ROARS THROUGH THE ROOM AND FILLS THE WHOLE HOUSE. THEN, TONGUES OF FIRE SETTLE ON THEM.

IN THAT HOLY MOMENT, JESUS' FOLLOWERS ARE FILLED WITH THE HOLY SPIRIT. THEY START TO SPEAK IN LANGUAGES THEY DIDN'T KNOW BEFORE.

JERUSALEM IS CROWDED FOR THE FEAST. WHEN PEOPLE HEAR THE SOUND, THEY COME RUNNING ...

WE HAVE TO SEE FOR OURSELVES WHAT IS HAPPENING WITH JESUS' FOLLOWERS.

THE PEOPLE FIND THE DISCIPLES AND LISTEN ...

IT'S TRUE! WE HEAR THEM SPEAKING IN OUR OWN LANGUAGES.

EVEN THOSE OF US FROM FAR AWAY—FROM EGYPT OR ROME OR ARABIA—WE HEAR THEM SPEAKING ABOUT GOD'S WONDERS!

THEY'VE BEEN DRINKING TOO MUCH WINE! THAT'S ALL IT IS.

PEOPLE WHO ARE DRUNK DO NOT SUDDENLY SPEAK IN FOREIGN LANGUAGES.

PETER SPEAKS OUT FOR ALL THE DISCIPLES.

WE ARE NOT DRUNK! WE ARE FILLED WITH THE HOLY SPIRIT, AS THE PROPHET JOEL PREDICTED, YOU CRUCIFIED JESUS, THE CHOSEN ONE OF GOD. BUT GOD RAISED HIM FROM THE DEAD, AND WE ARE WITNESSES TO HIS RESURRECTION.

PETER'S WORDS CUT DEEP INTO THE HEARTS OF THE PEOPLE. THEY REMEMBER HOW THEY HAD DEMANDED JESUS' CRUCIFIXION ONLY A FEW WEEKS EARLIER.

STOP YOUR SINNING WAYS! BE BAPTIZED IN THE NAME OF JESUS. THEN YOU WILL RECEIVE GOD'S HOLY SPIRIT FOR YOURSELVES.

BEFORE THE DAY OF PENTECOST IS OVER, 3,000 PEOPLE BELIEVE IN JESUS AND ARE BAPTIZED. AS THE DAYS PASS, MORE AND MORE PEOPLE SEE THE LOVE OF JESUS' FOLLOWERS. BELIEVERS BEGIN MEETING IN HOMES, SHARING MEALS AND EVERYTHING THEY OWN.

I'VE BROUGHT SOME FRIENDS WHO WANT TO LEARN ABOUT JESUS.

COME IN. WE'RE GLAD TO HAVE YOU HERE.

HAVE YOU HEARD? THE POOR WIDOW WE TALKED TO YESTERDAY NEEDS FOOD FOR HER CHILDREN.

I'LL GIVE THE APOSTLES SOME MONEY TO HELP HER.

THE FOLLOWERS OF JESUS TAKE CARE OF ONE ANOTHER'S NEEDS AND WORSHIP TOGETHER EVERY DAY. EVERY DAY MORE PEOPLE BELIEVE IN JESUS AND JOIN THE BELIEVERS.

WHAT DO YOU THINK ABOUT THESE FRIENDS OF JESUS?

I DON'T UNDERSTAND THEM, BUT I WANT TO FIND OUT MORE. LOOK AT HOW THEY LOVE EACH OTHER!

Stand Up for Jesus

BASED ON ACTS 3–4

ONE AFTERNOON WHEN PETER AND JOHN GO TO THE TEMPLE FOR PRAYER, THEY MEET A LAME MAN BEGGING AT THE GATE CALLED BEAUTIFUL.

HAVE MERCY! GIVE SOMETHING FOR THE POOR.

LOOK AT US!

IT LOOKS LIKE *BOTH* OF THEM MIGHT GIVE ME SOME MONEY.

I HAVE NO MONEY, BUT I'LL GIVE YOU WHAT I HAVE. IN THE NAME OF JESUS CHRIST, STAND UP AND WALK.

WALK? THIS MAN HAS NEVER TAKEN A STEP IN HIS LIFE! BUT AS PETER REACHES OUT HIS HAND TO HIM, THE MAN REACHES BACK ...

I CAN WALK! PRAISE GOD! I CAN WALK!

IN HIS EXCITEMENT, THE MAN RUSHES INTO THE TEMPLE, LEAPING AND SHOUTING FOR JOY.

LOOK! ISN'T THAT THE MAN WHO WAS AT THE GATE BEGGING?

YES, BUT ...

GRATEFULLY, THE MAN TURNS TO PETER AND JOHN. THE CROWD PRESSES IN, ANXIOUS TO KNOW WHAT HAPPENED.

WHY DO YOU STARE AT US AS IF *WE* MADE THIS MAN WALK? THE MIRACLE CAME FROM GOD THROUGH THE POWER OF HIS SON, JESUS. YOU KILLED HIM, BUT GOD RAISED HIM FROM THE DEAD.

SEEING THAT HE HAS THE ATTENTION OF THE CROWD, PETER CONTINUES ...

REPENT AND TURN TO GOD SO YOUR SINS MAY BE WIPED OUT. PREPARE YOURSELVES, FOR JESUS WILL COME AGAIN.

PRIESTS IN THE CROWD GROW ANGRY AS THEY LISTEN TO PETER'S TESTIMONY. AND THEIR ANGER INCREASES AS THEY WATCH THE GROWING INTEREST OF THE PEOPLE. THE PRIESTS GET THE HELP OF THE TEMPLE GUARDS ...

YOU ARE UNDER ARREST!

WITHOUT ANOTHER WORD, PETER AND JOHN ARE MARCHED AWAY TO PRISON, WHERE THEY SPEND THE NIGHT. BUT ALREADY 5,000 PEOPLE HAVE COME TO BELIEVE IN JESUS.

THE NEXT MORNING, THE JEWISH RELIGIOUS RULERS—THE SAME ONES WHO CONDEMNED JESUS TO DEATH—HAVE PETER AND JOHN BROUGHT TO THEM FOR QUESTIONING. THE HEALED BEGGAR IS WITH THEM.

BY WHAT POWER AND IN WHOSE NAME HAVE YOU HEALED THIS MAN?

FILLED WITH THE HOLY SPIRIT, PETER SPEAKS OUT COURAGEOUSLY.

LET ALL THE PEOPLE OF ISRAEL KNOW THAT THIS MAN WAS HEALED BY THE NAME OF JESUS CHRIST OF NAZARETH. YOU CRUCIFIED HIM, BUT GOD RAISED HIM FROM THE DEAD.

THE RELIGIOUS LEADERS ARE STUNNED. PETER AND JOHN ARE UNEDUCATED FISHERMEN; BUT THEY SPEAK AND ACT WITH AUTHORITY AND POWER.

TAKE THEM AWAY!

WHEN THE PRISONERS ARE OUT OF SIGHT, THE LEADERS DISCUSS THEIR PROBLEM.

EVERYONE KNOWS A MIRACLE HAPPENED. WE CAN'T DENY IT. BUT WE HAVE TO KEEP THE NEWS FROM SPREADING.

TELL THEM IF THEY SPEAK OF JESUS AGAIN, WE'LL PUT THEM TO DEATH TOO!

THE PRIESTS WANT TO PUNISH THE DISCIPLES, BUT THEY ARE AFRAID TO STIR UP THE CROWDS TO A RIOT.

WE WILL RELEASE YOU THIS TIME. BUT DON'T SAY ANOTHER WORD ABOUT JESUS!

YOU TELL US— SHOULD WE LISTEN TO YOU, OR SHOULD WE OBEY GOD? GOD HAS COMMANDED US TO TELL THE WORLD ABOUT THE THINGS WE'VE SEEN AND HEARD.

THE PRIESTS THREATEN PETER AND JOHN AGAIN, BUT LET THEM GO. PETER AND JOHN HURRY BACK TO THEIR FRIENDS, WHO IMMEDIATELY BEGIN PRAYING.

LORD AND KING, YOU MADE EVERYTHING. HELP US TO BE BRAVE AS WE SHARE YOUR MESSAGE.

AND MAY WE CONTINUE TO HEAL AND DO MIRACLES IN YOUR NAME, JESUS!

A Grave Lie

BASED ON ACTS 4:32–5:11

STRENGTHENED BY THE HOLY SPIRIT, THE DISCIPLES KEEP ON PREACHING. MORE AND MORE PEOPLE BELIEVE IN JESUS. ONE DAY A MAN NAMED BARNABAS BRINGS THE DISCIPLES A LARGE BAG OF MONEY.

WHY ARE YOU GIVING ALL THIS MONEY TO US?

I SOLD A FIELD. I WANT YOU TO USE THE MONEY TO HELP FOLLOWERS OF JESUS.

ANOTHER MAN, ANANIAS, WANTS TO APPEAR GENEROUS TOO. BUT HE ALSO WANTS TO KEEP MOST OF HIS MONEY. SO HE LIES ...

... BUT THE HOLY SPIRIT SPEAKS TO PETER.

WE, TOO, HAVE SOLD OUR LAND, AND WE'RE GIVING ALL OF THAT MONEY TO HELP THE CHURCH.

ANANIAS, YOU COULD HAVE DONE ANYTHING YOU WANTED WITH YOUR MONEY. BUT DON'T PRETEND YOU'RE GIVING ALL OF IT WHEN YOU'RE NOT. YOU HAVEN'T LIED TO ME; YOU'VE LIED TO GOD!

AT PETER'S WORDS, ANANIAS FALLS DOWN DEAD. SOME YOUNG MEN WRAP UP HIS BODY AND TAKE IT AWAY. A FEW HOURS LATER, HIS WIFE, SAPPHIRA, COMES. SHE DOESN'T KNOW WHAT HAPPENED. SHE ANSWERS PETER'S QUESTIONS WITH THE SAME LIE HER HUSBAND TOLD.

SAPPHIRA, HOW DARE YOU TRY TO TRICK THE HOLY SPIRIT? LISTEN! HERE COME THE MEN WHO ALREADY BURIED YOUR HUSBAND; YOU WILL NEED THEIR SERVICES AS WELL.

INSTANTLY, SAPPHIRA FALLS DEAD ON THE FLOOR. THE FOLLOWERS OF JESUS SEE THIS AS A WARNING TO ANYONE WHO TRIES TO DECEIVE GOD OR THE CHURCH.

Prison Break

BASED ON ACTS 5:12—6:11

THE THREATS OF THE JEWISH LEADERS DO NOT KEEP THE DISCIPLES FROM DOING GOD'S WORK. THEY KEEP ON HEALING IN THE NAME OF JESUS. FAMILIES BRING THEIR SICK INTO THE STREETS, HOPING THAT PETER WILL PASS BY AND CURE THEM. CROWDS ALSO GATHER FROM THE TOWNS AROUND JERUSALEM.

HE CAN'T WALK. PLEASE MAKE HIM STRONG SO HE CAN RUN AND PLAY WITH THE OTHER CHILDREN.

I CANNOT HEAL HIM, BUT JESUS, THE SON OF GOD, CAN. IN JESUS' NAME, I TELL YOU YOUR SON IS HEALED.

EVERYONE WHO COMES IS HEALED. THE HIGH PRIEST AND THE ONES WHO WORK WITH HIM ARE SO JEALOUS THEY CAN'T STAND IT. THEY HATE SEEING THE PEOPLE COME INTO TOWN TO BE HEALED. IN A FIT OF RAGE, THEY HAVE THE DISCIPLES ARRESTED AND THROWN INTO JAIL.

THIS TIME THEY'RE NOT GETTING OUT. WE'LL PUT AN END TO THIS NONSENSE!

DURING THE NIGHT, AN ANGEL OF GOD COMES TO PETER AND JOHN IN JAIL.

GO, STAND IN THE TEMPLE COURTYARD. TELL THE PEOPLE ABOUT THE NEW LIFE GOD HAS PROMISED TO ANYONE WHO BELIEVES IN JESUS.

THE NEXT MORNING, THE HIGH PRIEST CALLS THE JEWISH COURT INTO SESSION AND SENDS FOR THE PRISONERS. WHEN THE OFFICERS RETURN ...

THE PRISON IS LOCKED AND THE GUARDS ARE ON DUTY; BUT THE PRISONERS ARE GONE!

WHEN WE OPENED THE DOORS, NO ONE WAS THERE!

NOT THERE? *WHERE* ARE THEY?

THEN WORD COMES ...

THE MEN YOU PUT IN JAIL LAST NIGHT ARE IN THE TEMPLE TEACHING ABOUT JESUS!

THE HIGH PRIEST ORDERS THE DISCIPLES BROUGHT TO THE COURT AT ONCE.

DIDN'T WE WARN YOU *NOT* TO PREACH ABOUT JESUS?

WE MUST OBEY GOD, NOT MEN.

THIS ANSWER MAKES THE PRIESTS FURIOUS, AND THEY WANT ALL THE DISCIPLES KILLED AT ONCE. BUT A FAMOUS TEACHER NAMED GAMALIEL SENDS THE DISCIPLES OUT OF THE ROOM ...

BE CAREFUL WHAT YOU DO WITH THESE MEN. IF THIS TEACHING IS THEIR OWN IDEA, IT WILL SOON FADE. BUT IF IT IS FROM GOD, YOU CAN'T DEFEAT IT. YOU DON'T WANT TO END UP FIGHTING AGAINST GOD!

THE COURT IS FORCED TO ADMIT THE WISDOM OF THIS ADVICE. STILL FURIOUS, THE LEADERS ORDER THAT THE DISCIPLES BE BEATEN. THEN THEY RELEASE THEM WITH THE THREAT OF MORE PUNISHMENT IF THEY KEEP ON PREACHING ABOUT JESUS.

IT'S AN HONOR TO SUFFER FOR THE NAME OF JESUS.

WE CAN'T STOP NOW. WE HAVE TO KEEP TELLING THE GOOD NEWS.

THE DISCIPLES KEEP ON DOING THE WORK THAT GOD GIVES THEM TO DO, AND THE NUMBER OF PEOPLE WHO BELIEVE KEEPS GROWING. SO MANY PEOPLE WANT TO FOLLOW JESUS THAT THE DISCIPLES DECIDE TO CHOOSE OTHERS TO HELP LEAD THE WORK. THEY CHOOSE SEVEN DEACONS TO HELP CARE FOR THE PEOPLE.

ONE OF THEM, STEPHEN, SOON SHOWS THAT HE IS AN OUTSTANDING SPEAKER.

SOME JEWISH LEADERS BEGIN TO DEBATE WITH STEPHEN. TO THEIR EMBARRASSMENT, THEY FIND THEY ARE NO MATCH FOR STEPHEN'S WISDOM AND ABILITY TO DEFEND HIS FAITH. SECRETLY THEY PLOT THEIR REVENGE ...

WE MUST BE CAREFUL NOT TO TURN THE PEOPLE AGAINST US.

RIGHT, BUT PERHAPS WE CAN STIR UP THE PEOPLE AGAINST STEPHEN LIKE WE DID WITH JESUS!

THE COURT RISES UP IN FURY, BUT STEPHEN CONTINUES, FILLED WITH THE HOLY SPIRIT.

I CAN SEE HEAVEN! LOOK! THE SON OF MAN IS STANDING AT THE RIGHT HAND OF GOD.

STEPHEN'S WORDS ARE TOO MUCH FOR THE COURT. LIKE A PACK OF SAVAGE BEASTS, THEY SEIZE STEPHEN AND DRAG HIM OUTSIDE THE CITY, WHERE THEY THROW ROCKS AT HIM. AS THE STONES BATTER HIS BODY, STEPHEN CONTINUES TO PRAY ...

LORD, DON'T HOLD THIS AGAINST THEM!

FINALLY, STEPHEN TAKES HIS LAST BREATH AND DIES, SAYING, "JESUS, RECEIVE MY SPIRIT."

A YOUNG MAN NAMED SAUL* WATCHES THE STONING. (AND KEEPS AN EYE ON THE COATS.) HE IS PLEASED AT THE DEATH OF A FOLLOWER OF JESUS.

* HIS STORY BEGINS ON PAGE 686.

Stranger on the Gaza Road

BASED ON ACTS 8:1-4, 26-40

FOLLOWING STEPHEN'S DEATH, MANY ATTACKS BREAK OUT AGAINST BELIEVERS IN JERUSALEM. OVER THE NEXT FEW WEEKS, THOUSANDS OF JESUS' FOLLOWERS FLEE THE CITY, MOVING THROUGHOUT JUDEA AND SAMARIA AND TAKING GOD'S GOOD NEWS WITH THEM. THE JEWISH LEADERS HAVE UNINTENTIONALLY HELPED TO SPREAD THE GOSPEL. PHILIP, A DEACON, GOES NORTH TO SAMARIA.

ONE NIGHT AN ANGEL TELLS PHILIP: "GO DOWN TOWARD GAZA." PHILIP QUICKLY OBEYS ...

GOD HAS SENT ME ALL THIS WAY TO MEET THE PERSON IN THAT CHARIOT. WHO COULD HE BE?

AT THAT MOMENT, GOD'S SPIRIT TELLS PHILIP TO STAY CLOSE TO THE CHARIOT, SO HE DOES. HE HEARS A MAN READING FROM THE SCRIPTURES.

"HE WAS LED LIKE A SHEEP TO BE KILLED."

DO YOU UNDERSTAND WHAT THE PROPHET ISAIAH IS SAYING?

THE MAN IS AN IMPORTANT OFFICIAL FROM ETHIOPIA, TREASURER TO THE QUEEN.

HOW CAN I, UNLESS SOMEONE EXPLAINS IT TO ME? DO YOU KNOW, IS THE PROPHET TALKING ABOUT HIMSELF OR SOMEONE ELSE?

HE'S TALKING ABOUT JESUS CHRIST, THE SON OF GOD. HIS ENEMIES CRUCIFIED HIM, BUT GOD RAISED HIM FROM THE DEAD.

AS THEY RIDE ALONG, PHILIP EXPLAINS THAT GOD LOVED THE WORLD SO MUCH THAT HE SENT HIS SON, JESUS, TO DIE FOR OUR SINS. WHOEVER TRUSTS IN JESUS WILL LIVE FOREVER WITH GOD.

I BELIEVE IN JESUS, AND I'M SORRY FOR EVERYTHING I'VE DONE WRONG. WHY SHOULDN'T I BE BAPTIZED RIGHT HERE AND BECOME A FOLLOWER OF JESUS?

I'M SURE THAT'S WHAT GOD SENT ME TO DO.

SO PHILIP BAPTIZES THE MAN FROM ETHIOPIA. IMMEDIATELY AFTERWARD, THE SPIRIT OF THE LORD WHISKS PHILIP AWAY. HE FINDS HIMSELF IN THE NORTH, WHERE HE PREACHES IN TOWNS ALONG THE RIM OF THE MEDITERRANEAN SEA. EVENTUALLY, HE SETTLES DOWN IN CAESAREA, THE ROMAN CAPITAL OF PALESTINE.

ABOUT THIS TIME, SAUL, THE YOUNG MAN WHO WAS PLEASED TO SEE STEPHEN STONED, EXPERIENCES A MIRACLE THAT CHANGES HIS LIFE FOREVER. JESUS APPEARS TO HIM, AND SAUL BECOMES A FOLLOWER. INSTEAD OF PERSECUTING JESUS' FOLLOWERS, HE JOINS THEM. NOW THE DISCIPLES CAN TRAVEL ALL OVER PALESTINE TEACHING AND HEALING IN JESUS' NAME WITHOUT FEAR THAT SAUL WILL TRY TO ARREST THEM. HIS NAME IS CHANGED TO PAUL, AND HE BECOMES A GREAT MISSIONARY.

Sea of Galilee

CAESAREA

JOPPA

LYDDA

JERUSALEM

GAZA

The Dead Sea

MEANWHILE, PETER IS PREACHING IN LYDDA. THERE HE MEETS A MAN NAMED AENEAS.

More Miracles
BASED ON ACTS 9:32—10:2

I HAVEN'T BEEN ABLE TO GET OUT OF BED FOR EIGHT YEARS.

JESUS CHRIST HEALS YOU. GET UP!

WHEN THE PEOPLE OF LYDDA SEE THAT AENEAS IS WELL, THEY BELIEVE IN JESUS TOO. PETER CONTINUES PREACHING IN LYDDA, UNTIL ONE DAY TWO MEN FROM JOPPA ARRIVE ...

WHERE'S PETER? WE HAVE TO FIND HIM IMMEDIATELY.

PETER FINDS TABITHA'S HOUSE FILLED WITH WEEPING FRIENDS.

SHE WAS THE KINDEST PERSON I HAVE EVER KNOWN.

SEE THIS COAT? SHE MADE IT FOR ME.

I KNOW HOW MUCH YOU LOVED HER. NOW, IF YOU WILL PLEASE GO OUTSIDE ...

ALONE, PETER KNEELS DOWN AND PRAYS.

AS HE RISES, HE TURNS TOWARD THE BODY OF THE DEAD WOMAN.

LORD, ONLY YOUR POWER CAN BRING TABITHA BACK TO LIFE.

TABITHA! GET UP!

INSTANTLY, TABITHA OPENS HER EYES AND SITS UP. THEN PETER TAKES HER TO HER FRIENDS.

GIVE THANKS TO GOD. YOUR FRIEND IS ALIVE!

THE GOOD NEWS ABOUT TABITHA SPREADS THROUGH THE WHOLE CITY OF JOPPA, MAKING MANY PEOPLE BELIEVE IN JESUS. PETER STAYS TO PREACH IN JOPPA.

TABITHA IS ALIVE! PETER HEALED HER IN JESUS' NAME!

ONE DAY A STRANGE THING HAPPENS IN THE HOME OF CORNELIUS, A ROMAN CENTURION. HE LIVES IN THE SEACOAST CITY OF CAESAREA, 30 MILES NORTH OF JOPPA. IT IS THREE O'CLOCK IN THE AFTERNOON. CORNELIUS, WHO HAS LEARNED TO WORSHIP GOD, KNEELS TO PRAY ...

A New Menu
BASED ON ACTS 10:1—11:18

AS CORNELIUS, AN OFFICER OF THE ROMAN ARMY, KNEELS TO PRAY, HE HAS A VISION—AN ANGEL OF GOD APPEARS AND CALLS HIM BY NAME.

WHAT IS IT?

GOD HAS HEARD YOUR PRAYERS. HE CHERISHES YOUR GIFTS TO POOR PEOPLE. NOW, SEND SOME MEN TO JOPPA TO LOOK FOR A MAN NAMED PETER. HE IS STAYING WITH SIMON THE LEATHER-WORKER, IN A HOUSE BY THE SEA.

AFTER THE ANGEL LEAVES, CORNELIUS SENDS THREE OF HIS MOST TRUSTED MEN TO JOPPA. AS THEY APPROACH THE CITY, THE MAN THEY'RE LOOKING FOR GOES UP ON A ROOFTOP TO PRAY ...

WHEN PETER RETURNS TO JERUSALEM, THE JEWISH LEADERS THINK HE HAS SOME EXPLAINING TO DO.

IS IT TRUE THAT YOU'RE BREAKING JEWISH LAWS AND BEING FRIENDLY WITH GENTILES? WE HEARD YOU WERE EVEN VISITING THEIR HOMES AND EATING WITH THEM.

GOD TOLD A ROMAN CENTURION TO SEND FOR ME, AND GOD TOLD ME TO GO TO HIM.

WHILE I WAS TELLING THE GENTILES ABOUT JESUS, THE HOLY SPIRIT CAME TO THEM— THE SAME WAY THE SPIRIT CAME TO US ON THE DAY OF PENTECOST!

IF GOD GAVE THEM THE SAME GIFTS HE GAVE US, WHO WAS I TO STAND IN THE WAY?

THE CHURCH LEADERS AGREE WITH PETER AND PRAISE GOD FOR GIVING ETERNAL LIFE TO THE GENTILES. THE CHURCH CONTINUES TO GROW ...

Death to the Tyrant

A NEW HEROD COMES TO POWER. HEROD AGRIPPA WANTS TO PLEASE JEWISH LEADERS, SO HE BEGINS TO PERSECUTE JESUS' FOLLOWERS.

ARREST THE DISCIPLE CALLED JAMES. CHARGE HIM WITH STIRRING UP TROUBLE AND PUT HIM TO DEATH IMMEDIATELY!

SO JAMES, ONE OF THE FOUR FISHERMEN WHO LEFT THEIR NETS TO FOLLOW JESUS, IS KILLED TO SATISFY A WICKED KING'S STRUGGLE FOR POWER.

WHEN HEROD SEES THAT THE DEATH OF JAMES PLEASES THE JEWISH LEADERS, HE HAS PETER ARRESTED AS WELL. HE PLANS TO EXECUTE PETER AFTER THE PASSOVER FEAST.

CHAIN EACH HAND TO A GUARD. KEEP FOUR SOLDIERS ON WATCH AT ALL TIMES. THIS PRISONER MUST NOT ESCAPE!

IT'S PETER!

PETER? RHODA, YOU'RE SO UPSET YOU'RE IMAGINING THINGS.

THE GIRL INSISTS. FINALLY SOMEONE GOES TO OPEN THE DOOR.

IF YOU KNEW IT WAS PETER, WHY DIDN'T YOU LET HIM IN?

I WAS SO EXCITED TO TELL YOU THAT I FORGOT TO OPEN THE GATE!

A FEW DAYS LATER, HEROD APPEARS AT A PUBLIC CELEBRATION IN CAESAREA. WEARING DAZZLING SILVER ROYAL ROBES, HE SPEAKS TO THE PEOPLE. TO FLATTER HIM, THEY SHOUT:

HE HAS THE VOICE OF A GOD, NOT A MAN.

HEROD ACCEPTS THE PRAISE OF THE PEOPLE, WHICH SHOULD ONLY BE GIVEN TO GOD. IMMEDIATELY, GOD STRIKES HIM DOWN. HEROD LIES SICK FOR DAYS WHILE HE IS EATEN BY WORMS FROM THE INSIDE OUT. WITHIN THE WEEK, HE DIES.

WITH THE DEATH OF HEROD, THE PERSECUTION OF THE CHURCH STOPS FOR A TIME. THE GOOD NEWS OF JESUS CHRIST CONTINUES TO SPREAD THROUGH THE LAND OF THE JEWS ...

A Blinding Light

BASED ON ACTS 9:1-18

YEARS EARLIER, A BOY NAMED SAUL WAS BORN IN TARSUS. HIS PARENTS TAUGHT HIM TO WORSHIP AND OBEY GOD. SAUL BECAME A BRILLIANT STUDENT OF THE JEWISH LAW. LIKE MOST JEWISH LEADERS, SAUL REFUSED TO ACCEPT JESUS AS THE SAVIOR SENT FROM GOD. WHEN JEWISH LEADERS STONED STEPHEN, SAUL HELD THEIR COATS. SOON HE BEGAN HIS OWN ATTACK ON JESUS' FOLLOWERS. HE DRAGGED THEM OFF TO BE QUESTIONED, PUNISHED, AND EVEN PUT TO DEATH. THEN SAUL DECIDED TO LOOK FOR MORE BELIEVERS IN DAMASCUS.

SAUL RIDES TOWARD DAMASCUS WITH THE EAGERNESS OF A HUNTER ON THE TRACK OF HIS PREY. AT THE SIGHT OF THE CITY, HE URGES HIS HORSE ON—AS IF EVERY MINUTE COUNTS IN HIS SEARCH TO DESTROY JESUS' FOLLOWERS. SUDDENLY LIGHT FLASHES, A LIGHT BRIGHTER THAN THE NOONDAY SUN. HE FALLS TO THE GROUND, AND A VOICE CALLS OUT TO HIM:

SAUL! SAUL! WHY ARE YOU TORTURING ME?

WHO ARE YOU, LORD?

I AM JESUS, THE ONE YOU ARE PERSECUTING. GET UP AND GO INTO THE CITY. YOU WILL BE TOLD WHAT TO DO NEXT.

THE MEN TRAVELING WITH SAUL HEAR THE VOICE BUT DON'T SEE ANYTHING. TERRIFIED ...

SAUL, WHAT'S THE MATTER? WHAT HAPPENED?

MY EYES! I CAN'T SEE! HELP ME INTO THE CITY.

SO, BLIND AND AWED BY HIS EXPERIENCE, THE ONCE PROUD SAUL IS LED INTO DAMASCUS—TO A HOUSE ON STRAIGHT STREET.

WHERE ARE YOU TAKING ME?

TO THE HOME OF JUDAS, A FRIEND OF MINE.

FOR THREE DAYS, SAUL CAN'T SEE ANYTHING. HE EATS NOTHING AND DRINKS NOTHING THE WHOLE TIME. INSTEAD, HE SPENDS HIS HOURS SIMPLY PRAYING.

HAS A MAN NAMED ANANIAS ASKED TO SEE ME?

NO. WHAT MAKES YOU THINK HE WILL?

I'VE BEEN PRAYING, AND I HAD A VISION OF A MAN NAMED ANANIAS COMING TO GIVE ME BACK MY SIGHT.

WHILE SAUL IS PRAYING, JESUS APPEARS TO ANANIAS IN ANOTHER PART OF THE CITY.

ANANIAS, GET UP! GO TO STRAIGHT STREET, TO THE HOUSE OF JUDAS. ASK FOR A MAN NAMED SAUL. HE'S HAD A VISION THAT YOU WILL COME.

LORD, I'VE HEARD OF THIS EVIL MAN. HE HATES YOUR FOLLOWERS!

GO! I HAVE CHOSEN HIM TO WORK FOR ME. HE'LL TAKE MY GOOD NEWS TO ALL PEOPLE— NOT JUST THE JEWS.

ANANIAS OBEYS. AT THE HOME OF JUDAS, HE FINDS SAUL ...

BROTHER SAUL, YOU SAW THE LORD JESUS. NOW HE HAS SENT ME SO YOU WILL BE ABLE TO SEE AGAIN. YOU WILL BE FILLED WITH HIS SPIRIT.

ANANIAS LAYS HIS HANDS ON SAUL'S EYES ...

PRAISE GOD! I CAN SEE AGAIN!

IN JERUSALEM, PAUL BOLDLY DECLARES HIS NEW BELIEFS.

I BELIEVE JESUS ROSE FROM THE DEAD! I BELIEVE HE IS THE SAVIOR SENT FROM GOD.

WHAT HAS HAPPENED TO MAKE PAUL TALK LIKE THIS? MAYBE JESUS *IS* THE SON OF GOD.

WHEN PAUL'S OLD FRIENDS SEE THAT HE BELIEVES IN JESUS, THEY ARE FURIOUS!

STOP HIM! STOP HIM BEFORE HE STIRS UP THE PEOPLE.

DEATH IS THE ONLY THING THAT WILL SILENCE A MAN LIKE PAUL.

THEN WE HAVE TO KILL HIM.

JESUS' FOLLOWERS FIND OUT ABOUT THE PLOT AGAINST PAUL'S LIFE AND WARN HIM.

YOUR ENEMIES ARE POWERFUL, PAUL. THEY'RE TRYING TO KILL YOU. WE'LL HELP YOU GET AWAY TO CAESAREA.

I CAN GO TO TARSUS, MY HOMETOWN. I'LL SERVE THE LORD THERE.

PAUL ESCAPES TO THE SEACOAST AND SAILS NORTH TO HIS BOYHOOD HOME, TARSUS. THERE HE EARNS HIS LIVING BY MAKING TENTS—AND SPENDS ALL HIS FREE TIME TELLING PEOPLE THAT JESUS IS THE SAVIOR GOD PROMISED TO SEND.

ONE DAY A SHIP DOCKS AT TARSUS. A PASSENGER HURRIES DOWN THE PLANK ...

NOW TO FIND PAUL!

Foreign Assignment

BASED ON ACTS 11:19-30; 12:25—13:5

AFTER ESCAPING HIS ENEMIES, PAUL WORKS FOR SEVERAL YEARS AS A TENTMAKER IN TARSUS AND TELLS THE GOOD NEWS ABOUT JESUS. ONE DAY AN OLD FRIEND COMES TO SEE HIM ...

BARNABAS! WHAT ARE YOU DOING IN TARSUS?

I'M LOOKING FOR YOU, PAUL!

I'VE BEEN PREACHING IN ANTIOCH, AND THE CHURCH HAS GROWN SO MUCH THAT I NEED HELP. WILL YOU COME?

EAGERLY, PAUL ACCEPTS THE INVITATION.

WHEN YOU STARTED THE PERSECUTION IN JERUSALEM, SOME BELIEVERS WENT TO ANTIOCH AND STARTED A CHURCH THERE.

THANK GOD YOU ARE GIVING ME THE CHANCE TO ASK THEIR FORGIVENESS AND WORK WITH THEM TO TELL OTHERS ABOUT JESUS.

IN ANTIOCH, THE THIRD-LARGEST CITY OF THE ROMAN EMPIRE, PAUL AND BARNABAS CONVINCE BOTH JEWS AND GENTILES TO BELIEVE IN JESUS. JESUS' FOLLOWERS ARE CALLED CHRISTIANS FOR THE FIRST TIME. A TEACHER FROM JERUSALEM, AGABUS, MAKES A PROPHECY ABOUT A TRAGEDY.

GOD HAS GIVEN ME A WARNING! A GREAT FAMINE IS COMING. MANY BELIEVERS IN JERUSALEM ARE POOR AND MAY STARVE.

THE BELIEVERS IN ANTIOCH WANT TO HELP. THEY DECIDE TO SEND MONEY TO JERUSALEM FOR BELIEVERS THERE TO BUY FOOD. PAUL OFFERS TO HELP DELIVER THE GIFT.

BUT YOU HAVE ENEMIES IN JERUSALEM. THEY WANT TO KILL YOU!

THAT DOESN'T MATTER. WE HAVE TO HELP THE BELIEVERS THERE, EVEN IF IT'S DANGEROUS.

THE CHRISTIANS IN ANTIOCH GIVE GENEROUSLY, AND PAUL AND BARNABAS TAKE THE MONEY TO JERUSALEM.

WHAT WILL WE DO WHEN OUR FOOD IS GONE?

GOD WILL NOT FORSAKE US.

LISTEN! SOMEONE'S AT THE DOOR.

BARNABAS!

PAUL AND I BRING HELP FROM THE CHRISTIANS IN ANTIOCH. WE'VE BROUGHT MONEY FOR THE ELDERS IN JERUSALEM TO USE.

GO TELL THE OTHER ELDERS. WE HAVE MONEY TO BUY FOOD!

THEIR MISSION COMPLETE, PAUL AND BARNABAS PREPARE TO LEAVE JERUSALEM.

PAUL, THIS IS MY COUSIN, JOHN MARK. HE WOULD LIKE TO GO WITH US.

GOOD! WE CAN USE YOU, MARK.

IN ANTIOCH, PAUL AND BARNABAS MEET WITH OTHERS FOR PRAYER. GOD TELLS THE LEADERS OF THE CHURCH TO SEND PAUL AND BARNABAS TO TELL THE GOOD NEWS OF JESUS IN OTHER PLACES. THEY SET OUT WITH MARK.

THERE'S THE ISLAND OF CYPRUS!

AND THAT'S WHERE OUR MISSIONARY WORK BEGINS.

AFTER PREACHING IN SEVERAL CITIES ON THE ISLAND, THE MISSIONARIES REACH PAPHOS. NO ONE HAS GIVEN THEM ANY TROUBLE, BUT THEN ...

SERGIUS PAULUS, THE ROMAN GOVERNOR, ORDERS YOU TO COME WITH ME.

Silence, Sorcerer!

BASED ON ACTS 13:6–14:7

AFTER PREACHING AROUND THE ISLAND OF CYPRUS, PAUL, BARNABAS, AND MARK ARE SUMMONED TO SEE THE ROMAN GOVERNOR. TO THEIR SURPRISE, HE WANTS TO HEAR ABOUT JESUS. EAGERLY, PAUL TELLS ABOUT JESUS AND HOW GOD RAISED HIM FROM THE DEAD. THE COURT SORCERER TRIES TO KEEP THE GOVERNOR FROM BELIEVING.

LIES! *ALL* LIES! NO MAN CAN DIE AND LIVE AGAIN.

YOU CHILD OF THE DEVIL!

YOU'RE AN ENEMY OF TRUTH AND YOU TWIST THE RIGHT WAYS OF THE LORD.

NOW YOU WILL BE BLIND!

I CAN'T *SEE!* SOMEONE HELP ME!

ONLY GOD COULD DO THAT! I BELIEVE WHAT YOU'VE SAID ABOUT JESUS.

ENCOURAGED BY THEIR SUCCESS ON CYPRUS, THE MISSIONARIES DECIDE TO TRAVEL FARTHER. AT PERGA ...

PAUL SAYS YOU'RE GOING NORTH INTO ASIA MINOR. THAT'S TOO FAR FROM HOME!

I THINK IT'S TIME FOR ME TO RETURN TO JERUSALEM.

I UNDERSTAND, MARK. GIVE OUR FRIENDS A REPORT OF THE WORK WE'RE DOING, AND ASK THEM TO PRAY FOR US.

PAUL AND BARNABAS TRAVEL ALL AROUND THE MEDITERRANEAN SEA.

Black Sea

ASIA MINOR

PISIDIAN

PERGA

TARSUS

ANTIOCH

PAPHOS

CYPRUS

Mediterranean Sea

S Y R I A

DAMASCUS

CAESAREA

JERUSALEM

ON THE ROAD TO PISIDIAN ANTIOCH ...

I'M DISAPPOINTED IN MARK FOR LEAVING US.

HE'S YOUNG. HE'LL SERVE JESUS IN JERUSALEM, AND THAT'S IMPORTANT TOO.

IN PISIDIAN ANTIOCH, PAUL PREACHES IN THE SYNAGOGUE. HIS SERMON ABOUT JESUS IS SO EXCITING THAT THE PEOPLE URGE HIM TO SPEAK AGAIN. BUT THE NEXT WEEK, THE JEWISH LEADERS DON'T LIKE WHAT THEY SEE ...

LOOK! THE CROWD IS LISTENING TO EVERY WORD PAUL SAYS. HE'S GOING TO DESTROY OUR WHOLE RELIGION.

I'LL PUT A STOP TO HIM RIGHT NOW.

696

PAUL AND BARNABAS ARE IN DANGER, SO THEY SHAKE THE DUST OFF THEIR SANDALS AND LEAVE PISIDIAN ANTIOCH. THEY TRAVEL SOUTHEAST TO ICONIUM, ANOTHER CITY IN THE PROVINCE OF GALATIA. HERE JEWS AND GENTILES ALIKE BELIEVE IN JESUS. BUT THE JEWS WHO DON'T BELIEVE ARE FUMING.

THE MIRACLES THESE MEN DO PROVE THEY ARE TELLING THE TRUTH ABOUT JESUS.

WE HAVE TO GET RID OF THEM.

RUNNING THEM OUT OF TOWN ISN'T GOOD ENOUGH. WE'LL STONE THEM!

NO MATTER WHERE PAUL GOES, SOME PEOPLE ARE MADE ANGRY BY THE GOOD NEWS OF JESUS.

PAUL! BARNABAS! YOUR ENEMIES ARE PLOTTING TO STONE YOU. YOU MUST GET AWAY IMMEDIATELY.

THEN WE'LL GO TO LYSTRA AND DERBE AND SEE WHAT GOD WILL DO THERE.

WHIPPED INTO A RAGE BY MEN FROM ANTIOCH AND ICONIUM, THE PEOPLE OF LYSTRA TURN AGAINST PAUL AND STONE HIM. THEY DRAG HIS BODY OUT OF THE CITY AND LEAVE HIM FOR DEAD.

THIS WILL BE A LESSON TO ANYONE WHO TRIES TO MAKE TROUBLE IN OUR CITY!

AFTER THE MOB LEAVES, BARNABAS AND THE BELIEVERS OF LYSTRA GATHER AROUND PAUL'S MOTIONLESS FORM. AS THEY STAND WEEPING ...

HE'S MOVING! HE'S ALIVE! QUICK, HELP HIM!

WE THOUGHT THEY KILLED YOU!

THEY MEANT TO. BUT GOD SAVED ME. LET'S GO BACK INTO THE CITY.

The Greek Divide

BASED ON ACTS 14:20—15:1

THE NEXT DAY, PAUL AND BARNABAS LEAVE FOR DERBE, WHERE MANY PEOPLE BECOME CHRISTIANS. BUT PAUL'S EYES TURN BACK TOWARD ANTIOCH AND THE CHURCH THAT SENT THEM OUT ...

THE SHORTEST WAY HOME IS THROUGH TARSUS.

NO, WE MUST GO BACK THE WAY WE CAME SO WE CAN CHECK ON THE BELIEVERS AND SEE HOW THEIR CHURCHES ARE DOING.

ON THEIR FIRST MISSIONARY JOURNEY TO THE GENTILES, PAUL AND BARNABAS TRAVELED 1,400 MILES BY LAND AND SEA AND WERE GONE FOR ABOUT TWO YEARS.

A S I A   M I N O R

ANTIOCH
ICONIUM
LYSTRA
TARSUS
Galatia
DERBE
PERGA
ANTIOCH
ATTALIA

Mediterranean Sea

Syria

Cyprus
SALAMIS
PAPHOS

BACK IN THEIR OWN CHURCH IN ANTIOCH, PAUL AND BARNABAS ARE OVERJOYED TO SEE THEIR FRIENDS AND TELL EVERYTHING THAT GOD HAS DONE.

GOD HAS OPENED THE WAY FOR ANYONE TO BELIEVE IN JESUS!

WE'RE GLAD WE COULD HELP SUPPORT YOU AS YOU SPREAD THE GOOD NEWS.

WITH PAUL AND BARNABAS AS LEADERS, THE CHURCH IN ANTIOCH GROWS IN SIZE AND INFLUENCE. BUT ONE DAY A GROUP OF CHRISTIANS ARRIVES FROM JERUSALEM.

YOU GENTILES CANNOT BECOME CHRISTIANS UNLESS YOU ALSO OBEY OUR JEWISH LAWS.

WHAT? WHO MADE THAT RULE?

WE SPEAK WITH THE AUTHORITY OF JAMES, THE BROTHER OF JESUS, WHO IS THE LEADER OF THE CHURCH IN JERUSALEM.

HOW CAN THIS BE *TRUE?* PAUL NEVER SAID ANYTHING LIKE THIS.

I'LL NEVER GIVE UP BELIEVING IN JESUS, BUT I CAN'T OBEY ALL THOSE JEWISH LAWS.

THEN YOU CANNOT *BE* A CHRISTIAN!

THE ARGUMENT GROWS—JEWISH CHRISTIANS AGAINST GENTILE CHRISTIANS. BELIEVERS TAKE SIDES AGAINST EACH OTHER ...

Jerusalem Council

BASED ON ACTS 15:1-35; GALATIANS

LIKE A VIOLENT WIND, THE ARGUMENT BETWEEN JEWISH AND GENTILE CHRISTIANS RIPS THROUGH THE CHURCH. PAUL AND BARNABAS AND OTHERS FROM ANTIOCH TRAVEL TO JERUSALEM TO SPEAK WITH THE CHURCH LEADERS THERE.

THE CHURCH IN JERUSALEM WELCOMES PAUL AND BARNABAS.

EVERYWHERE WE GO, GENTILES BELIEVE IN JESUS.

GOD IS SHOWING HIS POWER BOTH TO JEWS AND NON-JEWS.

I AM CONVINCED THAT TO GOD IT DOESN'T MATTER IF YOU ARE GREEK OR JEW, MAN OR WOMAN, RICH OR POOR, BECAUSE WE ARE ALL ONE IN CHRIST.

SOME OF THE BELIEVERS HAD BEEN PHARISEES, EXPERTS IN JEWISH LAW ...

PEOPLE WHO ARE NOT JEWS MUST BECOME JEWS. THEY MUST OBEY THE LAW OF MOSES.

THEN THEY CAN BECOME CHRISTIANS.

THE APOSTLES AND ELDERS MEET TO TALK ABOUT THIS QUESTION. NOT EVERYONE AGREES. PETER STANDS UP TO TALK ...

BROTHERS, GOD CHOSE ME TO TAKE THE GOOD NEWS TO PEOPLE WHO AREN'T JEWS.

HE GAVE THEM THE SAME HOLY SPIRIT HE GAVE US. WHY DO YOU WANT TO MAKE IT HARD FOR THEM TO BELIEVE?

WE ARE SAVED BY THE GRACE OF GOD. THE GENTILES ARE SAVED THE SAME WAY.

THERE IS DEAD SILENCE IN THE ROOM ...

THE JERUSALEM COUNCIL FACES A QUESTION: DO GENTILES FIRST HAVE TO BECOME JEWS AND OBEY JEWISH LAWS BEFORE THEY CAN BELIEVE IN JESUS? AFTER ARGUMENTS FROM BOTH SIDES, JAMES, THE HEAD OF THE COUNCIL, STANDS UP TO SPEAK ...

WE'VE HEARD WHAT PAUL AND BARNABAS HAVE SAID.

WE'VE HEARD PETER TELL US THAT GOD LOVES PEOPLE WHO ARE NOT JEWS.

LET'S NOT MAKE IT HARD FOR NON-JEWS TO TURN TO GOD.

THE COUNCIL AGREES TO A FEW IMPORTANT RULES. CHRISTIANS, BOTH JEWS AND GENTILES, MUST AVOID EATING FOOD THAT WAS SACRIFICED TO FALSE GODS, AND THEY MUST LEAD PURE LIVES.

The Next Journey

BASED ON ACTS 15:36—16:19

WITH THIS QUESTION SETTLED, PAUL AND BARNABAS CAN GO BACK TO TRAVELING AND PREACHING ABOUT JESUS.

LET'S MAKE A TRIP TO VISIT THE CHURCHES WE STARTED.

GOOD IDEA. I WANT TO ASK MARK TO GO WITH US AGAIN.

NO, MARK LEFT US THE LAST TIME.

I KNOW, BUT WE SHOULD GIVE HIM A SECOND CHANCE.

PAUL DISAGREES. SO BARNABAS AND PAUL GO THEIR SEPARATE WAYS. BARNABAS TAKES MARK AND SAILS TO CYPRUS. PAUL TAKES SILAS TO VISIT THE CHURCHES HE STARTED.

PAUL RETURNS TO LYSTRA, THE CITY WHERE HE WAS STONED. THE CHURCH HAS BEEN GROWING, AND PAUL MEETS A YOUNG MAN NAMED TIMOTHY.

PAUL, I WANT YOU TO MEET TIMOTHY. HE'S BECOME ONE OF OUR BEST YOUNG LEADERS.

TIMOTHY, NEVER LET ANYONE LOOK DOWN ON YOU BECAUSE YOU ARE YOUNG. YOU CAN SET A GOOD EXAMPLE FOR OTHER BELIEVERS.

A GOOD WIND SPEEDS THE FOUR MISSIONARIES ACROSS THE AEGEAN SEA TO THE PORT OF NEAPOLIS. FROM THERE THEY WALK EIGHT MILES TO PHILIPPI, A ROMAN COLONY.

MACEDONIA

PHILIPPI
NEAPOLIS
THESSALONICA
SAMOTHRACE
TROAS
Aegean Sea
ASIA
ATHENS

PHILIPPI HAS NO SYNAGOGUE, SO ON THE SABBATH THE MISSIONARIES GO DOWN TO THE RIVER LOOKING FOR A PLACE OF PRAYER.

DO YOU HEAR THOSE WOMEN? THEY ARE PRAYING TO GOD.

THE MISSIONARIES JOIN THE WORSHIPPERS. SOON PAUL IS TELLING THEM ABOUT JESUS. A CLOTH MERCHANT NAMED LYDIA SPEAKS UP.

GOD HAS OPENED MY HEART TO RECEIVE YOUR MESSAGE. I BELIEVE IN JESUS. WILL YOU BAPTIZE ME?

ABSOLUTELY.

SOON ALL THE MEMBERS OF LYDIA'S HOUSEHOLD ARE BAPTIZED. LYDIA INVITES THE MISSIONARIES TO MAKE HER HOME THEIR HEADQUARTERS WHILE THEY ARE IN PHILIPPI.

THE ROMANS LOVE PURPLE. I SELL MOST OF MY CLOTH TO THEM.

AS YOU SELL TO THEM, TELL THEM ABOUT JESUS.

EVERY DAY AS PAUL AND SILAS WALK THROUGH THE STREETS OF PHILIPPI, THEY SEE A SAD SIGHT ...

THE POOR GIRL IS UNDER THE INFLUENCE OF AN EVIL SPIRIT. HER MASTERS EARN LOTS OF MONEY USING HER AS A FORTUNE-TELLER.

FINALLY, ONE DAY ...

YOU SERVE THE MOST HIGH GOD!

IN CHRIST'S NAME, COME OUT OF HER!

LOOK! SHE CAN'T TELL FORTUNES ANYMORE. OUR BUSINESS IS RUINED.

WHOEVER THAT MAN IS, HE'LL PAY FOR THIS. HE HAD NO RIGHT TO MEDDLE WITH OUR AFFAIRS.

Earthquake!

BASED ON ACTS 16:19-39

WHEN PAUL REMOVES AN EVIL SPIRIT FROM A SLAVE GIRL, HER OWNERS ARE LIVID. BECAUSE THE GIRL CAN NO LONGER TELL FORTUNES, THEIR BUSINESS IS RUINED. THE OWNERS DRAG PAUL AND SILAS BEFORE THE JUDGES IN THE PUBLIC SQUARE. A CROWD GATHERS ...

THESE JEWISH MEN ARE MAKING TROUBLE BY TEACHING AGAINST ROMAN LAW.

YES!

WE ALL HEARD THEM!

BUT I—

SILENCE! WE WILL NOT TOLERATE TROUBLE IN OUR CITY. GIVE THESE MEN A BEATING AND THROW THEM IN JAIL. SEE THAT THEY DON'T ESCAPE.

THE JAILER RUSHES DOWN INTO THE DUNGEON, SURE THAT HIS PRISONERS HAVE ESCAPED.

THEY'RE GONE! I MIGHT AS WELL KILL MYSELF.

NO! NO! WE'RE ALL HERE! DON'T HURT YOURSELF.

BELIEVING PAUL AND SILAS CAUSED THE EARTHQUAKE, THE JAILER FALLS DOWN IN FRONT OF THEM.

WHAT MUST I DO TO BE SAVED?

BELIEVE IN THE LORD JESUS CHRIST.

IN THE MIDDLE OF THE NIGHT, THE JAILER TAKES PAUL AND SILAS TO HIS HOUSE AND CARES FOR THEM. HE AND HIS FAMILY LISTEN AS PAUL TELLS THEM ABOUT JESUS. THEN THEY ARE ALL BAPTIZED!

EARLY IN THE MORNING, WORD COMES THAT PAUL AND SILAS ARE FREE TO GO.

THE JUDGES HAVE ORDERED YOUR RELEASE.

WE ARE ROMAN CITIZENS. WE WERE PUT IN PRISON WITH NO TRIAL.

NOW THE JUDGES THINK THEY CAN GET RID OF US QUIETLY? NO!

TELL THE JUDGES TO MAKE OUR RELEASE AS PUBLIC AS OUR BEATING WAS.

THE ROMAN JUDGES, WHO ORDERED PAUL AND SILAS RELEASED FROM PRISON, ARE SURPRISED WHEN THE OFFICER RETURNS WITH A MESSAGE FROM THE PRISONERS.

THOSE MEN ARE ROMAN CITIZENS. THEY DEMAND THAT YOU COME TO THE PRISON AND RELEASE THEM AS PUBLICLY AS YOU PUNISHED THEM.

THEY'RE *ROMAN CITIZENS?* AND WE PUNISHED THEM WITHOUT A TRIAL! THIS COULD MEAN SERIOUS TROUBLE FOR US.

FORGETTING THEIR DIGNITY, THE JUDGES GO IMMEDIATELY TO THE PRISON.

WE'RE SORRY FOR THE SHAMEFUL WAY WE TREATED YOU. NOW PLEASE LEAVE OUR CITY TO AVOID FURTHER TROUBLE.

WE FORGIVE YOU—AND WE'LL LEAVE TODAY.

Trouble in Thessalonica

BASED ON ACTS 16:40—18:11; 1 AND 2 THESSALONIANS

AT LYDIA'S HOUSE, PAUL, SILAS, AND TIMOTHY SAY GOOD-BYE TO THEIR FRIENDS.

THANK YOU FOR LEAVING DR. LUKE HERE TO HELP OUR CHURCH.

BE BRAVE. WE WILL RETURN SOMEDAY. HOLD ON TO YOUR FAITH IN JESUS.

TRAVELING ON ABOUT 90 MILES, THE MISSIONARIES REACH THESSALONICA ON THE AEGEAN SEA. AS HE USUALLY DOES IN A NEW CITY, PAUL GOES TO THE SYNAGOGUE TO PREACH.

THE SCRIPTURES PROMISED A SAVIOR WOULD COME. JESUS, WHO DIED ON THE CROSS AND ROSE FROM THE DEAD, IS THAT SAVIOR.

TO ESCAPE THEIR ENEMIES IN THESSALONICA, PAUL AND HIS COMPANIONS, SILAS AND TIMOTHY, GO ON TO BEREA, WHERE THEY CONTINUE PREACHING. UNKNOWN TO THEM, THE ENEMIES FOLLOW ...

WE'VE COME TO WARN YOU ABOUT A JEW NAMED PAUL. HE'S TROUBLE! GET RID OF HIM AS FAST AS YOU CAN.

WE'LL TAKE CARE OF THIS IMMEDIATELY.

BUT BEFORE THE ANGRY MOB CAN FIND PAUL, HIS FRIENDS HELP HIM ESCAPE ONCE AGAIN. THIS TIME HE GOES TO ATHENS. FROM THERE, PAUL SENDS WORD FOR SILAS AND TIMOTHY TO JOIN HIM AS SOON AS POSSIBLE.

ON THE SABBATH, PAUL PREACHES TO THE JEWS. ON OTHER DAYS, HE PREACHES TO THE GREEKS IN THE MARKETPLACE. THEY INVITE HIM TO SPEAK BEFORE THE COURT OF MARS HILL. PAUL ACCEPTS EAGERLY.

MEN OF ATHENS, I'VE SEEN YOUR STATUES HONORING A "GOD YOU DO NOT KNOW." LET ME INTRODUCE YOU TO HIM. HE IS THE ONE TRUE GOD WHO MADE ALL THINGS, AND HE PROVED THIS BY RAISING JESUS FROM THE DEAD.

NOBODY CAN BE RAISED FROM THE DEAD. THAT'S RIDICULOUS.

I'M NOT SO SURE.

Corinthian Court

BASED ON ACTS 18:12–19:22;
ROMANS; 1 CORINTHIANS

JEWISH LEADERS IN CORINTH ARE ANGRY BECAUSE SO MANY PEOPLE BELIEVE IN JESUS. THEY TAKE PAUL BEFORE THE NEW ROMAN GOVERNOR, GALLIO.

MOST EXCELLENT GALLIO, THIS MAN IS TELLING PEOPLE TO WORSHIP GOD IN WAYS THAT ARE AGAINST THE LAW. HE IS CHANGING THE JEWISH CUSTOMS THAT THE ROMANS ALLOW.

PAUL PREPARES TO DEFEND HIMSELF, BUT TO EVERYONE'S SURPRISE, GALLIO TURNS ON PAUL'S ENEMIES.

I AM NOT GOING TO GET INVOLVED IN YOUR QUARRELS ABOUT THE JEWISH LAW. THIS HAS NOTHING TO DO WITH ROMAN LAW. GET OUT OF MY COURT.

AFTER THIS ORDER BY THE GOVERNOR, PAUL PREACHES IN CORINTH WITHOUT ANY TROUBLE, AND THE CHURCH GROWS. PAUL WRITES ANOTHER LETTER, THIS TIME TO THE ROMANS.

Map of Paul's Work in Greek Cities

PHILIPPI
NEAPOLIS
THESSALONICA
BEREA
TROAS

ASIA

Aegean Sea

Black Sea

ANTIOCH
ICONIUM
TARSUS
ATHENS
Galatia
EPHESUS
LYSTRA
DERBE
CORINTH
MILETUS
ANTIOCH
SELEUCIA

Mediterranean Sea

CYPRUS

SIDON
TYRE

CAESAREA
JERUSALEM

PAUL'S LETTER
TO THE ROMANS ...

Everybody—Roman or Greek, Jew or Gentile—needs God, because everybody has sinned and fallen short of God's perfection. But we are no longer punished by the law, because Christ Jesus gave us the law of the Spirit of life, which sets us free from the law of sin and death.

PAUL VISITS JERUSALEM AND ANTIOCH. THEN HE BEGINS HIS THIRD MISSIONARY JOURNEY. IN EPHESUS, HE SEES THE GREAT TEMPLE OF THE GODDESS ARTEMIS.

LIKE THE PEOPLE OF ATHENS, THE EPHESIANS WORSHIP A GODDESS MADE WITH THEIR OWN HANDS. GOD, HELP ME TO TEACH THEM THE TRUTH.

THE PEOPLE OF EPHESUS LISTEN TO PAUL AND SEE THAT WHAT HE SAYS IS TRUE AND THAT THEIR MAGICIANS ARE FAKES. MANY PEOPLE BELIEVE IN JESUS AND BURN THEIR BOOKS OF MAGIC.

THOSE SCROLLS ARE WORTH A FORTUNE!

YES, BUT THEIR NEW LIFE IN JESUS IS WORTH EVEN MORE!

PAUL IS STILL REJOICING ABOUT THE GROWTH OF THE CHURCH IN EPHESUS WHEN NEWS COMES FROM CORINTH ...

SO PAUL SENDS A LETTER TO THE CHURCH AT CORINTH.

THE CHURCH IN CORINTH IS HAVING ALL KINDS OF TROUBLE. THE MEMBERS ARE TAKING SIDES AGAINST EACH OTHER. SOME OF THEM SAY *YOU* ARE THE HEAD OF THE CHURCH. OTHERS SAY APOLLOS IS THE BEST PREACHER. OTHERS SAY PETER IS THE REAL LEADER.

PAUL'S FIRST LETTER TO THE CORINTHIANS ...

I beg of you, my brothers, do not quarrel and divide the Church. The Church has only one head—Christ, who died on the cross.

Keep yourselves pure, because your body is a temple of the Holy Spirit. So whatever you do with your body, eating or drinking or anything else, do it to honor God.

We've all been given different gifts of the Spirit so that we can build up the church in different ways. But even if I had all the gifts possible—if I knew everything and could speak the language of angels—it would mean nothing if I didn't have love.

Ephesian Mob

BASED ON ACTS 19:23—20:5; 2 CORINTHIANS

THE CHURCH IN EPHESUS GROWS—ALMOST AS RAPIDLY AS THE BLAZE THAT DESTROYED THE BOOKS OF MAGIC. BUT THE PEOPLE WHO EARN MONEY BY SELLING THINGS TO WORSHIP THE FALSE GODS ARE NOT HAPPY ...

BUSINESS IS NO GOOD. PEOPLE AREN'T BUYING SILVER SHRINES OF ARTEMIS.

IT'S BECAUSE OF THAT CHRISTIAN PREACHER, PAUL. HE'S TELLING PEOPLE TO BELIEVE IN JESUS, SO THEY DON'T WANT THE THINGS WE MAKE.

PAUL TELLS PEOPLE ARTEMIS IS NOT REALLY A GODDESS, THAT IT DOES NO GOOD TO WORSHIP HER.

THE ANGRY MERCHANTS RUSH INTO THE STREET AND GRAB SOME OF PAUL'S FRIENDS.

WHERE IS PAUL? TELL US!

NEVER!

THE MOB SWELLS AS IT PRESSES THROUGH THE STREETS. SOON THE WHOLE CITY IS IN AN UPROAR ...

ARTEMIS OF THE EPHESIANS IS THE GREATEST!

THE MOB TAKES PAUL'S FRIENDS TO THE GREAT OUTDOOR THEATER.

IN ANOTHER PART OF THE CITY ...

PAUL! THE SILVERSMITHS ARE AFTER YOU FOR DESTROYING THEIR BUSINESS. THEY'VE GRABBED GAIUS AND ARISTARCHUS!

WHERE ARE THEY? I WANT TO HELP THEM.

NO! PAUL, THAT MOB WANTS TO KILL YOU.

THREATENED WITH ROMAN ACTION, THE RIOT BREAKS UP. PAUL SENDS FOR HIS FRIENDS.

THE MOB WAS REALLY AFTER ME. I DON'T WANT ALL OF YOU TO BE IN DANGER, SO I'LL GO TO PHILIPPI.

OUR PRAYERS GO WITH YOU.

SOON AFTER PAUL REACHES PHILIPPI, TITUS JOINS HIM WITH NEWS FROM CORINTH.

YOUR LETTER TO THE CHRISTIANS AT CORINTH MADE THEM GET BACK ON THE RIGHT PATH.

BUT NOW SOME PEOPLE CLAIM THAT YOU ARE NOT A TRUE APOSTLE OF JESUS.

ONCE AGAIN PAUL WRITES TO THE CHURCH IN CORINTH ...

PAUL'S SECOND LETTER TO THE CORINTHIANS ...

I can see that my first letter upset you, but I am glad I sent it. I don't want to hurt you, but to help you grow in your faith. I know that many of you are suffering, but take comfort: though we share Christ's pain, He also floods us with his comfort.

So don't lose heart! Our troubles only last for a moment, but they earn us eternal life. And life in heaven will quickly make us forget our earthly hardships. So don't focus on the things you can see—those things are temporary. It is the unseen things that are eternal.

For those who question my authority, remember this: I have been imprisoned and beaten; I have faced down death; I've been stoned and shipwrecked. And I've endured all that to carry out the work of Christ.

WHILE TITUS TAKES THE LETTER TO CORINTH, PAUL CONTINUES VISITING CHURCHES IN MACEDONIA. HE COLLECTS MONEY FOR THE POOR IN JERUSALEM. MONTHS LATER HE REACHES CORINTH, WHERE FRIENDS GREET HIM EAGERLY.

THIS MONEY WILL SHOW THE CHRISTIANS IN JERUSALEM THAT YOU'RE CONCERNED FOR THEM.

"Falling" Asleep

BASED ON ACTS 20:6—21:16

PAUL'S ENEMIES CONTINUE TO PLOT AGAINST HIM, SO HE CHANGES HIS TRAVEL PLANS TO AVOID THEM. HE AND HIS COMPANIONS TRAVEL THROUGH MACEDONIA AND ON TO TROAS. DR. LUKE JOINS THE BAND OF MISSIONARIES ONCE AGAIN.

AFTER WEEKS OF TRAVELING AND VISITING CHURCHES, PAUL HAS SO MUCH TO TELL THE PEOPLE IN TROAS THAT HE TALKS LATE INTO THE NIGHT. UNTIL ...

LOOK OUT!

EUTYCHUS FELL ASLEEP SITTING IN THE WINDOW!

PAUL RUSHES OUTSIDE ...

HE FELL FROM A THIRD-STORY WINDOW. HE'S DEAD!

DON'T BE ALARMED. HE'S ALIVE.

THANK GOD!

I'M SURE HE WAS DEAD! GOD HAS GIVEN PAUL AMAZING POWER!

PAUL TALKS UNTIL DAYBREAK, THEN SAYS GOOD-BYE TO HIS FRIENDS AND CONTINUES HIS JOURNEY.

AT MILETUS, PAUL SENDS WORD FOR THE ELDERS OF EPHESUS TO MEET WITH HIM. EAGERLY, THEY TRAVEL THE 35 MILES TO SEE PAUL AGAIN.

I AM GOING TO JERUSALEM, EVEN THOUGH IT IS DANGEROUS. MY LIFE MEANS NOTHING TO ME, SO LONG AS I FINISH THE WORK JESUS GAVE ME TO DO. SINCE I WON'T SEE ANY OF YOU AGAIN, REMEMBER WHAT I'VE SHOWN YOU: WORK HARD AND HELP THE WEAK. AS JESUS SAID, "IT IS BETTER TO GIVE THAN TO RECEIVE."

PAUL GOES ON TO TYRE, WHERE HE PREACHES FOR A WEEK. WHEN HE LEAVES, THE CHRISTIANS FOLLOW HIM TO THE BEACH FOR A PRAYERFUL GOOD-BYE.

DON'T GO TO JERUSALEM! IT'S TOO DANGEROUS. YOUR ENEMIES ARE WAITING TO KILL YOU BECAUSE YOU SAY JESUS IS THE SON OF GOD.

I MUST GO. I HAVE MONEY THAT THE GENTILE CHRISTIANS HAVE GIVEN FOR THE POOR IN JERUSALEM. I'M NOT AFRAID.

PAUL GOES DOWN THE COAST TO CAESAREA AND VISITS WITH PHILIP. THE PROPHET AGABUS JOINS THEM. SUDDENLY HE TAKES PAUL'S BELT AND USES IT TO BIND HIS OWN HANDS AND FEET.

THE HOLY SPIRIT TELLS ME THAT THIS IS HOW THE JEWS OF JERUSALEM WILL TIE UP THE OWNER OF THIS BELT. THEY WILL HAND HIM OVER TO THE GENTILES.

PAUL, CHANGE YOUR PLANS! DON'T GO TO JERUSALEM.

WHY ARE YOU CRYING? I'M READY TO GO TO PRISON. I'M EVEN READY TO DIE FOR JESUS.

Under Arrest

IN JERUSALEM, PAUL MEETS WITH JAMES AND OTHER LEADERS OF THE CHURCH. HE DELIVERS THE MONEY FOR THE POOR AND TELLS WHAT GOD HAS DONE IN OTHER PLACES.

I MUST WARN YOU, PAUL. YOU HAVE ENEMIES HERE WHO THINK YOU ARE A TRAITOR. EVEN CHRISTIAN JEWS HAVE QUESTIONS BECAUSE OF YOUR WORK WITH THE GENTILES.

I'LL WORSHIP WITH THEM IN THE TEMPLE TO SHOW THAT I AM TRUE TO THE FAITH OF OUR FATHERS.

JAMES' WARNING COMES TRUE WITHIN THE WEEK. WHILE PAUL IS WORSHIPPING IN THE TEMPLE, HIS ENEMIES MAKE FALSE ACCUSATIONS. THEY SAY HE BROUGHT NON-JEWS INTO THE PART OF THE TEMPLE WHERE ONLY JEWS ARE ALLOWED.

THERE HE IS—THE TRAITOR!

HE HAS MADE THIS HOLY PLACE UNCLEAN!

THE PEOPLE ANGRILY TURN AGAINST PAUL. A MOB DRAGS HIM FROM THE TEMPLE AND STARTS TO BEAT HIM.

LOOK OUT! ROMAN SOLDIERS ARE COMING!

NOW TELL US WHAT THIS MAN HAS DONE.

TAKE HIM AWAY! KILL HIM!

SINCE THEY CAN'T GET A STRAIGHT ANSWER, THE SOLDIERS TAKE PAUL AWAY. ON THE STEPS OF THE PRISON, PAUL STOPS AND TELLS THE PEOPLE HOW HE BECAME A CHRISTIAN. BUT WHEN HE MENTIONS PREACHING TO GENTILES, THE MOB GOES WILD.

KILL HIM!

KILL HIM!

HE IS NOT FIT TO LIVE!

Bound for Rome

BASED ON ACTS 23:23—28:16

TO KEEP PAUL SAFE, THE ROMAN COMMANDER AT JERUSALEM SENDS HIM TO CAESAREA, WHERE PAUL STAYS IN PRISON FOR TWO YEARS. THEN PAUL APPEARS BEFORE FESTUS, THE ROMAN GOVERNOR, AND DEMANDS HIS RIGHT TO A TRIAL BY THE EMPEROR, NERO, IN ROME. BUT FIRST FESTUS TAKES PAUL BEFORE A NEIGHBORING RULER, KING AGRIPPA, WHO IS VISITING THE CITY.

I ONCE OPPOSED JESUS AND IMPRISONED HIS FOLLOWERS. BUT THEN I SAW A LIGHT FROM HEAVEN, AND JESUS HIMSELF SAID TO ME, "I AM SENDING YOU TO TURN THE GENTILES AWAY FROM SATAN'S POWER AND BRING THEM TO GOD." I COULD NOT DISOBEY A HEAVENLY VISION!

I WOULD LIKE TO LET YOU GO, BUT YOU MUST BE SENT TO ROME.

UNDER ROMAN GUARD, PAUL BOARDS A SHIP BOUND FOR ROME FOR HIS TRIAL. DR. LUKE GOES WITH HIM. THE SHIP SETS SAIL, ONLY TO BE STRUCK BY A VIOLENT TEMPEST.

THE STORM RAGES DAY AFTER DAY. AFTER TWO WEEKS, THE SAILORS TRY TO DESERT THE SHIP.

STAY WITH THE SHIP! GOD PROMISED HE WOULD SAVE US. BE COURAGEOUS!

IN THE MIDST OF THE STORM, PAUL THANKS GOD FOR THEIR FOOD. HE PROMISES THAT EVERYONE WILL SURVIVE, BUT THE SHIP WILL SINK. AT DAYBREAK ...

LAND AHEAD!

HEADING TOWARD A BAY, THE SHIP HITS A SANDBAR. THE FRONT OF THE SHIP IS STUCK, AND THE POUNDING WAVES BREAK THE BACK OF THE SHIP TO PIECES.

ABANDON SHIP!

KILL THE PRISONERS! IF THEY REACH SHORE, THEY'LL ESCAPE.

BECAUSE OF HIS FRIENDSHIP WITH PAUL, THE ROMAN OFFICER SPARES THE LIVES OF THE PRISONERS. SOLDIERS, SAILORS, AND PRISONERS STRUGGLE FOR THEIR LIVES IN THE WILD SEA.

JUST AS GOD TOLD PAUL, EVERY MAN ON BOARD REACHES LAND SAFELY. PEOPLE ON THE ISLAND OF MALTA RUSH DOWN TO THE SHORE TO HELP THE VICTIMS OF THE WRECK.

WE'LL HAVE A FIRE GOING SOON.

I'LL GET SOME MORE WOOD.

AS PAUL LAYS STICKS ON THE FIRE, A SNAKE CRAWLS OUT FROM THE WOOD—AND STRIKES!

A VIPER! PAUL WILL DIE!

THIS MAN MUST BE A MURDERER! HE ESCAPED THE SEA, BUT JUSTICE WILL NOT LET HIM LIVE.

PAUL SHAKES THE SNAKE INTO THE FIRE. THE PEOPLE WAIT FOR HIM TO BEGIN SWELLING OR SUDDENLY FALL DEAD. BUT NOTHING HAPPENS. THE ISLANDERS CHANGE THEIR MINDS ABOUT PAUL AND BEGIN TO BRING SICK PEOPLE TO HIM TO BE HEALED. THREE MONTHS LATER, PAUL SAILS AGAIN FOR ROME AND A LONG STAY IN PRISON.

Prison Pen Pals

BASED ON EPHESIANS; PHILIPPIANS; COLOSSIANS; PHILEMON

FOR MONTHS PAUL IS UNDER HOUSE ARREST AS HE WAITS FOR HIS TRIAL BEFORE THE EMPEROR IN ROME. HIS CHRISTIAN FRIENDS IN ALL THE CHURCHES PRAY FOR HIM CONSTANTLY. ONE DAY ...

GREETINGS, PAUL!

I HAVE COME WITH A GIFT FROM THE CHURCH AT PHILIPPI.

EPAPHRODITUS! DON'T MIND THE GUARD CHAINED TO MY WRIST.

HE'S JUST MY CONSTANT REMINDER THAT I'M A SLAVE TO CHRIST.

WHAT KIND OF MAN IS ABLE TO JOKE WHILE IN CHAINS?

WHILE IN ROME, EPAPHRODITUS BECOMES ILL. CHRISTIANS IN THE CITY GLADLY TAKE CARE OF HIM.

THANK GOD YOU ARE RECOVERING. THIS LETTER IS FROM YOUR FRIENDS IN PHILIPPI. THEY ARE WORRIED ABOUT YOU.

I'M SORRY THEY WERE SO WORRIED.

HISTORICAL
BACKGROUND ...
IN THE YEAR 64, NERO, THE CRUEL EMPEROR
OF ROME, HAS MANY ENEMIES AMONG HIS
OWN PEOPLE. RUMORS SPREAD ABOUT
PLOTS ON HIS LIFE. SUDDENLY A FIRE
SWEEPS ACROSS THE CITY AND RAGES FOR
NINE DAYS. GREAT SECTIONS OF THE CITY
BURN TO THE GROUND, DRIVING THOUSANDS
OF PEOPLE FROM THEIR HOMES.

EVEN WHILE THE CITY IS STILL IN FLAMES, NEW RUMORS SPREAD.

EMPEROR! THE PEOPLE ARE SAYING YOU STARTED THE FIRE.

AND I SAY THE CHRISTIANS STARTED THE FIRE. ARREST THEM! TORTURE THEM! KILL THEM!

ANYTHING TO TURN SUSPICION AWAY FROM ME.

ARMED WITH ORDERS FROM THE EMPEROR, ROMAN SOLDIERS KILL HUNDREDS OF CHRISTIANS IN ROME. THE ORDER REACHES OUT ACROSS THE SEA FROM ITALY. ONCE AGAIN PAUL IS ARRESTED!

BY ORDER OF THE EMPEROR, YOU ARE UNDER ARREST!

ONCE AGAIN PAUL COMES TO ROME AS A PRISONER. THIS TIME HE IS CHAINED TO THE WALL OF THE PRISON. LUKE COMES TO COMFORT HIM.

I'M SURE I HAVE ONLY A FEW MONTHS TO LIVE. BRING SOME PAPER AND INK AND WRITE WHAT I TELL YOU TO TIMOTHY.

I'LL BRING IT THE NEXT TIME I VISIT YOU.

Fight the Good Fight
BASED ON TITUS; 2 TIMOTHY

PAUL'S LETTER TO TITUS ...

We followers of Christ must be good examples to the world. Be honest and serious, careful about what you say. That way, your enemies will be embarrassed, because no one will believe anything bad about you.

PAUL'S SECOND LETTER TO TIMOTHY ...

Be strong, like a soldier for Christ. Remember the truth you learned from me and the Scriptures. Keep preaching it, even though the time will come when people don't want to hear the truth. Follow Scripture, because it is all inspired by God, and it equips us to do good.

PAUL'S CASE COMES TO TRIAL. GUARDS MARCH HIM INTO THE COURT OF NERO ...

NERO CONDEMNS PAUL TO DEATH. GUARDS TAKE HIM OUTSIDE THE CITY TO BEHEAD HIM.

I HAVE FOUGHT THE GOOD FIGHT. I HAVE FINISHED MY COURSE. I HAVE KEPT THE FAITH.

SO DEATH COMES TO PAUL, WHO STARTED CHRISTIAN CHURCHES ON TWO CONTINENTS. MANY OF PAUL'S LETTERS BECAME BOOKS IN THE NEW TESTAMENT.*

BUT PAUL'S DEATH DOES NOT MEAN THE END OF SPREADING THE GOSPEL. THE TRUTH ABOUT JESUS MARCHES ON THROUGHOUT THE ROMAN EMPIRE AND ACROSS THE WORLD.

*ALTHOUGH THE BIBLE DOES NOT TELL US ABOUT PAUL'S TRIAL AND EXECUTION, EARLY CHRISTIAN TRADITION TELLS US HE WAS BEHEADED DURING NERO'S PERSECUTION.

The Final Letters

BASED ON HEBREWS—JUDE

THE LAST EIGHT
LETTERS OF THE
NEW TESTAMENT,
HEBREWS
THROUGH JUDE,
ARE MESSAGES
THAT JESUS'
DISCIPLES
WROTE TO GIVE
ADVICE,
COURAGE, AND
COMFORT TO
THE EARLY
CHRISTIANS.

THE BOOK OF HEBREWS
THE LETTER TO THE HEBREWS WAS
WRITTEN WHEN JEWISH CHRISTIANS
WERE BEING PRESSURED TO GIVE UP
THEIR FAITH IN JESUS AND RETURN
TO THEIR JEWISH TRADITIONS. THEY
ASKED THEMSELVES, WHICH IS RIGHT:
FAITH IN JESUS OR FAITH IN THE
RELIGION OF ABRAHAM, MOSES, AND
DAVID?

In the past, God spoke to our people through the prophets. But in these last days, He has spoken to us through His Son. All the faith heroes of the past looked forward to Jesus, even though He didn't come during their lifetime. Now that Jesus has come, throw away your sin and run the good race, because Jesus is waiting for us at the finish line. While you're running, remember what God said to us: "I will never leave you."

THE BOOK OF JAMES
THE LEADER OF THE CHURCH IN JERUSALEM, JAMES, THE
BROTHER OF JESUS, WROTE A LETTER TO ENCOURAGE
CHRISTIANS TO LIVE IN WAYS THAT SHOW THEIR FAITH.

Faith is meaningless unless you do something with it. Take care of the helpless. Ask God for wisdom, and keep your lives pure from the muck that surrounds you. Then your prayers will be powerful and change the world.

THE BOOK OF 1 PETER
PETER WROTE TO ENCOURAGE THE CHRISTIANS
WHO WERE BEING PERSECUTED. LIKE PAUL, HE
WAS ALSO EXECUTED BY THE ROMANS.

Face your hardships bravely. God chose you to be His royal priesthood and His holy nation. Even though the devil prowls like a lion to destroy you, stand firm.

THE BOOK OF 2 PETER

Don't be deceived by those who spread lies to mislead you. They'll get what they deserve when Christ returns. Don't be impatient waiting for Christ; God is taking His time so that people have a chance to repent.

JOHN, THE APOSTLE JESUS LOVED, WAS THE ONLY DISCIPLE WHO WAS NOT EXECUTED FOR HIS FAITH. HE LIVED TO AN OLD AGE, EXILED TO A GREEK ISLAND IN THE AEGEAN SEA. HE WROTE THREE LETTERS ABOUT GOD'S NATURE AND HOW CHRISTIANS SHOULD TREAT EACH OTHER.

THE BOOK OF 1 JOHN

God is pure light. Anyone who denies the truth of Jesus walks in darkness. If we pretend we've never sinned, then we're only lying to ourselves. But if we admit our sins, God forgives us and cleans us. My friends, make sure you show love to each other. Why? Because love comes from God, and by loving others we know God even better.

THE BOOK OF 2 JOHN

I am glad to hear that you are obeying God's commands and loving one another. Beware of enemies of the truth. These people say that Christ was just a man. Don't let them hang around you and do not invite them home! I have much to say, but not with pen and ink—I cannot wait to talk with all of you face-to-face.

THE BOOK OF 3 JOHN

You are doing right by receiving Christians into your home, especially traveling preachers. Your kindness helps in their work. Don't copy evil. Imitate what is good. Never let anyone stop you from doing good things. Peace to you.

JUDE WAS ANOTHER BROTHER OF JESUS WHO WROTE TO DEFEND TRUTH AGAINST FALSE TEACHERS.

THE BOOK OF JUDE

Dear friends, you must defend our Christian truth. Build up your faith, and pray with the help of the Holy Spirit. Have mercy for those who doubt, so you can save them from the fire of fear.

The Final Days
BASED ON REVELATION

MANY YEARS HAVE PASSED SINCE JESUS CAME BACK TO LIFE AND ROSE UP TO HEAVEN. PAUL AND PETER HAVE DIED DOING THE WORK OF THE LORD. JOHN—JESUS' BELOVED DISCIPLE AND FRIEND—IS THE LAST APOSTLE LEFT. JESUS VISITS HIM IN ONE FINAL VISION, WHERE HE REVEALS WHAT WILL HAPPEN AT THE END OF TIME.

DO NOT BE AFRAID. I AM THE FIRST AND THE LAST, WHO LIVES FOREVER AND EVER. I HOLD THE KEYS TO DEATH AND HELL.

IN THE END DAYS, FOUR HORSEMEN WILL RIDE FORTH. FIRST A CONQUEROR, ON A WHITE HORSE. THEN WAR, RIDING ON A RED HORSE. THIRD WILL COME FAMINE, ON A BLACK HORSE. AND FINALLY, DEATH WILL COME FORTH ON A PALE HORSE, WITH HELL FOLLOWING CLOSE BEHIND HIM.

AS THE FOUR HORSEMEN RIDE THROUGH THE SKY, AN EARTHQUAKE SHAKES THE LAND. THE SUN TURNS BLACK, THE MOON TURNS RED, AND THE STARS IN THE SKY FALL TO THE EARTH. MANY PEOPLE ARE KILLED BY WAR, PLAGUES, FAMINE—EVEN BY WILD ANIMALS!

AFTER THE FOUR HORSEMEN FINISH BRINGING THEIR SUFFERING TO THE EARTH, THE DEVIL WILL COME IN THE FORM OF A RED DRAGON. HE WILL PERFORM MIRACLES, RAINING FIRE DOWN FROM HEAVEN. THE PEOPLE WILL BE DECEIVED AND WORSHIP HIM.

BUT JUST WHEN ALL SEEMS LOST, THE HEAVENS WILL OPEN WIDE! JESUS, WHO IS FAITHFUL AND TRUE, WILL RIDE FORTH ON HIS WHITE HORSE OF JUSTICE. THE ARMIES AND ANGELS OF HEAVEN WILL FOLLOW CLOSE BEHIND HIM.

JESUS WILL SEIZE THAT ANCIENT DRAGON, THE DEVIL, AND LOCK HIM IN THE PIT OF FIRE FOR A THOUSAND YEARS.

THEN GOD AND HIS LAMB, JESUS, WILL RULE IN THE HEAVENLY CITY. THE RIVER OF THE WATER OF LIFE FLOWS THROUGH THE STREETS, AND THE TREE OF LIFE HEALS ALL THE PEOPLE. THERE WILL BE NO MORE SIN AND NO MORE NIGHT. AND GOD WILL REIGN FOREVER AND EVER.

WHOEVER IS THIRSTY, COME. ANYONE WHO WANTS IT, COME TAKE THE FREE GIFT OF THE WATER OF LIFE.

THROUGH THE PROPHECY IN REVELATION, JESUS GIVES JOHN A MESSAGE FOR THE SEVEN CHURCHES IN ASIA. SOME PEOPLE AT THOSE CHURCHES HAVE BEEN FAITHFUL FOLLOWERS. SOME HAVE TURNED AWAY FROM JESUS BECAUSE IT WAS TOO HARD TO FOLLOW HIM. AND SOME JUST WANT THINGS TO BE EASY. JESUS' WORDS TO THESE CHURCHES ARE STILL RELEVANT TO US TODAY.

"I KNOW WHAT YOU'VE BEEN DOING, AND IT'S NEITHER HOT NOR COLD. I WISH YOU'D BE ONE OR THE OTHER.

BECAUSE YOU ARE LUKEWARM—NEITHER COLD NOR HOT—I WILL SPIT YOU OUT OF MY MOUTH.

YOU THINK YOU ARE RICH, BUT YOU HAVE NO IDEA HOW POOR, BLIND, AND NAKED YOU ARE.

TAKE THE WEALTH I GIVE YOU, AND YOU WILL TRULY BE RICH. MY WHITE CLOTHES WILL COVER YOUR SINFUL NAKEDNESS. THE SALVE I GIVE YOU WILL LET YOU SEE!"

"HERE I AM! I'M STANDING AT THE DOOR AND KNOCKING. ANYONE WHO HEARS MY VOICE AND OPENS THE DOOR WILL SHARE MY FOOD AND MY THRONE IN HEAVEN!

JOHN'S VISION ENDS THE BIBLE, THE GREATEST STORY EVER TOLD.

JESUS STANDS AT THE DOOR AND KNOCKS. WILL YOU LET HIM IN?

BIBLE BOOK INDEX